Politics and Religion in Eastern Europe

To Nicolas and Marc

Politics and Religion in Eastern Europe

Catholicism in Hungary, Poland and Czechoslovakia

Patrick Michel

Translated by Alan Braley

Polity Press

First published as *La société retrouvée: Politique et religion dans l'Europe soviétisée* © Librairie Arthème Fayard, Paris 1988

This English translation
© Polity Press 1991

First published 1991 by Polity Press
in association with Basil Blackwell

Editorial office:
Polity Press, 65 Bridge Street,
Cambridge CB2 1UR, UK

Marketing and production:
Basil Blackwell Ltd
108 Cowley Road, Oxford OX4 1JF, UK

Basil Blackwell Inc.
3 Cambridge Center
Cambridge, MA 02142, USA

All rights reserved. Except for the quotation of short passages for the purposes of criticism and review, no part of this publication may be reproduced, stored in a retrieval system, or transmitted, in any form or by any means, electronic, mechanical, photocopying, recording or otherwise, without the prior permission of the publisher.

Except in the United States of America, this book is sold subject to the condition that it shall not, by way of trade or otherwise, be lent, re-sold, hired out, or otherwise circulated without the publisher's prior consent in any form of binding or cover other than that in which it is published and without a similar condition including this condition being imposed on the subsequent purchaser.

ISBN 0 7456 0797 7

The relevant CIP catalogue record for this book is available from the British Library or the Library of Congress.

Typeset in 10 on 12 pt Garamond
by Colset Private Limited, Singapore
Printed in Great Britain by
T.J. Press Ltd, Padstow, Cornwall.

Contents

Preface to the English Edition	vii
Introduction	1
An 'other Europe'	4
A historic break?	6
An approach that gives priority to civil society	10
Religion as a breach in totalitarianism	15
1 Concerning Time and Space	20
Towards a theoretical outline of the relationship between religion and government in a Soviet-type system	21
From theory to practice	27
Some waymarks	31
A marked propensity to seek compromise	34
An inescapable paradox	46
2 Religion and Scientific Socialism: A Sociological Analysis	49
Voluntarism in sociology: Czechoslovakia and Hungary	53
The healthy virtues of competition: Poland	62
3 Religion and Society: The Meaning of Modernity	71
Poland: beyond conformism and progressiveness	74
Morals and the economy	88
Religion and relations in society	95

vi Contents

4 Religion and Politics: Symbolism, Catacombs and Opposition 102

Behaviour and attitudes 104
Symbolism and politics: towards a political symbolism of forms of worship in Poland 108
Marginalization, catacombs and opposition 116

5 *Slavorum Apostolus* 131

The Slav Pope 133
A theology of the nation and of freedom 144
Slavorum Apostoli 156
John Paul II's third journey 162

Conclusion 171
Postscript to the English Edition 185
Appendix 197
Notes 202
Bibliography 233
Chronology 250
Index 311

Preface to the English Edition

The French version of this book was completed at the end of 1987, some three years before the English edition appeared. In the light of the events that have totally changed the political landscape in the central and eastern part of the continent of Europe during the intervening period, the question arises: should the book be reworked, or even completely rewritten? It was decided to leave the main text unchanged, and this for three reasons:

– The main intention of this work was to analyse, with the aid of specific examples, the relationships between politics and religion within the specific framework of soviet-type systems. The fact that these systems have now broken down in no way detracts from their inherent interest as a particular historical configuration, the study of which provides valuable lessons about the past, the present and the future. For there can be no doubt that the long endeavour to sovietize East-Central Europe will leave deep, long-lasting impressions in the mental structures of the peoples of the region. Moreover, in our view that collapse would appear to verify the hypotheses formulated on the threefold part that religion is capable of playing in the process of breaking down the soviet system – disalienation, detotalization and desovietization.

In the second place, while the work deals with Europe under the soviets, it also aims at raising, with the aid of specific examples, theoretical problems such as that of the relationship between religion and national identity or the problem of the historical forms of catholicism.

– Lastly, and perhaps most important, an analysis of the relationship between politics and religion in sovietized Eastern Europe raises questions about some of our theoretical categories in the West, and in particular the idea that politics is an independent sphere.

Rightly or wrongly, I believe that events have not invalidated the analysis on these theoretical problems and these questions. Therefore I have confined myself to updating the chronology and to adding a postscript, intended to place the whole discussion within a broader theoretical perspective, as warranted by the process of democratization now under way in East-Central Europe. The demolition of the Berlin Wall is proof that a major period of contemporary history is at an end. We can now begin trying to think of the period as a coherent whole, and to distinguish within it the various phases of which it was constituted.

PM
August 1990

Note

For technical reasons, the diacritical signs used in the writing and transcription of Russian, Polish, Slovak and Hungarian names are not reproduced in the typography.

Introduction

Father Juan Miguel Garrigues dedicated a recent book[1] 'to the memory of Pope John Paul I who in a pontificate of just thirty-three days dared to repudiate the silences of shame [2 Cor.4:2] and to call evil by its name, when he said: "It is untrue to say: "Ubi Lenin, ibi Jerusalem." ' It is unlikely that Christians in Eastern Europe would disavow such words, because for them Marxism-Leninism is not simply a political theory; it is a reality permeating and shaping everyday life. For how can one live and hold a dialogue with somebody who has this slogan posted up in a secondary school (at Trencin, in Czechoslovakia): 'There will never be any prosperity until the last priest has been killed by the last stone of the last Church'?[2]

And yet the state of affairs conjured up by these observations seems now to have been partly superseded. The election of a Slav Pope and the considerable interest aroused in international public opinion by the situation of the Church in Poland before, during and after the Solidarity period are all factors suggesting that the image of churches of silence and martyrdom should be replaced by that of resisting churches or even, in the case of Poland, victorious ones.

In fact, resistance has always been called for; was not the Church threatened with destruction? In the face of this destructive design a whole range of reactions was possible, and some of them were tried out more or less to the full. From the extremes of fomenting insurrection to advocating compromise, via the middle way of seeking an acceptable *modus vivendi*, the Church's attitude towards Soviet-type government was and still is aimed at ensuring its survival. What has changed over the past few years, or perhaps what is now better recognized, is that religion has succeeded in placing itself in a threefold 'active vector' of disalienation (at individual level), detotalization (at the level of society) and desovietization (at national level), while the churches, or at least some of them, have managed to create for themselves areas of freedom, thus prefiguring or promoting a process of reconstitution in civil society that makes it more self-reliant, emancipated, and freed from the grip of the government.

There are of course several reasons why this has happened. It is easy to understand that the Church should be seen as the natural enemy of Soviet-type power and should therefore resist the attacks mounted against it. One has only to study official statements by Soviet, Czechoslovak and other governments to grasp exactly the real nature of the long-term intentions cherished by these rulers concerning all religions and all churches. But the evidence shows that to leave it there would be to disregard what appears to be a major development, over the medium to long term, throughout Soviet Europe: the fact that the civil societies, or some of them, have chosen religion and the Church as ramparts and weapons in the struggle against the totalitarian system.

For quite a long time – exactly how long depends mainly on local situations and traditions – the churches, battered by the savage repression to which they were subjected, were almost exclusively concerned with ensuring their survival. Then a second phase commenced with attempts by the government to resort to subtler methods of weakening them, and during this phase they contrived to create a small area of freedom for themselves. A third and decisive phase came when human rights, whether civil, political, economic or social, were pursued as part of the Church's mission. It is this that prompted Alain Besançon's remark that, 'The question whether communism is atheist is a secondary one, for it is not condemned by the Church *primarily* on that account but because its radical falsity constitutes a threat to the human beings for whom the Church is responsible, or at least concerned, and whose natural rights it must defend'.[3] Undoubtedly the arrival at the Vatican of a Polish-born Pope did much to break the stereotype of the silent Church. Did not John Paul II himself declare, shortly after his election, that the silent Church no longer existed, since the voice of the Pope would in future be its mouthpiece?[4]

The Soviet rulers made no secret of the fact that this turn of events caused them some disquiet. As O. V. Borisov declared glumly, 'The Church, not only in Poland but also in some other socialist countries of Eastern Europe, has become appreciably more active. Religious centres and especially certain circles of political clericalism are encouraging the Church to go actively on to the offensive against Marxist-Leninist ideology, undermining the political and social order.'[5] No doubt this is why Mr Gorbachev, speaking to Party leaders of Uzbekistan at a meeting in Tashkent, said that it was necessary to 'carry on a resolute and unrelenting struggle against manifestations of religion'.[6]

Conversely, responsible leaders in the churches find reasons for satisfaction in the situation of the churches in Eastern Europe. As Cardinal Ratzinger observed:

> Paradoxically (or not so paradoxically) the faith seems to be more securely rooted in Eastern Europe, where it is officially persecuted. Doctrinally we have scarcely any problems with the Catholicism of these regions. The fact is that there they are in no danger of being converted to the viewpoint of a culture imposed by force: every day the people are paying a very heavy price in the sufferings of a society that has indeed tried to free itself – from God. It even looks as if the idea of a 'liberation theology' is emerging in some East European countries, but this time as liberation from Marxism. Of course, that does not mean that they are sympathetic towards the ideologies and mores that prevail in the West.[7]

In fact, so well-informed a lay observer as Leszek Kolakowski has no hesitation in saying that:

> In so far as we can speak of a workers' revolution, Solidarity was the first workers' revolution in history; the Bolshevist coup of 1917 has no claim to this title. It follows that the first workers' revolution in history was directed against a socialist state and has proceeded under the sign of the cross with the blessing of the Pope. So much for the irresistible laws of history discovered (scientifically) by the Marxists.[8]

Moreover, some of the latter exhibit a degree of openness towards a course of events of which they admit to being only partially in control. For example, Imre Miklos, president of the Hungarian State Office of Church Affairs (Minister of Cults), said to us in a relaxed manner: 'Marx could not provide all the answers to all the questions, including the question of the policy to be pursued *vis-à-vis* the churches at the end of the millennium in a socialist society.'[9] This eminently sensible admission well reflects the perplexity of Soviet-type power faced with the resurgence of a religious phenomenon that it had consigned to speedy decay. Under the effect of complex interactions, but primarily as a consequence of government doublespeak which professed to relegate religion to the sphere of private life while combating it in practice, religion has become one of the principal factors challenging the regime. Since religion is unsurpassed in its ability to (re)define and affirm an identity, the very fact that the state refuses for ideological reasons to have any truck with it makes it a formidable instrument of liberation. This explains why Emile Poulat's remark[10] that there is now no longer any specifically religious field applies so strongly in the case of Europe under the Soviets – a fact that inevitably poses some delicate problems. Indeed, we might almost be tempted to adapt for our purposes the question raised by Bruno Etienne concerning Islam: 'How can the religion of the Other be analysed with European concepts?'[11]

An 'other Europe'

This might appear to be a provocative question, especially now that the primate of the Catholic Church is a Pole. And yet any work dealing with East-Central Europe must begin with some attempts at definition. These attempts must include or even centre upon some points that might at first sight appear immediately comprehensible. Zdenek Strmiska, for example, observes that:

> It is significant that the national existence of the peoples of Central Europe is not lived as something to be taken for granted, without the need for any particular explanation. On the contrary, national existence is felt as a precarious reality, always uncertain and threatened. The feeling of national insecurity is one of the foremost characteristics common to the countries of Central Europe. It finds expression in consciousness of the 'national question'. Therefore it is not surprising that there exists in Czechoslovakia, Poland and Hungary a copious scientific and literary production on the national destinies of these peoples, on their national character, on the 'meaning' of their history. There are very few analogies to this production of comparable extent and importance in other national cultures.[12]

This context explains why it is natural that any conflict situation, whether overt or concealed, between a Church or a religion, which is heavily charged with symbolism in the context of the very existence of the nation, is immediately reflected or apprehended in terms of a historical ordeal having a purpose of its own, as an opening episode in a national quest for self-realization.

It is worth broadening the discussion: originally the Soviets planned to homogenize the vast European empire that had fallen into their hands at the end of the Second World War to the greatest possible extent. In Milan Kundera's neat phrase, the aim was to achieve 'the minimum of diversity over the maximum space' in a region that, on the contrary, was defined by 'a maximum of diversity over a minimum of space'.[13] The fact that this scheme had to be modified owing to the refusal of the populations concerned to bow to it does not mean that it has fundamentally changed. It is undoubtedly true that Soviet-type government is nowadays less disposed than in the past to undertake blind repression. It is equally true that it hardly bothers any longer to win the willing consent of its subjects. All it requires is resignation. Having failed to achieve perfect control of minds, it limits itself to requiring the bodies to obey the official rules and regulations. Based on appearances – the appearance of legitimacy, the appearance of normality – it effectively places an unbridgeable gulf between what people are allowed to think and what they are permitted to say or do. Totalitarianism, 'soft' totalitarianism, new, more or less enlightened authoritarianism, the label matters little; it cannot conceal the effectiveness of this levelling down, by resignation rather than by repression. Once that is in place, the increasing diversity between the different regions of the empire does not constitute a real threat to the system in the short term. That is not to say that the system adapts to the diversity, but it tries to exploit what it is unable to change. To acknowledge that there is something specific about things Hungarian or Polish is to recognize that the process of homogenization as originally conceived, elaborated and applied was meaningless or premature. To proclaim it today is nothing other than the alibi of maintaining an alignment even if, as in Poland, as a 'lesser evil' – the sole justification for General Jaruzelski's government since 13 December 1981. Yet the deployment of all these artifices cannot conceal the fact that growing diversification is signalling the breakdown of the attempt at in-depth Sovietization of the countries of Central and East-Central Europe. The rulers dreamed of transforming human nature, of creating a 'new man' subservient to them. Even though they have succeeded in installing powerful structures of domination and control, some more effective than others, the events of the past few years have demonstrated beyond argument that the pattern they aimed to impose appears to have been largely rejected by the civil societies concerned, which are resurfacing in strength, contradicting those who had somewhat prematurely marked them 'absent' from history.

The case of Poland is sufficiently well known to need no extended treatment; more than five years after 13 December 1981, the government has to tolerate such realities as an independent press and publishers widely distributed across the country, or the presence of declared opponents whom important visitors from the West to Warsaw demand to see, and do see. But beyond this single example, the presence of some 150,000 people at Velehrad in Moravia on 7 July 1985 to celebrate the 1100th anniversary of Saint Methodius constituted the largest spontaneous demonstration to have taken place in Czechoslovakia since the Prague Spring. The Czech Minister of Culture, M. Milan Klusak, was spat upon there by the crowd to shouts of 'Long live John Paul II', 'We want the Pope', when he spoke about the policy of his government. A gathering like that is a sign of the inner decay of the totalitarian system even in a country whose rulers tried to be more Soviet than the Soviets. It is not surprising that in this process of detotalization and desovietization that is occurring first at the mental level – the disappearance of fear – religion has a leading part to play; and it is plainly no accident that Eastern Europe has invented the new and decidedly strange phenomenon of the practising non-believer just when that of the non-practising believer is becoming increasingly widespread in the West.

A historic break?

The present study has a twofold aim, first to analyse the ways in which religion and politics, Church and state are confronting one another in East-Central Europe, and secondly to attempt an appraisal, forty years after the installation of Soviet-type regimes in this part of the continent, of the effects of this confrontation on each of the protagonists, taken separately and viewed in their relationship to the others (Church/state, Church/civil society, grassroots believers/episcopate, etc.), while at the same time taking into account the part played by the Pope and by the Vatican. However, the aim in view is not to paint a fully detailed picture óf the religious situation in Eastern and East-Central Europe. It is the more modest one of trying to understand how the complex relationship that exists between religion, politics and society on the one hand, and the Church, the state and civil society on the other, actually 'functions'. The intention is to investigate the very nature of Soviet-type states, the question here relating to the gaps, to one of the principal, if not the most important, defects that these states exhibit. For in fact the Soviet system and Catholicism are both potentially 'totalitarian' systems; one of them is in power and the other, by its very existence, challenges that power. Moreover, it is not simply ideologies that are at stake but also structures, *vis-à-vis* which, with which or against which civil society has to define itself. In drawing up a list of the main factors that condition the policy of the various communist countries towards religion, T.H. Rigby mentioned not only the historical traditions regarding the relations between Church and state and the circumstances in which the communists seized power, but also the connection that exists between the churches and patriotism, the problem for the state of assessing the international costs and benefits of its religious policy, the relation between religion and nationhood, and indeed the nature of the traditional religious beliefs, structures and practices.[14] Practically all these factors derive from the fundamental problem of the relation to history, and this could be reflected by a central question: to what extent did the installation of communist regimes in Central and Eastern Europe constitute a break with history? There is no simple answer to this problem of the time-relationship; there are of course many factors which, besides ordinary common sense, would weigh in favour of the theory of the break, and yet a certain continuity is also discernible in the attitudes of the protagonists in the struggle between religion and politics. Both in Poland and in Slovakia Catholicism constitutes, as it always has, a means of affirming national consciousness; in Hungary the communists contrived to reintroduce to their benefit the Habsburg system favoured by the Emperor Franz-Joseph, so much so that John Paul II repeatedly made public his feelings with regard to the 'pliability' of the episcopate in Hungary. It would appear that in these three cases the effect of the installation of regimes modelled on that of the Soviet Union has been to accentuate certain behavioural patterns of long standing rather than to change them. Of course, the Second World War played an important role in this respect, first because, as in Poland, the exemplary conduct of the clergy appreciably raised the esteem in which the Church was held,[15] but also because, as René Rémond observes,

> the confrontation with death and the seriousness of the circumstances have as it were enabled religion to be stripped down and have fostered discrimination between the core of the faith and the accretions due to its history, awakening the desire for a living, existential religion instead of a legal system. The desire to move forward from a Church that is a society and an institution to one that is a community, a people of God, a poor servant Church,[16] probably dates from those years.

This aspiration naturally became more widespread owing to the various measures taken by the authorities in the countries concerned with regard to church property. The example of Catholicism in Poland, of the underground Church in Slovakia, or the house churches in Hungary is there to attest this change, while another, contrary, endorsement is the conduct of the faithful themselves in opposing hierarchies that, like the bishops in Hungary, paid far too much attention to the institution and disappointed the hopes of the humble faithful. Then, as under the Habsburgs, priests and bishops found themselves relegated to the position of simple state officials whose task, like that of policemen, was to imprint the authority of the state upon the people. On the other hand, events in Czechoslovakia seem to have falsified this hypothesis of the persistence of one type of relationship between politics and religion, despite the incorporation of Central Europe into the Soviet sphere. For in fact in Bohemia a historic reconciliation appears to be coming about between the identity of the Czech nation and Catholicism. Since government policy is the well-tried one of 'divide and rule', it has provided fertile soil for an 'ecumenism of suffering' or, perhaps better, an 'ecumenism of struggle'. In this way the communist regime has performed the spectacular feat of harmonizing the Catholic and Protestant views of the present, if not the past, of Czechoslovakia.[17] This process, which bids fair to subvert behavioural patterns over 350 years old, is a complex one. It might be the result of the fact that, unlike Poland or Hungary, Bohemia underwent a historical fracture that gave rise to a profound change in the collective psyche. In our view, however, this fracture did not occur in 1948 with the 'Prague coup', but in 1968 when the Warsaw Pact troops intervened. It could be objected that Poland has undergone more serious crises than has Czechoslovakia, or that the suppression of the uprising in Hungary in 1956 took a greater toll than did 1968 in Czechoslovakia. But perhaps that is not the crux of the problem. Confrontation with Russia is one of the permanent themes of Polish history.

Hence popular movements seeking ever since 1956 to loosen the grip of the U.S.S.R. on Polish society are a natural feature in the history of the country, as are the risks of consequent intervention by the Soviet Union in order to protect its interests. By the same token, the Hungarians, a non-Slav people, who formed an integral part of a cultural grouping traditionally opposed to Russia, ended the war as a vanquished nation, occupied by the Red Army. It may well be that the signature in 1955 of the Constitutional Treaty granting Austria full sovereignty in return for neutrality was an incitement to the violent attempt of 1956 to shake off the yoke and escape from the Soviet camp. In this case too, the popular uprising went with the grain of Hungarian history – as did also the repression that followed, terrible though it was. The case of Czechoslovakia is different. In that traditionally Russophile[18] country, where communism had taken strong root even before the Second World War and where Munich had been seen as an unforgivable betrayal by a West with which Bohemia felt perfectly at one, not even the Stalin period had been able to undermine the feeling that, up to a certain point, communism and therefore the Soviet Union was not irreconcilable with the Czech national identity. Perhaps it is in this way that the profound despondency of Czech society in August 1968 has to be understood. The despair then experienced was the result, even more than the actual invasion of the country, of the realization that any expectation that Russia would understand the meaning of Czech history was misplaced. When this realization dawned, there seemed to be no point even in fighting, whereas it would have been natural for a Hungarian or a Pole to do so.

We have to go back a little way in order to try to verify this hypothesis. To quote Zdenek Strmska once more:

> The place of religion in the national . . . identity can be apprehended in terms of cultural models. Clearly, the distinction which has to be made between historical reality and ideological representation does not contradict such an interpretation, in which religious orientations correspond to axiological choices. . . . This question lies at the heart of the debate on the meaning of Czech history, which fuelled most of the philosophical and sociological discussions that accompanied the birth of Czechoslovakia, and in which Masaryk, Pekar, Chalupny and others took part by putting forward various ideological blueprints for defining the identity of the nation. Masaryk's vision made such a deep impression on the minds of his contemporaries that any attempt now made to analyse the Czech identity is bound to take account of it; for this identity has, so to speak, remodelled itself on the definition of it which he gave, in which the relationship between the nation and the problems of equality and democracy is so fundamental that he could even say that the national question 'was' the social question, and vice versa.[19]

And in truth, for Masaryk, 'it is no accident that the first and greatest mentors of the new Czech literary movement, Kollar, Safarik, Palacky, were, after Dobrovsky the freethinking priest, the descendants of the Czech Brethren and of their Protestant successors. Over against the Catholicism of the Counter Reformation, Dobrovsky, Kollar, Safaryk and Palacky proclaimed the humanitarian ideals of the Brethren.'[20] Masaryk also wrote that:

> The humanitarian ideal to which Dobrovsky and Kollar gave utterance, the ideal of our renaissance, is of profound national and historical significance to us Czechs. It is humanity, fully and truly understood, that impels us to renew our links with the best period of our past; that will awaken us from the spiritual and moral slumber of several centuries; that must make us march at the head of human progress. Humanity is for us the national task which the Brethren prepared and bequeathed to us. The ideal of humanity is the whole meaning of our national life.[21]

To read this text is to see how the Czech people has endeavoured to get back to its roots, beyond the wounds of the Stalinist epoch, and, since communism was there, to make it serve these ideals. It will be recalled that the aim of the Prague Spring was to create 'socialism with a "human" face'. Clearly the use of this adjective was significant; it conjured up the foundation ideals of the identity of the Czech nation and aimed at integrating the political experience through which the nation had passed since the end of the Second World War, or at least since 1948, into the all-embracing purpose of discovering the *meaning* of Czech history. In Masaryk's time, Catholic clericalism was perceived as the main adversary; according to the first president of the Czech republic, its aim was to 'overthrow in the people Palacky's philosophical bases of history, to eliminate his ideal of the Reformation'. 'We face here', he added, 'the great problem of all cultural development: our history shows us that this is so. . . . Because of its past, the Czech people absolutely cannot accept clericalism. Of course it will not be against the religion of love, but it always will and must be against clerical despotism.'[22]

Perhaps this explains the intensity of the repression of the Church by the Czechoslovak government virtually without interruption since 1948. Attacking Catholicism was a ready-made way of identifying with the history of the nation, of affirming oneself as a Czech – the more so since Catholicism had compromised itself with the Nazis in a Slovakia whose aspirations to self-government were best held in check as far as possible.[23] But it also shows the limits to such a course of action. And 1968 with its breach of the national history showed the Czechs very plainly that the main adversary of the humanitarian ideals they strove for was certainly no longer the persecuted Catholic Church: it was the Soviet-type system itself. More than that, a platform of historic reconciliation between Catholics and Protestants based on a common defence of human rights under attack came into existence in the country.

The case of Czechoslovakia well illustrates why any approach to the relationship between politics and religion that concentrates simply on institutions should be treated with the utmost reserve. Such an approach is usually governed by an apparent voluntarism, barely concealing the reality of the historic conditionings affecting each of the actors concerned. This is why we have not sought to retrace in detail the history of the relations between Church and state.[24] Apart from the fact that this task has already been undertaken for each of the countries concerned and for all of them together,[25] that was not what we had in mind. For as Moshe Lewin wrote, such a viewpoint is tantamount to giving in 'to the pressure of the Russian system itself, because by its profound "statism" it draws attention mainly to the instruments of power – the state, the rulers, the ideology. There is nothing intrinsically wrong in dealing with those aspects, except that this one-sided concentration on political power has detracted from a due consideration of "society" and its history.'[26]

An approach that gives priority to civil society

In point of fact, where relations between Church and state are concerned, the initiative is mainly with the latter in the sense that it is the state that decides in the last resort whether it is to be peace or war, the search for a compromise or repression. To adopt this approach often means confining oneself to the observation that phases of tension are followed by phases of easement, often separated from one another by indecisive periods – neither peace nor war, neither tension nor détente, but a combination of both. It has to be said that in most of the European countries under Soviet rule the phases of tension are tending to last for shorter and shorter periods, while the other two phases are lengthening. This of course is only a general observation, and would need a great deal of detailed qualification.

Above all, this approach seems to suggest that the state has complete freedom, that it is entirely free to decide whether to unleash an offensive against the Church or to call a halt. Even assuming that Soviet-type power has wide latitude in choosing its time for giving a fresh turn to its policy, the basic question is still that of its motivations. And the logic of these motivations cannot be discerned without taking into account the numerous constraints or pressures by which they are conditioned. Obviously the international context plays a major role, as do national traditions. But the deep religious revival experienced in Eastern Europe over the past few years cannot be understood apart from the fact that each of the countries concerned belongs to the same political system. The fact that this revival of religious consciousness is not without ambiguities and contradictions cannot hide the fact that the uniformization of the approaches and attitudes of the governments concerned is reflected up to a point in the uniformization of the approaches and attitudes of the civil societies.

For in fact the homogeneous political structures are based on a common ideology. In the last resort the Soviets are bent upon destroying religion and the Church, even if for a multitude of reasons the government has had to postpone the execution of this design. The very existence of the design ensures that there will be extensive common areas in the policies of each of the satellite governments, but it also means that there will be a tendency for civil societies possessing different historical and national traditions to adopt convergent attitudes with regard to religion. Clearly this sets the scene for an overall approach that must not be too reductionist. Above all, to give a proper account of the relationship between religion and politics in this part of Europe a resolutely comparative approach has to be adopted, one not confined to simply juxtaposing a series of national monographs, as all previous studies have done.[27]

However, adopting this approach has entailed limiting the field under study; it was impossible to give a proper account of the whole area. Therefore the analysis will relate only to the Catholic Church and to the three countries in Eastern Europe that have Catholic majorities, though of different sizes: Poland, Czechoslovakia and Hungary. The Catholic religion is the bearer of Latinity, anchored in the Western tradition yet also outward-looking, with its centre outside the frontiers of the Soviet bloc. But of course the dominant character of the Catholic religion is not the only factor giving cohesion to our selected field of study. There is abundant witness to the acceptance as a specific entity of this part of Europe situated 'geographically at the centre, politically to the East and culturally to the West', in the words of Milan Kundera,[28] of an Eastern Centre which 'is always leaning towards one or another of its neighbours, betraying one, adopting another, but also changing without much wanting to do so', as Fernand Braudel wrote.[29] Other such indications are the works of Istvan Bibo,[30] recently published in French, or of Jeno Szucs,[31] the meticulous comparison of the three experiments in 'normalization' undertaken in the Soviet bloc during the last three decades,[32] the links that have been established and the dialogue that has commenced between Polish, Czech and Hungarian intellectuals and their opponents, and the new topicality of the concept of 'Central Europe' itself.

Central Europe is distinguished from Germanic Europe (and hence from the German Democratic Republic), from Eastern Europe and from Balkan Europe both by its historical traditions and by the way in which it interprets the present situation. Thus Timothy Garton Ash, analysing writings of the Pole Adam Michnik, the Czech Vaclav Havel and the Hungarian Gyorgy Konrad, observed that:

> The new idea of *Central Europe* is not *solely* a reference to the past; it is also,

and perhaps primarily, an affirmation of the present. Broadly speaking one might say that the independent intellectuals of Eastern Europe have in common, *today*, a number of attitudes, of values, which in large measure are peculiar to them. . . . It seems that these characteristic attitudes are largely the result of the specific historical experiences of Eastern Europe – for example the trials that beset small nations enslaved to large empires, the tradition that impels the intelligentsia to unite for committed action in civil society, the employment of irony which is a daily lesson of defeat – but above all the experience peculiar to citizens of Central European states, a direct, unique, shared experience of life under Soviet communist type systems, ever since the Yalta partition. They are the only Europeans who, so to speak, really know what it is all about. Thanks to them we can learn a great deal, if only we listen to them. Central Europe is not a region the frontiers of which can be traced on a map like, say, the countries of Central America. It is a kingdom of the mind. 'Compared to the geopolitical reality of Eastern Europe and Western Europe' wrote Konrad, 'Central Europe only exists today as a political and cultural antithesis (*Kulturpolitische Antihypothese*) . . . to belong to Central Europe is to have a world view, not a nationality [author's italic].[33]

Having decided to consider only three countries we can of course reach only partial conclusions and, in view of the fluid situation, provisional ones at that. None the less we believe this approach does permit a clear delineation of the problem of the normalization and denormalization of the Church, and of the way in which both government and civil society try to instrumentalize it. Furthermore, it enables us to investigate the secularization or desecularization of these societies and to reflect upon the ways in which they act in the complex relationship governing relations between religion, symbolism and politics. Above all, since this is a comparative study carrying a considerable risk of being tempted to emphasize aspects of similarity and neglect the indispensable reference to the dissimilarity of the situations, it seemed more profitable not to attempt an exhaustive exposition but rather to try to illustrate the complexity of the situation by means of a small number of examples, which themselves exhibit dissimilarities. For instance, when considering Czechoslovakia one should distinguish clearly between the very different cases of Bohemia-Moravia which has a Protestant majority, and Slovakia, which is mainly Catholic. Similarly, both for Czechoslovakia and for Hungary an effort should be made to determine the effects of multiconfessionalism on the situation of the Catholic Church. Nevertheless, without underestimating these points it is clear that the appearance of this *ecumenism of struggle* mentioned earlier in connection with Bohemia considerably limits the differences inherited from the past between the various confessions. Along the same lines, the opinion of the Hungarian Minister of Religious Affairs that there are no longer any appreciable differences between the Protestant Churches and the Catholic Church concerning relations with the state[34] appears to be soundly based, inasmuch as the government has succeeded in controlling *all* Churches equally. In any event, our chosen method of confining the analysis to a comparison between the three countries in East-Central Europe that have Catholic majorities, namely Poland, Czechoslovakia and Hungary, raises some fairly serious problems of its own. Quite clearly, one major problem is the fact that there simply are no sources. It is easy to understand why the underground Church in Czechoslovakia refrains from publishing any very specific information about the way in which it operates, or why some priests in Prague refuse to see foreign visitors. But without going as far as that, statistical information on the faithful is often fragmentary and dubious even when it is available, both in Czechoslovakia and in Hungary. This being so it would undoubtedly be extremely useful to have access to the archives of the Ministries of Religious Affairs in the countries being studied. But for reasons that can be easily imagined, that resource is not available. For this reason Poland will occupy a more important place than the two other countries studied. This is partly explained by the 'specific weight' of Catholicism in Poland, which has given a Pope to the Church and may seem to be a veritable model for Churches in Eastern Europe. Other reasons are the opportunity of working there and the abundance of sources.

Thus a study of the work done on the sociology of religion in Poland, Czechoslovakia and Hungary very quickly leads to the conclusion that the results obtained in the latter two countries, where Marxist researchers have a near-monopoly, are at the least disputable, if not actually disputed. Poland is virtually alone in furnishing reliable social science material for analysis. Consequently, the materials available fall, broadly speaking, into four categories: Church texts, legal texts, the press and personal testimonies. Sources in the first of these categories pose a particular problem in that by their very nature they lay claim to a transcendental dimension. However, it did not appear necessary to preface the work by a sociological definition of religion. The classical and fully functional definition given by Rudolf Otto and Mircea Eliade,[35] that religion is the human enterprise that creates a sacred cosmos, has the operative feature that since it apprehends religion as a *human* enterprise, it enables it to be perceived as an empirical phenomenon and hence amenable to what appears to be the only valid method for a scientific approach. As Peter Berger writes, using a formula originated by Anton Jijderveld, 'any enquiry into religious matters which is confined to what can be apprehended empirically is bound to adopt the viewpoint of a methodological atheism'.[36]

This implies that the interpretation we place upon pastoral letters, sermons addresses and various notices given out by the dioceses concerned, or encyclicals, homilies and speeches by the Pope, is not only far from being the only possible one, but might indeed seem to be very incomplete, in so far as these texts are reduced simply to their earthly dimension. The constitutions and other legal texts define the status of the Church in the countries concerned; in particular the agreements signed between Church and state will be cited here more for reference than for use as working documents. In a situation where political practice means a great deal more than law, and always influences the latter considerably, things could hardly be otherwise.

The other sources pose delicate questions of scientific criticism, for all of them are to a greater or lesser degree directly functional in intention. This applies without qualification to official speeches such as statements, press conferences and various releases issued by the civil authorities of the countries in question, as well as the press. But a truly independent press does not exist legally (except in Poland, where Catholic publications merit this description), while clearly the underground press is not in the business of assembling data for scientific analysis.

For reasons that will be readily understood, the documentary collections existing in the West (in particular at Keston College in Great Britain, at the Centro Studi sull'Europa Orientale, in Italy, the Research Centre for Religion and Human Rights in Closed Societies, in the United States, or at Radio Free Europe) consist largely of documents produced and gathered for the purpose of documenting cases of anti-religious persecution, to enable the facts to be brought to the notice of public opinion in the various countries and thereby to bring about cessation of the action being taken against the individuals concerned.

The interviews we have had over the past few years with the protagonists under study, from the Hungarian Minister of Religious Affairs to the Czech member of the underground Church, from the Solidarity expert to the country priest in Poland, fit basically into the same framework, even if they help to modify or correct the impressions gained from a reading of the written sources. Thus, for example, if one wished to measure the influence exerted in Czechoslovakia by the underground Church one would have to be in a position to carry out a survey of a representative sample of the whole population using scientifically attested criteria, whereas in present circumstances one is (alas!) reduced to simple intuitions or suppositions based on the increased numbers observed taking part in a pilgrimage from one year to the next, or on assurances given by one or another member of the underground Church. In point of fact, it is 'simpler' to meet one of the latter than to carry out a formal sociological study. Yet it is undeniable that this limitation inevitably results in one's perceiving, if not the extremes, at least the prominent features of a sociopolitical landscape rather than gaining a complete overview.

Even in Poland, some interpretation of what is said is needed if one is to arrive at a proper assessment of the political weight of the Church. In a situation where the opposition is forbidden from the outset to formulate adverse judgements upon, or to criticize, the primate or the episcopacy, it is often necessary to read between the lines, or interpret a hint. This indicates how cautiously the material studied must be treated. Clearly this does not imply that the same weight of credence has to be given to what government says and the utterance (or utterances) of civil society. As Barrington Moore wrote:

> In every society the dominant groups are those which have most to hide about the way in which society functions. It follows that very frequently a serious analysis is bound to be a critical one, which seems to distance itself from an objective exposition in the conventional meaning of the term. . . . For all who study human society, sympathy towards the victims of historical processes and scepticism with regard to the shouts of the victors supply indispensable safeguards against the risk of absorption by the dominant mythology. Anyone who tries to be objective needs this as part of his normal working equipment.[37]

Religion as a breach in totalitarianism

As Pierre Bourdieu observes, 'every religious field is the theatre of a battle for definition, that is to say the delimitation of competences, competence being understood in the legal meaning of the term, i.e. as delimiting a province of jurisdiction'.[38] If what is religious is disseminated across a wider field, this 'battle for definition' is thereby transferred from a localized area to the whole of the sociopolitical field, that is, it enlarges its scope: from being purely religious, the 'province' becomes moral, and hence political. In effect, by claiming a monopoly of defining what is political, Soviet-type regimes evacuate that term of all meaning. Everything may be political, or may become so at any time. Above all, by refusing to set boundaries to what is political and to acknowledge an independent religious sphere, Soviet-type governments run the risk of seeing religion erected into a dimension where politics are redefined, through rejection of a 'perverted' politics, challenged in the name of ethics, morals, or even the authenticity of national traditions or else, quite simply, of the truth. The government cannot adopt a neutral stance in regard to religion without renouncing the ideology that legitimates it. If it cannot suppress religion it will make every effort to gain control of it. We shall formulate the hypothesis that religion, under the effect of the hostile policy conducted by the government, which seeks to marginalize it in the sociopolitical field, or even to expel it, will move in three different directions at once, reappearing both within and outside this field, which it then surrounds both *above* and *below*:

> 1—'Above' the sociopolitical field: by rejecting the rules of the political game as fixed by the government on the basis of the monopoly that it claims to possess, religion defines itself as the place of a moral witness which cannot suffer the least compromise. Hence it will affirm that·it is above politics, to which it will assign limits, for example

setting up human rights against the interests of the state. Its 'rejection of politics' or, if you will, its rising above politics, will find natural expression in the register of discourse, since it will function as witness.

2—Inside the sociopolitical field itself: a dissolution, or more accurately a fragmentation, of what is religious will take place. From now onwards, therefore, the religious as such will not be easy to discover in the sociopolitical field, with the result that this field will be coloured throughout by a moralism which, since obviously it will be turned against the government, confers a directly oppositional dimension on this fragmentation. Above all, since it will constitute an axis along which autonomous social dimensions can be formed, it helps to (re)create a civil society. Here we are in the register of social praxis.

3—From 'beneath' the sociopolitical field: in Daniel Beauvois's very apt words, 'underneath religion there is always a kind of sub-culture made up of ideological implications, which are never semantically neutral'.[39] The fragmentation of the religious within the sociopolitical field will reinforce the effect of this sub-culture, causing it to act as a symbolic referent, a symbolic material available to civil society in its search for a cultural and/or national identity. Here the register is that of the symbol.

Clearly, the most important feature of this phenomenon is the simultaneity of this resurgence. At a time when the state is endeavouring to secure the tightest possible hold over a field apprehended horizontally, it enables religion to bypass that dimension, and henceforward to traverse the sociopolitical field only vertically. Naturally the government will not be unaware of this development and will strive to enter into competition with religion by symbolic manipulation in the vertical plane. In doing so, however, it is engaging in direct competition, since it is abundantly clear that religion, if understood and lived in a certain way, can constitute in Eastern Europe one of the surest means of escaping from the referential framework of the dominant legitimacy. In other words, while the state may be able to spread confusion in the horizontal dimension by imposing its own rules, in the vertical dimension it is compelled to fight on ground where the use of force and the monopoly of definition no longer suffice. As Bruno Étienne said, 'The institutionalization of society is itself a product of the imaginary: the forces which make a social unit cohere are not reducible to constraint; they are symbolic forces. On this point, the mistake common to all positivists is to contrast the imaginary with the rational as illusion contrasts with the truth, whereas reality itself is a social invention because it is an effect of this constitution of society by itself.'[40]

In a Soviet system the Church by its very existence is a radical, and therefore an unacceptable, critique of the regime. In other words, in the eyes of Soviet-type power the very essence of the Church is to delegitimate it, though it may decide, as Stalin did in 1941, to use for its own purposes the symbolic charge carried by the Church. To do so it would of course have to enter into a working arrangement on a given basis and to make a substantial change in the objectives towards which it claims to be striving, even if only at the level of propaganda (in the example chosen: defence of Russian territory, not the Soviet system as hitherto).

The area of symbolism, where government, Church and civil society are going to position themselves and confront one another is where all the manipulations[41] and all the diversions take place. The most important thing is to find in that area ways of sustaining one's own legitimacy. But this field is of course a minefield. By choosing religious symbols to blazon its independence over against the government, which has done its best to monopolize all the available secular symbols, and pervert them, civil society delegitimates the state and legitimates the Church, though without thereby necessarily adopting in their entirety the values that the Church professes. That is no doubt the explanation of some inconsistencies that are observable in Poland, where churches are crowded for the mass yet a great number of abortions are carried out every year, or where more and more Poles, especially young ones, are saying that, 'The Church should not meddle in politics.' Moreover, the Church might find its own symbols turned against it, if ever some of its faithful supporters should come to believe that the government was manipulating its action and gaining respectability too cheaply.

It is in this field of symbolism that the fluxes and checks that will define social reality at any given moment are organized. This ceaseless flow of symbolic material explains why in the relationship between politics and religion, society plays the most important part. For it is civil society that determines in the last resort the extent to which the symbolic forces of which the institutional protagonists are trying to make use shall be invested with reality.

Taking up Foucault's contention that power passes through subjects as much as through rulers, Gilles Deleuze has written: 'It is any force which has the power to affect [others] and to be affected [by yet others], so that every force entails power relationships; and every field of force distributes the forces in accordance with these relationships and the changes in them.'[42]

Thus from this point of view the Church participates directly in the *exercise* of power, even if it quite obviously does not *possess* power. This is what renders its relationship to the state so ambiguous. And in fact, in the three countries in Eastern Europe under the Soviets where the majority of the population is Catholic, while the type of Church–state relationships is certainly different, it is none the less governed by certain common constraints. Each planning to outlive the other, Church and state enter into a sophisticated dialogue of time and space in which religion may be constrained to play simultaneously a stabilizing and a destabilizing role *vis-à-vis* the political system, in each of the countries considered.

The long-term dimension impels both state and Church to enter into spatial compromises that are indispensable. In so doing, the Church hopes that in course of time it may be able to widen the breach, transforming survival space into growing space. In fact, it would be more accurate to use the plural, for it is the conjunction of legal, religious, cultural, social, economic and symbolic spaces that forms the diffuse and labile geography of an independent area of freedom which may end up by organizing itself into a political space challenging the government. Naturally civil society throws its whole weight into this dialectic, which inevitably involves the institutionalization of the Church. For in the last resort it is society that has to define the acceptable threshold of the compromise or compromises, since on society also depends, in the last analysis, the prestige on which the Church may rely when confronting the civil power. That relationship is extraordinarily unstable, since the *thresholds of legitimacy* to which each of the protagonists can lay claim over against the others are constantly changing (see chapter 1).

Where our chief concern is with civil society, the analysis of religious attitudes and behaviour is extremely important. The study of the sociology of religion (official, independent and clandestine) in the three countries we are considering provides very many clues to an understanding of the way in which religion in Eastern Europe is politically *understood* and to a grasp of what is at stake in an undertaking in which the requirements of science pale before those of ideology. It is not simply a question of tracing a course of action or unearthing hidden presuppositions, but of demonstrating the directly functional nature of a production which, incidentally, faithfully reflects the development of official thinking about religion and reveals its inconsistencies and its objectives (see chapter 2).

The fact that 'scientific' production on religion is assessed only on the criterion of operational effectiveness would of itself be sufficient to warrant the hypothesis that things religious *produce* social phenomena. Verification of this hypothesis naturally leads to speculation about the effects of socioeconomic changes on the Church, both as to their perception and as to the adaptation of Church institutions to a new situation, and this clearly raises the problem of modernity: what meaning should be assigned to the terms 'progress', 'tradition', 'conservatism' or 'progressivism' in the context of a Sovietized country? Obviously such questions have a directly political bearing, in so far as they furnish an assessment of the effectiveness of religion in its specific role of a vehicle for the reconstitution of a civil society (see chapter 3).

The links between religious sentiment and national sentiment in East-Central Europe form one of the major dimensions of this viewpoint. When the historical or political factors responsible for this linkage are analysed, the contradictions or ambiguities, both theoretical and practical, that it contains become very apparent. But beyond the relationship between symbolism and politics itself, it is the very attitude of the government that condemns Czechoslovak, Hungarian and, to a lesser extent, Polish Catholics to the status of second-class citizens. This marginalization process can very easily create a dissidence that is the first step along the path to political opposition. This opposition may be directed both against the government and against the Catholic hierarchy itself, if the latter is suspected of compromise. At all events it is a means of escaping from the lies and schizophrenia of daily life, of bringing conduct into line with convictions. It warrants the hypothesis that religion has become one of the main – if not the main – adversaries of Soviet-type government, because it operates simultaneously in the register of discourse (or of witness), of values and social praxis. This also explains why secular oppositions have had to learn to take note of it (see chapter 4).

The threat to the government represented by the Catholic Church is the more serious because of its international structure, which means that each national Church has a fall-back, an overall coherence, that gives it a common objective and watches over it.[43] Consequently, and even if the Vatican's Eastern Policy had not been one of its main concerns, it was inevitable that the arrival of a Slav Pope at Rome should constitute a new and supremely important event for Christians in Eastern Europe. An analysis of John Paul II's pronouncements shows that he really has a great Messianic design for the spiritual reconquest of Europe, Russia included, which inevitably raises the question whether this is compatible with the pursuit of a diplomacy aimed at normalization (see chapter 5).

I cannot conclude this introduction without expressing my gratitude to Georges Mink, for the present study has a special connection with the works that have been written in collaboration with him. The first section of chapter 1 and the third section of chapter 3 incorporate many themes that we worked on together when writing *Religion et société en Europe du Centre-Est (Eléments de réflexion)*,[44] and whatever I am able to write about the situation in Poland is inseparable from the work done during the writing of *Mort d'un prêtre – L'Affaire Popieluszko: Analyse d'une logique normalisatrice*.[45] But my debt to Georges Mink extends far beyond the limits of particular works published under our two names. However, in the time-honoured phrase, I alone am responsible for any omissions and errors in the present work. To quote Peter Berger's felicitous expression, 'Sociologists are like thieves: the wolves may not eat one another, but they commit some crimes together and others separately.'

1
Concerning Time and Space

For too long the study of the confrontation between religion and Soviet-type regimes in East-Central Europe has been confined to an analysis of the relations between the Church as an institution and the state. This approach is of course essential, but it must be supplemented by aligning other approaches with it. For the contest is more than simply bipolar; civil society also plays a key role, reacting to the stimuli it receives from Church and state but also acting on them, forcing them to make adjustments, adaptations and long-term compromises. Above all, religion cannot be reduced to its established forms; it exhibits a tremendous propensity to overstep the bounds within which the institutionalized protagonists would like to confine it.

Religion is unrivalled as a producer and vector of axiological attitudes, which always carry ideological or political implications. It is capable of resurfacing in the most unexpected places, of creating and occupying social, aesthetic, symbolic or cultural space alike. In this sense there is not even a triangle of forces but a polygon, and each of these areas tends to become independent and to reproduce itself. Church, civil society and state are not homogeneous blocs. Rather, they appear as entities made up of composite elements, involved in a field of forces in which they move at different speeds towards objectives which, although sometimes convergent, may often be very different. This incessant movement is continually changing the shape of the space in which relationships between the various protagonists are made and unmade.

Moreover, it forces them to redefine themselves, both introspectively and also in relation to the others, changing the mode and the locus of their operation, breaking down patterns of behaviour, and reforming them elsewhere as new priorities dictate. In this constantly changing environment it does not follow that each of the actors necessarily has the same perception of what is urgent, and they therefore have different priorities. Consequently, the protagonists each have differing ideas on time management, or at least on the relationship between time management and what they believe to be achievable. Nor is the pressure exerted on these protagonists an invariable; it may change under the influence of situations, traditions, factors rooted in history, the weight of symbolism operating here or there, or even at times through the exemplary actions of a single person.

The interpenetration of the religious, social and political fields is even more significant in a system in which either everything or nothing is political, that is to say, where everything is always potentially political according to whether or not it is so designated. This makes it imperative to treat all definitions as provisional, and renders analysis a somewhat random operation especially since, as already indicated, many pieces of information are lacking.

Therefore we cannot provide a full conspectus of the problems here. We can do no more than outline a theory of the relationship between religion and government in a Soviet-type system, without claiming that it is exhaustive. With this approach, the study of one structure can be used to supplement, or even modify, the study of the others.

Towards a theoretical outline of the relationship between religion and government in a Soviet-type system

The basic texts of the different countries in the Soviet bloc follow the pattern of the Soviet constitution in enunciating the principle of religious freedom. Article 52 of the Soviet constitution guarantees citizens 'freedom of conscience, that is to say the right to profess any religion or none, to hold religious services or to conduct atheistic propaganda'; it states that 'any incitement to hostility and hate on account of religious beliefs is forbidden' and that 'the Church is separated from the state and the school from the church'.[1]

Thus, article 63 of the Hungarian constitution of 1972 guarantees to citizens 'freedom of conscience and the right freely to exercise their religious convictions. In order better to guarantee freedom of conscience, church and state are separated.' Article 82 of the Polish constitution of 1976 guarantees to citizens 'freedom of conscience and worship' and states that 'the Church and other religious organizations may freely exercise their religious functions. Nobody may compel a citizen to refrain from taking part in religious services. Nobody may compel a citizen to take part therein.' Lastly, 'the Church is separated from the state'.[2] Provisions of a repressive nature, such as those contained in article 70 (3) of the Polish constitution of 1952 which stated that 'misuse of freedom of conscience and religion for purposes harmful to the interests of the Polish people will be punished', were in general abolished during the widespread revision of constitutions that took place in the Soviet camp in the 1970s.[3]

But in substance the legal aspects are still secondary, for as the Polish bishops stated during their 151st plenary conference held on 18 and 19 February 1976, the most important thing is to see 'how the provisions of the constitution are interpreted and applied'. In the Soviet-type system, where the government aims to control the whole of the sociopolitical field, it is in fact impossible to envisage a situation in which Church and state are truly separated, whatever the constitution may say. The very existence of a Ministry of Religious Affairs in all of the states concerned, its director having a place in the Council of Ministers and possibly in the central committee of the Party itself, is sufficient proof of this.

And the fact is that, though the precise details may vary from country to country, the background to the picture is basically that of an anti-religion policy stemming directly from Lenin's idea that:

> religion must be declared to be a private matter: that is how the attitude of socialists to religion is usually interpreted. But it is important to determine exactly the meaning of these words, so as to avoid any misunderstanding. We demand that religion shall be a private matter over against the state, but we can in no way consider religion as a private matter in relation to our own Party.[4]

But this is the Party that under the constitution has to play a leading role in society. It therefore follows that, whatever the degree of normalization that has been achieved in institutional relationships between the church(es) and the state, there is an unavoidable conflict between religion and the Marxist-Leninist ideology as understood and applied in the Soviet Union and in Eastern Europe.

The attitude of Soviet-type regimes towards religion always follows the same simple rule: not to allow religion to be practised outside the control of the state. In fact, as soon as these regimes have accepted the principle of allowing the outward forms of freedom of conscience and worship to subsist,[5] they must be careful to take back more than they have conceded. And the disadvantages that arise from the existence of one or more churches are, from their point of view, very serious:

> 1—The very presence of a Church constitutes a breach of the uniformity on which Soviet-type regimes are based. The Church may become a centre around which an ideological outlook will form, a place that gives birth to, and protects, values felt to be incompatible with the official values. Thus it challenges the monopoly practised by the Party, and this is particularly unacceptable where the education of children and young people is concerned.

2—More often than not, the Church is the only legal structure that has both buildings, trained leaders and financial resources, however limited these may be, around which grassroots initiatives can crystallize. As such it forms a potential source of hostile questioning and of protection of the questioners. Therefore it is felt to be a potential or actual pole of political opposition.

3—The Catholic Church has links with a centre that is situated outside the country, and therefore beyond its control.

In view of these disadvantages, the government will weigh up the presumed usefulness of the Church in relation to the objectives laid down by the Party, in deciding upon its attitude. If it appears that the Church cannot be of any use, it will be appropriate to destroy it. If otherwise, either the Church will agree to collaborate and will be protected, or the Church will refuse or only collaborate with an ill grace, in which case it will be met with repression. Generally speaking, relations between Church and state in the countries of East-Central Europe fall into the two latter categories.

The control exerted by the state over religious life is aimed at limiting as far as possible the disadvantages just enumerated. Clergy will be required to swear oaths of loyalty or to make official declarations on the ideological primacy of the Party and the soundness of the objectives it is pursuing. Above all, efforts will be made to hamper religious indoctrination of children and the Church's scope for influencing the education of the rising generation. Limitations will be placed upon the resources available to the Church: building permits for new churches will be refused or issued in dribs and drabs; Catholic newspapers and publications will be hemmed in with severe restrictions such as paper rationing, censorship and so forth. Efforts will be made to instigate movements of 'patriotic' priests or laymen, such as Pacem in Terris in Czechoslovakia, Opus Pacis in Hungary, or Pax in Poland. Powers may be taken to exert pressure upon the clergy, by paying a stipend or granting privileges of one kind or another. Attempts will be made to utilize Vatican decisions against the national bishops, or manipulate the episcopate so as to make Rome change its stance; and if that does not produce the desired result, recourse will be had to persecution: permission to officiate as priests will be revoked, there will be a variety of harassments, or even imprisonment, physical attacks and assassination.

There is of course nothing exhaustive about this short catalogue; it could be greatly extended and embroidered. For the situation differs widely from country to country even though the initial constraints are similar. Whether in Poland, Czechoslovakia or Hungary, the initial pattern was doubtless almost identical: in all three cases two mutually exclusive aims were established – on the one side the will to destroy the Church and on the other side the will to outlive an atheistic government which, in the final analysis, was only a temporary vicissitude. But after several years of parallel development marked by all sorts of repressive measures, wide divergences have appeared. The government, perceiving the folly of hoping to crush the Church swiftly and completely, has refined its tactics considerably. It has everywhere been at pains to draw a distinction between religion, which is always denounced as an alienating factor, and the churches, which it has done its best to instrumentalize, playing upon their functions of symbolic legitimation or social stabilization. For their part, the churches have become aware of the need to survive for the long term, and hence to effect a compromise – the smallest possible – with the state in the short term. This said, the level of the threshold of compromise varies from country to country.

In Czechoslovakia there has been no normalization, and Church–state relations have gone from bad to worse. Repression of the Church has continued almost without respite since 1950. Eight of the thirteen bishoprics are without an incumbent, even though John Paul II is said to have appointed several bishops secretly. The Church is very closely monitored by the government, in particular through the organization Pacem in Terris, which enables the state to compel the Church to make common cause with certain political possitions. A Vatican decree of 1982 forbade priests to belong to organizations having political aims, and this has precipitated a process that is already well under way, causing a real tension between the Church and the government. More will be said about this later.

The situations in Poland and Hungary are very different. In those countries the overall institutional relationships between Church and state have been normalized. But whereas in the latter case this process has worked to the advantage of the government, which promoted it, in the former case it has come about as a result of changes in the balance of power which the Church has been able gradually to impose in its favour. Clearly, however, it is very difficult to measure the differences between the three countries: this would presuppose the availability of quantifiable, comparable data which the gaps in the statistics, research, or even information, whether deliberate or involuntary, make it impossible to assemble.

Tables 1, 2 and 3 are therefore designed simply to illustrate trends and to provide an outline of the political and institutional background to the relations between religion, the state and society. After inquiring as to the extent to which the Church is *dependent* on the government, we shall try to assemble the main indicators of its *cohesion* – that is to say, the ability of the different constituents of the Church to speak with a united voice and to aim for the same goals in action. This should provide a tentative yardstick of the *influence* of the Church in question; that is, its ability to affect and change reality.

Not surprisingly, in terms of the criteria of institutional dependence adopted here, the Church in Poland shows up as a model of self-reliance. The

Table 1 Criteria of institutional dependence

	Poland	Czechoslovakia	Hungary
Institutionalization of administrative control of celebration of services	+	+	+
Existence within the clergy of organized groups with pro-government sympathies	–	+	+
Clergy dependent on the state as regards appointment and/or remuneration	–	+	+
Hierarchy itself "policing" the institution	–	–	+
Transfer of legitimacy by inclusion of ecclesiastics in public institutions	–	–	+
Anti-religious repression confirmed by independent sources	–	+	–
Measures hindering religious instruction	–	+	+
Primate holds honorific distinctions conferred by the state	–	–	+

Table 2 Criteria of cohesion[a]

	Czechoslovakia	Hungary
Existence of groups forming a parallel or clandestine Church in disagreement with the official Church	–	+
Open attacks on members of the hierarchy by members of the clergy	+	+
Existence of organized groups of clergymen with a pro-government stance	+	+
Open attacks on the primate by the faithful	–	+
Catholic press and/or publications in disagreement with the hierarchy	–	+

The criteria adopted are in fact criteria of lack of cohesion rather than of cohesion, in so far as they indicate the presence of divisions within the Catholic community. In this sense, the Church in Hungary with 5 pluses is clearly less cohesive than the Czechoslovak Church, which has only 2.

Hungarian and Czechoslovak cases are more difficult to interpret. For example, tha absence of anti-religious repression in Hungary does not signify that the Church has more freedom *vis-à-vis* the state than the Czechoslovak Church; on the contrary, it could betray a situation of dependence such that the state had no need to adopt such methods. And in fact, whereas Cardinal Wyszynski, the ex-primate of Poland, and Cardinal Tomasek, primate of

Czechoslovakia, have always sidestepped the trap of even a symbolic integration into the official system, Cardinal Lekai, the Hungarian primate, was a holder of the Order of the Banner and, it seems, declined the government's offer of a seat in Parliament only after repeated and insistent representations by John Paul II.

Above all, the Hungarian bishops themselves ensure that priests who in

Table 3 Criteria of influence

	Poland	Czechoslovakia	Hungary
Religious identity facilitating identification with the nation	A	C	C
Monopoly or near-monopoly of a church	A	A	A
Freedom of conscience and worship recognized under the constitution	A	A	A
Catholic press and/or publishers legal and independent of government	A	C	C
Illegal churchbuilding	A	A	A
Confessional higher education independent of the state	A	C	C
Existence of groups of laypeople producing or reproducing a Christian ethos	A	A	B
Critical remarks by bishops regarding the government	A	B	C
Organization of Church-sponsored cultural events	A	C	C
Catholic youth movements independent of the government	A	C	C
Clandestine Catholic press and/or publications in agreement with the hierarchy	B	C	C
Access to the audio-visual media	A	C	C
Public discussion about political problems within the Church's sphere of influence	A	B	C
The episcopate expresses views on social and economic matters	A	C	C
Christians in opposition on account of their religious ideal	A	A	A
The opposition mentions the Church in its statements	A	B	C

A = strong trend
B = trend unchanged
C = weak or non-existent trend

any way endanger the terms of the compromise worked out by the government are disciplined.

Because the situation in Poland is so homogeneous, we can justifiably treat it as an example of institutional coherence. It is noteworthy that in Poland the terms 'episcopate' and 'Church' can almost be used as synonyms, which they clearly cannot in Czechoslovakia, and still less in Hungary.

A study of tables 1, 2 and 3 will reveal the significant differences between the situations in the three countries, and the need for a careful reassessment of the stereotyped ideas that prevail as to the supposed strength or weakness of the Church (the Church of silence – the Church triumphant). Nevertheless, we believe that any analysis of the functions of religion in East-Central Europe under the Soviets must take account of three facts which, though obvious, are also paradoxical: each situation may constitute a paradigm, but none of them is ever either immutably fixed or applicable to all three, and each situation may at a given moment represent a reference. It is within this general framework that the evolving relationship between religion and society has its being, whereas the differences caused by historical traditions may tend to become blurred or sharpened.

Thus in Poland a popular type of religiosity, in the sense that it was strongly associated with religious and national values, has given place, owing to special historical circumstances, to a more selective and intellectualized type of religion. In Bohemia, Catholicism is ceasing to be regarded as the negation of Czech national identity. Yet in Hungary, despite Mindszenty, 1956 and long years of persecution – or because of them – the Church, after the vicissitudes of war and a Soviet-type regime, has reverted to a subservient role in which it appears as an official Church serving the interests of the government.

From theory to practice

Although relationships between Church and state differ in the three Sovietized East European countries where the religion of the majority is Catholic, despite the constraints common to all those relationships, they nevertheless all seem to obey an ineluctable logic which leads the Church to play both a stabilizing and a destabilizing role with the respect to government.

As they face each other, both the Catholic Church and Soviet-type governments have had to learn how to coexist once it became apparent that neither could achieve its dearest wish – namely, the rapid disappearance of the other party whose existence was utterly repugnant to it. But such coexistence necessarily presupposes the long-term design of each of the protagonists to outlive the other. They therefore set the scene for this temporal arbitrage by spatial compromises: because the opponent could not be eliminated, he had to be confined to the smallest possible space. This led the government to define permitted or forbidden areas, while the Church endeavoured to break out from one or more of these cantonments, to enlarge some of them, to open up others or even to drive the state completely out of them, or to create totally new areas. This domestic pattern is reproduced at the international level; the prime objective of diplomacy aimed at normalization, of the Vatican's *Ostpolitik*, is to enable the local churches to survive in as good a condition as possible. It would be an exaggeration to say that this sophisticated dialectic of time and space was understood from the outset by each of the protagonists. The immediate post-war period was one of violent confrontation, and both participants had to suffer much disillusionment before the idea of conducting Church–state relations prudently, and as far as possible without ideological preconceptions, was accepted.

Nevertheless, some of the participants had the feeling at a very early stage that things were going that way. On 27 September 1953 Cardinal Wyszynski, two days after his arrest and detention at Rywald, in the north-east of the country, wrote:

> My analysis of the historical development of the October revolution has shown me that it is possible for policy towards the Church to become more flexible. In the Soviet Union the initial ferocity – the establishment of anti-God museums, the closure of churches, the theft of icons and so forth – gave place to the Dimitrov method. Just before the outbreak of the great national war the Soviet government concluded a 'tacit' agreement with the Orthodox Church. This deathbed transaction was evidence of the pressure exercised by social forces. Events in the USSR have shown that any kind of government, even the most barbaric, softens its approach appropriately when it comes up against difficulties that its executives cannot overcome without support from society. At that point it has to find ways of 'winning over' society. It was only to be expected that the Polish government, a more or less faithful copy of the Soviet system, would follow a similar course.[6]

However, Cardinal Mindszenty, the primate of Hungary, whose imprisonment lasted from 1948 until the very day in October 1956 on which Cardinal Wyszynski was released, drew very different conclusions from the Soviet experience. He notes in his memoirs that:

> The study of history taught me very early that any compromise made with [communists] is hardly ever of any use except to [them]. I have always respected – and still do – those who courageously hazard their whole life for the Church, in the knowledge that though one persecutor may follow another the Church outlives her enemies. Castles and citadels fall, but the Church, with all its human weaknesses, will never perish. The blood of the martyrs has always been the seed of the Church, and from it she arises again.[7]

These analyses, one bearing the imprint of realism and the other of intransigence, reveal the political directions that were chosen. Whereas the Polish primate favoured a step-by-step approach, Cardinal Mindszenty simply affirmed great principles from which there would be no retreat.

Thus, in Cardinal Wyszynski's view:

> We were so badly mauled at the end of the war as to be barely able to survive. Many priests survived imprisonment by the Nazis only to return to prison in Poland. We had to take this into account. There was no foreign example we could follow, for no other nation – neither Czechoslovakia, nor Hungary, nor even the Catholic part of Germany – had been ravaged to such a degree. . . . In view of the situation in Poland the bishops saw it as their duty so to lead the Church as to spare it further losses. We even feared that after these first *initia dolorum* changes in society might lead to conflict between Christians and unbelievers. To be ready for such an eventuality we had to gain time and rally our strength in order to defend God's positions.[8]

While the primate of Hungary proclaimed:

> I wish to be the conscience of my people. In my vocation as a guardian, I knock at the door of your souls. In opposition to the errors now appearing, I declare to my people and my nation the eternal truths. I wish to revive the sacred heritage of our people, without which the individual may perhaps live, but not the nation as a whole.[9]

Firmly maintaining that standpoint, the primate of Hungary refused to make any move whatsoever towards the new government:

> If I had felt that such a move might make life more tolerable for the people, I would have taken it upon myself to do as they asked. But it was to be feared that, after their bishops had taken such a step, the people would be led into error as to the intentions and even the spirit of the communists.[10]

The primate of Poland took the opposite course. He went promptly to the negotiating table to fend off the most immediate threats, without harbouring too many illusions:

> During standing discussions on the chance of reaching an agreement, we were not talking about agreements between Church and state but between the state and the Polish bishops. We would not have been competent to negotiate the former. *Causae maiores* are the preserve of the Holy See. The word *agreement* was inserted at the last moment. The main task was to find a *modus vivendi* between the bishops and the government. I was convinced that it was possible, even imperative, to set out certain essential points in such an agreement in order to remove the threat of a new accelerated extermination from the

Church. . . . I have never taken advantage of favourable circumstances. I have neither engaged in politics nor gambled upon 'survival'. I simply believed there was a need to lay down rules of coexistence between a Catholic nation and a Marxist state.[11]

Like Cardinal Wyszynski, the primate of Hungary denies wanting to engage in politics, but claims that circumstances compelled him to do so:

I have never been able to think very highly of the role of a priest as politician. But this made me all the more ready to fight against the enemies of the country and the Church, both in speech and writing, and to support Christian politicians with committed, quite specific, advice, of the kind I gave to the faithful. As for myself, however, I was determined to confine my activities to the cure of souls. I regarded politics for a priest as a necessary evil which had to be coped with from time to time. But since politics is able to attack the Church and imperil souls, I considered that part of a priest's duty was to be well informed about party politics, for only so will he be in a position to give guidance to those committed to his charge and to react against political movements hostile to the Church. It would undoubtedly be a mark of great weakness to leave the consciences of the faithful, so often deceived, alone to face what are often fundamental political and moral decisions.[12]

For the same reasons he is sorry that so little attention was paid to his views when the *Ostpolitik* was instituted:

When . . . Mgr Agostino Casaroli entered into negotiations with the Kadar regime on behalf of the Vatican, this regime had completely stifled the true Hungarian Church with the help of 'priests for peace' and of the National Office for Religious Affairs. That is why the Vatican diplomat heard so little of the Catholic point of view and why, in my opinion, the diplomacy of the Vatican, not accurately informed about the situation, allowed itself to be drawn into negotiations which were bound to offer advantages to the communists and seriously disadvantage Catholicism in Hungary.[13]

Naturally it is not our task to pronounce any sort of judgement on either of the two courses chosen by the leaders of the Polish and Hungarian Churches. Nevertheless, the attitude of the former primate is nowadays severely judged in Budapest, where some people say that Mindszenty was 'a holy but fanatical man who caused the Church great losses by his intransigence: he was made a pretext for repression'.[14] And afterwards, suffering from a veritable 'Mindszenty syndrome', the Church in Hungary rediscovered its old reflexes of infeudation. On the other hand, the prestige enjoyed by Cardinal Wyszynski well illustrates the fact that dialogue with the government does not necessarily lead to the charge of collaboration or capitulation. But beyond the particular historical experiences of Poland and Hungary in the years that followed 1945, the two types of relationships sustained by Cardinals Wyszynski and Mindszenty stand out. While the former claimed to have succeeded in reconciling the fundamental principles and the identity of the Church with the compromises it was bound to effect with the government, the latter appeared to riposte that any compromise is certain to degenerate into a surrender of principle. And the fact that Cardinal Wyszynski's gamble appears to have paid off does not mean that the primate of Hungary was necessarily wholly mistaken. But between the martyr Church and the compromised Church there stretches a large grey area in which the relationship between Church and state can develop step by step. In other words, adopting theoretical positions carries little weight compared with the concrete realities, national traditions, the history and the strategies, to say nothing of the personalities, involved.

Some waymarks

There are three themes that constantly recur throughout this attempt to explore the relationship between politics and the religion in East-Central Europe. The first, which has already been mentioned, is of course the question about history, about its meaning, and about the destiny of the nation. There are two others that flow from it and are themselves linked – the specific part played by the intelligentsia and the complex relationships maintained by Polish, Czech, Slovak and Hungarian society with the state. This is not the place to treat these subjects in detail; a whole book would not suffice for that task. Hence we can deal with them only briefly and fragmentarily, for the purpose of supplying a number of waymarks and introducing some of the key problems.

After 1918, Masaryk declared: 'I think it right to consider the nation and nationality as the goal of social trends, and the state as a means; it is a fact that every nation conscious of itself tends to acquire its own state.'[15] This way of putting it well encapsulates the manner in which the relationship between state and nation has been posed in this part of Europe. The two cannot be virtually identified, as they can in France or Britain. To say that the state is an instrument is to conjure up all the historical ambiguities connected with the way in which it is defined, and this is determined by a more or less conscious quest on the part of the nation, whose identity is worked out *without* the state, or even *against* it. How could it be otherwise, given that the national states had disappeared and been replaced by a dynastic link, with various degrees of acceptance in the different countries? Certainly the development of a national consciousness has been no straightforward process and appears to be heavily charged with ambiguities. For example, in what sense can one speak of national consciousness for a Polish peasant subject to the tsar at the end of the nineteenth century? Or for a Hungarian peasant of the same period? In both cases, consciousness of class ('The Pole is the Lord!') or religious identity, strongly experienced as an ethnic classifier (Polish *because* Catholic and Ruthenian *because* Uniate), appear to be dominant.[16] In the same way, it is essential to recall that during the nineteenth century and for the first half of the twentieth, the Polish, Czech and Hungarian societies were multinational, multiconfessional, multicultural and multilingual societies; that in them nationalism has been strongly tinged with xenophobia, anti-Semitism and exclusiveness; and that the Church, which was often invoked as a support for nationalism, has sometimes served as an alibi for nationalism in some of its most questionable manifestations.[17] Precisely in so far as a national identity was denied a state around which to crystallize, its favoured instrument was culture in the broad sense, and this was bound to give the intelligentsia and the Church a specific part to play. As things were, the former succeeded the nobility as a repository of national consciousness.[18] As Bernard Michel writes:

> In the national movement in Poland, the Libelts and the Mickiewicz replaced the members of the old aristocracy after 1830, such as the Czartoryski who still dominated life in Poland before the Partitions. In Bohemia-Moravia, the intelligentsia was forced to take the lead, almost single-handed, in a national movement which could not exist without it. Without Palacky, and later on without Kramar and without Masaryk, there is no Czech political life and no struggle for national values. Palacky had to be Hugo, Thiers and Jules Ferry all rolled into one. The nation's survival depended upon the intelligentsia's taking upon itself all these functions. For it had not only (as in France in the nineteenth century) to answer the questions society was asking itself about the meaning of the future and the existence or non-existence of God. It also had to utter the oracles of science and single-handedly to guide the nation into the way of applying those ideas in practical matters.[19]

This conception of the intelligentsia as having a *mission* with respect to the nation, an intelligentsia that claimed to *educate* the poeple, is itself not without ambiguity. Certainly it calls to mind the specific part these groups have to play in forming a *national culture* able to support a national identity.[20] But the enthusiasm with which the intelligentsia shoulders this task should not conceal the ambivalence of its relationship to society.[21] For example, it is well known that the attitude of the nobles, the bourgeois and the intelligentsia of Bohemia towards the French Revolution was almost identical: fear of losing their own privileges and a pan-Slav cult of an absolutist Russia. As the Hungarian Istvan Bibo observed:

> In these countries, the broad mass of the people for whom the national idea, then being formed, did not coincide with the historically existing reality of the

dynastic state, at first adopted a somewhat passive attitude towards the idea of the nation; but the national intelligentsia made immense efforts to 'teach' the people the 'lesson' of nationalism. Of course, only history was capable of successfully teaching this lesson, but in the meantime the contention of primary Marxism that the national idea acts as a draught-screen to the interests of certain restricted groups, represented a mortal danger which threatened to hamper the educational efforts of the national intelligentsia.[22]

So the ground is somewhat treacherous, because of the very considerable overlaps of national, religious and social motifs, each with a logic of its own, whose objectives it sought to impose upon the others as so many ultimate aims. The national theme is most frequently accorded priority precisely because of the perceived threat to the existence of the nation. It invoked an urgency and a priority to which the others could not lay claim. This gave rise to many ambiguities, not the least of these being the 'nationalization of religion' at the cost of a 'sacralization of the nation', to introduce expressions that will be encountered later on. The fact is that religion and the Church, which underpin human hopes and are evidences of continuity and pledges of perpetuity, were bound to face attempts to use them for political ends. Nevertheless, a distinction has to be drawn between the two.

In each of the three countries with which we are here concerned, the Catholic Church maintained organic relationships with certain groups in society: the Church's hierarchy was identified with the leading nobility, in many cases by blood relationships. As a large landowner, the Church had common interests with other large landowners; at a lower level, upward social mobility was facilitated by membership of the priesthood indeed, in the case of a young, poor Slovak it was almost a *sine qua non*. These close ties tended to affect the Church's image there, as anywhere else. Being rich and powerful itself, the Church was a natural ally of the rich and powerful in society, and this sometimes generated a strong current of anti-clericalism among the populace, of which some traces are still perceptible – even in Poland for all its devotion to Catholicism.[23] But even apart from the ambiguities connected with the perception of the Church in society, one has only to go back as far as the nineteenth century to find evidence of the great diversity of situations as regards its role in the national question:[24] in Poland alone, a different religious policy was followed in each of the three areas into which the country was partitioned, so much so that even today the sociological map of religious practices in the People's Republic of Poland could easily be interpreted simply by highlighting the exact boundaries of the Russian, Prussian and Austrian zones of occupation to explain the differences found between the various regions.[25] And whereas in Poland, taking all the zones together, the Catholic Church was able to underpin the slow formation of the national consciousness, in Bohemia it was felt to be an instrument in the service of central government. When the 'Bach absolutism' re-established the Church's supervision of education, Czechs saw this as the continuation of a process which, from the Counter Reformation to the present day, has identified the interests of the foreign state with those of the Catholic Church, to the disadvantage of the nation.

This being so, it is not surprising that the Church should have attracted bitter, stubborn criticism, and should have been regarded as an *enemy* by the nationalist movement. When therefore, as in Poland,[26] the church gave its support to such a movement, it was on social grounds that it was attacked.

Religion in turn has always been utilizable, once again at the cost of many misunderstandings, as a symbolic vehicle, either as a means of affirming a national identity threatened with destruction[27] or as a support for social demands, as witness the very strong connection between social and religious themes during the peasant rebellions that have occurred throughout the history of the region, or again as justification for a 'national messianism' aimed at giving hope for the future to peoples lacking such a hope. For in the last resort the crux of the matter is always the 'meaning'. That is what is really meant by all the references to *Poland, Christ of the nations*, suffering to redeem the sins of the world. Like every canonization, sacralization of the nation is intended to transform a defeat into a victory. The disappearance of national states, in Poland, in Bohemia or in Hungary, bore heavily on the collective mentalities of their peoples and proved fruitful ground for what Bibo describes as 'the burgeoning of confused political theories and philosophies which in the end submerge the political life of these communities paralysed by fear'.[28] Even the restoration of national independence would not transform this situation in depth, especially in a context in which the problems of coexistence between different nationalities would arise in particularly acute form. The imposition of soviet-type regimes, by once more abrogating national sovereignty, has helped to pose the same questions yet again under a new aspect, questions concerning the state, the role of the intellectuals and of the church, and, of course, the meaning of the nation's history.

A marked propensity to seek compromise

On 11 April 1963, John XXIII addressed the encyclical *Pacem in Terris* to the world. The new attitude adopted by the Pope with respect to Soviet-type regimes marked a radical departure from the uncompromisingly condemnatory tone adopted up to that time. Although the encyclical was favourably received in Moscow, it did not in fact introduce anything new in substance. But the tone was different.[29] Undoubtedly the basic idea both of the Pope and of Monsignor Casaroli, who was to be the chief architect of

Vatican policy towards Eastern Europe, was to avoid leaving the Church in the half of Europe dominated by the USSR and under constant attack, to its own devices with all the risks of schisms that course would entail. Direct negotiations with the governments concerned were, therefore, inevitable. In May 1963 Monsignor Casaroli therefore went to Budapest, thus initiating a policy that Paul VI later bade him continue, and from then onwards the contacts were never broken off. On 15 September 1964 the first agreement was signed in Budapest. On 19 February 1965, Monsignor Tomasek was appointed apostolic administrator of the archdiocese of Prague and the ex-primate, Monsignor Beran, was permitted to leave the country accompanied by Monsignor Casaroli. An agreement was signed with Yugoslavia on 25 June 1966. In 1967 Monsignor Casaroli made three visits to Poland, and in 1969 the episcopal hierarchy in Hungary was reorganized. In 1970 the protocol on diplomatic relations with Yugoslavia was signed, and on 2 February 1971 Monsignor Casaroli went to Moscow to sign on behalf of the Vatican the treaty on non-proliferation of atomic weapons. While there, he made contact with officials in the Ministry of Religious Affairs. M. Gromyko, the Soviet Minister of Foreign Affairs, had already met Paul VI on two occasions, in April 1966 and in November 1970. On 30 January 1967, M. Podgorny, chairman of the praesidium of the Supreme Soviet, visited the Vatican. These first steps are evidence of the relative speed of a process that was to lead within a decade to the normalization of relations between Church and state, to differing degrees in the various countries. Kadar, Gierek and Tito, as well as other dignitaries, also made the journey to Rome. In 1979, John Paul II went on an official visit to the land of his birth, the first Pope to tread the soil of a Soviet-bloc country. Moscow and the Soviet-bloc countries had very different reasons for playing along with this normalization. There can be no doubt that the new international deal and the demands of détente exerted a real influence by making it more difficult openly to repress believers in the interest of making a favourable impression on public opinion in the West. But internal factors were doubtless more important: religion, expected rapidly to wither away, was putting up unexpected resistance, and harassment, far from diminishing it, magnified its influence and power tenfold. Moreover, the need for moral standards was often painfully evident, given that the state itself did not provide a credible example. But it does not follow that the general attitude of the existing governments in East-Central Europe towards the Church had undergone a sea change. On 15 August 1986, at Czestochowa, the primate of Poland, Monsignor Glemp, accused the authorities of wishing to destroy the Church.[30] In July the primate of Czechoslovakia, Monsignor Tomasek, declared that the government was trying to 'reduce [the Church] to slavery'.[31] All that has happened is that policy on religion has become more shrewd and has diversified from country to country while adhering to the same objective. Smothering by normalization, as attempted in Hungary, has as its counterpart smothering by physical constraint as practised in Czechoslovakia. Neither of these techniques was suitable for Poland, where the government was constrained to innovate, and this it did with great pragmatism. This being so, a brief review of the situations in the three countries in the mid-eighties may prove useful.

Hungary: a normalized Church

When asked to describe the situation in Hungary, Laszlo Makkai, professor of history at Budapest University and a very respected member of the Calvinist Church, spoke of 'maximum possible freedom'.[32] This opinion is also found within the Catholic Church: 'The nightmare is over – said a priest in Budapest who, like many others, was imprisoned and forbidden to officiate some thirty years ago. Everything can be done in this country – services, preaching, teaching, concerts, etc.'[33] And indeed a real consensus has been established between the Church and the state, due both to the wish of the former for a cessation of physical persecution and of the latter to offer the population some material and symbolic compensations for the frustrations that have accumulated since the 1956 revolution was crushed. In essence, the challenge of consumerism was a gamble aimed both at normalizing the Church and neutralizing it. By and large, this aim has been achieved. No doubt there has been a decline in religious observance, though it is still somewhat above the levels usual in Western Europe,[34] but the Church in Hungary can carry on its normal activities, many books are published dealing with relations between Marxism and religion, and Cardinal Lekai, the primate of Hungary, had no hesitation in saying:

> From the ideological point of view, the people of our country do not all see eye to eye, but every day brings proof that harmony can be created in the common interest of the country if in going about our work we do not look at what separates us but at what unites us. . . . Dialogue is an open road which will bring us closer together, without compromising our ideological convictions, in common action dictated by the good of our country.[35]

Imre Miklos, president of the State Office for Church Affairs, had almost the same message:

> Developments in society have convinced the Church that there is no future in simply standing on the conviction that ideological reconciliation is impossible – a conviction which we share. For there are many things in socialism worthy of encouragement. We must try to save people from feeling schizophrenic, half religious and half not. Do not let us divide man: a citizen can both experience religious feelings and build socialism. We are not asking the

Church to stop what it is doing, but to recognize the good things that have been achieved. In return, we do not promise to renounce ideology; the ideological struggle is going on in the consciousness of the people. But it is not a situation of war or confrontation. At the beginning of the fifties we prophesied that the Church had not long to live, but the Church said the same about us. Now each has begun to learn what were the values of the other, even though the path to understanding was not smooth. Time has wrought change in us; we have learned to talk to one another. Some matters are perceived differently with the passage of time. Discussion is not confrontation but creative meeting. Common interests must be in the foreground, even if there is still a background. Solutions will be found by compromise.[36]

This pragmatism is not a pretence; today normalization is a reality in Hungary. There is now a full complement of bishops: each of the dioceses is administered by a bishop, and there are altogether 2,700 priests in charge of 2,300 parishes, as well as 200 religious responsible for the eight Catholic high schools. There are five seminaries training 280 seminarists and 400 students are taking courses at Budapest theological faculty.[37] There is no doubt that this normalization offers distinct advantages to both sides. It enables the Church to carry on its normal activities, besides giving it appreciable material advantages. Church dignitaries draw a salary equivalent to that of a minister, and priests can live comfortably on the salaries and pensions paid by the state.[38] For its part, the government succeeds in neutralizing forces that are potentially in conflict with it, and in directing them towards useful objectives such as peace, moral values, patriotism, and so on. In this way, by making use of the long-standing method of the Habsburgs, it contrives by setting the various Churches against one another and, in each of them, the grassroots against the hierarchy, to obtain a very firm control over religious activity.

Above all, the onset of consumerism has had some undesirable effects, and these have made the state realize how useful the Church could be to it in laying down an ethical line which could serve as a moral basis for society. As Laszlo Makkai observed, in language that would not be repudiated by Imre Miklos, 'religion is a social necessity recognized by the state, and secularized Christian morality is the only moral code common to the whole of Europe; it is the only one from which moral training can be given to children, in the absence of a secular model'.[39] The problem is the danger that a normalized Church may lose its credibility and that its moral teaching may be perceived by the people as a crutch provided for the government. Be that as it may, the spiritual vacuum from which Hungarian society is suffering frightens both the political leaders and the Catholic hierarchy, and the opponents themselves deplore the relative cynicism of a working class that is more concerned about maintaining a material standard of living which it knows to be higher than that of the other bloc countries than it is about winning social or political rights. In the words of Miklos Haraszty, a member of this opposition, 'it would be deluding oneself to lead workers who don't want to be led'.[40] According to the sociologist Miklos Tomka, the field of religion in present-day Hungary is marked 'by religiosity in the lower levels of the social, cultural and political structure, by the end of ecclesiastical hegemony, the spread of ideological indifference and the rise of new base communities, new forms of religiosity'.[41] The fact is that although there are still some points of tension[42] between Church and state, by and large the episcopate seems to be content with the situation, and many grassroots Christians view this as capitulation pure and simple on the part of the hierarchy, which is thereby discredited in the eyes of the most active among the faithful; indeed, this disaffection can extend to religion itself. As one historian put it, the Church, accused of compromising itself and of serving the interests of the government,

> would be better advised to listen to the complaints of our dissatisfied Christians and to make an effort to meet their spiritual needs. Political and intellectual anarchy is offering the Church a golden opportunity of bringing about a spiritual renewal, whereas the state is playing with a delayed-action bomb. If it is not careful the Church will find itself, as usual, on the wrong side of the barricades.[43]

This conclusion is vindicated by the facts; the base communities movement, the main characteristics of which will be described later, also claims to be a search for a style of living which is authentically religious because it is not perverted and is a vehicle of renewal. Understandably, the episcopate will have nothing to do with such a movement.

Czechoslovakia: a Church that is becoming radicalized

On 17 March 1968 a petition signed by 22,317 Catholics was sent to Alexander Dubcek. It contained a list of twelve anti-religious government measures, declared that the main provisions of the period of the 'cult of personality' were still in force, and expressed surprise 'that such a state of affairs is still possible in Europe, among highly civilized nations'.[44] This action bore witness both to the very difficult situation of the Church in Czechoslovakia and to the hopes aroused by the 'Prague Spring' then unfolding. In actual fact, there had been some slight improvements during the 1960s. Two Slovak bishops had been allowed to attend the council held in 1963, and Monsignor Beran, the archbishop of Prague, was released from house arrest. Two years later he left the country and Monsignor Tomasek, until then auxiliary bishop of Olomouc, was appointed apostolic administrator of the Prague archbishopric. In 1967 Monsignor Casaroli had several meetings with Karel Hruza, the official in the Czechoslovak government responsible for religious affairs. However, at the same time the central committee of the Party was issuing secret internal instructions about the intensification of the struggle against the Church. During the 'Prague Spring' several bishops and priests who had been interned were allowed to return to their dioceses or parishes. At the end of March 1968, Hruza was replaced by Erika Kadlecova, a sociologist from the Academy of Sciences who was said to favour dialogue between Christians and Marxists. At the end of May, Kadlekova published in *Rude Pravo*, the official organ of the Czech Communist Party, an article that aroused considerable comment, inasmuch as it contained a disavowal of the anti-religious policy that had been followed since 1949. The Church's activity was reorganized both in Bohemia and in Slovakia, beginning with the Peace Movement of Patriotic Clergy, an organization dedicated to close surveillance of religious affairs by the government. The governing committee was removed from office, the *numerus clausus*, which limited the number of seminarists, was abolished in practice, and the Church began to make preparations for the reopening of the religious houses, which had been dissolved since 1950. But, as Robert Aigner wrote:

> The Prague spring did not last long enough to enable religious life in Czechoslovakia to be regulated or regularized, on a basis of legality, let alone by the passing of laws. There was a certain incoherence about events, as indeed about the whole process of liberalization in the country. The officials responsible for monitoring the Church, the secretaries for religious affairs, were still in office. They had not become excessively active, but were letting things take their course. . . . So developments in the Church had been tolerated, but nothing more. Therefore when normalization was resumed, all the instruments for controlling the Church were already in place.[45]

And in point of fact, despite certain favourable signs that had been noted after the Soviet troops entered the country, the attitude of the government hardened immediately. Karl Hruza returned to his post. The Post-conciliar Renewal Foundation, set up in order to encourage the study and implementation of the Vatican II decrees, was proscribed and the diplomatic talks with the Holy See were called off, not to be renewed until 1972.

Some twenty years after 1968, the situation of the Church in Czechoslovakia is still confused and difficult. It has been said that eight of the thirteen bishoprics are without incumbents, and only three are validly filled: Prague, where Cardinal Tomasek was officially appointed only on 10 January 1978 following lengthy negotiations between the Vatican and the authorities, Banska Bystrica (Monsignor Jozef Feranec) and Nitra (Monsignor Jan Pasztor). Two others are managed by apostolic administrators, Trnava (Monsignor Julius Gabris) and Olomouc (Monsignor Jozef Vrana). It must also be said that some of these appointments are by no means universally approved. As Alexander Tomsky emphasized:

> Putting the most favourable construction on it, the bishops who were appointed in 1973 believe that it is impossible to do anything; at worst, they are corrupt, unscrupulous time-servers [like bishop Vrana of Olomouc]. Their outlook was formed during the terror of the fifties; their aim is to survive without causing any violent reaction on the part of the state, in the hope of seeing the Church outlive the present regime. They know that their priests are spied upon by informers who make their reports to the local religious affairs office and they are afraid of losing even more priests, who will go to swell the ranks of those who have a titular position but are unable to perform their pastoral task. Their main concern is to preserve the official institution of the Church, as a structure necessary to its survival and a powerful symbol in a totalitarian society.'[46]

And yet during the 1970s it looked as if progress was being made in Czechoslovakia, as in other countries, towards the establishment of a *modus vivendi* between Church and state, even though it was the Church that was making the running. The condemnation of Charter 77 by Cardinal Tomasek set the seal on the growing influence of the organization Pacem in Terris, presided over by the bishop of Olomouc, Monsignor Vrana. In 1972 Mr Lucan, vice-president of the Slovak government, speaking at a meeting of the ideological committee of the Party, was able to express his pleasure at the progress made:

> Since April 1969 there has been a far-reaching change in outlook. . . . The most encouraging fact is that a party of churchmen have expressed their loyalty towards the state, the possibility of working together with the state and their desire for a good understanding between the Church and the government. This movement has found expression in the organization *Pacem in Terris*.[47]

This was certainly not the opinion of the great majority of Czechoslovak Catholics. In 1979, 350 of them sent John Paul II a letter in which they complained that they could not 'call upon the heads of our Church. Our association of priests which claims to speak on behalf of Catholics in reality serves the purposes of the state designed to snuff out religious life in this country. Every attempt to obtain justice from the authorities has so far ended before the public prosecutor.'[48]

This appeal, signalizing an attempt by believers at the grassroots to exercise on the episcopate a counter-thrust to the pressure exerted by government, was a sign of radicalization. Hence the obligation placed upon priests by the 1982 decree to leave Pacem in Terris hastened a process that had already largely begun and opened a new phase of severe tension between the Church and the government. Notwithstanding the efforts of the government to prevent publication of the text of that decree, and the refusal of the organization to disband, it appears that half of its membership of priests resigned from it.[49] Moreover, Monsignor Tomasek adopted a much stronger line. In July 1982 he did not hesitate to denounce the secretariat of Pacem in Terris for 'infringement of religious discipline' and to order the official Catholic weekly *Katolicke Noviny* to publish the text of the papal decree in full. When the periodical refused to comply, the cardinal withdrew its 'religious authorization' on 1 November 1982 and removed its 'religious controller', Jan Lebeda, from his post. These decisions drew the wrath of the authorities upon the primate, whom they had often violently attacked in the press. In an article published on 17 December 1982 by *Rude Pravo*, the official organ of the Party, M. Hruza described the Vatican's position as 'a blatant attempt to interfere in the affairs of Czechoslovak citizens . . . attacking priests who support the struggle for peace and for building their country whereas it praises those who are trying to destroy socialism'.

From then onwards, the primate had become radicalized along with grassroots Christians. Thousands of copies of clandestine publications circulated and original methods of protest made their appearance, such as cutting out from *Katolicke Noviny* articles that, in the readers' opinion, had no place there and sending them back to the editorial staff. Clearly, the emergence of an underground Church was part of this movement.

Nor did the government stand idly by. More and more priests had their work permits withdrawn, more and more priests or laymen were accused of 'illegal religious activities'. In January 1983 Helena Gondova and Frantisek Novajesky were sentenced to a year in prison for 'making preparations for incitement to rebellion'. On 27 May of that year a priest, who had already been deprived of his working permit, was arrested. On 1 June, the police carried out an extensive search in a house for retired nuns at Prelouc, east of Prague. In March some Franciscans were arrested and accused of 'clandestine and illegal religious activities'. On 11 December 1983 three young people, two of them students and one a worker, were arrested in Slovakia, accused of having illegally crossed the Polish frontier carrying religious literature. In March 1984 a campaign of intimidation was mounted against the 17,000 signatories of a petition asking that the Pope should visit Czechoslovakia. In March 1985, three young Catholics were sentenced to periods of imprisonment by the Bratislava court for having caused religious literature to be brought into the country illegally. In April an extensive police operation aimed at the underground Catholic press was unleashed.[50] And these are only some of the known cases, which have been publicized by VONS, Charter 77 and the Western press. Furthermore, the authorities are strongly pressuring priests to rejoin Pacem in Terris, especially in Slovakia, under threat of withdrawing their permits to practise in case of refusal; this would compel them to find secular employment or to go underground. And in any event, since the police have the right to scrutinize work engagements, such a priest would have to accept manual work, as a labourer or car washer, if he wished to avoid being charged under laws punishing 'social parasitism'. Lastly, the government misses no opportunity of criticizing John Paul II. On 28 March 1984, *Tribuna*, a weekly published by the central committee of the Czech Communist Party, denounced 'one of the most reactionary Popes of this century', who 'calls on Catholics on Central Europe to take as their example the reactionaries of the Polish Church', and who 'during his travels, always concludes that communism and the Soviet Union must be destroyed'. Yet this statement was published barely a month after Monsignor Poggi, the itinerant Papal Nuncio for Eastern Europe, had visited Prague, a revealing sidelight on the continuing state of tension between Church and state in the country. In spite of that, however, the Church succeeds in assembling numbers of up to 200,000 of the faithful for pilgrimages to Levoca, Velehrad or Sastin,[51] most of them young people forthrightly punctuating their march with unambiguously political slogans, thus adding to the unease of the government.

Poland: the ambiguities of power

Poland is a nation for which history has taken the place of geography; it has its own peculiar relationship with space. The era of partition, during which to be Polish was not a nationality but a *destiny*, in the words of Adam Mickiewicz, has deeply influenced people's thinking. This is illustrated by the persistent rumour circulating at the end of 1980 that Russia, East Germany and Czechoslovakia had reached an agreement to divide out the spoils of their rebellious neighbour. The political leaders are past masters in the art of harping on this theme; they try to use it to underpin a legitimacy that is, to say the least, doubtful.

Catholicism, with its 14,000 churches, disputes part of the national territory with the state and anchors Poland in a Latinity from which certain fundamental values of the nation derive. The conflicts between government and the Church about religious processions which, the laws in force decree, may not take place elsewhere than on Church premises, are a good indication of what is at stake. A church, a chapel, an oratory, even the simplest cross, bear witness to an allegiance and lay claim to ownership of a place.

Thus it is that the pictures of Our Lady of Czestochowa and the portraits of John Paul II when posted on the railings of the Gdansk shipyards were meaningful at several levels. They signalized the essential part played by the Church in the moves towards the formation of what later became Solidarity, and in the awareness that had crystallized around the Pope's first visit. They claimed that history was on the side of the workers and their movement. In fact, the reference to the Pope, who in a survey conducted at the end of 1980 was said by 73 per cent of respondents to symbolize the best in present-day Poland,[52] takes us right back to the baptism of Mieszko in AD 966, through the Swedish wars of the seventeenth century and the *Flood* (Potop) to the affirmation of a national identity the characteristics of which clearly had little in common with the values extolled by the authorities.

Two of the tasks assumed by the Church before the appearance of Solidarity were, first, to be the bearer of a certain national legitimacy, a guardian of the fundamental interests of the nation;[53] relying upon its prestige and its strong roots in the people, as the only legal institution having an infrastructure and means of expression not controlled by the state, it constituted the only autonomous area that government could not claim to include within its sphere. What is more, it is the Church that gives hospitality in its publications to secular opponents, providing them with a platform; it is the Church that lends rooms in which meetings of the Flying University can be held, thus helping society in the search for its own history. And lastly, it is the Church that, more generally, participates in the reconstitution of a social geography which the state had been doing its best to disperse.[54]

Of course Solidarity, 10 million members strong, had no need of protection and was not prepared to shelter under anybody's wing. Assuming the defence of the interests of society as a whole and insisting on the moral nature of its action, it took over from the Church in challenging the legitimacy of the government, depriving it of that monopoly, confining it to the role of an adviser, and even going so far as to contest its right to play an overtly political role, by placing the accent on its spiritual vocation. Thus Polish society underwent a certain secularization during the period when the trade union was legal. Some internal factors were involved, for example the death of the charismatic leader Cardinal Wyszynski, and the commitment of very many young priests side by side with their parishioners, as well as the internal factor of the emergence of Solidarity. Nevertheless, it is very difficult to arrive at an accurate judgement of this process.[55]

This process was abruptly halted on 13 December 1981, after which the Church regained the central position it had occupied before August 1980. For from the morning on which the clampdown occurred, it was to the churches that the Poles went of their own accord to find refuge,[56] and to exchange information. It was the Church that assumed the task of organizing and distributing aid to the families of those who had been interned. But although everybody praises this aspect of the Church's action, the ambivalent attitude of the bishops was sometimes more than a little suspect. By agreeing to enter into negotiations with the government in order that the Pope's visit might take place, and by giving absolute priority to the maintenance of civil peace, even at the price of accepting, even implicitly, the process of normalization, were not the bishops running the risk of dividing the Church of the Poles, of creating a rift between the hierarchy and the more radical lower clergy – in fact, of becoming trapped in a process of collaboration similar to that in Hungary? As soon as *martial law* had been imposed, the head of the Polish Church issued an appeal to the faithful to avoid any sharp confrontation between society and the government:

> It matters little that the Church can be accused of running away, of temporizing or of softening radical attitudes. It is the Church's duty to defend every human life and hence, in a state of war, she will issue a call in favour of peace, for a cessation of violence, wherever than can be done, in order to exorcise fratricidal conflict, should matters come to that. Nothing is so important as human life![57]

Many people in Poland interpreted this declaration as nothing more than the justification of a surrender.[58] Such people barely concealed their indignation at certain attitudes adopted by the primate who, after having called for calm, went on television to advise striking actors to return to work, and made statements that were thought ill-timed, to say the least, on the eve of the general strike organized by the underground movement on 10 November 1982, and to give repeated signs of goodwill towards a government that gave nothing in exchange, to condemn the installation of American missiles and, to conclude the recital, to move the priest Nowak, vicar of the parish of Ursus and a man hated by the authorities.

That explains the criticisms levelled at Cardinal Glemp, whether by the clergy themselves[59] or by society. For example, in 1984 an open letter was in circulation, published clandestinely in Warsaw and signed with the pseudonym 'Father Olaf', criticizing the primate for his excessive 'submission' to the government and begging him not to 'take the path of patriarch Pimen'.[60] This text illustrates the worsening of the distrust felt no doubt by many Poles – though it is hard to say how many – towards the head of the Polish Church. His policy of social peace 'at any price' was misunderstood all the more because people found it difficult to see any compensating advantages. For example, some of the delegates taking part in the national conference of the Party on 16, 17 and 18 March 1984 still felt called upon fiercely to denounce the 'intolerance' of the Church.[61] Similarly, the government decided to introduce the 'science of religion', that is, 'scientific' atheism, as a compulsory subject from the commencement of the 1986 school year in secondary education, though this did produce a sharp reaction from Monsignor Glemp.[62]

There is no doubt that, as *Wola*, an underground publication, complained, the primate 'puts the interests of the Church as an institution first, instead of the interests and aspirations of the nation as a whole'.[63]

However, doubtless from the Church's point of view the two were identical. Thus, from December 1981 until June 1983, all the efforts of the episcopate were directed solely towards making possible the visit of the Pope to his country of birth. In pursuit of this priority a policy of appeasement had to be followed towards the authorities. This choice explains the appearance of a certain disharmony between a hierarchy anxious for the survival of the institution and hence careful to see that the boat was not rocked, and priests close to the day-to-day worries of the people, who adopted a more radical tone.[64] The assassination of Father Popieluszko in October 1984 both highlighted this dissonance and lessened it, because it forced both the hierarchy and the Church as a whole to become more radical.[65] The ties between the feelings of the nation and Catholicism, the powerful ecclesiastical structures,[66] the special place held by priests within the society, and the coming together of secular opposition and the Church in the 1970s have combined to ensure that the Church is still the accepted locus of faith and the expression of religion, and the only legal structure around which new movements in civil society have been able to organize themselves since 13 December. The Church provides society with the symbols and the vocabulary that enable it to express its rejection of normalization. Moreover, it is a rampart against normalization, especially in cultural matters, since it provides venues for exhibitions, literary evenings, concerts and theatrical performances. It also acts as a go-between, enabling the government to save face by not having to negotiate with a trade union that has been dissolved, with opponents who have been proscribed, or with foreign institutions unacceptable to other bloc countries. For example, representatives of the episcopate discussed with the government the fate of the eleven detainees whom the government did not know what to do with.[67] Doubtless, as Cardinal Wyszynski said in his Christmas sermon in 1977, in Poland 'Catholics are more enviably situated than in other countries where the churches have been closed.[68] Clearly, it is only the power of the Polish Church that has compelled the government to compromise with it, even though it is obvious that this makes no difference to the long-term objectives of the government and that there are still a considerable number of 'hardliners' within the state organizations who find the very existence of the Church intolerable.[69]

The price to be paid for this power, or its ambiguity, consists in the responsibility that the Church must accept. As a central actor on the stage of Poland, the institution of the Church is a permanent bone of contention between society, which has great difficulty in grasping that the Church might cherish aims not *completely* identical to its own, and the government which, being unable to reduce it, dreams of instrumentalizing it to its own advantage.

An inescapable paradox

What makes the Church symbolically the guarantor of the truth is the vigour with which it plays the part of a denouncer of lies. It is the freedom that it manifests that enables it to embody freedom. But since opting for the long term entails accepting normalization, the Church finds itself boxed into the logic of institutionalization, compelled to give priority to its stabilizing role to the detriment of its potential as an alternative power centre, even though by so doing it loses some of its prestige and its influence on society,[70] and hence some of its ability to bring pressure to bear on those in power.

What this means is that the Church is constantly confronted with the problem of defining the equilibrium threshold between institutionalization and non-institutionalization, normalization and non-normalization, given that there is no definitive situation and that the other actors on the socio-political scene can at any time raise questions about something that might appear to have been settled.

Ideal of the government[71]	Church institutionalized, normalized and influential, helping to disseminate the official values.
Ideal of the Church	Normalization and institutionalization with a maximum of advantages and a minimum of concessions so as to ensure both survival and influence
Ideal of civil society	Church institutionalized, not normalized and influential, defender and bearer of the values of society

In other words, we have the paradox that the more a Church is institutionalized and normalized, the less powerful it is; yet the less institutionalized and normalized it is, the less powerful it is. To escape this contradiction, the Church must contrive to combine, in different degrees from country to country, institutionalization and non-institutionalization, normalization and non-normalization.

It would be a mistake to think that the Church is free to deal with this dilemma as it alone sees fit. Both civil society and government are also concerned with it, though naturally for different reasons. The former does indeed need an institutionalized Church, one that can provide welcome and refreshment, and supply symbols that it may lack. At the same time, if these symbols are to remain attractive, the Church must not be perceived as compromised with the government. The latter for its part has of course a strong interest in neutralizing the Church through a process of institutionalization and normalization. But it would lose all the benefit from this operation if, at the end of the day, the Church were no longer capable of exercising the stabilizing role that it looks for.

Quite evidently, to attain its ideal the Church must overcome a major contradiction which is seen nowhere more clearly than in Poland. Even before the rise of Solidarity, Cardinal Wyszynski was regarded by Gierek as an interlocutor *par excellence* especially since, as it appears, many of their meetings took place in secret. As for Cardinal Glemp, he was received in a blaze of publicity by General Jaruzelski. Moreover, although the government might on occasion mount very violent attacks on the 'reactionary clergy' or 'extremist priests', or denounce 'clerical activists', some of its leading members have no hesitation in crossing thresholds that would have been considered unimaginable some years earlier. For example, M. Lopatka, Minister of Religious Affairs, stated on 4 June 1983 in an article published in the weekly *Polityka* that the authorities 'no longer held the opinion that the Church should keep out of politics', provided that it behaved 'in accordance with the constitution and respected the international interests of Poland'. The significance of this statement is apparent if it is compared with statements made by the minister's predecessors. In 1969 Dr Skarzynski stated that 'as a religious leader, the primate has the right to speak freely on religious matters, as long as he shows respect for the law. But what he cannot do is to speak, as a religious leader, about political matters. That we shall not tolerate.'[72] On 19 May 1976, again Mr Kakol stated: 'We shall not allow the Church to have any influence whatsoever on cultural and social life.'[73]

Clearly there has been a considerable change, and this may be the result of the Warsaw government's imperative need of assistance in implementing its policy of normalization, assistance that is so sadly lacking. For it is quite obvious that the Church is the only possible intermediary between the government, aware of the realism that the episcopate can display, and society. On 8 June 1983, a few days before the Pope made his visit, the fortnightly *Zycie Partii* ('The life of the Party'), the journal of the central committee circulated only to militants of the PZPR (Polish Unified Workers' Party) wrote: 'Polish communists are aware of the mass nature and the millennial tradition of Catholicism in Poland', and drew the conclusion that 'the place of the Church in socialist Poland' had to be recognized.

But at the same time, the government cannot give up its endeavour to fulfil the ideological requirement of combating the Church, and consequently it cannot enter into any permanent compromise with it. The affair of the Agricultural Modernization Fund is a good illustration of this dilemma. In bare outline, there was a scheme to make available to Polish agriculture large sums of money (up to 2,000 million dollars in the initial project) for the purpose of financing its modernization. The German and

American Churches contributed largely to this fund, but there were also other sources, such as the money from Lech Walesa's Nobel prize. These funds would have been administered by a board independent of the state, and some of its members would have had Church connections.

This splendidly original idea had been accepted by the government and a Bill had been adopted by the Council of Ministers and subsequently passed by the Diet on 6 April 1984, providing the project with a legal framework. There can be no doubt that it was calculated to give immediate, practical aid to an agriculture that was in real difficulty. But it would also have placed the Church in the position of co-managing the system, thus enabling it to acquire a certain amount of economic power, with all the consequences that might flow from such a development. This innovation, giving the Church joint responsibility, was bound to lessen the effects of any denunciations of the system that it might subsequently utter. And yet the government raised one obstacle after another, jeopardizing the agreement already reached and doing everything in its power to sideline the project and take control of it. The primate of Poland realized what was happening and, noting that 'the power of decision conferred upon the minister of agriculture' was irreconcilable with 'the principle of autonomy' of the fund, decided to give up the whole operation.[74]

2
Religion and Scientific Socialism: A Sociological Analysis

The advent of Soviet-type political regimes in East-Central Europe has resulted in the introduction of ideological standards in the most diverse areas of social life and individual or collective activity. Naturally, Sovietization has affected the sciences; its effects have been felt in all disciplines, particularly in sociology. Just as historians were given the task of rewriting the national histories, deleting references to the conflicts with Russians and other Soviet nationalities and placing the stress on co-operation with the USSR, so sociologists had to get down to describing a harmonious society in which the old dichotomy of the exploiters and the exploited had vanished. Naturally such language savoured more of Utopia than of reality, since these descriptions had no basis whatsoever in scientific observation.

The onset of conflicts between the working class and a Soviet-type government raised serious deontological problems and exacerbated a feeling of frustration. The epistemological break represented by the uprising of the proletariat against a state that in theory represented it led sociologists to forsake the area of consensus of a harmonious society from which all anachronistic phenomena had been eliminated. The government itself, understandably disturbed by the turn of events, redoubled its efforts to get to grips with reality and became an avid customer of the social sciences in its desire better to control those whom it governed. The sociology of religion had from the outset been subject to the same voluntarist logic. The 'groan of afflicted creation' ought quite naturally to fade away as its affliction was ended by the establishment of a system of government in which 'mankind was the most valuable good'. The fading away of religion was to be the proof of the success of the communist enterprise of the creation of a new man, and since the process leading to this birth was under way, obviously the task of the sociologist was to chronicle the progress and record the signs of the decline of religion. Hence a sociologist of religion was *ipso facto* in a very singular occupation, since the very subject of his study and observation was in the process of disappearing. If he subscribed to the Marxist postulate of man's alienation through religion, or more accurately of religion as a symptom of man's alienation, he had to record the progress achieved in implementing the essential political aim of the government – the elimination of religion. This sociological determinism was accompanied by a more directly normative dimension. The sociologist had to be not only a witness but also an actor and a militant. The specific task allotted to him by the government was to help in initiating the process of the decline of religion by informing government of the objective conditions whereby this could be hastened, and even telling it how to create such conditions.

There was however an initial period, lasting from 1947 to 1956 (and even to 1966–7 in Czechoslovakia), during which this normative role was almost meaningless. As a subdiscipline, the sociology of religion was as much divorced from reality as its parent discipline. For were not religious attitudes nothing more than survivals fit to be observed by ethnologists? And was not religion itself a phenomenon under sentence, destined to disappear at a pace determined by the material progress of societies and the implantation of the new sociopolitical system? What then was the use of wasting time (and public funds) studying something that was bound to appear as an archaism lacking any real meaning? The result of such an attitude was a total sterilization of scientific observation.

In 1956, with the first major conflicts between working classes and socialist states[1] and mindful of the role played both in Hungary and in Poland by the primates of the Catholic Church, Cardinal Mindszenty and Cardinal Wyszynski, the government had a requirement for sociological observation, inasmuch as the information collected, however objective, needed to be organized into a series showing that progress in the desired direction was being made. This wishful thinking is of itself sufficient to explain why the ongoing results of this project do not exactly tally with what the international scientific community regards as an authentic sociology of religion, meeting generally accepted criteria, not the least of which is the neutrality of the observer. On the contrary, the official sociology produced by Soviet-bloc countries on religious matters consists of an astonishing synthesis between a propaganda text, a declaration of intent and a political platform, in the pseudo-scientific dress of a commentary on data as to which, incidentally, there is frequently no indication on how it was gathered. Some fieldwork, a very selective use of data, extensive borrowings from the Party theoretical reviews, and a certain strength of conviction, admittedly owing much to the Coué method, such is the general picture of the sociology of religion in East-Central Europe.

However, we must beware of generalizing. Whereas up to 1956 this area, like all the others, was characterized by a veritable homogenization of societies and attitudes, brought about by the Sovietization and the Stalinization of East-Central Europe, the periphery of the Soviet empire, after that year a real diversification began to take place. In Czechoslovakia, no development was permitted; in Hungary and in Poland a growing number of sociologists began to do work on religion, even though they adopted the voluntarist viewpoint described earlier. But in Poland there arose at the same time an independent school, in competition with the official sociology, and its work compelled the state institutions to be more prudent in their collection of data and less cynical in presenting their conclusions. In fact, the existence of an independent – read 'Catholic' – school provided the means for comparing results.

This diversity was reinforced by the work of sociologists in other countries, whether exiles or simply foreigners. Though it must be emphasized that, in the almost total absence of direct observation on the ground, this work was based on the results published in the countries themselves. In other words, most of the time it consisted of a *critique* of these results, though some of this work was nevertheless of high quality.

The diversification was to become even more pronounced in the late 1970s. The normalization that was carried out after the sudden ending of the 'Prague Spring' led the new Czech and Slovak authorities to step up their anti-religious propaganda and hence to endeavour to give it greater credibility, and to intensify their anti-religious policy.[2] To do this they had to collect the information they needed as to the numbers of believers, their behaviour and their values. Thus there was some slight contribution to sociological observation, even if it was made by police officials.

Part of the fall-out of this operation was the appearance of a pseudo-sociological literature, though based on actual observation carried out for the purposes of suppression. Although this output is not of great value, it nevertheless deserves close examination, both on account of the information it supplies, sometimes by default, and above all because it betrays in negative form the apprehensions of the government when faced with a phenomenon that it did not succeed in bringing under control despite increased administrative surveillance, and which it found disturbing.

In Hungary the process of normalization had precisely the opposite effects. Seeking the broadest possible consensus, Janos Kadar's team was constrained to enter into a compromise with the Churches, to regularize its relations with the Catholic Church, the largest Church in the country, and to suggest a draft 'social contract' to the bishops and the faithful – liberalization instead of neutrality and loyalty or even collaboration. It was not long before the effects of such an attitude were felt in the field of research. The unexpected strength of religion was taken into account by sociology; instead of repeating forecasts that were falsified by the facts, sociologists began to make observations based on them, even though the conclusions they drew were still coloured by their former presuppositions and fixed ideas.

Lastly, in Poland, where the course of events itself was enough to convince the authorities how vain were their hopes regarding the decline of religion, they were in no position to prevent the development of independent research, and furthermore they themselves were aware of the need to obtain serious scientific information about the Church owing to its growing importance in politics.

Thus each of the three countries studied here is at a different level on a scale running from simple negation of the religious phenomenon to an effort to gain understanding for purposes of control, via determinist observation. Poland went through all three phases in succession, and it even combined the last two, in varying degrees depending on the authors. Similarly, Hungary went through all three stages, even though there still remain considerable survivals of the second stage in its production of sociology. As for Czechoslovakia, it is stuck between stages one and two.

There is of course very little to say about the *negative phase* with its refusal to face reality and its propagandist outlook; but the second phase, which we have dubbed the phase of *determinist observation*, is worth closer study, in that it gave birth to a shoal of publications based on theories of secularization and laicization, which enabled a scientific gloss to be imparted to what was no more than the expression of a political voluntarism. In this connection, Marxist sociologists of religion showed a great deal of interest in the development of Western societies, taking them for the nonce as so many models.

This may well have evidenced a very rapid decline in religious behaviour accompanied by a noticeable lessening of the impact of the traditional religious values, under the influence of an accelerated urbanization coupled with the fact that ever-widening circles of the population were gaining access to mass consumption. This attention was to have lasting effects even in the political field: both in Hungary and Poland, where the then Minister of Religious Affairs, M. Kazimierz Kakol, explicitly stated in 1976 that both the installation of a socialist system of mass consumption and the satisfaction of the ever-increasing material needs of the population were interpreted as being means of accelerating the disappearance of religion and the Churches, as had happened in the West.[3] Quite clearly this was to underestimate the importance of motivations peculiar to the individual, to say nothing of the transcendental dimension of the faith.[4] It was also to forget the interactions between religious factors, such as faith and the community of faith – and hence the Church as an institution – and the political system. Moreover, it took the governments both in Poland and Hungary many years to realize that, given a certain ideological context, the Church proves to be more alive when subjected to persecution than when it is simply ignored. In other words, the more the Church is attacked the greater its prestige, just because the attacks against it bear witness to the government's efforts to increase its ideological hold over a civil society which, to escape that domination, tends to take refuge in religious values beyond the reach of the political system.

The Hungarians did not fall into this trap. They made radical changes in their policy towards the Church, replacing persecution by an infinitely more skilful policy aimed to some extent at integrating the Church with the state apparatus; and this policy has already been partly crowned with success. Even so, Hungarian society has gone through a process that is puzzling sociologists, in that secularization is being overtaken by desecularization.

It is impossible to give a full list here of official and independent sociological production in Poland, Hungary and Czechoslovakia, nor is this our purpose. Nevertheless, a brief overview of this production and a few direct glimpses of the most representative among its works will serve to verify and illustrate the foregoing observations and to highlight certain broad trends. We shall, too, constantly remember that the changes that have taken place in the sociology of religion in Eastern Europe, its twists and turns and changes of subject, do not add up to a specific chronology but are parts of a threefold development: that of sociology, or of the social sciences in general, that of relations between Church and state, and lastly that of the political history of the societies in question. Under this aspect events such as 1956 in Hungary and Poland, 1968 in Czechoslovakia, 1980–1 in Poland, or the election of a Pope of Polish origin, have obviously had a major influence on the partial development sketched below.

Voluntarism in sociology: Czechoslovakia and Hungary

When we look at the 'sociology of religion' in Hungary and Czechoslovakia we are bound to conclude that, however policies concerning religious observance may have developed elsewhere, the strong ideological bias has been constant here, faithfully reflecting the fundamental objective of the Party – namely, to eliminate the Church and religion. Broadly speaking, what we have is a *zero state of sociology*. We need spend little time cogitating the ideological, political or scientific neutrality of a writer who publishes, for example, in the Czechoslovak review *Ateizmus*.

Miklos Tomka drew up for the review *Social Compass*[5] a well-researched bibliography of works on the sociology of religion written by Hungarians living in Hungary (hence excluding exiles publishing in Hungarian). This bibliography, listing the publications for the period 1945–79, shows 33 items out of a total of 161, of which the very titles are a political declaration of intent and the contents confirm that they are little more than propaganda pieces. Under cover of sociology, the aim pursued by the authors is obviously to make their contribution to the edifice of the government's fight against religion.

For example, in 1974 Mihaly Muranyi published in Budapest in the Kossuth series a work entitled *Vallas es Illuziok* (*Religion and illusion*) in which, basing himself on the postulate that religion is only a product of society, he reached the conclusion that anything to do with religion can only be a deception and a fraud. In 1977, in the review *Vilagossag* (no. 8–9 1969, pp. 458–60), the same author replied to the question 'Mi a szekularizacio?' ('What is secularization?') by calmly asserting: it is the *necessary* route to the extinction of religion.

The same normative, voluntarist temper is encountered in the works of Eva Csoregh ('Elpatolnak e az ifjak istentol?' – 'Are young people turning away from God?' – in *Vilagossag*, no. 8–9/1969, pp. 544–51), which concludes an article on education, reporting on about a hundred non-directive interviews with schoolchildren by affirming the *necessity* of a more strictly atheistic education. One Peter Jozna writes of religion as not only an irrational phenomenon – a view that could doubtless be defended – but as being pathological in certain cases, a theme for wide-ranging discussion ('A falusi vallasossag fenomenologiahoz' – 'Towards a phenomenology of rural religiosity' – in *Vilagossag*, no. 2/1970, pp. 118–21).

The sociology of religion in Czechoslovakia, or more accurately what passes for the sociology of religion there, is even more grotesquely distorted by ideological bias. The article entitled 'Tendencia pohybu religiozity v podmienkach Slovenska' ('The development of religiosity in the Slovak reality') published by Peter Prusak in the review *Ateizmus* (no. 5) is fully representative of this literature, and for that reason will repay a detailed analysis.

It begins with the bald statement: 'The increasingly rapid and ever-deepening process of secularization which characterizes all the socialist countries is at work in Slovakia as well.' The author then launches into a long exposition, justifying his observation by the effects of the far-reaching social changes and of technical and scientific progress. From this he logically deduces that, 'Religion and the Church are increasingly at odds with the needs and demands of the building of socialism. Believers are objectively constrained to try to resolve this contradiction, which they manage to do by giving religion a smaller place in their thinking and feeling.' To illustrate this trend, Prusak cites a survey made in 1971 purporting to show that 32 per cent of persons aged between eighteen and twenty-four in the sample studied claimed to be believers, against 64 per cent of persons aged over fifty-five. However, no information is given as to the technical characteristics of this survey – who carried it out, by what method, the size of the sample, or, of course, who commissioned it. There is no assurance that the sample studied was a representative one.

Prusak goes on to affirm, 'Nowadays people are much less religious than they used to be', as is confirmed by 'sociological surveys'. As an example, it is stated that there are only half as many believers among those who have had a secondary education as among those who have been to primary schools. Then the author plunges into a more elaborate analysis, giving details of each socio-occupational group. The surveys (still the same ones) show that 44 per cent of employed persons are atheists, while 38 per cent stated that they were believers. With regard to the last-named group, it is stated that their faith is characterized by 'introversion, individualization and theological speculation'. Prusak then admits, with obvious regret, that 57 per cent of workers said they were believers. He hastens to make some corrections to this order of magnitude: many of them (how many is not stated) are really 'indifferent to religion'. Moreover, 25 per cent of what – all the workers, or the 57 per cent who said they were believers, which would then mean 14.25 per cent of the workers?) are believers only because they were baptized at birth. The author does not ask himself why persons in this category nevertheless said they were believers. Was this question even asked? At all events, in this case as in the other no information is given as to the way in which the inquiry was conducted; not even the date is mentioned.

Even its formulation raises a problem. For example, when the author writes: '25 per cent of the rural population has given up religion', what about the 75 per cent who have not done so? Then again, what is the precise meaning of the term 'giving up', as to which at least a rough definition might be expected? In fact, Prusak concludes:

> The data show that the larger the city the more differentiated is sociocultural life and the lower the level of religiosity. Thus urbanization favours differentiation between individuals, destroys religious usages and traditions and the cult of saints. Hence the problem is to create sociocultural conditions which will promote the overall development of the personality in town and country.

Here we are well and truly immersed in the Sovietized, normative and determinist theory of secularization. This outrageous article would not be worth a second glance, but for the fact that it inadvertently supplies some useful information. For it is certain that the shadowy nature of the sources from which the author draws his information does not mean that the figures quoted were invented. Prusak obviously has access to information that is not made public, and that could only have been compiled by the relevant department of the state apparatus, in this case the Office of Religious Affairs. And it would be surprising if state agencies of this kind were to accept incomplete or doctored data, given their well-known links with the secret police.[6] They surely have a statistical databank at their disposal, if only for the purpose of identifying their targets or task-setting, though it is of course difficult to say how sophisticated this tool may be. And it is only to be expected that the thinly disguised plain-clothes agents charged with surveillance of religious services should make headcounts, even rough ones. It is a proven fact that records are kept on the faithful in these countries; any Christian who has been called in for interview could confirm this after listening to a recital of the religious gatherings in which he has taken part. It would not strain credulity to suggest that officials of the Religious Affairs Department obtain from their statistical material the data for a pseudo-sociology, and that writers such as Prusak convey some idea of their content.

It is however necessary to stress that the figures cited by Prusak or used in this or that study published officially in Czechoslovakia should be treated with considerable reserve. As the Czech sociologist in exile Jaroslav Krejci observed in an article published in *Sociological Analysis* in 1975, commenting on a survey published in Czechoslovakia in 1967,[7] 'it is permissible to doubt the veracity of the replies given by persons who have a good social position, and hence have more to lose. This goes some way to explain the very small percentage of believers among white collar workers and professional.' (Prusak correctly observed that the largest reduction in religious observance had occurred in this segment.) Krejci also mentioned one of the disturbing features common to all surveys officially published in Czechoslovakia – namely, the very high rate of 'no reply' or don't knows. To take only employed persons as an example, 44 per cent of atheists and 38 per cent of believers only add up to 82 per cent . . .

However representative Prusak's article may be of the general run of official writing on religion in Czechoslovakia, it illustrates only one of the trends of Marxist sociology of religion in Eastern Europe. But the underlying ideological bias remains, for any change of direction or broadening in the themes played upon by institutional sociologists is always directed towards a modification of the policy towards the Churches as a whole. For example, the publication in Budapest in 1979 by the Forras publishing house of Andras Balint's book *Rabizom magamistenre. Beszlgetes vallasos fiatalokkal* (*I Rely on God – Talks with Young Believers*) could not possibly have been published by a state publishing house in Prague. It was possible in Budapest only because of a change of tactics, not of aim, by the government. Nevertheless, such a book by its very title is a sign of the way in which political practice in Hungary has trimmed with regard to Soviet orthodoxy. There is no pejorative connotation, the words *young* and *believers* are juxtaposed, and the permission to publish is itself an implicit recognition that faith is not necessarily a negative phenomenon and that what young people claiming to be believers have to say is of sufficient interest to society to warrant to use of a product as scarce as paper. The development of Jozsef Lukacs is an interesting pointer to this trend. In 1960 this Marxist author published in *Vilagossag* an article entitled 'Technika, maganyossag, vallasossag' ('Technology, solitude, religion'), arguing the thesis already mentioned that social alienation and personal solitude are the two factors that explain religion. Naturally this second source, which no government, even a socialist one, has been able to bring under control, can be used to explain the persistence of religious attitudes under a Soviet-type political system.

In 1969 Lukacs advanced, in *Tarsadalmi Szemle* (pp. 7–8), a theory of secularization ('Tarsadalmi struktura es vallasi szabalyozas' – 'Social structure and religious regulation'). In 1976 he deplored the underdevelopment of the sociology of religion in his country ('Harmine esztendo a magyar vallaskritika torteneteben' – 'Thirty years of history of the critique of religion in Hungary', in *Vilagossag*, no. 4, pp. 201–9). Then in 1978 he edited a work published by Corvina and entitled *Reasoning Together*, dealing with the dialogue between Christians and Marxists, Church and state. More than the personal development of the author, this bibliographical selection clearly illustrates the successive modifications of the Hungarian government's policy *vis-à-vis* the Churches. This is proved by the publication, also in 1978, of an article signed by Lukacs in the Soviet review *Voprosy Ateisma*, entitled 'Sekularizatsia i religioznost pri sotsialisme' ('Secularization and religious observance in socialism', Kiev, no. 14, pp. 7–18), the content being what one would expect to find in a journal of this nature. A subject analysis of the bibliography drawn up by Miklos Tomka shows how typical this development of Lukacs was. In order to study the changes that had gradually occurred over the years in the choice of subjects studied, one had first to divide the publications into broad subject categories. Inevitably this division is an arbitrary one, and the result does not lay claim to complete rigour, being intended only to illustrate general trends. It is shown in table 4.

However rough and imperfect this division may be, it nevertheless calls for some comments. To begin with, it is noteworthy that a bibliography of works on the sociology of religion includes publications that are capable of influencing the *political* relations between Church and state. There are, for example, articles signed by government office-holders, such as Mr Aczel, the right-hand man of Janos Kadar, or Miklos, president of the Office of Cults. But in fact it is hardly surprising that Tomka saw to it that he included texts that, over and above their ideological, political or propaganda content, opened up new prospects to scientific activity and the establishment of less strained relations between Church and government which were bound to confer increased freedom on the sociologist, hence enabling him to obtain a better grasp of reality.

Unsurprisingly, two of the three most important categories deal with secularization, a major theme of the Marxist sociology of religion, and with the influence, or the degree of influence, of religion on young people and in the educational process. It is clear that these two themes are intimately connected, since the fading away of religion that the theory of secularization

58   Religion and Scientific Socialism

Table 4

Works dealing with secularization	35
Works dealing with relations between religion and society[a]	33
Works dealing with the relation between religion, education and youth	30
Works dealing with the theory of the sociology of religion	28
Works dealing with Church-state relations	14
Works dealing with the sects	14
Others (history of religion, sociography of the clergy, etc.)	10
Total	164[b]

a 'Religion and society' is understood to mean works dealing with: desecularization; religion and morals; religion and social stratification; religion and social behaviour patterns (marriage, rites, suicide); religion and minorities (gypsies).
b The total is greater than the number studied, because some publications fall into two or more categories.

is at pains to identify, presupposes the constant erosion of religious beliefs and behaviour among the group that constitutes the future of socialist society.

On the other hand, one is struck by the comparatively small number of works dealing with the theory of the sociology of religions. Could this be a consequence of the fundamental ideological bias of the discipline? As the scientific nature of the sociology of religion is overlaid by the requirements of the instrumental role assigned to it from above, it would in fact be understandable if by the same token epistemological or theoretical considerations were relegated to second place, as nobody attributed more than a minor importance to them in comparison with the much weightier political issues at stake. Lastly, following on from the foregoing, one is bound to point out how marginal is what one does not venture to call the 'Hungarian school' in relation to the great discussions which have stirred and still stir the international scientific community concerning the sociology of religion: 122 out of the 161 publications listed deal with religion *in general*, 14 being targeted on the sects, 14 on Catholicism alone, and 11 on Protestantism (7 of which deal with Calvinism). There are few or no studies of the comparative development of the various confessions, few or no analyses based on Weber's themes, or discussing those themes, few or no publications dealing with *popular religion*. Here too, the dominant impression is that of a discipline in which the imperatives of propaganda outweigh scientific considerations or discussions. Moreover, when Istvan Kemeny, one of the best Hungarian sociologists, now in exile in France, is asked about the state of the sociology of religion in his country, he simply shrugs his shoulders and quietly replies that this branch of sociology does not exist in Hungary, even if he then goes on to mention some works worth reading.

The division into subjects enabled an analysis of the chronological development of subject choices by Hungarian sociologists of religion to be drawn up, and this is shown in table 5.

Even if we ignore the very small amount of work published between 1945 and 1956, we cannot fail to be struck by the large increase in production, since in the five years 1975–9, seventy works were published, almost as many as during the preceding twenty years. But although this acceleration undoubtedly reflects a resurgence of interest, it conceals some real disparities between different subjects. For in recent years the category 'religion and society' has attracted more attention than work bearing on secularization and the relations between religion, youth and the educational process. In this regard it would be more accurate to speak of tactical and political constraints than of ideological fanaticism; it is clear that these shifts in subject choice were the result of the new conditions governing relations between Church and state from the middle of the 1970s onward. Emphasis was placed more on research into what could unite them, rather than on factors that might increase the tension. There was analysis of the role of the Church in promoting moral values. Published work became more 'neutral', and tried to keep closer to reality.

Thus in 1977, in reporting the results of a survey carried out among 3,000 villagers, Istvan Kiss was able to demonstrate a 65–70 per cent rate of religious observance.[8] Some authors went so far as to emphasize the dangers of the process of secularization – for example, Laszlo Nemeth who regarded the growth of the sects as a perverse effect of this process.[9]

Table 5

Period	Secularization	Religion and society	Education and youth	Theory of sociology	Church/state relations	Sects	Total
45–56	–	1	2	–	–	–	3
56–75	27	7	22	13	5	6	80
75–9	8	25	5	15	9	8	70
Total	35	33	29[a]	28	14	14	153[b]

[a]Number less than the number studied, as a date is not given.
[b]Number less than the number studied, because the negligible category *Others* has been omitted.

Even though some writers nevertheless continued in the former attitude,[10] generally speaking the sociology of religion in Hungary was at pains to appear more flexible. In 1976, presenting in *Vilagossag*[11] the result of his research on the value orientations of young people in Budapest (800 young people aged from eighteen to twenty who had received secondary or higher education), Muranyi distinguished up to five types of attitude: traditional religiosity, modern religiosity, agnosticism, ordinary atheism and scientific atheism. The diversification reveals some analytical effort, which contrasts strongly with the fairly crude distinctions formerly used. Nevertheless, the conclusions, namely that 70 per cent of the sample believed neither in the existence of God nor in the desirability of such existence, still bore the imprint of ideological prejudice by the very way in which they were formulated. For example, this sentence hardly needs any comment: 'There is however a small minority, of the order of 30% [*sic*], for whom religion constitutes a problem [*sic*].'

However, one other conclusion is noteworthy: 'The withering away of the traditional system of values does not necessarily lead to a scientific-atheist system of values.' One is bound to detect in this sentence an acknowledgement of the failure of the state in its attempt to inculcate Soviet values into the nation's youth.

We are entitled to ask a number of questions as to the value of the results presented. In regard to education, for example, J. Bango, a Hungarian-born sociologist working at Louvain University, after having observed that sociological surveys had *all* been carried out by Marxist researchers and that Western specialists confined themselves to reproducing unverifiable figures, pointed out the abnormally high rate of 'don't know' replies. In fact, on the basis of surveys carried out between 1963 and 1969, this figure amounted to nearly 41 per cent, compared with 12 per cent of believers and 47 per cent of atheists.[12]

At this point the problem of *dual education* is crucial. The child learns at home values different from those that it is taught at school. Furthermore, it very quickly learns to adopt a certain type of behaviour towards the outside world that does not necessarily represent its true beliefs or those of its family. One illustration of this is provided by the figures for the number of pupils taking religious education lessons at school from 1950 to 1970 (since then the rate has levelled out) (see table 6).

As will be seen, in a single year, 1950–1, the number of pupils receiving religious instruction at school was divided by two in primary schools and by eight in secondary schools. It will also be seen that after the 1956 revolution, this number increased by more than 18 per cent in primary schools and by nearly 16 per cent in secondary schools. This is a fair indication of how natural was the choice of parents to send their children, or not to send them, to religious-education classes. No doubt the latter duly imbibed the moral of

Table 6

Year	Primary school %	Secondary school %
1950	86.0	80.0
1951	43.9	10.5
1952	27.0	12.5
1953	27.1	0.7
1954	35.5	1.9
1955	29.4	0.8
1956	30.2	0.5
1957	48.8	16.4
1958	39.7	4.4
1967	12.0	2.0
1970	04.0	1.0

the story, knowing by experience what reply to give to such and such a question asked of them.

Still on the subject of the limits of the surveys, the highly directive nature of the questionnaires should be emphasized, added to which the conditions under which the surveys were conducted are never made clear. The Catholic journalist Bela Hegyi, criticizing the results of official surveys on the religious attitudes of students, carried out a counter-survey, in which 24.4 per cent of the students questioned simply refused to answer.[13]

Without doubt it is difficult to draw any conclusions from all this. But one may be permitted to think that the religious belief and conduct forged in Hungary as a result of these political constraints has become both more personal, less ritualized, more selective and conscious. Less openly paraded, it is undoubtedly resistant to the sociological approach, at least as now practised. What indeed is the use of asking for trouble by replying 'believer' when it is so easy to pass as a 'don't know' or an 'atheist'? Hence the high proportion of 'don't knows' might be explained by the rejection both of the government, which is being told that faith is a matter for the individual in his privacy, and of a hierarchical Church that is condemned for its compromises and its paternalism, as will appear later.

One of the few independent surveys carried out secretly in Czechoslovakia among a sample of 342 persons during the second half of 1985[14] showed that 25 per cent of the respondents had no ideological leanings whatsoever. Moreover, often very fragmentary ideological affiliations are reported; for instance, those claimed to be 'liberals' are obviously not interested in identifying themselves with democracy. And yet two regular series stand out from this overall picture of a deep aversion from ideology: the 5 per cent of communists and the 17 per cent of believers. Only the last category exhibits a specific profile, revealed in answers to the eighty-five questions contained in the questionnaire, indicating more independent activity and a greater openness to commitment.

But independent surveys of this kind are very rare, precisely because of the difficulties surrounding them and the risks they carry for their promoters. And this means that for a long time to come any analysis of the sociology of religion in Hungary and in Czechoslovakia will perforce be confined to criticism of presuppositions and ideological conditioning. It does not, however, mean that the entire production in these two countries should be rejected out of hand, for some Hungarian authors, such as Miklos Tomka or Zsuzsa Horvath, are undoubtedly worthy practitioners of the discipline. But the former, who describes himself as neutral since he is neither a Marxist nor committed to the Church, is extremely isolated in the institutional research of his country, while the latter has been dismissed from the post she held at the Academy of Sciences, and both are wellnigh deprived of resources for their work. The same is true of Czechoslovakia, except that it would be impossible for Tomka's works to be published officially there. In that country the only option for a sociologist who means to be a researcher rather than a spokesman is to work in secret, with all the risks attendant upon that choice.

In Poland, of course, the situation is very different.

The healthy virtues of competition: Poland

In presenting a report on 'the situation of the sociology of religions in Poland compared with that in other socialist countries in Europe', Andrzej Swiecicki, professor of the Catholic Theological Academy of Warsaw, set out to list 'the main lines of enquiry both in sociology and related social sciences, in particular political science, and to point out the most substantial findings of such research'.[15] He said that his analysis would cover three aspects: the laicization of the populations, the institutions for propagating religion, and the process of the secularization of the Church and its capture by the state. Clearly, the methodological bias and the choice of subject-matter were not fortuitous. They simply pointed up the impossibility of giving an account of the sociological development of the religious situation in Poland without reference to the political context, especially the state of relations between Church and state. The author said in conclusion:

> To sum up, one has to report that, *sociologically*, the following facts explain the religious situation in Poland:
> – a pronounced separation from the state, in the sense of financial autonomy of the community of believers and practising churchgoers in respect of the

Religion and Scientific Socialism 63

maintenance of the clergy and of catechetical teaching and less state influence on appointments to ecclesiastical positions than in other socialist countries;
– a marked process of secularization, in the sense of a withdrawal of the Church from many areas of secular activity such as schools, hospital and welfare institutions; this applies also to other socialist countries;
– the presence of religious ideas in the culture and above all in the intellectual equipment of the young generation.[16]

At this point the sociological analysis manifestly leads very directly to a political finding. Concluding his intervention, Swiecicki mentioned two texts that also have a considerable bearing on this matter, the sermon preached by Cardinal Wyszynski on 27 January 1974 on 'homo politicus' and the so-called Mielec speech by Edward Gierek on 3 September 1976. These two texts are intended to illustrate what the author calls 'the state of pragmatic equilibrium and reciprocal autonomy between Church and state',[17] a concept that could in fact be more simply expressed as 'the power of the Church in the Polish context'.

It is this power that explains why studies in the social sciences of religion are more developed in Poland than anywhere else in the socialist bloc. Thus the abstract of a randomly selected issue of *Studia Religiologica*, a scientific publication of Cracow University, shows both the richness of the field scanned and the very close connection between social sciences of religion and political preoccupations. Besides articles of an ethnological nature such as 'popular demonology'[18] or 'religiosity as reflected in Polish proverbs',[19] one finds more historical texts on 'the battle of Catholic philosophy in Poland against the secular culture in the years 1918–39',[20] or on 'the political origin of the stereotype: Polish = Catholic';[21] lastly, the contents list includes studies on the formation of a Marxist-Leninist world-view,[22] or on 'the attitude of the Polish episcopate towards some principles of the political system of the People's Republic of Poland'.[23]

But apart from the social sciences of religion, other branches of sociology take an interest, for obvious reasons, in the influence that religion and the Church may exercise on Polish society, and the large-scale surveys 'Polish 80' and 'Polish 81' included some questions bearing on this subject. In the same way, writers on political science evince a marked and equally understandable interest in this problem.

For instance, in presenting the conclusions of a major survey carried out in 1984 by the Political Sciences Institute of Warsaw University, Professor Stanislaw Gebethner spent a long time detailing the place, the role and the image of the Church in Polish political life. Certainly, in replies to the question dealing with statesmen of the twentieth century who had given most meritorious service to the Polish state and nation, Cardinal Wyszynski came first with 62.9 per cent of replies, while the runner up, Sikorski, obtained only 46.8 per cent, and the third – and the first communist to be mentioned – Gomulka, received only 35.4 per cent.[24] Similarly, in reply to the question: 'Who deserves confidence?', Pope John Paul came first with 97.4 per cent of yes replies against 0.1 per cent of noes and 1.5 per cent of don't knows, followed by the primate, Cardinal Glemp, with 81.2 per cent of yes replies against 7 per cent of no and 10.8 per cent don't knows. General Jaruzelski obtained 54.3 per cent yes replies against 28.2 no and 17.1 per cent don't knows.[25]

Commenting on the results of the survey, the author stated prudently:

> In my opinion [the fact that] 82.4 per cent of replies state that they have confidence in the Church still does not prove that four-fifths of the population form a community of Catholics with deep faith and devoted to the ideas of the Catholic religion on the world and life.[26] The replies indicate political attitudes more than ideological or doctrinal conviction. It is certain that those stating that they have confidence in the Church include many members of Solidarity which was formerly legal. Either these people do not want to be identified with the underground Solidarity, or they are against this form of illegal activity.[27]

Doubtless there is some validity in these reservations. All the same, Michal Pietrzak, one of Professor Gebethner's colleagues, who is a specialist in the problem of Church–state relations, has no hesitation in describing the Church as the guarantor of ideological pluralism in society.[28] What is more, society is well aware of this fact. Stanislaw Gebethner is entitled to point out that whereas 'more than a third of the respondents (38.8 per cent) are against an increase in the role of the Church in the public life of the nation whilst 46.6 per cent are in favour of an increase . . . the most important fact is the change compared with 1980 and 1981: the proportion in favour of a greater role for the Church is decreasing and the number of those against is increasing', he has to admit that 'on the one hand the Church has already attained so strong a position in the public life of contemporary Poland that most people see no reason to ask for a greater role; and furthermore, the Church has plunged so deeply into political life that it is naturally susceptible of losing the support of some of its adherents who have for various reasons become disillusioned in view of the political activity of the Church or of certain priests'.[29]

Whether one agrees with this finding or not, it goes far to explain the interest aroused by the Church, its believers and its clergy, and by the attitudes of Poles to religion. The government cannot ignore the phenomenon, and the Church has the resources to engage in self-scrutiny.

In sum, Polish sociology of religion is the only one that truly deserves the name in the Soviet-bloc countries of Eastern Europe. Its voice is heard in the most important international conferences and symposia (in particular at the International Conference on the Sociology of Religions),[30] and in the major reviews such as *Social Compass*, *Concilium*, etc. Moreover, it would be very difficult to embark upon an inventory of works on the sociology of religion in Poland (as could easily be done in the case of Hungary or Czechoslovakia), for it would overflow several volumes.[31]

Even more remarkable than the volume of this production is the variety of its contributors, who include sociologists working either for Catholic institutions (the Catholic University of Lublin (KUL), with, in particular, Piwowarski, Radwan and Ryczan; The Academy of Catholic Theology of Warsaw (Swiecicki and Slonomska); the great seminaries, above all those of Cracow, Katowice and Wroclaw (Majka); then the orders, foremost among which should be mentioned the Pallottins (Zdaniewicz)) or for Marxist institutions (the Social Sciences College at the Central Committee of the Polish United Workers' Party, the Philosophy and Sociology Institute of the Polish Academy of Sciences (Darczewska), Warsaw university (Ciupak), Cracow university (Kubiak), and the university colleges of education, especially that of Rzesow (Jadam)).[32]

According to Wladyslaw Piwowarski, the sociology of religion in Poland, whether official or independent, tends to follow one of five main directions: the fundamental dimensions of religious feeling, religious communities or institutions; religion among different strata of society; the relations between religion and the other areas of human activity; and the influence of cultural and social changes on religious sentiment.[33]

Considerable areas are however as yet still unexplored, no programmed and systematic work having been done in them.[34]

Both Catholic and Marxist sociologists use the same investigative techniques – surveys, interviews, observation and analysis. The only difference is that generally speaking these sociologists do not have access to the same loci. A Catholic will experience considerable difficulty in obtaining permission to conduct a survey among schools or universities, while a Marxist will have only very partial access to ecclesiastical sources. And naturally enough, their works are published by different houses.

However, although, as has been seen, there is little difference between official and independent sociologists as regards fields of inquiry or methods, there is on the other hand a stark difference between their respective definitions of what the sociology of religion should be about.

Catholics believe that the sociology of religion should be a scientific discipline, a branch of sociology. In 1946, L. Halban published in Lublin a work entitled *Opotrzebie badan etno-szocjologicznych nad religijnoscia* (*The Use of Ethno-sociological Research on Religion*). But because of the political context of the Stalinist era, it was only at the end of the 1950s that a sociology of religion began to develop in Poland. Jozef Majka at the Catholic University of Lublin provided the initial impetus, by his efforts to popularize the works of Gabriel Le Bras. The influences that have impinged upon the development of this discipline in Poland have been very diverse: they of course include Durkheim and Weber, but also the works of French sociology of religion or of Polish authors such as Czarnowski or Znaniecki.

Alongside the development of an independent sociology, a growing interest on the part of the authorities became evident. The appearance of Nowakowski's publication 'Religia jako przedmiot badan sociologicznych' ('Religion as a subject of sociological research') in *Kultura i Spoleczenstwo*, no. 1, 1957, p. 233, was immediately continued in the work of organizations such as the Euhemer Centre, the radio and television research centre on public opinion, or the review *Czlowiek i Swiatopoglad* (*Man and the Vision of the World*).

But Marxists see the sociology of religion primarily as a branch of scientific atheism rather than as a scientific discipline, though this does not prevent some writers from being concerned about credibility in view of the existence of a competing 'school',[35] as is evident from what Piwowarski says about Ciupak, one of the principal Polish Marxist sociologists:

> It seems that although this author adopts the Marxist position in his statements, he does not hold to it in his publications. In general, it can be said that although in his popular writings on the sociology of religion Ciupak maintains a firmly Marxist position, the important things in his scientific publications are: a. the specific facts gathered in the social milieu, b. the sociographical analyses, c. some conclusions of limited scope. As will be seen, Ciupak is an accurate [*sic*] researcher into religious life.[36]

Nevertheless, despite the greater rigour in work done by Marxists on religion, when compared with the situation in Czechoslovakia or Hungary, sociology is still instrumentalized. As Jerzy Godlewski has written, 'The Polish United Workers Party considers secularization, understood in the positive sense taught by Marxism-Leninism, to be a task of the first importance. In the pursuit of this task the Party bases itself upon a scientific world-view, on socialist morality and on knowledge of social, philosophic and religious problems.'[37]

In an article that appeared in 1972, Ciupak defined the criteria of a Marxist sociology of religion by three imperatives. Such a sociology must concern with transformations of the structure of society and with the process of forming a socialist social consciousness; it must deal with religion via the categories of Marxist theory; and it must be characterized by its instrumental nature. In fact, its results are at the service of a particular social praxis, in particular that of guiding policy with regard to religion or the course of the process of laicization.

He also drew up a list of gaps in Marxist sociology of religion in Poland, distinguishing four in particular:

1 the inadequate amount of data regarding changes in the religious outlook of workers and the intelligentsia;
2 the lack of any interest in ways of forming the Marxist outlook on the world in the various socio-professional groups and in the influence of ideological teaching of the masses on the outlook at work and in politics;
3 the absence of any in-depth studies on the process of modernization, which the Church has carried out on a large scale in the contemporary conditions of the Polish social system;
4 the arguments due to the results of works of non-Marxist sociology, in particular studies carried out by catholics.[38]

This last point is especially striking, inasmuch as the peculiar feature of the situation in Poland is that a dual operationalization of sociology is taking place there. As Andrzej Potocki observes:

> When programming and carrying out their studies, Catholic institutions look upon their pastoral utility as being one of the major methodological directives. It is true to say that whereas up to the middle of the 1960s the sociology of religions was far from arousing the interest of most of the clergy, nowadays the situation is different.[39] This is evident from the large number of priests who were taking specialist studies in the sociology of religions at the Catholic University of Lublin and at the Warsaw Academy of Catholic Theology, and from the fact that sociologists are finding employment in the bishoprics. This change is partly due to the "modesty" of sociology, which does not (as was at first suspected) arrogate to itself the right to formulate pastoral directives. Catholic sociologists have succeeded in convincing their theologian colleagues that the usefulness of sociology in pastoral care has to be filtered through pastoral theology, which must attempt to interpret theologically the results gathered by the sociologists and to formulate suggestions directed to the clergy.

'In the same way', observes Potocki, 'Marxist institutions make no secret of the fact that their research too has to have a strategic aim, namely laicization.'[40] Hence it is hardly surprising that Marxist sociology devotes a good deal of attention to young people.[41]

Another feature peculiar to the situation in Poland is that Marxist authors are on the defensive there. As was remarked by an observer working abroad, at the end of a publication dealing with the sociology of religion in Poland:

> An examination of the concept of secularization as used in Polish publications reveals three main points: this concept is utilized by the civil authorities as an instrument of anti-religious policy and of repression; the available data do not clearly confirm the claim that society is secularized; on the contrary, there is evidence providing very good support for the view that Poland is desecularized.[42]

This being so, it is understandable that official sociologists are at pains to provide theoretical justification for the persistence of religious attitudes in Polish society. In this respect, Ciupak's attitude is revealing, for he writes:

> In the structure of religion Marx distinguishes clearly two series of phenomena – those that depend on the class structure and can be accounted for on the basis of the theory of the class struggle understood in the broad sense, and those that are more distant from the process of the social antagonisms. This distinction is important because it enables us to see in the development of religion which of its functions are located *within* the class society and which are of a more general, more universal nature, connected with needs whose non-satisfaction is linked not only to transformations in the class structure of society but also to the transformation of the human personality. In general it can be said that the Marxist critique of religion is the scientific proposition of a study of the social processes from which the need for a compensation arises, of the alienation of desires that are not satisfied in the given historical conditions. The transformation of the conditions of human existence eliminates this need of compensation, though this does not signify that religion itself disappears.[43]

This recourse to the psychology of religion in an endeavour to account for the gap between reality and what is desired has a singularly reductionist appearance. To reduce religion simply to a register of individual aspirations in this way amounts to just another attempt to avoid posing it as a political vector of affirmation of values opposed to the official values.

Wladyslaw Piwowarski is undoubtedly nearer the mark when he notes:

> As regards changes in religious attitudes, it would appear that the development of modern civilization exercises a greater influence than does the propaganda of the Marxist-Leninist Party. It may therefore be presumed that the way in which these changes will occur will resemble that which is seen in the highly developed countries of Western Europe. The sole effect of the conditions specific to Poland is to make them occur more slowly and with some differences. It is difficult to foresee how long the present situation can be maintained and what will be the future of religion in Poland with the type of pastoral care that has predominated during the last thirty years.[44]

The implication here is that the part played by religion in Poland is in some sense beyond the political and socioeconomic development of the country. Moreover, both Stefan Nowak and M. Misztal have emphasized the absence of any appreciable correlation between religious and social attitudes.[45] Rather, the problem would appear to inhere in the realm of symbolism. Piwowarski has written: 'In the Polish context, popular religious sentiment functions as a common value inherited from the forebears, a sentiment which for the overwhelming majority of Poles is what is what underpins meaning and identity.'[46]

For the official sociologists, however, to entertain such an idea would be to admit to the ideological bankruptcy of the regime in its claim to embody the nation. And so they deploy a curious combination of frankness in presenting the results of the surveys with theoretical acrobatics to explain those self-same results.

Thus Kazimierz Sopuch, commenting on a survey carried out on the Baltic coast in 1979–80 by sociologists from Gdansk University on a sample of 1,182 persons, representative of the three towns of the region (Gdansk – Gdynia – Sopot), of a medium-sized township (Ostroleka) and of two rural localities, stated that 'even Party membership does not have a significant influence – as might have been supposed – on attitudes with regard to religion: among members of the Party, 51 per cent said that they were regular or irregular practicants, 22 per cent said that they were non-practising believers and only 27 per cent described themselves as non-believers'.[47] Similarly, Franciszek Adamski of Cracow University admits, in a review published by the Polish Academy of Sciences, that, '[in socialist bloc countries] the spontaneity of the process of laicization, intended to reduce human beings solely to the material sphere, is singularly accentuated by a campaign programmed from above and carried out with an enormous use of resources'.[48] But although Zenon Kawecki, reporting on a survey carried out in the industrial region of Oploe among 800 workers, admitted, with evident regret, that only slightly more than 10 per cent of the workforce declared themselves to be 'indifferent or atheists', against 52 per cent of 'regularly practising believers' and 37 per cent of 'occasionally practising believers', the only possible explanation according to him was that their public statements did not accord with their private beliefs, and he wrote: 'The religious attitude of the individual is based on the authority of the family and on the pressures of the surrounding milieu.'[49] Here is indeed a surprising reversal, for whereas in Czechoslovakia or Hungary independent observers questioned the sincerity of the replies given as regards faith because of the pressures exerted upon the surveys, in Poland it is the official sociologists who complain of these same pressures to explain results that did not come up to their expectations.

This is in fact a signal illustration of the observation with which Andrzej Potocki ended his analysis of the philosophical conditioning of the sociology of religions in Poland: 'The situation of Polish sociology of religions as practised in Catholic institutions reflects in large measure the situation of the Catholic Church in Poland, and the situation of Marxist sociology corresponds to the problems facing the ruling class owing to the existence of a spiritually and structurally ineradicable Catholicism in a communist state.'[50]

This instrumentalization of the sociology of religion by Catholics and

Marxists alike, in a context in which there is a strong correlation between religious identity and politics, is obviously bound to raise some doubts concerning the analyses advanced in scientific works whencesoever they come. For example, some Catholic sociologists have no hesitation in inferring from the situation existing in Poland a 'model' that could be applied in foreign countries, particularly Western ones. Such a view clearly sits lightly to reality and draws a veil over many ambiguities and contradictions. Nevertheless, it seems that the Solidarity period has favoured the development of a new generation of sociologists whose works aim *primarily* at understanding the religious attitudes and behaviour of Poles, without worrying too much about their transposability into practice, and who, while naturally not at home in the official sociology, also distance themselves from the results of sociological research undertaken in the Catholic institutions.[51]

3
Religion and Society: The Meaning of Modernity

The West has created for itself an inconsistent image of the Catholic Churches of Eastern Europe which, although not entirely false, nevertheless leaves out much that is true. The inconsistency consists of juxtaposing two pictures that are mutually exclusive: that of the Church humiliated, arrests, persecution and silence, with that of the Church triumphant, omnipresent at the heart of the greatest social change to have swept across this part of Europe since the war. But although Western opinion does not always succeed in overcoming this inconsistency, there is at least one point on which it is in agreement and which enables it to arrive at a viewpoint possessing at least a modicum of homogeneity: whether suppressed or in power, the Catholic Church in Europe is seen as the very model of conservatism. There is no denying that over the years its leaders have themselves repeatedly made statements that lend colour to this opinion. Thus Cardinal Lekai, ex-primate of Hungary, was fairly representative of bishops in Eastern Europe when he said that he was suspicious of 'all these novelties that reach us from the West'.[1]

But in truth the reality is infinitely more complex. The fundamental question is not whether or not the Churches in Poland, Czechoslovakia and Hungary are conservative, but what they intend to retain or to change, and for which reasons, and how far they are in a position to do so. If we ask this question, we immediately have to eliminate Czechoslovakia from the analysis, for there the persecution aimed at the Church compels it to think about its future purely and simply in terms of survival, and this clearly leaves little scope for grand theoretical discussions. The control exercised by the government even over the celebration of worship means that practice has to remain traditional, if not routine, and priests who try to innovate are at risk of having their state licences withdrawn.[2] Then again, the fact that the hierarchy is not only incomplete but contains some high-ranking members considered by the faithful to be merely government agents does not favour the emergence of a coherent and credible discussion among the higher clergy about the emergence of an amicable relationship between the Church and society. This does not mean that no thought has been given to the matter but, as will be seen, this has been possible only outside the official Church.

For different reasons the situation in Hungary is very comparable; the normalization of relations between Church and state rests on the Catholic hierarchy's obligation no longer to claim to exercise real influence on society. This renunciation, marked by passivity and adherence to the orthodox line, pervades all the pronouncements of the institutional Church and leads to what the sociologist Tomka calls 'the end of the hegemony of the church'.[3] It is worth quoting the following text at length in order to show how true this is:

> After the Second World War a new economic, social and political order was established in Hungary. Besides bringing about a radical change in Hungarian life, it also directly affected all the Churches. That is how the social and political influence of the Catholic Church came to an end. The new socialist economic order stripped the Church of its large landholdings which provided it with a strong financial basis. Public order was now founded on atheism, a philosophy which was to determine the direction taken by public policy. To this was added the historical incubus of the pre-existing tension between the Church and Marxism, a legacy from the previous dispensation. This being so, social order could not be established without overcoming an opposition. Socialist public order was fearful for its conquests and for its future development, while the Church was afraid it might not be able to live in a structure of law and government based on atheism and the Marxist ideology. This was the environment within which official relations between Church and state had nevertheless to be established.
>
> After the Liberation, the Catholic Church exhibited a certain hardening. Whereas official contacts with the other Churches were established by 1948, only in 1950 was an agreement signed with the Catholic Church. This tardiness cost the Church many of its institutions, beginning with the right of the religious orders to practise. Despite the signature of an agreement, both sides continued to manifest a degree of tension. A fresh stage in Church–state relations was reached in 1964, when a partial agreement was concluded between the Vatican and the Hungarian People's Republic. Under this agreement the Vatican went so far as to commit itself officially to dialogue. One important consequence of this agreement was that one by one all the bishoprics were filled.
>
> The appointment in 1976 of Laszlo Lekai to the post of cardinal and archbishop of Esztergom, the main episcopal see of the country, marked a fresh turning point. This period was characterized by close collaboration in mutual understanding and respect in the endeavour to achieve common goals.
>
> For both sides, it was a growing awareness of the realities of the situation that enabled events to take this turn. In seeking common ground between their various points of view, the two interlocutors were trying to develop already existing relations.

> The Church of today appreciates the achievements of socialism and is striving to carry it forward. . . . At the present time some possibilities favourable to the life of the Church are taking shape and there is growing hope for the future.[4]

This author clearly regards the influence of the Church on society as being definitely at an end. It is the government that gives the orders, and the Church is seen as a disturbing factor, even if the 'disorder' it creates is justified or explained by the disquiet it feels. The government is as fearful as the Church (which would tend to suggest that both of the protagonists are in possession of the same weapons and are equally capable of influencing the situation). But it was the government that showed goodwill: it is the Church that 'evinced a certain hardening', and her 'delay' in entering into dialogue with the new authorities was the cause of the loss of her institutions. It is the Vatican that is 'officially entering into dialogue', which is tantamount to saying that before 1964 the Vatican opposed dialogue. And the proof of this goodwill on the part of the government is that as soon as the Vatican showed that its intentions were good, the vacant bishoprics were filled. The arrival of Monsignor Lekai was a good sign. The new situation at the head of the Church militated in favour of understanding – which obviously means that heretofore the Church was responsible for the misunderstanding.

It is clearly more than a mild criticism when the text contrasts a 'present-day Church' which 'is striving to carry forward socialism' with an 'old Church', with respect to which we will simply note that the name of Cardinal Mindszenty is not even mentioned. In any event, the Church is striving to carry forward a system concerning which the author explicitly states that it is based on atheism, a philosophy that determines 'official state policy'. It would need only a simple syllogism to suggest that the Church is striving to carry forward. . . . atheism, a circumstance that seems all the more surprising since the author in question is none other than Monsignor Laszlo Paskai, who in 1987 succeeded Monsignor Laszlo Lekai as primate of Hungary and was formerly archbishop of Kalosca.

Further on in the document we may read that, 'Hungarian law guarantees to all children the right to religious instruction if their parents state that they wish to have it. . . . Although we have no accurate statistics, we are sad to note a drop in attendance at these religious instruction courses . . . due mainly to lack of interest on the part of the parents.'[5] At this point it is strange that this factor is emphasized while nothing is said about the pressures exerted on families by the authorities.

Persecution and powerlessness in Czechoslovakia, renunciation and conformism in Hungary are without doubt simply justifications for conservatism. This makes it all the more important to look more closely at the attitude and the pronouncements of the only institutional Church in Eastern Europe that stands above the arguments about modernism, and hence justifies the special attention given in this book to Poland.

Poland: beyond conformism and progressiveness[6]

> If our black brethren can praise God in their own way, let us be allowed to worship him in ours. Let us beware of purist scholars who try to cleanse the Church from the wealth of its traditions on the pretext of maintaining the purity of the faith. . . . We have . . . the right and the duty to guard sedulously our religious traditions deeply rooted in the faith of our people which seeks to express theological truths in its own way.

This is how Cardinal Wyszynski summarized at Christmas 1961 the position to be adopted by the Polish bishops at the Vatican II council.

'Guard', 'maintain', 'traditions', 'rooted' – all these terms are revelatory of the attitude of the Polish Church and its primate, who, moreover, had no hesitation in saying calmly: 'The Polish bishops have spoken out in favour of Latin in the canon of the mass. We have special reasons for doing this, dictated by the history of our people.'[7] This statement alone is sufficient to explain why the Polish Church was dubbed 'conservative' and 'traditionalist' during the council. For was not the 'special position' claimed by Cardinal Wyszynski in direct conflict with the aim of reconciling the Church with the modern world? Was not the maintenance of traditions the comfortable alibi for a refusal to undergo a development that would be disturbing and would upset existing habits and privileges?

However, the reference to 'black brethren', to an African world the presence of which was one of the great novelties of the council, inevitably suggests other interpretations. In using these expressions, was not Cardinal Wyszynski aiming to denounce a certain kind of Eurocentrism within the Church, about which Poland too had reason to complain? It may be objected that, unless we are mistaken, Poland is a part of Europe by its geography, history and culture. But in claiming the same right of difference for Poland as for the African Churches, Cardinal Wyszynski was putting the Western Churches on notice that his country was orbiting in a mental universe very different from the one that had hitherto been the norm throughout Europe.

Twenty years later, in a general context of the rise of religious indifference, which is becoming the 'first religion of Europe',[8] Poland has given the universal Church a Pope, sends missionaries abroad, and gives to the world the image of an ecclesial institution powerfully sustained by its people. Furthermore, this institution appears to be in a position to exert a great deal of influence on sociopolitical developments in the country and enjoys considerable prestige and rights of consultation. And yet it is still widely seen abroad as 'retrograde' or 'conservative', popular and clerical, hence quite unlike the 'intellectual' pattern in vogue in France or the Netherlands.

There are those, even in Poland, who are inclined to agree with this interpretation:

> For some time the notion of *French* Catholicism has been in fashion. It is contrasted with a *Spanish* Catholicism, mentally associated with the attitude of traditionally minded Catholics and the wish to preserve in Poland a *people's* Catholicism which differs from the French variety by its emotional colouring, its forms of service and the imagery that it utilizes, all of which run counter to the French preference for theorizing and intellectualization.[9]

But the author of those words is not a Catholic intellectual anxious to see Polish Catholicism develop in the direction of positions that are assumed to be more open. The writer is a communist, Dionizy Tanalski, who, in a publication that appeared in 1978 in the very official *Panstwowe Wydawnictwo Naukowe* (State Scientific Publishers) saluted the 'increasing intellectual dynamism of a socially progressive Catholicism', giving special mention to the works put out by the Pax publishing house, which is 'reissuing the works of Maritain, de Mounier and other Western writers who are anti-traditionalist or frankly pro-socialist and publishing Polish authors who adopt similar positions'. Lastly, this author expressed anger at 'the reaction of the conservative bishops, who hold that the Pax reviews are losing the feeling for religious authenticity, for true Polishness, and blindly imitate the "little Western experiments" (*nowinki*), a *French* Catholicism that is foreign to the spirit of Polish Catholicism'.[10] Hence official opinion in Poland contrasts the *progressives*, those members of the Church who are prepared to enter into dialogue with the communists, with the *conservatives*, bishops who are hostile to progress in ideas and societies. This attitude has something in common with that of the West, which feels a certain unease in the presence of a Church that is at the same time both backward-looking and full of life, a fact that would go some way to explain the observation of Cardinal Wyszynski in a speech delivered on 6 January 1980 in St John's Cathedral in Warsaw: 'It sometimes happens that the foreign press places a quite different interpretation upon pastoral letters of the Polish bishops from the meaning they originally had.'[11]

In fact, the Polish Church faces Catholics and sociologists with the same kind of problems as Solidarity raises for trade unionists and left-wing politicians. The latter find it hard to understand the religious songs, the photographs of the Pope, or the masses celebrated in firms on strike, for these are manifestations that had very little place in the traditional forms of workers' protest. In the same way, it is not easy to analyse the Polish Church by the use of concepts such as conservatism or traditionalism, which belong more to Western categories than to those appropriate to a part of Europe which for some forty years has been under the sway of Soviet-type government.

A specific context

In Poland more than in the countries of the West, the Church has a multiplicity of functions, which means that it has various objectives and operates at several different levels. These objectives and fields of action, though they may overlap at some points, do not necessarily coincide. In addition to the religious, social and cultural role that, by tradition, it plays, the Church has acquired a quite specific dimension as a result of political developments in the country since the end of the Second World War. In the absence of any institutional counterweight, it constitutes an area of freedom in which the anti-totalitarian aspirations of a whole people find sanctuary and expression. Moreover, this does not necessarily imply that government in Poland has remained totalitarian in the same way as it was during the Stalinist years – but the utopia of which it is the expression is still totalitarian. Consequently, no 'liberalizing' developments should be allowed to obscure the fact that the government still has the option of reverting at any time to the use of the panoply of totalitarian instruments at its disposal.

Cardinal Wyszynski used the speech that he made during the 4th session of Vatican II to emphasize in the strongest terms the unique position held by Sovietized East-Central Europe in the world of Catholicism, when he said that 'the Council speaks on behalf of an institution that is present in the modern world'. It is a world governed by ideas with very differing contents – some of them diametrically opposed. 'Thus we are not dealing with one world, but with a number of different worlds. . . . There is the world shaped according to the traditional ideas of law, the state, and freedom. . . . It is essential to realize that there is in existence another "modern world" which gives a quite different meaning to the concepts of law, the state, and freedom. This is the world shaped by the principles of dialectical materialism.'[12] In this world, and in the conditions pertaining in post-1945 Poland, the very existence of a Church that is not servile to the state represents a counter-utopia for society, a standing, automatic reference to the values of freedom that the nation professes. So it is hardly surprising that the government has been constantly at pains to circumscribe the influence of the Church, for want of the power to eliminate it completely. It also has to be admitted that, despite a balance of power that has undeniably moved in its favour, the Church is often reminded in statements made by government spokesmen that the government's objective is still 'to extirpate religion from human consciousness and thought'.[13] Therefore, added Cardinal Wyszynski, 'no agreement concluded with a state professing dialectical materialism makes the Church secure, no rule in force today safeguards the human person against the violations of tomorrow. This being so, there is only one thing that counts: the moral authority of the Church, the faith and constancy of the faithful.'[14] A speech like that was bound to arouse some misunderstanding abroad. Thenceforward the primate of Poland was fully aware of that fact:

> Many writers, especially journalists who deal with these problems in Western countries, are misled because they apply to countries ruled by dialectical materialism the meaning of law prevailing in their own countries. That is perhaps why so many of our bishops are so often accused of harbouring retrograde ideas, of obscurantism and attachment to feudal privileges. In fact it has nothing to do with privileges or feudalism. It is about living or surviving.[15]

In the light of this, it can be appreciated that the concerns of the council may not have been apprehended in quite the same way by the bishops from Eastern Europe, and Poland in particular, as by those from the Western world. For the universal Church, the overriding priority was to try to find a response to the challenges of a course of events that appeared to cast it in the role of 'anti-modernism'. The first requirement for Vatican II, at least as seen by the majority, was to break the mould in which the Church was cast as archaic in opposition to the 'modern world'. Seen in these terms, the situation in Poland was nothing less than atypical. In a system of ideas impregnated by a Soviet-type ideology, words are booby-trapped and whole areas of the vocabulary have been emptied of their meaning, perverted and taken over. 'Progress' and 'modernism' are some of the values that the government has arrogated to itself, for its sole use and profit. Official pronouncements are aimed at relegating the Church to the past and excluding it from the future, from 'the meaning of history'. The government is striving towards a new world, in which the industrialization, urbanization and even the establishment of a socialist society of mass consumption would result in the same downward trend for the Church as in Western societies.[16]

In the Polish context newness, progress and modernism simply represent categories of official discourse aimed at the disappearance of the Church. The Vatican council may have been intent on reconciling the Church with modernity, but in Poland such an undertaking would entail first dispossessing the state of the role of guardian of the meaning of modernity which it had unilaterally assumed. Thus the 'archaism – modernity' debate was largely outdated, for the problem was not to be modern but to shape a convincing response to the totalitarian utopia. The challenge was not to be more modern than the government, but to construct a counter-utopia that would be capable of rendering the official utopia nothing more than an empty form. In other words, the customary categories of modernity and archaism, progress and conservatism were and still are in Poland largely non-operative.

In reality, while modernity may signify a deepening of the hold of a

Soviet-type pattern on society, it is quite evident that society by and large will refuse to see this as true progress. To take only one example, 'progressive priest', an official buzz-word, means to the generality of people 'liquidator of the Church'. Pax, the association of progressive priests, has been perceived ever since it was formed as an attempt to destabilize the Church in the interests of the government. The very perversion of the meaning of the word 'new' is a good indicator of the Polish Church's distrust of change. Before adopting it, the bishops are bound to consider what consequences it may have, in a context in which the government would not hesitate to use the smallest breach in order to weaken the Church. That is why the Polish hierarchy is often very indignant about criticisms of its alleged 'conservatism' coming from abroad; the irritation expressed shows that its members are convinced the West does not understand what is actually at stake in Poland. Cardinal Wyszynski said just that when he emphasized:

> Not everything that priests do abroad can be imitated in our country. . . . Those who desire a renewal of the council should recall that true renewal is not so much the new thing as holiness in the spirit of Christ, and that it is necessary to begin by sanctifying oneself. . . . Renewal of the council is not a screen from behind which one can shout foolish shibboleths for unconsidered reform. The endless dialogue masks an aversion from work, effort and sacrifice, 'patter' without thorough knowledge and without a viable plan of action, a mentality of opposition and indiscipline. . . . The intelligentsia which looks to the Church for renewal should also bear these truths in mind. For the renewal of the Church begins with ourselves. . . . When you are demanding progress from the Church, call to mind that 'progress in the Church means not novelty but saintliness'. It is not endless sterile discussion, the production of words and the pursuit of novelty and change, the destruction of what existed and exists, but personal holiness. And holiness begins with ourselves. . . . Remember that conciliar renewal will come about not by a change in the institutions of the Church but in a renewal of minds, hearts and personal lifestyle. You want to be teachers of the whole world. Then be holy yourselves.[17]

These words were not without effect in society. On 10 November 1980 Lech Walesa, together with representatives of Solidarity, saluted the primate of Poland as 'the man who has no right to lie, who has to know the truth and show it to others'. This indicates how outmoded is the debate between conservatism and progressiveness, traditionalism and modernism. And in fact, even if the Polish bishops make no secret of their distrust of the experiments conducted in the West, or proclaim their allegiance to a Marist Catholicism which is bound to be an obstacle to ecumenical rapprochement, even if Cardinal Wojtyla is a more 'acceptable' Pope than was Paul VI to Western traditionalists, it is impossible to account for the way in which Poles think about the Church with the aid of these concepts.

For although it is hardly surprising that an ecclesiastic, Father Boniecki, should consider the Church to be 'indispensable',[18] it certainly could be to hear a member of the secular opposition, Adam Michnik, state: 'It is impossible to imagine Poland without the Church and its enormous influence on society',[19] and even more astonishing when the communist Minister of Cults, Adam Lopatka, admits: 'It is clear that the Roman Catholic Church has contributed and is still contributing much to the national culture of Poland. It exercises a great influence on the mentality of society.'[20] This curious unanimity is a clear sign that the Church constitutes a major sociopolitical force, and that it would therefore be somewhat difficult to imagine that it could remain aloof from the world and modernity, frozen in conservative attitudes. But is it really likely that an institution cut off from reality would be able to draw 300,000 miners to every pilgrimage at Piekary or to lead 45,000 persons, for the most part young ones, to make the pilgrimage from Warsaw to Katowice on foot?

But if it is wrong to feature a debate between conservatism and progressivism, it would nevertheless be a mistake to conclude that such a debate would always have been out of place. For in the period leading up to the First World War the first generation of Polish intelligentsia did indeed initiate a realization of the fact that traditional Catholicism was stuffy and out of date. The literary critic Stanislaw Brzozowski protested, in his *Legenda Mlodej Polski*, against Jesuitism, the dependent position held by the laity compared with the clergy and the lack of vitality in the Church. He virulently rejected 'a Catholicism complete and ossified since the Council of Trent'. Plater-Syberg denounced a 'narrow, partial and formal' religiosity, Henryk Sienkiewicz, a Nobel prizewinner for literature, denounced 'a dead, mechanical faith', and Marian Zdziechowski 'a clericalism contrary to the spirit of the Church', while Professor Wlodimierz Czerkawski castigated 'a Catholicism which gives up the struggle and withdraws into the narrow confines of conservatism'.[21] These various pronouncements bear witness to the fact that a Polish type of modernism came to birth at that time, having affinities with movements in France and Italy but differing from them by its comparative lack of interest in theoretical researches. Doubtless the special situation of Poland, a country without a state, a nation partitioned between three occupiers, explains why the Polish modernists preferred to concentrate on areas in which the Church could exert a practical influence.

The publication in 1907 of the encyclical *Pascendi*, 'victory of traditionalism over modernism in the Catholic Church',[22] led to a challenge to religious orthodoxy by the Polish intellectual elite and to serious conflicts. The Mariavites separated from the Church, and the inability of the Church to come to terms with the new social groupings resulting from the rise of industrialism was to lead to a radicalization of the socialist movement. No doubt this last statement should be hedged with some provisos: the effects differed from one zone of occupation to another; the policies in regard to Catholicism pursued by Germany, Austria and Russia respectively had different effects, and as a result of the pastoral work undertaken in Silesia among the workers, they were firmly anchored in the Catholic faith.

Nevertheless, the basic trend, at the dawn of the twentieth century, was towards the distancing of progressive intellectuals from an institution that seemed to have no capacity for development. Despite this, the Polish people – with a literacy rate of only 26 per cent in the Kingdom of Poland (the Russian part) – was only capable of assimilating the traditional faith.

When national independence was regained after the First World War, the Catholic Church came to occupy a prominent place in the machinery of state. Regarded as the tool of the monied classes and felt to be violently opposed to progress, the Church was identified in the mind of a socialist such as Jerzy Zawieyski with 'anti-Semitism, fascism, obscurantism, fanaticism and with all anti-progressive and anti-cultural phenomena'.[23] And indeed, in the multinational Poland of the inter-war period Catholicism often served as a distinguishing mark from Jewishness, while the privileges enjoyed by the clergy gave rise to a strong anti-clerical sentiment among the common people. The Second World War constituted a radical break. In 1945 the Catholic Church certainly emerged from the conflict in an atmosphere hostile owing to the progressive seizure of power by communists under orders from Moscow, but it had some strong cards – a newly born prestige connected with the part it had played in the resistance, the loss of its possessions making it a poor Church (and therefore the Church of the poor), the homogenization of the population, which was now nearly 100 per cent Polish and Catholic owing to the tragic disappearance of the Jewish community and to territorial changes, and lastly, with a new function to perform *vis-à-vis* the government. As the only free space in a totalitarian world, the Church came to take sides with the resistance, to the point where the cardinal-primate was arrested in 1953. Gradually the Church acquired a new image in society, until in the end the secular opposition too was expressing its admiration of the good work being done by the Church. A milestone in this reappraisal was the publication of Adam Michnik's widely acclaimed book *Kosciol, Lewica, Dialog* (*The Church and the Left – The Dialogue in Poland*). He gave reasons for his reconciliation with an institution that many of his comrades in politics still regarded as irremediably backward-looking:

> We shall be told that the winds of change blowing since the Vatican council have not reached Catholicism in Poland. Such talk astonishes me. I fully understand and sympathize with the journalists of *Tygodnik Powszechny* and of *Wiez*[24] (but not with the so-called reformers of Pax), demanding change within the Catholic Church, but I cannot understand why outsiders should use arguments like that. Although, as an ignoramus, I am the same as all who

> deplore the conservatism of the Polish bishops and contrast them with the enlightened, progressive bishops of the Vatican, I am obviously not as daring as they are, and so I shall not enter the debate as to whether the Polish episcopate is or is not conservative. For in fact, what are we talking about? Liturgical reform? The cult of the Virgin Mary? The attitude to celibacy? Joint responsibility for attitudes adopted in the Church? The dismissive attitude of the bishops to the Dutch catechism? I don't understand! I can understand Catholics getting worked up about such questions; and we can all understand why some scoundrel of a journalist deplores the conservative attitude of the Polish bishops, but haven't my friends on the secular left really anything better to worry about? Would they prefer the kind of progressive attitude represented by Monsignor Casaroli, an envoy of the Vatican, who according to current rumour tried to induce the primate of Poland to adopt a more 'flexible' attitude towards the government – i.e. to capitulate? Let me remind you that this same Casaroli suggested that Spanish bishops who were criticizing the policies of General Franco should adopt a more 'flexible' attitude towards the government . . .[25]

This extract makes it clear that ever since the early 1970s, and even more after 1976, the Church had come to occupy a central position on the sociopolitical scene in Poland, enjoying considerable prestige and a very favourable balance of power. Cardinal Macharski, archbishop of Cracow, wrote:

> Christianity, as we are living it now, has broken down the idea of Christianity as an alienating factor, and has marked the end of the complexes of inferiority, backwardness and never being in step with history. The Pope no doubt had in mind this forward-looking, committed attitude of the Church in the difficult times through which we are passing when he said in November 1980 in Cologne cathedral that the Church, hitherto accused of hostility to reason, freedom and progress, had now become the defender of reason, freedom and progress, and that all eyes were turned to her. I have no doubt that in Polish society the gospel, as proclaimed and accepted, had been the inspiration of the defenders of the social, scientific and economic life, according to the categories of reason, freedom and progress, without inverted commas, that is to say according to the categories appropriate to the dignity of each person and their inalienable rights.[26]

A pattern for the Church?

It appears impossible, in the circumstances peculiar to a country subjected to a Soviet-type political system, to conceive of a 'pattern for the Church' as a specifically religious institution, in isolation from the social reality out of which it arises and which it reflects. In the case of Eastern Europe, it is evident that the presence of a hostile government, which has consciously adopted as its ultimate aim the abolition of all Church structures and the eradication of religious attitudes, is a primary datum, indispensable for decoding statements and attitudes.

It is, for example, difficult to make sense of the strong radication of the cult of Mary in Polish Catholicism, which forms one of the main characteristics of popular religion in the country, unless its role in the affirmation of a national identity is also understood. The reference to 'Mary, queen of Poland' is from the outset a way of drawing the frontiers of the 'imaginary territory of a free Poland'. And when John Paul II said at Czestochowa that 'here we have always been free', he was saying that the sphere of religion is also the place of national independence, precisely because the government cannot in any event claim to 'recapture' it. By the same token, to go to mass on Sunday or take part in a pilgrimage is also, in a country where there is no electoral consultation worthy the name, a way of 'voting with one's feet'.

It is moreover obvious that the Church in Poland cannot afford the luxury of internal dissensions.

> The reason why there are not, and have never been, disputes is that as the Church is situated, the external threat is so obvious to every priest that he realizes that any action he may take against his bishop will be used against the Church. In the Church's situation of 'to be or not to be' there is a dialogue, sometimes a very difficult one, and there are some malcontents and some priests who resign from the priesthood.[27]

There are some 20,000 priests in the Polish Church; clearly such a large group could not possibly be completely devoid of differences. The clergy is shot through by the same differences as the society from which it springs. Indeed, when Solidarity replaced the Church as the chief interlocutor with the government, from August 1980 to December 1981, this helped to show up some of them. The disappearance of Cardinal Wyszynski, a charismatic leader with an unchallenged authority, aggravated this trend, so much so that Monsignor Glemp was challenged by the priests of his own diocese in December 1982 at a stormy meeting.[28] But one Solidarity militant who came out of prison at that time after several months' internment regarded the publicity given to the affair as 'a success for official propaganda', so evident is it that the situation of the Church is still that of a besieged citadel.

What this means is that the fate of the entire Church is in the hands of every priest. 'The Church in Poland', observed Father Boniecki, 'is based on the priests. On the qualities of the priest depend the life of the parish, the teaching ministry, commitment in the life of the sacraments and the liturgy, the attitude of Christians to society. That is not the result of a paternalist attitude on the part of the priests themselves, but the wish of the laypeople who want above all to see their priest as a leader.'[29] This very special role thrust upon the clergy in Polish society, and further strengthened by the assassination of Father Popieluszko, is a key to the understanding both of the attachment to the wearing of the ecclesiastical habit, sign of the presence of the Church in society in the words of Cardinal Wyszynski, and of the almost complete identification between the Church, the clergy and the episcopate. In order to survive, the Church must feel itself to be a solid nucleus. Whatever internal differences there may be, the unity of the institution, sole guarantor of the maintenance of its power position over against the government, must remain unbroken. And the important point is that this is not only a *sine qua non* of the survival of the Church: it is also a demand made by all sections of Polish society without distinction. The consequence is that the secular opposition by and large refrains from challenging the Church, the primate or the bishops, even if on occasion one or other of them adopts an attitude of which the opposition might disapprove. Naturally this general trend does not exclude some isolated criticisms, but any such criticisms are always limited in scope, prudent and restrained. The truth is that Cardinal Wyszynski's authority was based not on his position as a religious leader alone, but rather on the fact that this position, added to his powerful personality, made him a national leader, a man with whom the whole nation could in some sense identify. When the primate spoke, it was the whole Church speaking with one voice and thereby giving expression to the fundamental values of the nation.

In June 1979, during his first visit to Poland, John Paul II mentioned the hierarchy seventeen times during his speech to the conference of bishops meeting at Czestochowa. In particular he said:

> The hierarchical organization of the Church has become not only the centre of its pastoral mission, but also a visible support for all the life of society, for the nation aware of its right to exist and which, as a nation Catholic as to its vast majority, also looks to the hierarchical structures of the Church for its support.[30]

As if echoing these words, Stefan Wilkanowicz, a respected Catholic intellectual, said during a speech to a Western audience:

> We Polish Catholics certainly have a more developed (or less weakened) sense of authority and discipline than you have here. Circumstances militate in favour of the strengthening of this sense. We need the structures of the Church, we want to see the institutions of the Church developed. They are necessary both to the pastoral work and to our defence, for the defence of the rights of man. We are far from criticizing them or fighting against them, as happens with you. Our safety depends upon our unity. We realize that this unity and discipline may sometimes lead to a certain closeness or rigidity, that they may hinder the creativity and freedom which are also necessary in the religious life. Therefore what we have to seek is a pluralist unity, not a monolithic one.[31]

Cardinal Wyszynski also called for this attitude:

> Our unity is neither a uniform nor a bureaucratic one. . . . We place a high value on pastoral dialogue and we desire that many more discussions should take place at parish and deanery level. Know that we are far from being unreceptive to your observations and proposals, especially when they are confirmed by experience and they bear fruit. Do not forget, however, that the overall view we have of our dioceses seen from our observation posts is a far more detailed and complex one than what is seen from one or a number of parishes. Therefore pastoral prudence and wisdom should take into account not only temporary successes; they should also look into the future and work towards harmonious cooperation for the coming of the Kingdom of God.[32]

The cardinal went on to say:

> We are well aware that the reforms instituted by the council call for certain changes and a pastoral recasting of our institutions and structures. However, this renewal must take place gradually and without hiatus. Nobody has the right to destroy existing structures before having tried out better methods and introduced them. We must beware of violent, premature changes because there is a danger that they will weaken the existing structures before better forms of apostolate have had time to mature. Moreover, the zest for novelty is no substitute for the genuine and systematic day-to-day ministry.[33]

Whereas the problem of the Churches in the West, as seen in the debates at the Vatican council, was largely that of trying to bridge the gap between their own development and that of their society, in Poland the aims of Church and society were to a large extent identical, and this became increasingly clear during the 1970s, when the Church and the secular opposition began to work together on the common platform of the defence of human rights. Is this difference sufficient to substantiate the view that there is a Polish pattern of Church – state relations? Assuming that it is, this pattern would undoubtedly consist in the ability of the Church to combat the atomization of society and to create spaces in which society can restructure itself – to invent new social forms. The Church has contrived to meet the threatened secularization of society brought about by the process of industrialization and urbanization with an effective pastoral operation directed towards all the groups of which Polish society is made up – peasants, workers, intellectuals and, above all, young people. To a large extent, the Church has long since won the ideological battle with the state for the control of youth, and the state has implicitly acknowledged this by modelling its efforts to restructure its own youth movements on the Catholic organization Oasis, founded in the 1950s by Father Blachniki.

By making use of a powerful material and human infrastructure of a very dense teaching network often equipped with the most modern techniques including transparency projectors and video cassettes, and of a press without its equal in Eastern Europe, the Church has been able to articulate a message in the economic, social or ethical sphere with which the population could identify. What is more, the Church has moved into most of the 'autonomous areas of society' left vacant by the disappearance of Solidarity as a legal organization. Nowadays there are few cultural or social activities in the broadest sense that are carried on outside the ambit of the Church. The government that set out to limit the Church's role to conducting religious services has had to resign itself to the inevitable. In 1966 Cardinal Wyszynski, commenting in Warsaw on the decisions taken by the Vatican council, said:

> The Church must be present in the modern world. Let it be given the resources for this! The pastoral constitution contains an important chapter on economic and social life. Naturally the Church is not going to make suggestions about the organization of production – that is the business of the state; but the Church possesses moral principles which can be of great assistance to those who organize economic life as well as those whose contribution is their work. These principles champion the just rights of the worker, so that he may be able to enjoy the fruits of his labours, which he really needs for the development of his personality and the maintenance of his family.[34]

The explicit reference to Christian values in the Solidarity programme is a sign of the failure of government to put forward a convincing Marxist ethic for society and, conversely, the success of the Church's efforts to avoid being pushed out of areas over which the state claimed to exercise exclusive rights. We shall return to this subject later.

Undeniably there are some archaic elements in Polish Catholicism, both as regards external appearances or its institutional organization and also its conception of the relations between the Church and the world. There is a strongly ritualistic tinge to religious behaviour, seen in the large numbers attending divine service and the greater frequency of confessions than in Western Europe. Material objects, especially images of saints, are used as supports to faith, and large numbers go on pilgrimages. But there can be no doubt that this attachment to the past, to history, tradition and the rite is an essential ingredient in the vitality of an institution that has succeeded in creating an astonishing synthesis of past, present and future, all of it oriented towards a social praxis. Poland and Poles have indeed good reason to be distrustful of all theories, however appealing they may be, and this explains the muted welcome given to certain initiatives that have reached them from the West, such as the neo-catechumenate or the charismatic renewal.[35]

In this sense it would be more appropriate to speak about a meeting between this institution and a particular sociopolitical configuration rather than about a pattern, and this meeting has resulted in specific attitudes and behaviour. On this reading, the power of the Church is a direct result of the challenge presented to it by the government. That at least is what Cardinal Wyszynski thought:

> It is the communists who teach us the love of God and a trust without limits! It is the communists who have taught us to rely far more on providence than on this world's goods! It is to the communists that we owe having accepted the spoiling of our earthly possessions for God with joy. It is thanks to them that we are constantly seeking to deepen the forms of our ministry, above all our teaching ministry.[36]

That is a counter-utopia, even something of an opposing force. The Church represents for society a place, in both the material and the symbolic meaning of the term, of national resistance. It is clear that such a situation forms the basis of its power. It is what enabled Father Lewandowski to go so far as to categorize the process of fostering atheism begun some forty years earlier by the government as a *crime* against the nation[37], thus echoing Cardinal Wyszynski who, on 26 August 1980, at the feast of the Virgin of Jasna-Gora, said: 'The attempt to instil atheism into children and adolescents both in schools and in social or public life has shaken the confidence placed in those who, perhaps in good faith, have not understood that certain values on which the nation is founded and by which the nation can live must not be subverted.'[38] However, this identification between the Church and the nation is not without its problems. For the instrumentalization, or the 'temporalization of the Church', over against the 'sacralization of the nation', to borrow the phrase of Jerzy Mirewicz,[39] raises the question: To what extent is this a misunderstanding? To what extent is the ambiguity deliberate? The 'political' power of the Church in Poland is directly linked to its ability to articulate the deep longings of the nation, of the nation as a whole. Yet it is clear that these longings are not wholly the same as those of the Church. It is only too apparent that a large proportion of the population of Poland does not abide by the moral standards set up by the Church, even when these standards are not rejected out of hand. For example, Monsignor Alfons Nossol, bishop of Opole, has admitted that 30–40 per cent of young Poles refuse to abide by the moral teaching of the Church on sexual relations, and there have been many examples to show that the authority of the Church has lessened when its pronouncements have diverged too widely from the perceived general interest in favour of formulating its own priorities, especially on political questions.

In this sense the Church appears somehow to be the hostage of society. But it is clearly significant that this society has had no other option than to use religious symbols in order to assert its rights and make its voice heard. In the final analysis, the symbols have a life of their own. They become more and more self-authenticating until at last they impose on those who make use of them a meaning that is not necessarily the message that the symbol was originally thought to convey. Thinking about the world in Christian categories is not a value-free activity. At the end of the day, even if initially these categories had a purely functionalist purpose, they go on to 'create meaning' and make it impossible to 'think outside them'. Functioning as a symbolic machine, as a producer and supplier of meaning, the Church in turn makes use of society. It would be naïve to think that this was not done consciously. But, as Adam Michnik wrote, 'the People's Republic of Poland is not a democratic, secular state. It is a totalitarian state subject to a particular ideology. For it to be secularized and laicized, it is essential that its totalitarian structure should be abolished.'[40] In the same way, Church leaders know that the power of the institution they are directing is partly based upon an ambiguity that some people regard as the 'heart of the drama of Polish Catholicism'.[41] No doubt this is why in the peroration of his speech to the plenary assembly of the Polish episcopate meeting at Wroclaw on 17 October 1966, Cardinal Wyszynski elected to quote a passage from the constitution on the presence of the Church in the modern world:

> The Church makes plain to the world that a true visible social union flows from the union of hearts and minds, that is to say from that faith and that charity whereon, in the Holy Spirit, its unity is indissolubly founded. For the energy that the Church is capable of breathing into modern society is found in this faith and in this charity effectively lived and does not rest on any external sovereignty exerted by purely human means. . . . What we desire above all is the power to develop freely, to the advantage of all, under any regime which recognizes the fundamental rights of the person, the family and the imperatives of the common good.[42]

This aspiration obviously carries implications for politics as well. The Polish Church has the Vatican to thank for helping it to regard itself not as a hierarchical institution but as a community of the people of God, a conception that clearly met the requirements of a situation in which official propaganda refused to see it otherwise than as an ecclesiastical hierarchy. The Church tried to foster the image of an open, tolerant institution, working for human rights. When questioned in 1976 by J.-M. Domenach, Cardinal Wojtyla, at that time archbishop of Cracow, simply stated that the defence of human rights was a priority for the Church.[43] And if the Church's pronouncements on economic and social matters are examined, this is seen to be true.

Morals and the economy

In an important homily delivered in Warsaw on 6 January 1978, Cardinal Wyszynski, speaking about the situation in Poland, where Christian reality met the ideology of materialism, said: 'Everybody knows that even in economic and social life the principles of the gospel ethics are necessary.' He went on to say that, 'today in order to overcome our various faults, our weaknesses, we must not only "save the economy", production, we must rescue man. We have to come back to man and remind him of his duties dictated by the Gospel of Christ, by common sense and by the sense of national resistance.'[44]

By this threefold appeal to daily life, national life and the religious life, the primate was pointing out the failure of the government to impose a moral code governing personal and working life based on the ideology deriving from Lenin's paradigm of 'socialist man', a completely new man motivated by the spirit of service to and sacrifice for the community.

More than three years later, when Alain Touraine's team, during a hasty on-the-spot visit to gather information about the social movement of 1980–1, interviewed at Gdansk Father Jankowski, the priest of Sainte-Brigitte, a parish bordering the Lenin shipyard,

> he said that the idea of a close interrelation between industrial action and a religious activity unambiguously affirming its Polish character was accepted without question by all. Zenon (one of the members of the group) recalls how, as early as day four, he telephoned the abbé to come and give a sermon, which he considered to be 'very mature politically' and the abbé, after explaining that he shared his time equally between the parish and the trade union, related how, after thinking about it, he had organized his sermon around the theme 'work as a blessing and work as a curse'. The Gdansk group relived with this interviewer the historic moments of the struggle and the impression left on him from this part of the meeting was of an indissoluble interpenetration of the problems of work and the affirmation of a Polish Catholicism. Thus the consciousness of workers, whether management or manual, is linked to a national consciousness defined either in terms of a rejection of foreign domination or in terms of religious affirmation.[45]

The Church's activity in the sphere of labour takes many different forms, not amenable to a simple classification. Similarly, the reaction of the state to this activity is not uniform; it varies from the denunciation of unacceptable interference to a recognition that certain aspects of these activities are helpful. The workplace, a social crucible filled with people, producer of wealth and generator of tension, is a supremely important prize for which state and Church contend.

'We must have done with the belief that there is no connection between the national economy and Christian morality', said Cardinal Wyszynski in 1978.[46] Already in 1977 he had vigorously affirmed the need

> to be conscious of the fact that at present there is less and less hope of solving the proletarian problem by Marxism. The utter ineffectiveness of this doctrine is being shown up and in the final analysis it is becoming clear that Marxism brings about the rebirth of capitalism by making man an appendage of the productive system and hence condemning him once more to slavery.[47]

Quite clearly, the Polish authorities take a very different view from that of the cardinal, even though, back in 1971, the deputy minister A. Skarzynski, at that time director of the Religious Affairs Bureau, said in a speech delivered on 3 October to members of Pax, that 'he believed that in the field of social morality there are problems of fundamental importance for the future of the nation, on which Marxists and Catholics, animated by a common patriotism, have convergent views, even though these are based on differing ideological or philosophical presuppositions'.[48] It is true that that was at the beginning of the Gierek era, when the task of building the Second Poland, which needed help from everybody for its successful conclusion, was just then getting under way. Despite that, the state was not unaware that it could not do without the help of the Church in its endeavour to solve certain widespread social problems, such as alcoholism or integrity at work. At the same time, to acknowledge that at certain points the collaboration of the Church was desirable or even valuable was to open a considerable breach in the conception of religion as a 'private affair' and, besides developing a dialogue acceptable to the state, provided the bishops with an opportunity to take action in an area from which they were supposed to be excluded. Besides, the Church could state conditions and, by analysing the causes of the situations that the state was requesting it to remedy, call government policy into question:

> We all understand that today the contribution of the Church to our life is all the more important in that we are doing our best to overcome all the defects that have arisen in the course of our enslavement for so many years. Slavery always produces social and moral deformities. . . . But in order to raise the moral tone of our society we have to obtain conditions in which the Gospel is not up against atheist propaganda.[49]

In this way, starting out from the fight against a duly identified social scourge, the Church comes to make a bid for the complete remodelling of Polish society: 'Alcoholism is connected with the feeling of lassitude and with the lack of natural communities and free cultural or religious associations.'[50] And, starting from the premise that 'without a return to a moral order, the

Polish chariot in the grip of a crisis will not be able to advance any further', the Church forecasts that:

> If the moral level of our life is not raised, we are in danger of seeing not only the life of the state but that of the nation atrophied in the end. Even though a people has admittedly a stronger power of survival than a state, since the nation itself has survived in the absence of a Polish state, nevertheless if private, family and working life are demoralized this may lead to the destruction of the life of the nation.[51]

The link that the cardinal here establishes between 'moral level' and 'life of the nation' finds a very precise application in the analysis made by the Church of the relationships between work and morals, ethics and economy:

> The results obtained [by Poland] so far in its economic expansion are extremely inadequate and far below what could be achieved. The efficiency of the economy leaves much to be desired, whilst output per worker is only 25 to 30 per cent of output in the developed countries (with a ratio of skilled management comparable and in some cases even better). In consequence we have a relatively low standard of living, below what society desires and could achieve, and this causes tensions, conflicts and crises. There is an enormous wastage of labour and production resources, high materials consumption and inadequate product quality and technical level.[52]

This severe judgement on the state of the Polish economy comes not from the opposition but from the government press office, in a publication issued in 1982. The finding is quite correct, but the analysis of the underlying causes of the 'enormous disproportion between the potential of the economy and its real efficiency and productivity'[53] is very far from adequate. Emphasis is laid on economic mechanisms 'which do not create sufficient incentives to high productivity' and on social aspects – the rigidity and bureaucratic nature of the system, 'controlled by means of administrative directives'. Yet not a word is said about the profound malaise felt by society before August 1980, which affected the whole of economic life. How much more important was the observation made by Cardinal Wyszynski on 24 October 1980 when, refusing mechanistic explanations, he said to a meeting of senior priests of the Warsaw archdiocese: 'Today we can compute our debts amounting to billions, but do we know how much of those billions are made up of thefts, wastage or the destruction caused by a lack of honesty which has become the general rule? . . . The misdeeds of individuals extend right across society.'[54]

The call to moral conduct to which this text bears witness has been a constant feature of the vast movement of social renewal that swept through Poland from August 1980 to December 1981, underestimated by the government and often misunderstood by onlookers. The 21 points of Gdansk, setting out the claims of the MKS at the beginning of the movement, gave a large place to demands of this kind, in emphatically calling for 'the introduction of the principle of the appointment of managers based on qualification and not on Party membership; the abolition of the privileges of the militia, the secret police and the Party apparatus by equalization of family allowances and the ending of the system of reserved sales' (point no. 13); 'publication of full information as to the social and economic situation' (point no. 6A); 'persons dismissed for standing up for workers' rights to be given back their jobs' (point no. 4A); and above all, of course, 'the acceptance of free trade unions, independent of the Party and of the employers on the basis of convention no. 87 of the International Labour Organization concerning the freedom of trade unions, ratified by the People's Republic of Poland' (point no. 1). For the workers were becoming increasingly dissatisfied with trade unions having the sole function of acting as transmission belts for the Party in industrial enterprises and carrying out their duties more in accordance with political criteria than social ones. Staszek, one of the first organizers of the strike at Ursus, says that the formation of Solidarity represented 'an act of faith in people against the ruling apparat, in integrity against corruption, in Christian values against a materialism highhandedly imported from abroad'. He regarded the new trade union as 'the return to reality, to the faith of the people, to the will to national existence, to respect for work'.[55] This moral dimension is a basic feature of Solidarity: since the Party had hijacked and discredited the vocabulary of politics and its values, the Polish workers chose to take their stand on the ground of ethics, and for months on end they refused to consider the question of power. For years, starting from the proposition that 'the regime may be democratic, but the organization of work is still capitalist',[56] the Church was the only voice having the ear of government that was raised in defence of the interests of the workers, and it associated itself with the various approaches and initiatives of other actors on the Polish scene who had the same aims in view. The bishops condemned corruption ('to rise above the bad habit of allowing oneself to be bought or enriching oneself often at the expense of society'[57]), dishonesty ('you have only to read a newspaper to see how much dishonesty, unscrupulousness and lawbreaking there is, and not only in high places but also in the sphere of industrial and agricultural work, especially in the state-owned sector'[58]), and incompetence:

> Just now when promotion has become so easy for one class of persons and absolutely impossible for another class, it is difficult to persuade people that they ought to give up the idea of acting crookedly, of being a slave to oneself, of oneself, of abjuring. . . . Generally speaking, we are demoralized by the search for easy advancement . . . without regard to whether we have the necessary experience and skill. The result is that there are very many people with

certificates, degrees and doctorates, but very few competent people capable of managing, of teaching others to lead an upright life, of transmitting lasting values.[59]

At the same time, the Church was at pains to explain the causes of the moral lapses it complained of. For example, it pointed out the connection between a lack of workplace integrity and recompense:

> As soon as we give society our hard work, our knowledge, our time and our energy, we obtain the right to receive a recompense of the same value. . . . Solidity for solidity, honesty for honesty, one value for another – that is justice. . . . Let us not forget those who in return for their hard-earned pay receive only valueless products.[60]

Again in 1980, analysing the causes of the situation of the country in an address given in Warsaw, the primate said:

> We feel deeply that all the turmoil in the world of labour comes from the violation of the moral principles of the organization of work, principles which ought to be acted on by employers and employees. The monopolization of the whole of economic life by the Party, the fact that the workers have been deprived of freedom of opinion and the means of standing up for their rights, and above all the fact that the labour code depends on economic programmes, all this has created abnormal situations which have engendered strife.

And he added:

> For a long time now, the Polish Church has had this problem under study. . . . For many years we have been drawing the attention of the government and the Party to the sub-standard conditions in the workplace. We have pointed out that to urge people to increase productivity by exerting undue pressure on them led to serious distortions. Human work, which ought to be a social task, has become the breeding-ground of an unbridled lust for gain. Those in charge of economic life, in their desire to increase production, have created temptations for additional gain, especially in the mining sector. Such a system took account neither of the physical stamina nor of the mental state of the workers, nor of their obligations to their families, to education or religion. . . . Huge wage increases were awarded to certain sectors of production while there were no goods on which those wages could be spent, and this is one of the reasons for the increase in the scourge of alcoholism, leading to the destabilization of family life, and the wave of divorces.[61]

Reading an analysis like this, one is not surprised to find that the Church placed conditions at work in the forefront of its concerns, fighting against what Cardinal Wyszynski had no hesitation in calling 'the violation of every principle of human safety and hygiene at work',[62] sending letter after letter to the authorities to 'defend workers who are losing their strength and their health following an overload of work, and denied the opportunity of serving God' and noting that 'these people are subjected to monetary incentives that make them work beyond their strength to the extent that some of them die prematurely or become seriously ill. Young miners also frequently suffer heart attacks or other industrial illnesses.'[63]

In fact, the doctrinal basis of the bishops' conceptions regarding the morality of work consists in promoting what Cardinal Wyszynski calls *the spirit of service*:[64]

> In your work, do not forget that you are not working only for yourselves, but for the whole nation as well, just as others work for you. That should awaken in you a sense of responsibility for the work done, of application, of responsibility for the public asset entrusted to you – machines, tools, materials, raw materials, technical installations – which you do not own but which belong to working people as a whole.[65]

The response evoked by this message of social solidarity in 1980–1 is a matter of history.

Because of its importance for society, the problem of alcoholism is a matter on which the Church has on several occasions delivered a very pointed message, with the same urgency as for the defence of living and working conditions. 'Give battle uncompromisingly to alcohol and to the squandering of your hard-earned money . . ., above all at your workplace remain sober and masters of yourselves so as not to become a cause of accidents, catastrophes or misfortunes in which innocent lives are lost',[66] was the clear message put out by Cardinal Wyszynski in 1967. Earlier still, in 1965, an analysis carried out by the Polish bishops had reached the conclusion that 'alcohol is the cause of enormous biological, economic and social, cultural and spiritual losses, even more serious than the losses caused by war'.[67]

And indeed alcoholism does appear to be a scourge: 'In the years 1933–1937 we Poles drank about 1 litre of pure alcohol per head, in 1945 about 1.5 litres, in 1950 3 litres, in 1957 over 4 litres, in 1969 5.3 litres, in 1971 5.5 litres (including children).[68] In 1977 the annual consumption per head was of the order of 8.2 litres. There are an average thirty shops selling alcohol for every 25,000 inhabitants, compared with one in Sweden.[69] The situation is so worrying that the censor's office has been instructed not to publish any global data on this subject and only to divulge partial information.[70]

In 1947 the bishops declared:

Whenever attempts have been made to weaken the Polish people physically and morally, the oppressors have tried to plunge the nation into alcoholism so as to make oppression easier. . . . That is what happened barely a century ago when the tsarist government suppressed the temperance movement organized by the Church in the dioceses; it was the same during the German occupation when alcoholism was encouraged by every possible means, by turning a blind eye to illicit stills and paying bonuses to peasants in the form of alcohol. . . . We note with sorrow that alcoholism is taking hold among all classes of society. Alas, even women – and students – are drinking.'[71]

At this point the text is perfectly clear: over and above the problem of alcoholism, the government is identified as an oppressive force and, what is more, is placed on the same footing as the tsar or the Nazis. By making this comparison, it is the Church in its role as guardian of the national identity that embodies the permanence of Poland. It is the Church that is fighting for the survival of a people whose government is held up as the representative of foreign interests. 'What is a nation worth that gives itself over to alcohol?' asked the bishops in the same year. 'It destroys its possessions, weakens and denatures itself, diminishes itself spiritually, loses all mental acuity, suffers moral decline, loses the resources wherewith to build its culture and its civilization, sees its creative faculties disappear, becomes indifferent to public affairs and is in danger of catastrophe. A nation of drunkards turns into a horde of slaves.' And the pastoral letter concluded with the hope that 'the state, which should be concerned for the health of society, would reduce the sale of alcohol so as to save the nation from incipient degeneration'.[72]

In actual fact, as the use of the conditional mood shows, the Church appears to have had few illusions about the state's willingness to put an end to the process which, progressing from lassitude and aversion from alcohol, led people into slavery and ever more pronounced degeneration. It is not without significance that the workers at Gdansk banned the consumption of alcohol on the premises of firms on strike in August 1980, or that the Church repeatedly launched widespread campaigns in favour of abstinence, during which tens of thousands of written pledges were collected. The causal connection between alcoholism and servitude established shortly after the Second World War by the Church is also a way of affirming the links between religion and the national identity in Poland and of demonstrating that the Church was consciously the guarantor of values that the government could not defend because it did not have the necessary legitimation. From this it is clear that the problem of the extent of the impact of the Church's moral pronouncements is of quite secondary importance here. Doubtless it is true that this influence soon reaches its limits, both as regards ethics in the workplace and the care of social property and with regard to sexual morals or temperance. But in so far as no alternative pattern exists, Catholic standards enjoy a *de facto* monopoly which necessarily gives them the status of a reference point. Church pronouncements are intended to fill a gap.

In 1979 the 171st plenary conference of the episcopate in its final communiqué singled out as elements in the moral crisis 'the absence of truth in interpersonal relations, the worsening of dishonesty in society – work badly done, a lack of a sense of the public good, corruption, alcoholism – the prevailing discouragement, increasingly pronounced indifference to the needs of individuals and of society in general, the lack of goodwill in human relations'. And the bishops observed that, 'it has reached a point where it is not competence, effort, the results of the work and integrity that count, but acceptance of the ideology'.[73] This amounted to saying that the degree of moral consciousness in a society is closely related to its independence of the state.

In fact, some time after the birth of Solidarity the sociologist Stefan Nowak, of Warsaw University, observed:

> Observation of everyday life in Poland during these last few months reveals that interpersonal anger and aggression have in large measure disappeared. . . . If the disappearance of the signs of frustration and aggression is confirmed by systematic surveys, that will show that essential needs of the population have been met. As these satisfactions cannot be economic ones (in that area the frustrations are worse than before) another explanation must be sought. It could be due to the restructuring of an atomized society, to the disappearance of a feeling of helplessness and to the re-establishment of the dignity of a nation.[74]

It is quite obvious that the peremptory stop that was put to this process on 13 December 1981 can only have had disastrous effects on morale: for how and why should citizens trouble themselves about ethical standards in a country in which they are denied any right to monitor the way in which society is run?

Religion and relations in society

Any consideration of the relation between religion and society in the context of a Soviet-type political system is bound to pose the question what really happens to the content of social relations under such a system, given that all the empirical studies describe it as an atomized grouping. It is true that this trend appears to be undergoing a reversal in certain countries, especially in Poland. However that may be, in such a system the political swallows up the social: the state tries to transform all the bonds and orders of social life so as to control them as completely as possible. Whether or not they are successful, the party-state and its organs for enrolling or coercing the citizens have the task of subjugating or taking over any independent collective movements as soon as they appear or, failing that, of destroying them. It is as if a gigantic suction pump were constantly at work, emptying every kind of independent social life of its substance. No group of people, however small, escapes or is supposed to escape government control, according to this system.

That of course is the theory, which is nowhere fully actualized, especially because of the resistances encountered by the party-state during the steamrollering process on which it has embarked. One such resistance is the survival of religion, since for ideological reasons the state could not try to take it over. What the situation in Poland has shown us is that one of the main, albeit unexpected, effects of the confrontation between scientific socialism and religion is that religion takes a hand in setting the scene in society.

This configuration does not fit very well into the traditional analytical patterns of the relationship between society and religion.[75] It opens up a fresh field for analysis, calling for a combination of the study of the political relations between Church and state with consideration of the specific functions of religion in a Soviet-type system.

Religiousness and the functions of religion

The Polish sociologist W. Piwowarski defines religious sentiment as 'a totality of beliefs, values and institutionalized symbols and of attitudes with reference to them, shared by a group of people, deriving from the distinction between empirical and extra-empirical reality and of subordination of the meaning of things coming from empirical reality to the things of the extra-empirical reality.'[76] Clearly, a Marxist intellectual would have difficulty in finding his way about this definition since it brings in an order of subordination unacceptable to a materialist. For all that, it does delimit a field of observation – religious sentiment as a generator of social relationships – that has a rather widespread application in Poland, reaching as far as the representatives of the Office of Cults or to official sociologists. Even in Czechoslovakia, where the institutional situation of the Church is very different from that in Poland, the presence of several tens of thousands on pilgrimages is clearly felt by the government to be a threat to the social and political balance that it imposes and seeks to maintain.

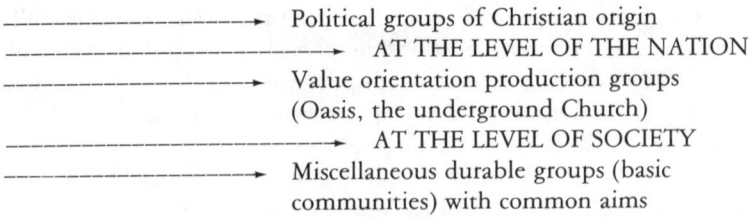

Religion and Society 97

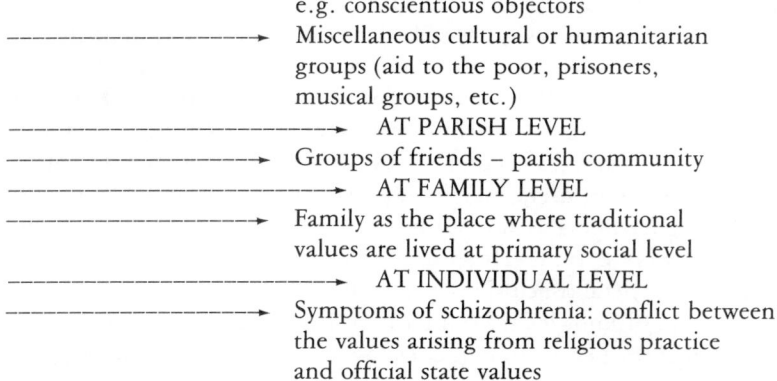

```
                                      e.g. conscientious objectors
------------------------→  Miscellaneous cultural or humanitarian
                                      groups (aid to the poor, prisoners,
                                      musical groups, etc.)
------------------------------→  AT PARISH LEVEL
------------------------→  Groups of friends – parish community
---------------------------→  AT FAMILY LEVEL
------------------------→  Family as the place where traditional
                                      values are lived at primary social level
---------------------------→  AT INDIVIDUAL LEVEL
------------------------→  Symptoms of schizophrenia: conflict between
                                      the values arising from religious practice
                                      and official state values
```

Continuum from − to + from the least structured to the most complex forms

It is not easy at this point to distinguish what is religious from what is social, the more so as the meaning of the words differs according to the political context in which they are used. At all events, the encounter between the sacred and the secular takes place in this sphere of values and behaviour, and results in the appearance of more or less structured and complex forms of autonomous social relationships. Naturally enough, these forms are not fixed, since they vary in accordance with the current balance of power between the Church, the government and society.

The lowest point on this scale of complexity of forms of social life arising from religious sentiment and practice are of course simple psychological attitudes. Either the individual will be able to identify directly with the value system provided by the Church or else he will suffer internal torment from the daily conflict between his inner convictions and his formal acceptance of the official system. Once the psychological obstacles have been surmounted, individuals have a natural tendency to form organized groups. There is a very wide range of forms from the circle of friends to organized political groups. But the balance of power at any one time is always precarious and may be upset by one protagonist or another, above all by a strengthening of the anti-religious drive of the government.

There are of course different configurations in each of the three countries considered in this book. In Czechoslovakia there are very many cases of direct identification with underground groups, these being the only alternative to what is perceived as a suffocation: 'Drink or believe! Those are the two remaining solutions in the void surrounding us', said a young nurse in Prague who, encouraged by a chance encounter, finally joined a small group of Christians meeting at regular intervals. Though unable to define the links between the official Church and the underground Church to which she belongs, she is none the less quite sure that some priests and ministers are showing exemplary behaviour. She mentions in particular the evangelist Karacek, forced into exile 'because he was being too successful'. An artist, not a believer, says that 'he feels himself to be at one with the Christians because, like me, they are fighting for moral values'. A woman photographer, also a non-believer, tells how purely out of curiosity she went to hear the sermons of a priest in Prague. She was not surprised that he had been arrested and deprived of his work permit: 'He spoke the truth.'[77]

Obviously no general conclusions can be drawn from a few cases which, in our present state of knowledge, cannot even be said to be typical. But the intensification of the persecution in Czechoslovakia during the past few years seems to constitute a proof *a contrario* of the movement that Cardinal Tomasek reflected in an interview published in the Austrian daily *Kurier* on 30 July 1986:

> The religious influence of the Catholic Church has never been so strong; more and more young people are thinking deeply about the fundamental question of the meaning of life. It is not without interest to note that the line taken by the Czechoslovaks to escape from the schizophrenia of daily life involves activities that have already been tried out elsewhere: as was done in Poland during the 1960s, even Party members have their infants baptized. The primate observes that these baptisms 'often have painful consequences for those concerned'.

This unexpected resurgence of religion is not the only thing about Czechoslovakia: 'A few years ago', observes Tomka, 'the theory of religions, in Hungary as elsewhere, was based on the premise that religion would wither away. Current research in this area contests this theory or relegates the event to an unimaginably distant future. The trends concerning religion that can be detected at present are not in line with previous ideological forecasts. Even the theoretical pattern of secularization is only faintly discernible. Secularization appears to have been overtaken by a process of desecularization.'[78] No doubt the clue to the turn of events reported here is to be found, as in Czechoslovakia, in the frustration felt by Hungarian society with the pattern offered by the government, while the comparative success of the venture into consumerism undertaken in Hungary is also an aggravating factor. Furthermore, in what is only an apparent paradox, the high degree of normalization of institutional relations between Church and state in Hungary has resulted in an interiorization of the conflict of values which even goes so far as to produce dissidents within state as well as Church organizations.

To come now to Poland, the Church has succeeded in putting forward a prospect of transcending the internal conflict, by membership of the mass organizations that it creates or protects, and support of certain broad objectives that it defines. No doubt this is the symbolic meaning of the widespread practice of building illegal churches, the best known example being at Nowa Huta in the suburbs of Cracow. The building of a church, virtually without money and without a building permit, implies that sufficiently strong social bonds have been re-established for each member of the group to accept the constraints, in time and money, and the risks for the individual resulting from the collective action. What this means is that an entire people must have become aware at a basic level of the urgent need to reconstitute a social space expunged by the government around a voluntarily selected centre. The building of a church or chapel is the crucible in which individual consciences bestir themselves in collective praxis, strongly bonding the links that until then were only embryonic and creating or recreating a social consciousness. Fundamentally, all that the building that is erected does it to concretize the existence of a new social geography, strengthened and newly centred, as a symbol of the collective will which, in coming to expression, founds the community.

The experience of Oasis is another illustration of the same line of action. We have already mentioned how very successful it has been; its influence is even felt beyond the frontiers of Poland, particularly in Slovakia. It began as a simple youth organization, gathering small groups for holidays, but it soon progressed to having a stable, well-established structure. It is true that Oasis was a reply by the Church to the challenge issued by the government, which thought that the best way to make the population dissatisfied with the Church would be to improve living standards. Therefore the bishops encouraged a movement whose aim was to lay the foundations for a new model of religion, more structured and detached from the traditional type of piety, by starting with young people. But, beyond this first objective, Oasis promoted the rise of a new collective consciousness with standards that appealed to groups other than the one originally targeted.

In fact, both in Czechoslovakia, where the underground Church played an important part, and in Hungary through the base communities, and certainly in Poland, a new form of religious belief and practice is being worked out. Indifference to religion is increasingly being counterbalanced by a deepening of faith, the main characteristics of which are described by Polish sociologists as follows:[79]

1 a more intellectual and individual approach to religion;
2 an increasingly widespread need of spiritual living and religious experience;
3 a growing turning to the Church as a community (frequently found in young people and the intelligentsia);
4 a developing orientation towards a 'socialized' Church, that is to say,

a Church committed to the creation of a social order based on strong ethical values, ensuring respects for the human person, the emancipation of the individual and of society through work and public life under the influence of the spirit of Vatican II, the personalist philosophy and the progress of the modern national consciousness.

It is easy to show how these trends bring the government face to face with the failure to which they are the implicit witness.

Intellectualization is at the opposite pole to ritualization, a series of empty gestures and forms in which the authorities wanted to confine religion. Furthermore, it shows that the Church is alive and has a future. The search for a community Church that is involved in the life of society is an unequivocal disavowal of the regime, inasmuch as it shows up the void in the life of society and the unattractiveness of the goals proclaimed by the government, and erects freely chosen membership and trust into cornerstones of communal life. And lastly, the partner in this search for values on which the life of this community can be organized is a Church reconciled with the modern world and capable of influencing its development. It needs no emphasis how ill such an outlook consorts with the philosophy and praxis of a Soviet-type system.

Polish sociology (which, as we have said, is in many respects the most advanced in this part of the world) has even endeavoured to question various social groups on the functions they assigned to religion. The interesting point about this survey is the ranking of the functions indicated by the replies. It is perhaps not surprising that a third of the skilled workers who are members of socialist youth groups thought that religion did not contribute anything of importance to their lives, but nearly half of the young workers and students stated that religion was a psychological support and provided a strong moral basis. Besides providing a social cement, it is a school of character and a means whereby values can be transmitted from one generation to another. It was also mentioned as being an aid to the integration of the nation, a road leading to mystical experience, an instrument of knowledge and a means of acquiring aesthetic experience, these attributes being mentioned in decreasing order of importance.

These opinions are of course constantly being modified under the influence of a variety of factors such as industrialization, urbanization, the extension of the educational network, widening access to cultural treasures, atheist propaganda, the economic and political situation, etc. External influences also play a part; the impact made on Catholicism in this part of Europe by the appointment of a Pope born in Poland needs no emphasis. But, even though the conclusions of this survey point to trends that undoubtedly exist, it is not possible in the present state of sociological knowledge to extrapolate them to other social groups, to Polish society as a whole and *a fortiori* to the other two countries studied. Nevertheless, in our view one point that applies to the whole of East-Central Europe stands out clearly from the foregoing analysis. Religion is acknowledged to have a detotalizing effect, and on this account it constitutes an essential instrument of desovietization. Our task is now to develop this conclusion under a more directly political aspect.

4
Religion and Politics: Symbolism, Catacombs and Opposition

Religion is a vehicle of desovietization and detotalization in East-Central Europe on several counts. Peter Berger has observed that, speaking generally, 'throughout history the quest of religion gives a profound revelation of the urgent and intense need that drives man to go in search of meaning. The huge projections of the religious consciousness, whatever other meaning they may have, represent the greatest human endeavour in history to find a meaning to human life at all costs.'[1] In the specific context of countries with a Soviet-type regime, this search for meaning is all the vaster and more urgently pursued because the clash between the dominant ideology and reality has resulted in a perceptible erosion of the former. There can be no doubt that after the events of 1956, 1968, 1970, 1976 and 1980–1, Marxism-Leninism is passing through a serious crisis in the East, to say the least. This turning away of course relates to the all-embracing explanation of the world which that ideology claimed to provide. But it also extends to the description of the ultimate aim that Marxism in power set before it in order to justify the methods of government it used. By and large, all that the ideology aims to do nowadays is to save appearances, in a face-saving exercise that was at first supposed to be only an instrument but that has become an end in itself. The government machine no longer has any other aim than to keep itself in power, thus preserving the privileges of those who are the embodiment of that power. Hence it is not surprising that the search is on for other systems of explaining the world, putting forward a different meaning and serving a higher aim. The 'discovery' or even the conversion to Christianity of 'disappointed' Marxists is quite a good illustration of the way in which religion can provide a way of escape from a daily round perceived as wellnigh intolerable, and can provide existence with values that it needs in order to justify itself in its own eyes.[2] In this sense the appearances are against it. To quote Peter Berger once more, 'although religion displays a strong propensity (very understandable in theory) to justify alienation, it is also possible for disalienation to be justified by religious motivations, in certain special historical situations'.[3]

Such a process entails a preliminary redefinition of the very content of politics. The Soviet-type political system claims to provide the whole of this content by itself; in other words, to monopolize politics. Moreover, it claims sole authority to define the limits of politics. Somewhat paradoxically, in appearance at least, the 'entry into politics'[4] of a believer takes place via a rejection of politics as defined by the government. More accurately, such a move will involve a subordination of politics to a higher, spiritual and moral register. Hence entering the field of politics means *ipso facto* assigning limits to politics, and these limits will apply not only in respect of the government alone, but also to the Church as an institution, which will not be permitted to take part in a power struggle in which the individual or collective aspirations or needs of the faithful and, beyond them, of society at large, are set at nought. This questioning of the self-styled pre-eminence of politics in the technique of government or in corporate jockeying is evidence of the search for new values around which a social fabric in course of reconstitution can be articulated.

In fact, it is doubtless a personal dawning of awareness that causes individuals to go against the government and against a reality that no longer makes sense. But it is unlikely that such an awakening will have any practical consequences unless it is accompanied by an effort to spread conviction. From this point of view, the base communities in Hungary well deserve their name, being signs of an outreach towards a community Church based on mutual trust and coming 'from the grassroots'.

Certainly believers are well prepared to challenge the monopoly of politics over society, since by their very nature they subscribe to a view that gives unquestionable priority to spiritual things over politics. This is well illustrated by the large numbers of believers active in the opposition movements in Czechoslovakia. But this process also affects non-believers; in their case politics is subordinated to morals or to law.

Moreover, the problem of the responsibility of government is also relevant here. By treating Christians as second-class citizens it helps to marginalize them. In employing repressive measures it criminalizes them. Hence the decision to live by faith almost inevitably leads to becoming an opponent of the government on the basis of a simple moral requirement to bring one's actions into line with one's convictions. Then again, the very status of the Church is not free from contradictions. The faithful, and more generally society as a whole, want it to witness by its very presence to the existence of a reality above politics or at least not subordinate thereto. Consequently, there is considerable risk of misunderstandings occurring when the Church takes upon itself to play politics in the name of the symbol that it constitutes. Just as in the case of the government, the pursuit of its own objectives as an institution must be subordinated to moral requirements defined as being higher ones, irrespective of the situation, whether the Church as an institution is powerful as in Poland, compromised as in Hungary, or suppressed as in Czechoslovakia.

Behaviour and attitudes

We can obtain an overall view of these problems by trying to identify the behaviour and attitudes of believers in the sociopolitical arena. Unfortunately, there are as yet few sociological studies dealing with this subject. However, we believe it is possible to identify the main types of behaviour occurring in the three countries covered by our study, on the basis of the semi-participating observation carried out during our fieldwork.[5] In this study the sociopolitical field is divided into four quadrants by means of two axes at right angles. The first quadrant arranges attitudes from the most passive to the most active, and the second from the most dependent to the most independent.

DEPENDENT-PASSIVE (AREA OF SUBMISSION TO GOVERNMENT):
The conformist: submissive to order and hierarchy, whether religious or civil, his faith tends mainly to be reduced to mere ritualization. He finds in the sacraments a factor of traditional integration with the community of which he is a part. He is often hostile to any innovation, either through ignorance or by choice. In this case, his options are determined by his anxiety to give no grounds for being accused of anticommunism. As an example one might mention the ex-primate of Hungary, Monsignor Lekai, and a large part of his Church.

DEPENDENT-ACTIVE (AREA OF MANIPULATION BY THE GOVERNMENT):
If the government can play its hand cleverly, the dependent-active can very well be instrumentalized. According to his degree of awareness, he will fall into one of the three following categories:
– The manipulated person: being naïve, he pays attention to what the government says about the need for dialogue between Christians and Marxists. By conviction, he supports the peace objectives officially put forward. He is a conciliator. He is a member of Pax in Poland, of Pacem in Terris in Czechoslovakia, of Opus Pacis in Hungary, or he feels an affinity with those organizations without always going along with everything they do. He may feel sorry about the disapproval shown them by society. There is for example the priest in Prague, a leading member of Pacem in Terris, most of

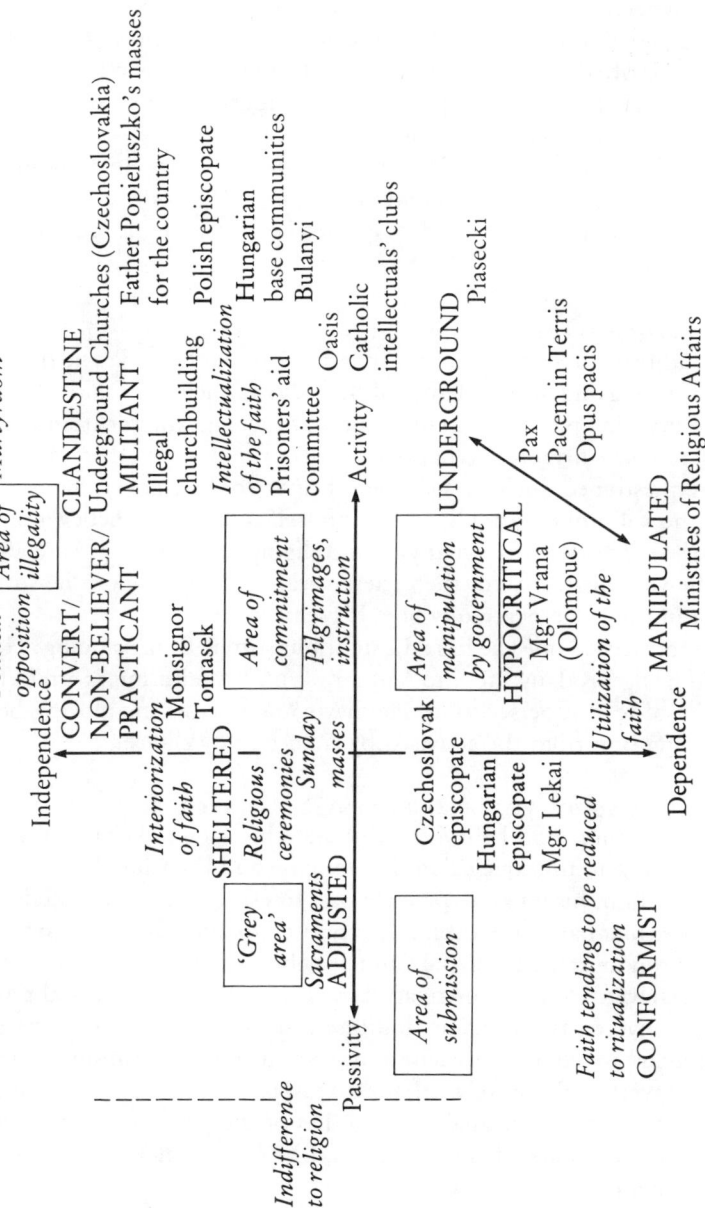

whose sermons were taken up by a fervent plea in favour of the outcasts. The dramatic nature of such a psychology needs no emphasis.

– The hypocrite: he is a member of the same organizations, but has joined them not out of conviction but of calculation. He knows that people are wondering whether he is still a believer. He is much attached to the privileges he enjoys. He may occupy a position of considerable responsibility (such was Monsignor Vrana, bishop of Olomouc).

– The submarine: he is a fully conscious manipulator. He pretends to be a believer, but is trying to liquidate the Church. He works in close collaboration with the authorities and may exercise considerable power (Piasecki, founder of Pax).

INDEPENDENT-PASSIVE ('GREY AREA'):

– The adjusted one: his distinguishing mark is that he makes no distinctions. He wants to avoid all problems, while not renouncing his faith. Depending on the situation prevailing in his country, he will or will not attend mass, will or will not have his children baptized, will or will not send them to catechism. When questioned during a sociological survey or by a government questionnaire, he will unhesitatingly declare himself to be a non-believer or a don't know. He considers that in any event religion is a strictly private affair. He may be very distrustful of the ecclesiastical hierarchy, whom he suspects of compromising. He peacefully goes his schizophrenic way.

– The tormented one: he has adjusted, but suffers from so doing. He would like to bring his daily life into harmony with his faith but is afraid to do so because of fear of persecution. He may come to cross the moving boundary separating him from the activists, by chance or by choice.

INDEPENDENT-ACTIVE (AREA OF COMMITMENT AND AREA OF ILLEGALITY):

– The practising non-believer: cultural, ethical or political considerations have led him to the conclusion that religion and the Church are 'indispensable'. For him, his religious practice is a protest against the utter falsity of the official secular pattern. He sends his children to catechism and pays attention to the pronouncements of the Church, while stoutly maintaining that he is not a believer. He is often engaged in anti-government political activity.

– The convert: as his name indicates, he comes from elsewhere, from indifference to religion, or even from atheism and communism. He may have been converted for purely religious reasons, or his conversion may have resulted from a process analogous to that of the practising non-believer. In any event, the mark of the convert is a high level of activity and a strong commitment.

– The militant: whether he is an intellectual or not, an innovator or a lover of tradition, a priest or a layman, it is his faith that has led him to try to influence events at whatever level (ethical, social, cultural or political). He may, as in Poland, work in harmony with the hierarchical Church, but his convictions may lead him into conflict with it, as in the case of Father Bulanyi. His activities always lead to a more or less open confrontation with the government.

– The underground opponent: whether he is a priest or a layman, the only thing that distinguishes him from the militant (with whom he may be confused) is that he gets the wrong side of the law, generally in connection with the political situation of the country. He may be obliged to go underground – for example, as a priest deprived of his permit to officiate in Czechoslovakia, or by choice, on the pattern of the martyr Church. He is like a moral beacon. His commitment to religion inevitably has political repercussions.

Obviously it is impossible to provide quantitative data in support of this typological sketch. Naturally enough there are far more passive church people than active ones, for whom they constitute, as it were, a 'reservoir'. In practice, movement is often from passivity to activity, and the transition is not always the result of individual choice; it may be caused by external factors. For example, repressive action by the police may cause a Czech citizen to move from the 'grey area' to that of commitment; in the same way, action by the civil authorities may cause one high-ranking ecclesiastic or another to move from simple passive dependence to a situation in which he will be manipulated or used. But apart from this factual observation that illustrates the very fluid nature of such a classification, it is incontestable that the course of events in East European societies is tending to reduce the number of those whose behaviour is confined to a ritualized faith. There is a corresponding increase in the categories of religious indifferentism and of interiorization, though in the absence of trustworthy sociological surveys this distribution cannot be quantified. But in any event, when religion is interiorized this leads to a more or less acute conflict between official values and the values of the individual. In some sense the ritualization of faith is a way of making a clear distinction between the sacred and the secular. In an environment in which the sacred no longer has any place other than the heart of the individual, the secular may at any time be besieged by it. Thus religious symbolism may take on a very directly political meaning, even if not 'enunciated'[6] as such, in a situation where the atheist government has renounced its use, thereby assigning itself a limit that it will not transgress. Hence also the transition to political opposition may occur on the basis of an ethical demand, when believers and civil society set bounds that the government must not pass. We shall now investigate these two directions.

Symbolism and politics: towards a political symbolism of forms of worship in Poland[7]

The signs of Catholicism are everywhere visible in Poland; Churches, chapels, oratories, wayside crosses or simple niches in the walls of private houses all witness to the fact that the sacred permeates Polish society. The present monograph, which is based on a field survey carried out in the district of Zywiec, south-west of Cracow, is not intended to furnish conclusions that can be considered valid for the whole of Poland and, *a fortiori*, for the two other countries analysed. Its purpose is the more modest one of trying to establish the possibility of interpreting religious symbolism politically and thereby verifying 'the symbolic efficacy' mentioned by Claude Lévi-Strauss.[8]

In this district – which covers some 20 square kilometres, has 146,000 inhabitants, and is socially very diversified – we were able to count 405 religious buildings of all kinds, which equals twenty to each square kilometre or, more accurately, an average of one for every 100 metres, by the roadsides and in the villages, thirteen churches and twenty-three chapels having been built since the Soviet-type regime was installed, some of them illegally and only after a trial of strength with the authorities.

For a very long time the consecration of a church or a chapel in Poland was done solely by the local lord, or his chaplain, under the more or less distant patronage of the bishop. Such is no longer the case. Since the temporal government no longer, or very seldom, finances the building of a religious edifice, the budget is met largely by the generosity of the parishioners as far as their means allow. When the building is completed, their names will appear in the doorway. This then gives them a right to be consulted in matters concerning the parish. It also effects a considerable change in the relationship between the priest and his parishioners. The Church in the village of Cisiec, which was built illegally in twenty-four hours in 1972, despite police pressure,[9] was consecrated, naturally not by chance, to Maximilian Kolbe, a man who stands for strong will and a refusal to give way to arbitrary power, even at the cost of life itself. It is a sign of the will to resist.

Not all ascriptions and dedications can be so easily interpreted: the method of consecrating an oratory is very different from that of a church consecration. A church is consecrated with all due ceremony and, furthermore, the state is involved by first granting a building permit and then by the interim and final building inspections. So there is a long, complex and involved legal procedure. An oratory, on the other hand, is usually the result of a private decision; it is built on privately owned land and no building permit is required; it receives such consecration as its owner pleases to give it; usually the priest's part is confined to blessing the building. Hence the problems are of a different kind. Nevertheless churches, chapels and oratories, as signs of the sacralization of space, show that it has been claimed for the Church. They are waymarks and invitations; they initiate a dialogue. Their function, a purely external one, is to organize the human geography and link it together.

From the inventory drawn up in the field[10] we were able to construct ranking tables for the cults, showing their respective importance. In order not to overload the text, the basic data representing four series of two tables have been shown in the Appendix (see p. 197). Table 7 summarizes the cultic buildings (churches, chapels, oratories and niches), while table 8 sets out the presence of the cults as shown by the number of buildings. The four series in the Appendix contain respectively the person and the life of Christ (I, 1 and 2), the Virgin (II, 1 and 2; in this one a distinction has been made between liturgical titles and 'popular' titles), saints (III, 1 and 2; classified into 'traditional Polish saints', 'saints of the soil', 'saints of the Counter Reformation' and 'saints of contemporary devotion'), saints (IV, 1 and 2). However, we show here a summary (table 7) from which a graph has been constructed. Finally, table 8 gives a breakdown of post-1945 forms of worship according to the types of buildings, using the same classification as before.

This approach has two limitations: in the first place buildings cannot constitute absolute indicators of the number of adherents of a form of worship; hence the raw data have to be interpreted. Secondly, the essential historical dimension contains uncertainties (buildings that have disappeared, a margin of error in data gathered in the field that is difficult to quantify). Nevertheless, the results recorded appear to say much about the trends they reveal. Any errors would not appear to be such as to invalidate the conclusions derived from a reading of the tables.

On a first listing, with all the buildings taken together, the distribution of cults for the Zywiec district is as follows:

Christ and divinities   12 per cent
The Virgin   66 per cent

Table 7 Summary of cults revealed by the presence of buildings (churches, chapels and oratories)

	(I) Christ	(II) Virgin	(III) Saints	(IV) Saints	Total
16th century	–	1	8	2	11
17th century	1	2	4	1	8
18th century	8	14	9	1	32
19th century	42	64	18	6	130
20th century	11	55	14	3	83
Total	62	136	53	13	264

Table 8 Cults as revealed by the appearance of buildings (1945–1978)

Oratories	Christ	4
	Matka Boska	5
	Virgin with Child	2
	Czestochowa	2
	Immaculate Conception	1
	Virgin of the Rosary	1
	Saint Nicholas	1
	Saint Jadwiga	1
	Saint Bernadette	1
Chapels	Ascension	1
	Matka Boska	5
	Czestochowa	8
	Virgin of the Rosary	3
	Sacred Heart of Mary	2
	Our Lady of the Angels	1
	Our Lady of Perpetual Succour	1
	St John the Baptist	1
	St Elisabeth	1
	St Bernadette	1
Churches[a]	Christ the King (P)	1
	Sacred Heart (P)	1
	Sacred Heart of Mary (P)	2
	Our Lady of the Rosary (P)	1
	Our Lady of the Angels (P)	1
	Czestochowa (S)	2
	Holy Name of the Virgin (S)	1
	Mary Queen of the World (S)	1
	Our Lady of Perpetual Succour (S)	1
	Saint Stanislas (P)	1
	St Maximilian Kolbe (P)	1
	St Michael the Archangel (P)	1
	St Jospeh the Worker (P)	1
	St Florian (P)	1
	All Saints (P)	1
	St Anthony of Padua (S)	1

[a] (P) indicates a principal title and (S) a secondary one. Hence there are 18 names for 12 buildings.

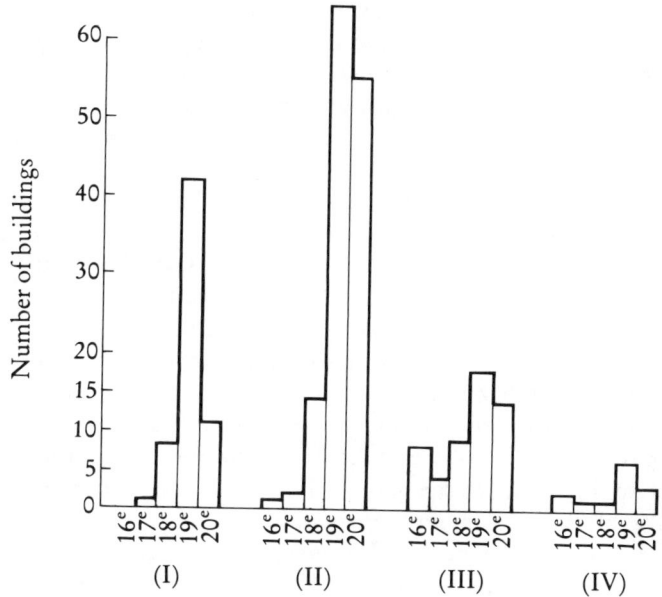

Appearance of cults revealed by the presence of buildings (churches, chapels and oratories)

| Saints (male) | 15 per cent |
| Saints (female) | 7 per cent |

Fifty-three buildings in the district were identified with the veneration of saints: eight for the sixteenth century and the preceding period, four for the seventeenth, nine for the eighteenth, eighteen for the nineteenth and fourteen for the twentieth centuries. There is no doubt that the relative decline in the cult of the saints is closely correlated with the growth of the cult of the Virgin, as is also shown by the fact that there are no pilgrimages or processions in the district devoted to saints. In our opinion this growth is also the reason for the sparseness of the cult of 'native saints', which make up only 15 per cent of the total of buildings dedicated to saints, including niches. One might have expected more devotion to be paid to Saint Wojciech (Adalbert), who suffered martyrdom on the Baltic coast, Saint Stanislas, slain by the king at Skalka, or Kazimierz Wielki (the king St Casimir the Great). But doubtless the cult of these national saints would have been an unnecessary duplication, since, as will be shown below in connection with

Our Lady of Czestochowa, the cult of Mary itself is a direct reference to the idea of the nation.

No special comment is called for by the respective proportions of the traditional saints and those of the Counter Reformation (64.5 per cent and 15 per cent of the total of all buildings, including niches): the cults of St Anthony of Padua (which sometimes covers that of St Anthony the Egyptian), Saint Francis of Assisi and of Saint Michael the Archangel are common to Catholics everywhere, while the cult of St Nicholas needs little explanation in this part of Europe.

As regards saints currently venerated, Maximilian Kolbe has already been mentioned in connection with the church of Cisiec (although he had not yet been canonized when that church was built). The style of the church of Ujsoly, Saint Joseph the Worker, is one such example of acculturation. Ujsoly is a village, the population of which has grown considerably since the end of the war. Since it specializes in cutting and working wood, it is not in the least surprising that its inhabitants consecrated their Church, when they were able to build one, to Saint Joseph. But the fact that they coupled St Joseph's name with the term 'worker' is interesting because of the many meanings that can be given to the term. On the one hand, the building permit was obtained in the wake of the agreement signed on 7 December 1956 by Wladyslaw Gomulka and the bishops, which enabled a real liberalization of the life of the Catholic community in Poland to come about. For some years following that agreement, Catholics enjoyed a somewhat easier situation; besides being permitted to form Christian social associations and to publish periodicals, they were granted permits to build religious edifices. It was in a gesture of recognition of this liberalization that the style of 'Worker' – suggesting the possibility of coexistence between Christians and communists in a socialist Poland – was adopted. But at the same time, differences arose between the state and the Church as soon as the agreement had been signed and it was not long before the government, which would not accept the refusal of the Vatican to acknowledge the frontiers of Poland as redrawn after the war, refused to give back to the Church the ecclesiastical buildings it had acquired in the western territories and forbade the teaching of religion in schools.

So the style of the church at Ujsoly could equally be interpreted as a reminder addressed to the authorities that Catholics *too* were workers; and as almost the whole population of the country were members of the Church, the Church was as much a mass organization as the Party, if not more so – 'of the people' in the strictest sense of the term. It is this equivocal meaning that constitutes the fecundity of such a dedication and gives it a potentially political application.

Little more need be said about the cult of saints. It is very sparse, accounting for only some 5 per cent of all religious buildings, and appears to be closely connected with that of the Virgin, through the cult of Saint Anne.

The following observations are relevant to buildings dedicated to Christ. There are far fewer of these than of buildings consecrated to the Virgin (62 compared with 136). Moreover, the disparity widens with time: there were nine buildings dedicated to Christ at the end of the eighteenth century compared with seventeen to the Virgin, fifty-one compared with eighty-one at the end of the nineteenth century, eleven buildings consecrated to Christ built during the twentieth century compared with fifty-five to the Virgin; of these, the figures for the period 1945-78 are six and thirty-six respectively. This is indicative of the Marilization of divine worship, in which Christ is worshipped through his mother (eight buildings dedicated to the Virgin with Child). This leaves only three churches in the district dedicated to Christ, whereas the Virgin has eighteen principal or secondary dedications.

In fact, 66 per cent of all churches, oratories and chapels in the district are dedicated to the Virgin, and the growth of her cult over the centuries speaks for itself. There were fourteen buildings in the eighteenth century, sixty-four in the nineteenth, and fifty-five for the period from 1900 to the present, of which thirty-five dedicated between 1945-78 alone.

Hence at Zywiec the cult of Mary, since the Virgin is commonly identified with Our Lady of Czestochowa, carries the marks of an absolute presence. To this the detail of the dual attributions of churches built since 1945 bears witness (table 9).

With just one exception, all the main titles also have a dedication to the Virgin; this applies to five buildings out of six. Seven other churches have been consecrated since 1945: three to the Virgin, one to the Sacred Heart, one to Maximilian Kolbe, one to St Michael the Archangel, and one to Saint Joseph the Worker. Hence the Virgin appears nine times out of twelve buildings.

This proportion is confirmed by the detail of the apportionment of the niches, which are a good indicator of popular fervour. This is as follows:

Christ and divine persons   15 niches
The Virgin   66 niches

Table 9

	1st attribution	2nd attribution
Kamesznica	Our Lady of the Rosary	Holy Name of Mary
Lesna	Saint Michael	Mary Queen of the World
Lipowa	Saint Stanislas	Our Lady of Czestochowa
Sporysz	Christ the King	Our Lady of Perpetual Succour
Zablocie	Saint Florian	Our Lady of Czestochowa
Zarzecze	All Saints	St Anthony of Padua

Saints (male)   13 niches
Saints (female)   1 niche

In addition, eleven out of the eighteen oratories created since 1945 and twenty out of the twenty-four chapels are dedicated to the Virgin.

What is the explanation of the intensity of this devotion to Mary? The first thing to note is that to a large extent the network of parishes in Poland was established after the end of the Middle Ages. The strengthening of this network, linked to developments in Europe during the fourteenth and fifteenth centuries, highlights the fundamental part played by the regular mendicant orders. This Franciscan form of religion was to leave a deep imprint on popular religion in Poland, and this imprint crystallized on the persons of Christ and of Mary. It was in this period, a crucially important one in the history of Poland, that some of the features of present-day popular fervour began to be formed. Many examples of this are to be found in art (sculpture) and in singing (canticles). Also during this period the Holy Trinity became identified with the Holy Family; this identification still persists, as has been repeatedly evidenced in the field, and elevates the Virgin to the rank of a divine personage.

Deeply embedded in the mentality, especially of the ordinary people, since the fifteenth century, devotion to Mary was not harmed by the Reformation because of the particular way in which the Catholic Church reacted to it. Protestantism found favour mainly with the nobles and never succeeded in gaining a firm foothold in society at large.[11] Catholicism, on the other hand, appears to be deeply rooted in the countryside, even if, as Jerzy Kloczowski suggested, it indicates a love of ritual or simply the fact that, slowly and at length, Christianity has taken hold.[12]

In the second place, there can be no doubt that it is Catholicism that places Polish culture within the European and Western cultural family. From this point of view, Poland has experienced, in greater or lesser degrees, the changes that took place in Europe in the eighteenth and nineteenth centuries, in particular the development of the cult of the Virgin. This trend found fertile soil in Poland, and flourished. As we have seen, at Zywiec the number of buildings consecrated to her rose from three at the end of the seventeenth century to seventeen at the end of the eighteenth, and eighty-one at the end of the nineteenth century. Today, in accordance with this trend, most of the buildings are dedicated to Mary.

Devotion to Mary, a consequence both of Polish history and of a development common to the whole of Western Europe but accentuated by conditions in Poland, is one of the basic components of the faith of the people. But besides this, because it is linked to national sentiment it constitutes a means of affirming the national identity.

In the district of Zywiec, the number of buildings dedicated to Our Lady of

Czestochowa increased from one in the seventeenth century to six in the eighteenth century. There were eighteen in the nineteenth century and twenty in the twentieth century, twelve of these having been built in the period since the end of the Second World War, if we include two secondary titles. There is perhaps no need here to retell the story of the sanctuary of Jasna Gora which houses the famous icon of the Black Virgin of Czestochowa. Suffice to mention that at the end of 1655 the Swedes were compelled to raise the siege they had begun against the citadel. The country was then solemnly consecrated to Mary 'queen of Poland' in Lwow cathedral on 1 April 1656. Eight days later, at Warka, the Swedes suffered a heavy defeat as a result of which they withdrew in large numbers. It was the end of the 'Deluge' (*Potop*) and the liberation of the national territory, thanks to the 'powerful intercession' of the Virgin. From that time the cult of Mary became effectively identified with the affirmation of national sentiment: to dedicate a building to Our Lady of Czestochowa is above all to make an ideological reference to the national idea, and this identification as a whole (Czestochowa = resistance to the invader, whoever he is = affirmation of the Polish nation) functions as a perfectly coherent system.

At Zywiec, for example, the style Mary Queen of Poland is only very weakly represented, with a single nineteenth-century building. But it is virtually a synonym of Our Lady of Czestochowa, and hence is not as such essential. Similarly, the style of Our Lady of Perpetual Succour appears to have a very direct connection with Czestochowa. To refer to it is to claim constant protection, which is in turn a reminder of the background of national history, even though the reference is a veiled one. Thus the predominant image is that of a majestic, protective Virgin, very closely linked to the history of the nation.

Furthermore, and still on the subject of Zywiec, its proximity to Czeztochowa, which is only 90 kilometres away as the crow flies, has without doubt been a factor in the spread of the cult. It is likely that the existence of a pilgrimage, undertaken on foot, has had a similar effect. The erection, not far from Gilowice, of a sanctuary called Jasna-Gorka (literally 'little Jasna-Gora') is a visible sign of the close relationship between Zywiec and Czestochowa.

The attitude of the Polish government towards Jasna – Gora is ambiguous from the outset. The government, while denouncing the superstitious nature of devotion to the image, also exhibits a vague, unavowed awareness of the important part played in history by the sanctuary as a popular symbol of Polish independence. Thus Czestochowa is both a national sanctuary – hence one that the government cannot afford to ignore, since it claims to incarnate the legitimacy of the nation – and a religious sanctuary. When John Paul II said to the crowd on 4 June 1979, 'Na Jasnej Gorze, tu zawsze bylismy wolni' ('at Jasna-Gora, we have always been free'), he was identifying a place with a value, a procedure that could not be other than intolerable to the government. Indeed, at the Millennium, in 1966, the government had forbidden churchmen to take the image out of the sanctuary, a clear acknowledgement of the symbolic power it knew the image to possess.

In the second place, if following the image is an act of faith, it is also an affirmation of attachment to a specific and distinctive element in the culture of the nation. But it may equally be a protest against the official culture and a demonstration of the rejection of that culture, and of the will to reincorporate religion into the common heritage.

Lastly, it is obvious that the great popular gatherings of Jasna-Gora, which prove religious sentiments to be a mass phenomenon in Poland, have a political aspect. For various strata of the population, for young people in particular, the journey to Czestochowa is at the same time a means of foregathering, a chance to speak more freely and openly and an opportunity of affirming a solidarity – indeed, of putting out a message. When Cardinal Wyszynski made Czestochowa on 15 August a platform reaching well beyond the sanctuary, he knew what he was about.

In conclusion, we may note that it is not only civil society or the Church that, consciously or unconsciously, makes symbolic use of religion for political ends. It has already been mentioned that in Bohemia, where ever since the White Mountain and the Counter Reformation Catholicism has seemed to be the very negation of the Czech sense of history, it was difficult not to interpret the constant repression of the Church by the government in so many ways as the expression of a sustained effort on the part of the government to appear *symbolically* in the eyes of the people as the guarantor of an identity and the instrument of the nation's revenge on history. The present course of events within the country would tend to show that the government has been caught in its own trap, and that by claiming to incarnate the nation when it is widely identified with foreign interests, it appears actually to be performing the feat of reconciling Catholicism with the meaning of Czech history.

Marginalization, catacombs and opposition

On 23 January 1977 the journal *Katolicke Noviny* published a text from the cardinal-primate of Czechoslovakia, Monsignor Tomacek, in which he said: 'We, bishops of the socialist republic of Czechoslovakia, wish to remove all possibility of doubt. We must say clearly that we are not signatories of the Charter.' Some days later Father Josef Zverina, who had been in prison several times since the Soviet-type government came to power in the country, sent the cardinal a letter uncompromisingly affirming his disagreement with the position adopted by the bishops:

> By allowing yourselves to be manipulated by the propaganda of Department of State, you have ranged yourselves on its side by stating that civil and religious

human rights are guaranteed and that the Church can develop freely. It appears to me that you do not realize the implications of what you say. You have ranged yourselves against the hopes and desires of your fellow believers and of those who yearn for justice. In so doing you have discredited Pope Paul VI and Catholic opinion, and lost the support of world opinion. You have put your false certitude into the scales against the pastoral preoccupations of Cardinals Koenig, Bengsch and Wyszynski. In sum, by this declaration, what have you done to enhance the prospects of the increase of religious freedom, since this has been rendered possible by the incorporation into our legislation of the international conventions of human rights? You have closed the door. That is why many priests now wish to add their names to Charter 77, so as to erase this shame. . . . Your statement is not inspired by the Gospel, but by the shameful needs of propaganda and by the hysterical witchhunt mounted against those who have dared to demand that the laws be obeyed. In your pastoral letters you seek to justify this attitude. We search them in vain for the spirit of the Gospel, and find only a dead letter. They even contain passages that could not be read in a Church, in the spirit of the Gospel. But, as you know, priests who refuse to read them lose their state licences. That is why many priests choose to read these letters after mass has finished, so as not to lose the last of the faithful.

And Father Zverina ended his letter with these words.

Watch over the weak brethren to whom you have given a bad example, these half-broken beings who have been given false promises, subjected to threats, pressure, weakness and cowardice! Take care of those who are traduced and persecuted, seize the last chance offered to you by our constitution and international agreements to save the Church from the shame and from gradual disintegration.[13]

This letter, which doubtless had some influence on positions subsequently adopted by the primate, particularly his denunciation of the monopoly exercised by the priests of Pacem in Terris on *Katolicke Noviny*, clearly shows the disquiet felt by some Christians on seeing compromises that they judged to be surrenders of principle. The reference to Cardinal Wyszynski at this point is no accident. Associated with the rejection of official values, the refusal to fall into line with the submission practised, willingly or unwillingly, by the bishops and seen as nothing less than the liquidation of the Church led to the installation of new structures outside the official ones, structures through which his religious convictions could be more authentically expressed.

Nowhere in East-Central Europe is this pattern seen as clearly as in Hungary. In that country:

after hard years of persecution all that are left to lead the Churches are men who are broken, terrorized, full of distrust for each other, or else unscrupulous careerists. These people do not ask for freedom of religion; all they want is safety and the outward trappings of the ecclesiastical hierarchy – and the Church now grants them that. In exchange, they themselves undertake to curb those among the faithful who look for a more authentic religious communion, and pastors who are anxious to be missionaries.[14]

This statement made at Budapest by the Methodist pastor Gabor Ivanyi on 24 April 1980, would doubtless be classed as one of those 'generalizations' that Imre Miklos spoke to us about. And because of this, it is said, the Churches, subsidized by the state, are allowed to carry on their activities as normal, to hold services, train their future leaders, and distribute publications. But the state allows these freedoms only on condition that the churches police themselves, that all initiatives come from the hierarchy, and that the grassroots are strictly monitored. This compromise has worked, and still works. In 1979, Alain Woodrow related the opinion of one Hungarian he spoke to that, 'The Church has been humiliated, decapitated. It is a living organism without a head, marked more by mediocrity than cowardice.'[15] And Bernard Lecomte noted: 'The Church hierarchy is sometimes accused of having replaced the state itself as regards censorship, or else of being a little too fond of receptions and black Mercedes.'[16] That explains why 'the temporal stances of the Church are rejected. People stand outside them, in a kind of return to the catacombs, especially the young. But the diplomacy of the Church leaders forces compromise down the throats of the lower clergy as well, with the result that they too are rejected.'[17]

There is nothing new about this process, and Marx himself, in his study on *The 18 Brumaire of Louis-Napoleon Bonaparte* showed how the peasants in the communes, in revolt against Napoleon's authority, finally took their stand against a Catholic Church that had compromised itself with the government. As Michèle Bertrand wrote:

When the ruling class uses religion it takes up a double-edged weapon. . . . The surrender of the Church to the government renders it *unfaithful* in the eyes of those who are under this government and are oppressed. And as that is what happens within the Church between believers, it is on the religious ground that the Church will be fought. Then the class struggles penetrate into the community of faith, not as class struggles but indirectly, as a spiritual fight, the fight of the true faith against a perverted faith, one that has lost direction.[18]

It is true that the Hungarian government succeeded in installing an arrangement very similar to what might be called, in Emile Poulat's phrase, the return to the constitutional Church. There is no doubt that this improved the image of Hungary abroad. But this process was rejected by a great number of the faithful. One of the clearest expressions of this rejection is to be found in the base communities of the Piarist Father Gyorgy Bulanyi. The work he did from 1945 onwards to found the communities led to the withdrawal of his licence to officiate in 1951, followed by a sentence of life imprisonment in 1952. Freed in 1961 after an amnesty, he set to work again, also earning his living as a labourer. From 1952 to 1970 everybody who worked with the base communities was arrested, and there were more than 300 of them.

In Bulanyi's own words, the movement originated in 'some plain facts taken to their conclusions':[19] 'The world must be rendered more human, it is preferable to go to prison than to risk killing one's neighbour, we have to rediscover that what it means to be a Christian is to serve others.' It was not long before the Catholic hierarchy found that they could not put up with Bulanyi's activities. In the first place he was calling into question the compromise reached with the state, by acting beyond the control of the official Church. And indeed, although the movement has always stated that it is subject to the authority of the bishops, it does not maintain structural links with the parishes. Consequently, the Hungarian bishops regard it as a threat to the unity of the Church. In 1979 Cardinal Lekai had issued a warning on behalf of the entire episcopate in which he reminded the communities that they must not separate from the parishes, for 'such a breach might become extremely dangerous for the integrity of their faith and bring them into temptation under the inspiration of the Evil One. As Catholics [members of communities] should always and in all things accept the directives of their pastors so that everything should be done decently and in order.'[20]

By 1976 the primate was asking the vicar-general of the Piarist order to send Father Bulanyi out of Hungary. He refused, and the bishops then started a long war of attrition against priest; this led in June 1982 to the suspension of his licence to officiate, the final decision being submitted to the Congregation of the Doctrine of Faith in Rome for its opinion, as this was the only body authorized to act as a final court of appeal in deciding whether the actions and writings of Bulanyi were comfortable to Catholic orthodoxy or not.[21] In October, on the occasion of the visit *ad limina* of the Hungarian bishops to Rome, the bishops submitted to the Pope a long list of accusations against Bulanyi and his communities, and they repeated these actions at the beginning of 1983. On 3 June following, the conference of bishops issued a fresh list of complaints. The priests who were members of the communities, numbering about forty, were asked to sign a declaration of submission. They refused to do this, declaring that they were obedient to the bishops in so far as the orders given to them were not contrary to the doctrine of Christ and to their own consciences.[22]

The truth is that the state and the Church shared a common disquiet concerning the way in which the communities under the Bulanyi banner were operating.[23] Each community consisted of some fifteen members, and they had a very advanced form of internal democracy. The priests, considered by

Bulanyi already to have the privilege of celebrating the mass, do not exercise any special authority; they are just members like the others, with the same rights and duties. A unanimous vote is required for the admission of a new member. Leaders are elected, for, according to Bulanyi's motto, 'appointed leaders are of the devil'. Members, including women, take it in turn to head the community. Groups meet for an average of six hours a month and for four consecutive days during summer, always in a private apartment. The chairman opens the meeting with a reading or meditation followed by a period of silence at the end of which discussion begins. Nobody may interrupt a member who is speaking.

Quite clearly there is nothing subversive about such a procedure, either for the government or the Catholic hierarchy. Above all, many members of the communities refuse to do military service and demand that the state should allow them to perform civilian service. In the recent past the state has made this concession to a small Protestant Church known as the Nazarenes. But since the basic communities claim loudly and clearly to belong to the Catholic Church, if the benefit of the agreement made with the Nazerenes were to be extended to their members, this would in effect open the door to claims by two-thirds of the population for a status of something like conscientious objection, and the government does not seem likely to contemplate this.

This demand caused Cardinal Lekai himself some concern in 1982:

> I, primate of this country, am disturbed to note that certain extremist priests and members of our Church are inciting young people not to do their duty by refusing to perform their military service. What is worse, these persons take their stand on the Bible and the teaching of the Church; they encourage our young people to refuse military service, just because they are Catholics animated by a deep faith. And I am not only disturbed but scandalized when I find that some young people are listening to these siren songs.[24]

There is no doubt as to the cause of this problem – the risk of destabilizing the relations between the state and the institutional Church, accused of failing to police itself as it is bound to under the 'contract' it has entered into with the government.

And in fact it is all very well for the Minister of Cults, Imre Miklos, to affect a detached attitude[25] when asked about the basic communities and to say:

> I must say that I don't understand the importance attached to this matter. Everybody asks me, as if we were talking about scientists, journalists or politicians. I don't understand. What's new about it, for goodness' sake? In the Church, movements aiming at renewal are as old as the Church itself. Some of them have disappeared, while others still exert a powerful influence, like Protestantism. Like every living organism, the Church needs renewal. The communities are a requirement of our age, born of a search for direct contacts, a

religious phenomenon. I'm sorry that people are trying to tell us we have difficulties. It's like the movement of the sea: some people like to be borne along by the waves. The problem arises when someone thinks he has made the wave. The conflict between the Church and the communities is not due to the need felt by some to be religious in a new way, but to the fact that they consider the old way to be feudal.

But as far as the state is concerned it comes to the same thing whether people express their religious sentiment within the Church or outside it. The conflict is not with us, but between a small part of the communities movement and the ecclesiastical order. It is an internal matter of the Church, and we have nothing to say about it unless public order is disturbed. We did not will this confrontation to happen, and people want to make us responsible for it . . .

What is more, attempts are made to identify Bulanyi with the communities. That is not true: the decisions taken against him were taken by John Paul II, for the sake of the unity of the Church. It is said that Lekai is under our influence, but the same certainly can't be said about the Pope or Monsignor Casaroli! It is also said that the main problem is that of military service and pacifism. That's just as wrong! There are only a few extremists. And on that point, the confrontation is not only with us but with the official Church.[26]

This conclusion by the minister is not contested by the communities. In an 'open letter to Pope John Paul II' they had no hesitation in saying:

[Our] disobedience constitutes a severe test for the ideas to which the bishops subscribe, since they cannot reveal to Catholics, and to non-Catholics, or even to national and international public opinion, that what they have against Father Bulanyi and his friends is that they will not obey the atheist state and its mish-mash of a policy. The state's objective is to incite the bishops to 'cut off a little slice of salami', then to cut a second slice, then a third, and so on. . . . It is just because Father Bulanyi is against this salami policy that he refuses to leave the country, that the communities will not give up their spiritual exercises in the parishes and in other places on the pretext that they want to obey, and that members of the communities called to the colours would rather go to prison than deny the command of Jesus which tells us to love our enemies.[27]

This open letter even went further, for it said: 'The state may be glad to see the cardinal and his faithful bishops showing themselves increasingly enterprising in pursuing the "salami policy", to the point where they end up by pursuing it unrestrainedly and of their own accord.'[28] The letter concluded with a solemn warning:

A policy that consists of giving in to the demands of the adversary is certainly non-viable anywhere in the world. If his wishes are met, then the adversary has purely and simply won. And that remains true, even if certain ecclesiastics see in such an outcome their own victory – or at least say they do – not because they hope that this ploy will bear fruit in the future but because they believe it will have immediate beneficial effects, namely that it will put a stop to persecution. But if the Church makes its actions dependent on this consideration, how can it identify itself with those to whom Jesus said: 'You will be persecuted'?[29]

Such language finds an echo in Prague. As Ladislas Hejdanek, a member of the evangelical church of the Czech Brethren and formerly spokesman of Charter 77, said:

> It is not surprising if Christians who talk about an evil, who condemn a wrongdoing or injustice, but who personally distance themselves, adopting the stance of an honest broker, of someone who has nothing to do with the situation, who is free from any fault, from any share in causing the evil thus discovered, are suspect. And the same thing applies where, not confining himself to his own person, he tries to free his own church, or Christianity as a whole, from responsibility.[30]

It is from this point of view that Pastor Jakub Trojan can say:

> [The Church] must judge things dispassionately and realize that she will enter into opposition to the government and will probably not escape suffering. The sooner she realizes that the two things are linked, the better for her. The strong suit of this government is its ability to manipulate, to *move* not only things and persons, but also consciences. We all sell our soul to the devil, we all become instruments of the government; power eats into us, corrupts us, hustles us into duplicity of heart and mind. Power in its present form is like the Grand Inquisitor ('men cannot bear freedom'), Shakespeare's Iago, playing people off one against another in a permeditated series and with a brutality reminiscent of Herod's, prepared to kill not only his adversaries but even new-born babies. It is the Church's vocation to educate this power – real and ineluctable as it is – and to induce it to adopt the modest role of a co-ordinating factor in the labyrinth of social relationships. . . . No power in the world likes to be called to account, yet from time to time they all have to be reminded of the *Mene, mene, tekel upharsin* of Belshazzar's feast. Unless this is done, the proliferation of power can only end in universal ruin. To wish to resign from this witnessing role is to deny our common responsibility with the powerful who, in their own special way, are no less in need of it than are the powerless.[31]

This will to assign limits to power is at the very origin of Charter 77. In a famous text entitled 'What Charter 77 is and what it is not – Why the signatories have right on their side and why action to suppress them will not succeed',[32] the philosopher Jan Patocka emphasized the fact that:

> It is impossible to place trust either in custom, trying to convince us that a *de facto* order will become second nature to us, or in the power of constraint without the internal assent of the people. If humanity is to develop in

accordance with the potential of a technical, instrumental reason, if progress in knowledge and capacities is to be made possible, people must be convinced of the unconditional validity of the principles, which are 'sacred' in this context, valid always and for all, and capable of defining the ends to be pursued. In other words, there has to be something that is ultimately non-technical, uniquely non-instrumental, there has to be a self-evident ethic, not one controlled by circumstances, an unconditional ethic.

This means that salvation, so conceived, cannot be looked for only from political power, from the state, from the 'thrones and dominations'.

And he added:

How happy would be persons who believe in facts as being alone capable of supplying the means to freely chosen ends, to exchange part of their too evident truths for a very modest moral truth capable of really carrying conviction! But that is an impossibility. All the accumulations of simple force during our century have been allowed to call the tune more than ever before in history. The result, as regards people's convictions, has been the opposite of what was intended. That ought to be clear today.

No society, however well equipped technically, can function without a moral basis, without a conviction not based on convenience, on the circumstances and the benefits expected. And yet morals are not there for the purpose of making society work, but simply in order that human beings may be human. It is not man who defines them as his needs, wishes, trends and desires dictate. On the contrary, it is morals that define man.

This is far from being the first time that such sentiments have been expressed. In 1873, during his last journey in Moravia, Palacky deplored the fact

that the moral foundations, in humanity and therefore also in our nation, have been shaken. Without those foundations the whole of society, and hence our nation too, perishes. It is only on moral convictions, only on the basis of religion that we can progress towards the goal. . . . What makes me happy is that you are learning self-cultivation and that the door is opening to education, even among the lowest classes. I see that victory cannot for long be denied us; reason, convinced by so many examples of our spirit, cannot do other than give us our due, in accordance with law and justice. Wait, but with tenacity and with united strength.[33]

The moral demand governing the course of action evoked in Patocka's words is not confined to opposition intellectuals, persecuted believers or Chartists. A survey carried out in secret in Czechoslovakia, the findings of which were published by *Listy*, showed that out of sixty-three young people questioned (forty-one men and twenty-two women, with an average age of twenty-one), fifteen stated that they were believers; faith appeared as an antidote to the deep disillusion revealed by the replies to the questions. For example, many people answered the question 'In whom or what do you believe?' by saying 'in nothing', 'in nobody', 'not even in myself'. A young woman of twenty-two said, 'being impressed by Christians, provided they are sincere'. To the question 'What do you miss most?' the most frequent replies were 'freedom', 'truth'.[34] It is in this context that believers state that

> the Church is irreplaceable only if it makes a real effort to live in truth and solidarity. Only by so doing can the Church prove that it is different, and holy. Only unconditional faithfulness to the truth, which would at the same time be a manifestation of authentic solidarity, enables it to escape from the ossified ways of thinking and the trivial round of ecclesiastical bureaucracy.[35] Then it would become a true Church of God in the truth, and this means above all having the courage to bear unconditional witness to the truth. All tactical and strategic considerations must be subordinated to this. Our home Church must resolve the problem posed by the claim of the regime to a monopoly of the world-view officially associated with the socialist way of life.[36]

The demand for unconditional obedience seems to echo Cardinal Wyszynski's exhortation: 'Be ye holy!'[37] To pose the problem in these terms is tantamount to opposing a counter-utopia to a totalitarian utopia, setting up the community of faith as an alternative pattern to the official system (see table 10).

Some attempts have already been made to work out this counter-utopia. The three main thrusts of the 'programme' sketched out by Jakub Trojan show the extent to which it impinges on the area of politics:

1 The Church has been entrusted with a unique mission which is universal in scope.
2 The otherness of the Church is the world's safeguard. Its otherness and its sanctity make of the Church a radical critic of existing conditions.

Table 10

Official system	Community of faith
Imposed obedience	Chosen obedience
No true community	Chosen community
Distrust of all	Trust in the other
Tormented individual	Reconciled invidual
Irrationality	Rationality
Fruitlessness	Witness[38]
Conflicts internalized	Conflicts externalized

3   The Christian as Christ's witness is a symbol of the new man and the Church is an alternative for a new humanity.[39]

Uniqueness, universality, otherness, saintliness, radicalness are all constitutive values of the alternative pattern that the underground Church in Czechoslovakia seeks to embody, using religion as a means of rejecting official values and applying this means to each tense of time – to the past as a referential deposit, to the present as a situational critique and a call to commitment, and to the future as a promise. One cannot but be struck by the way in which these themes harmonize with John Paul II's exhortation to rise above fear and with the spiritual programme that he outlined when he visited Poland in 1983.

Not only does the underground Church endeavour to make up for the quantitative and qualitative[40] inadequacies of the official Church; it can also be viewed as a model that might well be copied by the whole of civil society. This is well illustrated by the title of Father Josef Zverina's book *Odvaha byt Cirkvi* (*The Courage to be the Church*[41]). For in fact the undertaking is attended by real risks, as big as those assumed by members of Charter, of whom Patocka reminded us that they know 'that it is necessary . . . to undergo unpleasant experiences, to run the risk of being misunderstood and even to hazard physical danger'.[42]

In Czechoslovakia it is in fact the attitude of the authorities themselves that drives the faithful into illegality. Since all religious activity other than the strict performance of divine service in forbidden, even a meeting, a private celebration of the mass, and the writing, holding or transmission of religious texts are considered actions hostile to the state and as such attract penal sanctions. To withhold or withdraw a priest's or pastor's work permit places him in a situation in which he has to choose to go underground or submit. Furthermore, any person in contact with a presumed member of the underground Church is suspected of also being a member. This explains why the movement is growing and why it is causing increasing concern to the government.

A document published in the Catholic samizdat bulletin *Informace o Cirkvi* (*Information about the Church*) set out the main characteristics of the movement, and it is worth quoting at length:

> There are four main phenomena that cause government leaders anxiety:
>
> 1 An increasing number of young people are turning to religion and, despite the risk of official punishment, decide to seek the company of people of the same persuasion and to consult a priest whom they can trust. Many of these young folk are telling their friends about their religious experience, awakening in them a fresh interest in religious matters and even leading them to faith. A Church that did nothing more than hold services could not satisfy the needs of these young people in their spiritual interests. They are looking for religious

teaching and for a brotherhood not found today in Czechoslovakia except in the illegal groups.

2 The many hundreds of priests and secular religious men and women who are forbidden to follow their vocation and who consequently have taken up secular work are having an influence on those with whom they rub shoulders. The human and Christian example given by these women and men often influences colleagues at work who were formerly believers and encourages them to think anew about their attitude to faith. Hence religious cells are sometimes formed in factories, and this is beginning to influence other workers. These 'priest-workers' (and there are even some bishop-workers) have the opportunity to do a great deal more than the priests officially installed in the parishes, whose activities are severely restricted.

3 There is a remarkable network of communication and information which the authorities have been unable to dismantle despite trying to do so for several years, because whenever one is discovered, somebody else immediately takes his place. This system both enables illegal religious groups to become acquainted with one another and to obtain details of what is happening in other parts of the country, and also enables people outside Czechoslovakia to learn about these events. For example, especially in Slovakia practically every district has a Catholic layman in charge of this information network. Because each of them has contact with only a few other persons and because the network has no central organizing office it is almost impossible for the secret police to discover more than one or two threads of the network. Naturally the international reputation of Czechoslovakia is severely damaged if foreign media can make use of carefully verified facts and of actual cases to show how religion is persecuted in the country.

4 A kind of movement for the defence of religious civil rights has grown up, whose members are no longer prepared to tolerate attacks against the Church without showing some resistance. It is becoming more and more common for private individuals and groups to lodge complaints and petitions with the state authorities, drawing their attention to the measures taken against the Church by state officials and the authorities in contravention of the constitution and the law. Formerly there had been very few people willing to take the risk of lodging such complaints, but such cases become common knowledge among the networks and serve as examples. It is difficult to employ repressive measures against the complainants, because they use official channels and, far from violating the law, they are demanding that it be applied. It has to be said that these complaints are seldom crowned with success, though this sometimes happens: nevertheless they do have some effect: they show other people that it is possible, and perhaps necessary, to resist injustice.[43]

This text does not call for any comment; it is very explicit. Generally speaking, each of the groups of which the underground Church is composed effectively operates quite autonomously and has no standing relationships with the other groups. There is a core of some ten or twelve persons and none of the groups has more than twenty members, since any greater number would expose the group to charges of plotting against the security of the state. Meetings take place in private houses, at intervals that vary in accordance with the situations and opportunities. Naturally there is no set form for them, usually they include common prayer, readings and open discussions. There may also be addresses on various theological, philosophical, historical or other subjects given by a member of the group, or in some cases by an outside speaker. Also the mass may be celebrated, usually by a priest deprived of his official licence and more free in his movements than a priest in an official position; it seems, however, that such celebrations are rather infrequent.

It is of course impossible to arrive at a precise idea of the numerical strength of the underground Church in Czechoslovakia. The confident statements by its members that the movement is 'snowballing' could be disregarded, were it not for the fact that the state lends credence to them by intensifying its repressive measures. As *Informace o Cirkvi* states:

> Apparently, since unlike the governments of neighbouring communist states, the political leadership in Czechoslovakia seems to have decided against improving relations between Church and state, it sees police persecution as being the only way to prevent the spread of the underground Church. This is the only possible explanation for the fact that an enormous force of police has been sent to Slovakia for the express purpose of crushing the underground Church. Following a decision taken by the Slovak Minister of the Interior and by the provincial committee, all the investigating sections of the secret police at Bratislava have been ordered to direct their activities from October 1980 onwards against the secret Church and the lay apostolate. A team of thirty advisers has been attached to the city's security police. For the performance of their task they have been allotted ten full-time advisers in each of the four administrative districts of the Slovak capital. Their work is co-ordinated by a special operational branch of the secret police.[44]

Most of the time, these police trawls bring priests and laymen of the underground Church before the courts. To take just one example, on 15 April 1982 two Czech Franciscans, Father Barta and Father Trojan, aged sixty-one and seventy respectively, were sentenced by the Liberec district court to eighteen months' imprisonment for the former and fifteen months' suspended for the latter, on a charge of having organized a clandestine seminary.

There are, however, good grounds for believing that the police go much further than that. For example, a Moravian priest, Father Premysl Coufal, who had been forbidden to officiate and was working as an engineer at Bratislava, died in suspicious circumstances on 24 February 1981, after having been subjected to several interrogations and, according to his friends, refused to collaborate with the police. The official verdict at the inquest was suicide.

Facts such as these explain why Christians occupy an important place in the opposition, either because the authorities goad them into such action by the repressive measures used against them, or because their cases are 'taken up' by Charter 77 and VONS,[45] in their campaigns for the defence of human rights.

Beyond doubt, Charta 77 is one of the most remarkable examples in Eastern Europe of the coming together of men and women of all political persuasions, social origins and religious allegiances for 'the only form of political action [in Czechoslovakia], the struggle for human rights'.[46] Christians, Catholic or Protestant, make up about half the signatories, and there are in the Charter some dozen Catholic priests and about fifteen Protestant pastors. 'This is important', said Vaclav Maly, a Catholic priest of some thirty years' standing a formerly a spokesman of the group, 'because they are influential and restrained, and this gives our movement a certain credibility. Many believers who have not themselves signed nevertheless have quite a favourable opinion of us.'[47] In the same way, an opposition party in Hungary could establish links with the 'masses' thanks to the Catholic base communities, which are constantly in direct contact with workers and peasants. Janos Kis, who has spoken out in favour of this idea, is convinced that this would be the way to overcome the separation between the opposition intellectuals and the people. Obviously this assimilation only serves to increase the unease of those in Hungary who regard the base communities as being a political movement by definition. Such an interpretation was rejected by Patocka, pre-empting the accusation brought against the Charter of being an attempt to destabilize the regime politically under cover of a defence of human rights. He expounded his reasons at length when he wrote:

> The relationship . . . between the sphere of morals and the social and political sphere of the government clearly demonstrates that Charter 77 does not constitute any political act in the strict meaning of the term. Its signatories do not contemplate any invasion of or competition with any function of government. The Charter is neither an association nor an organization; its basis is purely moral and personal, as are the obligations undertaken by signing it. . . . This means that the signatories of the Charter are in no way acting for personal interest but are motivated solely by duty, their only strong foundation being an order above political rights and obligations. This by no means signifies that it cannot be harmonized more or less completely with the political order, in so far as that order freely acknowledges its supremacy.
>
> The signatories to Charter 77 do not claim any political functions or prerogatives whatsoever; but they also disclaim any pretension to represent something like a moral authority, a 'conscience' of our society. They do not think themselves superior to anyone or condemn anyone. Therefore their efforts are confined to emphasizing that there is a higher authority to which individuals in their personal consciences, and states whose representatives have signed international agreements of fundamental importance, are subject. They insist that this obligation is not a matter of convenience, governed by the rules

of political expediency, but that their signature carries the obligation to make politics subject to law and never law subject to politics.⁴⁸

Although faced with an extremely active campaign of police repression, Charter has taken many initiatives, mainly in defence of freedoms within the country but also expressing solidarity with the opposition in Poland, for example by sending a letter to Jacek Kuron and to the KOR-KSS in February 1981.

In a famous article Pierre Bourdieu has written:

> The history of the transformation of myth into religion (ideology) is inseparable from the history of the formation of a body of producers of religious speech and rites, that is to say from the progress of the division of religious labour, itself one dimension of the progress of the division of labour in society, one of the consequences of which is to dispossess the uninitiated of the means of the production of symbols.⁴⁹

This fits the present situation very neatly, in the sense that we are now witnessing a reinvestment by the intellectuals (clerics) of their political capacity, with the result that the rulers (laymen) are being dispossessed of the symbolic instruments of production of which they claimed to have a monopoly. It fits all the better because some of the protagonists do not hesitate to establish a kind of oppositional relationship between themselves and the Church, such as Gyorgy Konrad when he wrote: 'Without disputing the Church's right to its name, I feel that nowadays a veritable Catholic universalism, subsuming all the particularisms, is represented more authentically by the international intellectual aristocracy. Nowadays it is not enough to pray for peace. One has to think for it, not piously but radically.'⁵⁰

This is an extreme statement of the idea of the specific mission of the intellectual as being a watchman for the nation and society: denunciation of an *immoral* power leads to *opposing* it, which presupposes having first reflected on where this power is to be found, and having succeeded in finding it inside oneself, so true are the words of Vaclav Havel that 'the domination of a large number of people without power by a small number of people who possess it has long since ceased to be the most typical of the characteristics of totalitarianism. What is characteristic nowadays is the hold taken by a part of ourselves over another part of ourselves.'⁵¹

In setting forth what the Charter and VONS has contributed to Czechoslovak society, Libuse Silhanova noted, in reply to a question by Eva Kanturkova:

> I don't wish to exaggerate. I know, or at least I believe, the attitude to life and the viewpoints of our fellow citizens, and I know that very many of them know

practically nothing about the Charter and wish to know nothing, that it is of no interest to them. But for the many who look at our society with a *critical* eye and who take an interest in the conditions under which we are living and shall live, the Charter represents a certitude that perhaps something may change – that there is a little group out there who see further than the general run of folk and who, although they do not have power, may perhaps be able to envisage solutions, to achieve something. . . . It lifts the spirit just to know that there are people like the Chartists and that they are trying to do something for other people. Because the world of Kafka and of Orwell has long since ceased to be just a literary fiction, an absurdity, because it is reality that is absurd and is a threat not simply to us, but to all the rest of the world. The intrusion of such a world is the most dangerous thing possible. Every responsible being should work against it, even if only at a snail's pace and in his own little sphere.[52]

Dana Nemcova says that she 'does not believe in sudden upheavals. The change must come about in people's thinking; it must spread from person to person'.[53] That is an observation with which John Paul II would most certainly agree.

5
Slavorum Apostolus

Jerzy Turowicz concluded an article in *Tygognik Powszechny* celebrating the twentieth anniversary of the council by recalling what man represented in the thought of John Paul II: the 'way of the Church'.[1] This is more than a chance observation. In a system characterized by its total inability to think through the relationship between the individual and the collective, giving a central place to man is bound to constitute a fundamental vote of no confidence in the system. The Church confronts the daily lie of purely formal acceptance demanded by the government with a 'speak the truth', reconciling man with himself and restoring to him a lost dignity. To the false community that is a society made up of a multitude of atomized groups, in which man is constantly driven back into his own solitude, the Church opposes a conception of the relationship of the individual with the whole in which each man is the brother of all the others, a unique and irreplaceable member of the people of God. To the despair and lassitude of a nation deprived of its history and compelled to live outside time, the Church opposes its conviction that nothing is final, that the division of Europe into two hostile political camps will not last for ever, and that in any event, man is unconquerable.

It is therefore no surprise that, plunged into an experience of such tragic depth, the Polish people should have rediscovered certain great Messianic emphases of the nineteenth century, when their poets established a parallel between the crucifixion of Christ and the martyrdom of a nation sacrificing itself in order to save humanity. As Krasinski wrote, in a letter dated 2 January 1847 to Trentowski, 'the real reason for the existence of Poland is to realize on earth the kingdom of heaven, to merge politics and religion, to found the future church of humanity and to show the whole world that sovereignty does not reside in a king or in a people but only in the nation'.[2]

Clearly it would be an exaggeration to say that this conviction is shared by the majority of Polish Catholics, but it is not an exaggeration to think that it may have vaguely permeated the Church and, through the Church, Polish society. On 3 September 1970, in a speech celebrating the fifteenth anniversary of the 'Miracle on the Vistula', Cardinal Wyszynski reminded his hearers: 'We suffered many things in 1965 and 1966,[3] but we have shown that the Church of Poland and the Polish bishops think in truly eschatological, universal terms, that their views are wide open to the future. A great battle is in progress here, in the East and in the history of the Polish people in order that the Holy Church may be present there!' The primate went on to say that in order to win the battle:

> We have to prevent the Catholic Church from becoming 'Westernized'. Such thinking is present in the mentality of many bishops in the Germanic and Latin world. So where is the Slav world of which Otto III spoke? It isn't even visible. To my sorrow I felt this during the conference of European bishoprics [held in Rome in 1970]. The Germanic and Latin bishops were invited to this conference, but not a single Slav bishop. . . . If there were only Germanic and Latin Churches without the Slav Church, then the Church would no longer exist. At that time nobody understood me. They thought that the Church was Italy, Germany, France, Spain and . . . nothing more. We must remind the Western Church that there are Slav peoples who have made a great contribution to Christianity in Central and Eastern Europe, that it was thanks to them that Christianity penetrated to Kiev and Moscow.[4]

It is quite clear that the election of a Polish-born Pope in 1978 was bound to strengthen the vaguely held belief that a special role was assigned to Polish Catholicism. The closing words of Father Jerzy Lewandowski's book on the 'theology of the Nation' are revealing in this connection:

> The Polish nation is conscious that God is assigning a twofold task to it: one is internal, concerning itself, the members of the nation, and the other is external, concerning other nations, the whole economy of God.
> In each case Poland has both general and special tasks to accomplish . . . Thanks to her identity and her individuality, she serves the other nations, making up what they lack and what the whole Family of Nations lacks.[5]

From this point of view, the election of Cardinal Wojtyla was bound to be seen as a sign. John Paul II himself lends colour to this hypothesis in his frequent references to himself as 'the first Pope called from Poland, and hence from the heart of the Slav nations'.[6] At all events there is no doubt in his mind that there is a contrast between the vitality of Christianity in Poland and the 'crisis' of the Western churches. And the encyclical *Slavorum Apostoli* is proof that he is serious in his bid for the spiritual reconquest of Europe, and especially of Russia:

Ever since the nineteenth century when the first lineaments of a new face of Europe began to appear, Saints Cyril and Methodius have offered us a message which is now seen to be completely relevant to our age in which, just because of the many complex religious and cultural, secular and international problems, the search is on for a living unity in a true communion of differing constituent parts. . . . They too are the authors of the appeal to build communion together, an appeal addressed to Christians and to the people of our time.[7]

Paradoxically, this grand design of unity, of the reconquest and recatholicization of Europe, of which the Church in Poland is at once the starting point, the powerhouse and the ideal, involves the Church in real risks. John Paul II must now be strongly tempted to subordinate developments in Poland to the success of his overall project and, for example, to grant in Poland concessions that would forward the project elsewhere, perhaps especially in the Soviet Union. The consequences of such an attitude as they affect Church and state relations in Poland might be seen by civil society as a retreat, which would almost certainly result in diminishing the prestige of the Church. And that raises the double problem of what are the limits of tolerable compromise and how much real autonomy have the Polish bishops *vis-à-vis* the Pope, especially since Cardinal Wyszynski is no longer with them. But it would be premature to attempt a reply to this question before studying the pronouncements of the 'Slav Pope' himself in greater depth.

The Slav Pope

The election of a Slav Pope created a new situation for Christians in the East. The consequences of this change are difficult to foresee; they are bound to be important, although criteria for judging its impact are lacking. Enthusiastically hailed in Poland itself and a source of some national pride (which extended to government circles), this appointment, and the first official visit of a Pope to a Soviet-bloc country, made a deep impression on Polish sentiment. Nobody doubted that the visit of John Paul II to his native country in June 1979 had a direct bearing upon the emergence of the immense social movement that was Solidarity. The huge attendances at the Pope's public appearances, the faultless control maintained by the organizers over these crowds, and the disciplined behaviour of the crowds themselves, together with the conviction of those millions of people that they all shared the same feelings, problems and hopes, were the crucible in which Solidarity, the social and national movement, was founded. What is more, during this visit it was the Pope, the Church and Catholicism that provided the Poles with a significant proportion of the symbols, the words, themes and motivations that they needed. A society atomized by the government was reconstituted around the Pope – or rather, the Pope's visit was only one stage in a process that had begun some time previously, but one that revealed how far the movement had come and set the seal on the new alliance between the different groups of which civil society in Poland was composed.

It is even more difficult to assess the effects of the arrival at the Vatican of a Polish-born Pope in the other East European countries. The Czech historian Radomir Maly called it a

> major event for us, for it signifies that the Church will make human rights a part of its mission. By choosing a Slav, the Church has borne witness to its universal significance. Our Church suffers from the historical complex of the Hussite schism, and Catholics believe that they can only exist on the fringes of society. The Habsburg counter-reformation in some sense disqualified Catholicism in our eyes, made it something foreign, only connected with Latin culture. A Pope who comes from Poland can help Czechs to understand that the Church is not limited to one part of the world, for in its eyes all nations, including the Czechs, have equal rights.[8]

On 3 June 1979 at Gniezno, before the cathedral of Saint Adalbert, who was bishop of Prague before converting Poland to Catholicism, some young people unfurled a streamer in front of the Pope. 'That's a good sign', said John Paul II. 'I have before my eyes a sentence written in the sister language, the language of Saint Adalbert. This is what it says: "Father, do not forget your Czech children!". This Pope, who has received the message of Saint Adalbert, cannot forget his children. And I ask all Poles – I hope they all hear me – not to forget their Czech brothers and sisters.'[9]

In fact, on 5 November 1978 John Paul II said: 'There is no longer a Church of silence: now she speaks with the voice of the Pope.'[10] Some months later, at Gniezno, he announced the encyclical *Slavorum Apostoli*, in which he spoke of his task as 'the first Slav Pope':

> It may be for this that God has chosen him, so that he may introduce into the communion of the Church the understanding of the words and the languages which still fall strangely on ears that are used to romance, Germanic or Anglo-Saxon sounds. . . . Does not Christ wish, does not the Holy Spirit dispose, that this Pope who bears deeply imprinted on his heart the history of his nation since its origin and also the history of the neighbouring, brother people, manifest and confirm in a special way in our time their presence in the Church and their special contribution to the history of Christianity? Does not Christ wish, does not the Holy Spirit dispose, that the Polish Pope, the Slav Pope, should at this particular time manifest the spiritual unity of Christian Europe, heir to the two great traditions of the West and the East – one faith, one baptism, one God and Father of us all, the Father of our Lord Jesus Christ?

And the Pope went on to enumerate Croats, Slovenes, Bulgars, Moravians, Slovaks, Czechs, Serbs and Lithuanians. Finally, he said: 'This Pope comes to speak before the whole Church, Europe and the world of these often forgotten nations and peoples. He comes to shout aloud.'[11] On the preceding day, in Warsaw, during his homily, he had cried out: 'There can be no just Europe without the independence of Poland.'[12] Since he associated the destiny of his own country so closely with that of its sister nations, these words were clearly intended to mean: there is no just Europe without independence for Poland *and* for her sister nations.

The Czech government, at least, got the message. Although Cardinal Tomasek, archbishop of Prague and the primate of the Catholic Church in his country, had been given a permit to go to Cracow on 7 June to take part in the ceremonies in honour of the Pope's visit, ordinary citizens could not cross the frontier, because they were unable to obtain Polish currency, which had become unobtainable in the foreign exchange kiosks.[13]

Nor were the Soviets under any illusions. In a report published on 11 June 1979 the first secretary of the Communist Party of the Ukraine, Wladimir Shcherbitsky, issued an appeal for the strengthening of atheist propaganda and of the struggle against ideological diversion.[14]

In fact, the spokesman of the Polish ministry of foreign affairs was almost the only one who described the 'political aspects' of the Pope's speech as being 'very positive':

> He emphasized the Auschwitz speech, on declarations for peace. The Pope's ideas have much in common with ours. We are also glad the Pope emphasized on several occasions the unity of the Polish nation, on the basis of the family and of labour. He also mentioned religion, but that is a personal matter that we shall not go into. We are not against religion but for tolerance and freedom of religion.[15]

This view of the matter was by no means shared in Prague. Writing about the Pope's visit to Poland in *Ateizmus* (no. 3/1979), Jan Milota wrote at the beginning of his article:

> Reaction is looking with renewed vigour for new ways in which to recover its former influence, to regain its positions and the sovereignty it has lost. In this search a special role has been assigned to the religious organizations because of the influence they have traditionally exercised in many countries over wide strata of the population and of the part they have played in history.

After referring to the serious loss of prestige by the Catholic Church because of 'the sympathy shown by the Vatican to fascism', the author, after a long dissertation on the part played by the Church as 'an integral part of the machinery of repression' of workers' aspirations and their movement, reaches the following dual conclusion: 'The Vatican has come to realize that the working class in the countries of our [socialist] community recognizes the existence of the socialist regime'; 'the revolution has created the indispensable room for personal freedom of opinion, whether atheist or Christian, because people are free to take part in religious life, or not to do so, religion being a private affair of each citizen'. The implication was that this freedom is contrasted with 'the intolerance and fanaticism' manifested by the Church over the centuries.

Will John Paul II pursue the *Ostpolitik* of his predecessors since John XXIII, without altering its meaning? If so, replies Milota:

> This would be a great disillusionment for all the forces of imperialist reaction, anticommunism, antisovietism, for all who would wish to use the Vatican for their own purposes of destabilizing the socialist countries and interfering in the affairs of socialist countries, to whip up tensions and conflicts between churches and governments. Certain people, in the capitalist countries, have welcomed the election of Karol Wojtyla with the declared hope of a renewal of the confrontation between the Catholic Church and the socialist countries because, they say, the man now on the pontifical throne has in the past been noted for the firm attitude he has adopted towards the Polish state.

After trying to make out whether these hopes are justified or not, Milota draws a parallel between what the Pope said during his visit to Mexico, where he says that John Paul II advised the clergy to avoid any political commitment, and what he said during his visit to Poland. As regards Latin America, he considers that by stressing the 'religious, non-political and non-social' nature of the Church's mission, John Paul II has 'rendered distinguished service to the reactionary regimes in those countries and above all to the United States': 'Not surprisingly, these statements have shown that the Pope has chosen to take the side of the oppressors, to back the conservative wing of the ecclesiastical hierarchy which supports the most reactionary regimes, such as the Stroessner and Somoza dictatorships.' Lastly, writing about John Paul II's pilgrimage in Poland, Milota juxtaposes the good intentions of the Polish government, the *proclaimed* good intentions of the Vatican, and the way in which the visit was exploited by the West. Thus he features the statement of Cardinal Koenig, who said that John Paul II's journey would be 'the beginning of a political earthquake in Poland and in neighbouring socialist countries'. Using the well-tried technique of quoting from others what one would like to say oneself, Milota quotes long extracts from the Western press (*Financial Times*, BBC, *Le Figaro*, *La Cité*, *International Herald Tribune*), and draws from them the conclusion that this journey by the Pope was a manifestation of Polish Catholic clericalism and of its anti-socialist bias.

Furthermore, he maintains that this visit will confirm the Church in its objective of the coming struggle against the government. Such, at least, is the conclusion of the press, according to Milota, who writes that, 'nevertheless it has to be admitted that some of the Pope's statements or observations can be exploited by anticommunist propaganda. By their vagueness and ambiguity, they have given ammunition to Western journalists for this propaganda.' He goes on, 'It is understandable that the Polish bishops should have wished to use the Pope's visit to demonstrate the close links of a not inconsiderable part of the Polish people with the Catholic Church.' But he immediately adds: 'When they go beyond this objective, when the bond between the Church and the citizens is perverted and presented as the platform of an opposition to the state, on the pretext of a struggle for freedom, then there arises the danger of tension between the Church and the state.'

And the author exclaims:

> Saint Stanislas or John of Nepomuk are to be an example, are to encourage war against the state government, are to incite the ecclesiastical hierarchy not to *sink into conformism*. Listen to that! In a socialist country! God forbid that priests should collaborate with a government like that! Is it possible for the *Ostpolitik* to be combined with ideals like that? Or should it be considered as purely and simply an imposture?

And Milota quotes John Paul II's views on the unification of the Slavs as a driving force for European renewal, on union between East and West, on the task assigned to the Polish nation, as an 'audacious challenge to communism'.

This stylistic exercise, in the grand Soviet tradition, would be boring if it did not lead to a very interesting conclusion: 'If the Vatican appeals to history, that has a special significance for our nation, our state. At the decisive moments of the millenary history of our people, the Vatican has always been on the side of our enemies.' And after having mentioned the confusion of the White Mountain, the Habsburgs, the tension between Masaryk and the Vatican, the 'clerico-fascism', Milota attacks the streamer shown at Gniezno: 'It is only too plain that all this little game was prepared in advance . . .' Everything is OK in Czechoslovakia, and those who believe that scientific socialism can be destroyed are deceiving themselves!

What lessons can be learn from reading this? First of all, Milota must be given credit for a certain ability to see into the future. If he feels it necessary to say that socialism cannot be destroyed, that is because the danger exists, and it is here linked with the Pope. When he sees in Pope John Paul II's journey an attempt at political destabilization, this Czech author is not worried only about the fate of friendly Poland but also, quite evidently, about the situation in his own country. Hence he is fully aware that the Pope intends his speech to be heard everywhere in Eastern Europe. So he ends with a dissociating act, which might be crudely summarized as follows: What is happening in Poland is not good. But there is less reason to fear that it might happen here than there was for it to occur in Poland. In any event, it must not happen here and we shall defend ourselves tooth and nail against any attempt to make it happen.

But this recital also reveals all the matters that disquiet the Czech government: the weakness of the Polish authorities, guilty of having allowed a journey to be undertaken which, not content with challenging the legitimacy of the Polish government alone, was an affront to every government in the bloc; the strength of the Polish Church and the increasing strength of Catholicism being viewed as a potential source of political opposition; the popularity of a Pope who, by saying loud and clear 'Don't be afraid!' undermines the very basis of the power of Soviet-type regimes; the arguments advanced by John Paul II who, by affirming the cultural, historical and religious unity of Europe, uncompromisingly set his face against the efforts of bloc governments to compel universal recognition of the finality of the division of the old continent into two separate entities.

And yet . . . to keep on repeating that those who predict 'political earthquakes' are mistaken is to betray the fear that they may not be mistaken – as history has often shown.

If John Paul II's journey was a source of unease to governments, by the same token it was a source of immense hope to the Churches of Eastern Europe. He was too familiar with the words and methods of Soviet-type governments to be taken in by promises. As a scion of the Polish tradition, he know how to make a robust riposte. In any event, his very presence in the Vatican constituted an extraordinary revenge for the Churches reduced to silence, who would from then onwards have an incomparably good platform (and John Paul II had not yet revealed to the full his talents as a user of the media . . .).

However, the reality is not as simple as that, as witness the slight feeling of unease induced by a reading of some texts originated by leading churchmen in Eastern Europe, notably in Hungary. In an interview that he gave to the journalist Karoly Doromby, published by the review *Vigilia* (no. 8, August 1979), the cardinal-primate of Hungary, Monsignor Lekai, who recently died, gave his impressions after the Pope's journey to Poland of some of the public events in which he had taken part. This interview reveals a distinct difference of tone between the enthusiasm of the Poles, the Western visitors and even the Hungarian pilgrims or 'tourists' who frequently demonstrated during John Paul II's appearances, and the more reserved attitude of the head of the Hungarian Church.

Asked about the overall impression he had formed of the tour, Cardinal Lekai immediately stressed the 'agreeable suprise [provided by] the excellent organization' of the pilgrimage. He went on to speak about all the apprehensions both on the part of the Church and of the secular authorities regarding the assembling 'of so many thousands of persons, their feeding and the sanitary and hygiene arrangements'. Only after that did the prelate refer to 'the satisfaction of spiritual needs', emphasizing that that was 'clearly the most important thing'. The fact remains that he gave pride of place to an aspect that, on the face of it, was of minor importance compared with the religious significance of the journey, to say nothing of its political dimension. Nor is it without significance that pride of place was given to the 'assembling of thousands of persons'. It will be recalled that this was one of the main worries of the Polish government, and the departments concerned did not scruple to announce that if the crowds got out of control the consequences could be unforeseeable. In short, it was the spectre of disorder in the streets, or even more or less spontaneous insurrection, that was troubling them. And that was precisely the subject to which Cardinal Lekai gave priority when he afterwards praised 'the admirable discipline of the crowd of the faithful'. What is put forward here is the Church as a power for order, religion as a calming factor, ecclesiastical organization as a stabilizing force.

In what followed there was not a single reference to what Pope John Paul II said, simply an enthusiastic statement about 'the disarming[16] humanity of the Pope . . . and his personality which created a magic climate around him'. And Monsignor Lekai went to the sources of this magic, 'composed of innumerable small gestures, of the timbre of his voice'. The singer, not the song! Above all, not the song. No word of what John Paul II may have said was reported in this interview, nor did it contain any reflection on the content of what the Pope said. After having spoken of the magic of the words and the man, the cardinal confined himself to recalling, in concluding his reply to the first question: 'The Pope always emphasized that his visit to his country was of a purely religious nature . . . .'.

Clearly this constant harping on order and the refusal to see anything political are both rooted in the cardinal's interpretation of the situation in Hungary and the relations between Church and state in that country. When the journalist interjected that part of the world press had placed much more emphasis on the political aspects of John Paul II's journey than on the religious aspects, the primate of Hungary replied with a statement that might have been echoed by the entire official press of the Soviet bloc, denouncing 'that part of the international press which has done its best to distort the meaning of the Pope's visit from the direction of appeasement to that of confrontation', flinging a passing gibe at the 'harder ecclesiastical line' which, in Poland itself, supports those who are bent on tension. But fortunately, said the primate, 'the great wisdom [of the Pope], his political intelligence and his tact' had served to cool the atmosphere. And Monsignor Lekai emphasized that the Pope was accompanied by Cardinal Casaroli, which he saw as a sign of the continuity of a policy that had been initiated by John XXIII and carried on by Paul VI, and that John Paul II was continuing to follow.

The next two questions more directly concerned the part taken by the Hungarian Church in the Pope's journey. They gave Cardinal Lekai the opportunity of speaking at great length of the kind attentions the Holy Father had bestowed upon him, the cordiality with which he had received the respects the cardinal had paid him. The letter of invitation had an 'extrarodinarily cordial tone'. 'The Holy Father shows a very warm interest in the historical links' between Poland and Hungary; Monsignor Lekai had been able to sit next to the Pope, who had been kind enough to single him out for a particularly warm welcome and to send his good wishes to the Hungarian Church and people, etc. And the cardinal concluded: 'The Holy Father showed me unremitting kindness and attention. He always granted me the privilege of his love and cordiality.'

Qui nimis probat nihil probat . . . To devote more than a third of an interview intended to report upon an event as important as the first visit of a Pope to a Soviet-bloc country to enumerating each of the Holy Father's attentions to one's own person or to the institution one represents, compels the observer to ask certain questions.

We may dismiss at the outset any suspicions of immodesty. Apart from the fact that this would be unbecoming in a churchman, the cardinal's dwelling on certain themes would appear to have more deep-seated motivations. The fact is that Monsignor Lekai's constant references to the kindnesses shown him by the Pope are doubtless intended to say loud and clear to his own clergy and his own faithful that he is legitimate, since John Paul II himself considers him to be such. All we now have to ask ourselves is why Monsignor Lekai should have to proclaim his legitimacy in this manner. The explanation is given in his reply to the last question, on the importance of the Pope's journey from the double viewpoint of relations between the Vatican and the socialist states and, within each of the countries, relations between the Church and the government.

For Cardinal Lekai, there is no doubt as to this importance. But he immediately states that it is 'necessary to clarify certain fundamental questions'. And he recites:

> Although the bishops and the episcopal conferences of the different countries cannot remain indifferent towards the situation of the churches in the other countries I, as president of the Hungarian episcopate, know best the situation in Hungary. . . . The situation of churches living in socialist countries is very diversified, as are the different stages of historical development. Nor is there any one single pattern of ecclesial polity which can be transposed to all the countries. . . . We are bound by a fraternal relationship, united in love and

respectful of the characteristics of each of the local churches. Such is the main lesson I have learned from my extraordinary and unforgettable pilgrimage.

With thoughts so clearly expressed, comment is superfluous. The 'Polish model' may be good for Poland, but it is meaningless elsewhere. The Pope was talking to the Poles, not to the Hungarians (doubtless that is why there is no point in repeating what he said). Let each one hoe his own row. Other than that, just a brief reminder that the Church mission is 'to make Christ's message penetrate into men's hearts', and not – this is the implied corollary – to descend into the political arena. It is difficult not to see here a veiled criticism of the man whom he had just showered with compliments.

The two statements examined here come from very different authors, belonging to worlds far apart and in many respects hostile. What can an obscure Czech propagandist have in common with the primate of the Catholic Church in Hungary? And yet the two texts do exhibit some convergences. In both, the Western press is criticized and accused of attributing a political significance to the journey that it does not have. And even though this exercise leads Cardinal Lekai to dismiss the political significance whereas Milota, in his own way, gives weight to it, the procedure employed leads both of them to do scant justice to what John Paul II really said.

Furthermore, both pieces come to the same conclusion, namely, that Poland is Poland and that what happens there is not relevant for other countries. Both in Czechoslovakia and in Hungary the situation is different, as are the traditions and history. What the Pope said is *foreign* to the realities in these two countries. In short, the important thing is to preserve the *status quo* and to avoid any destabilizing developments that might upset the balance which, though of course for different reasons, each of these two authors believes to be in some sense to his advantage.

The Pope is a nuisance – that is basically what Cardinal Lekai is saying when he dwells on the attentions paid to him by the Pope. And Milota writes the same thing, only more openly.

In the nature of the case, the attitude of the Polish communists could not be the same as that of Czechoslovak or Soviet communists. The considerable strengthening of the Polish Church that resulted directly from the election of Karol Wojtyla was bound still further to weaken the Gierek regime. Therefore his government displayed a very cautious attitude at first; pride was expressed because Poland had provided the world with its first non-Italian Pope for centuries and circumspection practised as to the consequences of such an event. When asked when the visit of the new Pope to his native land might take place, Kazimierz Kakol, director of the Office of Cults, replied: 'The date and time of this visit will certainly be determined by bilateral and multilateral circumstances'.[17] This was an admission that Poland was under pressure from its allies, who were disturbed by the turn of events (for example

M. Bilak, the Czechoslovak number two, had twice visited Warsaw during the few months preceding the Polish official's statement). The party was then faced with the task of learning to deal with the major contradiction inherent in the presence of a Polish Pope in the Vatican, *ipso facto* recognized as final judge, as the most prestigious of all the Poles. So the government had to amass more information, and to think carefully about it. It is known, for example, that before the 1979 visit the government commissioned a sociological study of the religious sentiments of soldiers. This survey, the results of which have never been published, was clearly designed to measure to what extent the army could be relied on in the new, explosive context of a visit by John Paul II. But even in 1978 the central committee of the Party had asked a group of researchers to produce a study of social problems in contemporary Catholicism. The publication of the conclusions of this research in the form of an article signed by Dionizy Tanalski in *Człowiek i Swiatopoglad* (no. 3, Warsaw, March 1980) gave a better insight into the way in which Polish officials integrated the presence of the former archbishop of Cracow into the contemporary political landscape.

The first point to mention, paradoxical as this may seem, is the wish to minimize the particular qualities of John Paul II and to emphasize continuity rather then discontinuities. They did indeed concede that he has a special 'personality' and 'warmth', and admitted that he had made certain 'doctrinal advances', but only to note that these 'did not extend beyond the bounds laid down by his predecessor'. This was because 'in actual fact the doctrine of the Church is not a private matter: every Pope . . . has to take account of the reality of the situation in which he is operating and of the overriding interest of the Church'.

In addition to the commonsense consideration that John Paul II is acting in the context of a situation in which there are many constraints, in which the universal Church cannot be administered as though it were simply the diocese of Cracow, one cannot but detect in such language the hope, vivified into a certitude, that his accession to the pontificate will moderate Karol Wojtyla's excessive ebullience. He will have to take account of the existing framework, the structures of the Curia subject to international power relationships: in other words, it is being assumed that he has lost some of his freedom of action. But is this just wishful thinking, or is it a coded message to someone out there? Is it intended for Polish society and/or the sister countries? In point of fact it seems to have more than one addressee. The Party is being told: 'Don't be alarmed; we are equipped to handle the situation'; civil society is being warned: 'Don't harbour any illusions: the Pope cannot get the better of the sociopolitical facts of life here, even if he is your compatriot.' And the bloc is being told: 'There's no danger; the Pope is motivated more by patriotism than by anti-communism.'

This approach to the problem was of the greatest interest, since by using it the government might hope to win at all levels. By setting up Karol Wojtyla primarily as a patriot, it could suggest to the allies that pledges had to be given to the national sentiments of the Poles both at home and abroad, so as to defuse the time bomb the Pope was thought to be. 'We note', said Tanalski, 'the emphasis placed by the Pope on patriotism and his wish that Poland should receive special consideration from world opinion.' 'That shows', he wrote, 'the patriotism of a Polish Catholic who has had experience of the complex of Slav "provincialism" in Europe.' But this patriotism 'is not opposed to socialism (as an economic and political programme)', and 'it is plain that the Pope makes no secret of a certain pride in the economic, political and cultural successes of [Poland] since the Second World War'. The conclusion is clear. Leave Poland alone to its special position, give it more freedom of action! That will satisfy the Pope who, once this tribute is paid to his patriotism, will speed up the process of normalization between the state and the Church, and this the regime can only welcome since from this aspect it will strengthen the government's control over society. As to society itself, it is bound to be grateful to a government whose first concern appears to be to further the cause of national independence. Thus this hand, if well played, could result in lowering the prestige of the Church, provided that it could be sufficiently compromised.

This is why Tanalski emphasizes in his article mainly what unites the Vatican and the socialist government rather than what divides them, and dwells rather on points in the Pope's speeches that can be used for the government's ends than on those that are a dead loss to it. He recalls 'the search for peace, the humanism to which both socialism and Catholicism can lay claim, the fact that the Church speaks of "the cultural and creative function of social relationships and hence also of the class struggle" '.

In a word, the report was an attempt to sum up the visit of John Paul II to Poland. It is worth quoting at length from the passage, because it illustrates so well the effort made by the Polish authorities to turn the election of Karol Wojtyla to their advantage:

> Plainly this is what the new Pope believes: there is a need to awaken the Church and Catholics, whether clerical or lay. A need to re-endow them with a missionary, crusading spirit. The Pope wants do draw all the clergy along behind him, and to do that he refers to the Polish clergy whom he rates as the most active and missionary-minded of any in the Church throughout the world. . . . According to John Paul II the Catholic Church has played a creative role nationally and on the cultural scene, in Poland and throughout the Slav world. According to him, Poland and the Slav world have made their entry into the world cultural arena on the basis of a specific contribution, 'Slavo-Christian culture', and by making its own unique call to a creative unification of Europe

in Christian culture. This would be a new Europe organized in accordance with Christian principles by a remarkable international organization, the Catholic Church, with its numbers of 'officers', well organized and very disciplined.

Tanalski even goes so far as to give the figures: 813,181 persons in Europe, 2,460,326 persons throughout the world, according to Vatican data as of 31 December 1976.

There can be no doubt that this relatively low-key description of John Paul II's alleged design helped to reassure those among the rulers of the Soviet bloc who were worried. Yet clearly that was not its purpose. The object in view appears to have been to convince them that the obstacle was a formidable one, that the problem was not simply how many divisions the Pope had. . . . For the Pope had both a coherent programme and the means of executing it. Thus a frontal attack was out of the question – it might prove very costly. The wiser course was to seek an acceptable compromise, and this would inevitably entail making some concessions. Was not this Pope at heart a reasonable man, since 'he had acknowledged the value of the communist programme for transforming the life of society'?

The accession of Cardinal Wojtyla to the pontificate was pregnant with new risks and possibilities. It was a factor of hope for Christians in Eastern Europe, but also a source of apprehension for certain leaders of the Church, something to make the ruling powers tremble, but also a pretext for one of them to gain more freedom of action. In the last resort, would he prove to be a *stabilizing* factor or would he by his very presence and words upset hard-won equilibria? There has not yet been sufficient time to give a reply to this question which, even in 1983, was central to any discussion on John Paul II's second visit to Poland. Yet even by then Solidarity had emerged in the wake of the first visit . . .

A theology of the nation and of freedom

Originally John Paul II's second visit to Poland had been scheduled to take place in August 1982. It was postponed by the Polish government because of the situation that followed the imposition of martial law on 13 December 1981, and it finally took place on 23 June 1983, in very difficult circumstances. Even though all Poles were at one in regarding it as a manifestation of the Pope's solicitude for his country, and though many of them drew consolation and strength from it, some wondered whether such a visit was not 'objectively normalizing', whether it did not provide *a posteriori* justification to General Jaruzelski's heavy-handed action and give him the cloak of respectability he so sorely needed.

It is not certain that John Paul II saw the problem in those terms. He gave about twenty public speeches, homilies and addresses during his stay in Poland, and these did not touch only upon current events; they were also designed to adumbrate more distant prospects. From this point of view it would seem that the journey was anything but an encouragement to normalization, for the Pope's itinerary both testified to a free and awakened Poland and revealed its true dimensions. An analysis of what he said shows that the aims of his journey were couched as much in symbolic as in political terms. Wherever he travelled, the Pope exalted the nation. Even in the speech he made at Warsaw airport on his arrival, he made 22 direct or indirect references to Poland in a text barely 600 words long (*Poland* occurred 6 times; *fatherland* 7; *Polish earth, native soil, native earth*, 5; *Pole*, 3; *compatriots*, 1). The count can even be raised to 27 if one includes 5 references to Jasna-Gora, which, as we have seen, does duty as a symbol for the nation. For comparison, *state* occurs only 3 times, *the episcopate* twice, and *the Church* only once. Only the word *pilgrimage* is repeated 5 times, but that was the official purpose of the Pope's visit. And even this word was indissociable from Czestochowa, the high place of the nation's resistance to the foreign invader and symbol of his defeat by the Poles thanks to the intercession of the Virgin, who, for this reason, was proclaimed 'Queen of Poland'.

John Paul II also celebrated three beatifications during his stay in Poland. The biography of the three blessed ones, even in summary form, gives cause for thought. Mother Ursula Ledochowska, who cared for young people and their education, carried out her apostolate at St Petersburg from 1907 to 1914. She was the niece of Cardinal Mieczyslaw Ledochowski, who was the primate of Poland, and of whom the Pope said that 'at Poznan he opposed the Prussian Kulturkampf, in defence of the faith, the spirit of Poland and the autonomy of the Church in Poland; because of this he was persecuted and imprisoned'.[18] Rafael Kalinowski took part in the insurrection of 1863 against Russia, for which he was sentenced to forced labour in Siberia. Released under an amnesty in 1874, he devoted himself to the evangelization and pastoral care of young people at Wadowice. The third, Albert Chmielowski, also fought against the Russians in 1863, lost a leg in the uprising and managed to escape to France where he waited until the amnesty of 1874 before returning. He then devoted himself to work among the poor and underprivileged. Need one say more? In all three cases, the struggle of the nation for independence was clearly involved, and in all three cases the Church was involved in this struggle. What is more, in all three cases Russia was involved too, either as adversary or field of evanglization. In two of the three cases, the apostolate was directed mainly towards young people. Struggle, nation, independence, Church, Russia, apostolate, youth, all of them markers that make of the message delivered by John Paul II more an exhortation to resistance than a call to resignation. At Niepokalanow, in the same spirit, the Pope celebrated the memory of Maximilian Kolbe, a symbol of the triumph of humanity over totalitarianism, and the memory of Saint Stanislas, symbol of the rejection of arbitrary action and absolute power.

We shall say more about three texts in particular from the 1983 journey. They are not selected at random, though inevitably by personal choice. By choosing the homily at the Czestochowa mass on 19 June 1983, the address to the plenary meeting of the Polish episcopate on 19 June 1983, and the Pope's reply to General Jaruzelski's speech in his honour on 17 June 1983, it was possible to analyse the positions adopted by John Paul II towards each of the three great actors on the Polish scene – civil society, the Church and the government. To this basic corpus has been added the address given on 17 June by the Party chief, which was useful for reference purposes.

The Pope and the general: the nation between Church and State

On that day the Pope was received at the Belvedere Palace at Warsaw by the great officers of state, headed by the president of the council of state Mr Jablonski and the head of the government and the Party, General Jaruzelski. The general's speech was published in Polish in *Dziennik Ludowy* for 18–19 June 1983, and the Pope's reply, also in Polish, in the *Osservatore Romano* for 18 June 1983.[19] The speeches were of about the same length, the general's running to about 14,000 signs and the Pope's to 13,000, and they enabled each of the protagonists to summarize their views of the situation of the country a year and a half after 13 December, and to say what they expected to happen and what they intended to do.

Words are always carefully chosen, especially when it is known that the speeches will be published, and studied and analysed throughout the world. Beyond doubt much thought had been given to every jot and comma of these speeches, from the dual viewpoints of their expected impact on opinion in Poland and the effect they would have abroad. After diligent study of the texts a list of all the nouns, proper or common, used by the two speakers has been made and arranged in four series which represent the way in which the Pope and General Jaruzelski spoke of Poland, its international surroundings, the actors on the Polish scene, and the standards by which the country should be guided.

Poland was accorded a larger dimension in the Pope's speeches than in those of the general. Whereas the latter chose for preference official terms (*People's Republic of Poland*, 8; and more simply *Poland*, 16) or geographical ones (*country*, 8; *Polish earth*, 4; *territory*, 1), John Paul II preferred to refer to the *nation* or to the *homeland* (12 and 9). In point of fact, whereas for General Jaruzelski the word *Poland* clearly functioned simply as an abbreviation of *People's Republic of Poland*, for the Pope it was quite obviously a synonym for the *nation*. For instance, when the head of the Polish

Communist Party welcomed the Pope with the words: 'I cordially welcome Your Holiness to the country of the Poles, to the People's Republic of Poland',[20] John Paul II replied: 'I should like to assure the representatives of the highest authorities of the People's Republic of Poland of my gratitude for all they have done to prepare my meeting with the nation and with the Church of my country.'[21] John Paul II countered General Jaruzelski's initial appropriation of Poland by the state by making a radical distinction between the authorities and the state on the one hand, and the nation, the Church and the country on the other. What is more, by making it clear that he was talking about *his* country, the Pope implicitly refuted General Jaruzelski's contention when he said that 'for the second time, the pilgrim's road has led the head of the Catholic Church to his birthplace, to Polish 'soil',[22] intended to convey very respectfully to the Pope that he could now only claim a past connection with the country, and that the Poland of John Paul II was not the country in which Poles were now living.

So the Pope's 47 references and General Jaruzelski's 53 references to Poland were couched in very different registers, suggestive of almost completely opposite conceptions. Whereas the latter had a political and geographical connotation, identifying Poland with the state and the state with frontiers and security, the former were couched in terms of feeling and morals.

'Today real alliances contribute to the external security of the state', said General Jaruzelski. 'Nowadays, unlike so many epochs in our history, the frontiers of the Republic are not aflame. They are all frontiers of friendship. Not a single centimetre of Polish soil will ever be in dispute. On that, all Poles are agreed'.[23] This is pure Soviet doctrine: since the end of the Second World War Polish communists have made much of the guarantee of territorial integrity, presenting it as a fundamental source of legitimacy, even at the price of subjection. The argument is certainly ambiguous, since the nation is asked to be glad it is subject to an alien pattern in the interest of its very survival. But it is the keystone of an implicit and permanent blackmail: the only alternative to our being in power is for the country to disappear. And it is in the name of this so-called choice that General Jaruzelski seeks to unite (*all* Poles!).

John Paul II countered this argument with international morality. 'Poland has not only a right to existence and to the sovereignty of a state; more than that, in her place she is necessary to Europe and to the world.'[24] And, later on: 'The Polish nation has confirmed, at very heavy cost, its right to be sovereign mistress of the land it has inherited from its ancestors.'[25] This is obviously a riposte to the argument of the Soviets about the millions of soldiers sacrificed to deliver Poland from Nazi occupation, an argument that General Jaruzelski himself used as early as paragraph three of his text.[26] But in addition, the Pope's speech was intended to point out that a Poland cut off from half the continent was no longer fulfilling its vocation and hence was losing an identity that comes fully into being only in interaction with Europe and the world.

That is what makes the references to the international environment in the Pope's utterances (16 against General Jaruzelski's 6) so important. *Europe* is mentioned 10 times, *the world* 5, *the West* once. On the other side, while *the world* was also mentioned on 5 occasions, *Europe* was mentioned only once, and *the West* not at all.

As regards the actors on the Polish scene, however, there was a real symmetry, even though General Jaruzelski nearly always refers to the Church as the Roman Catholic Church, certainly a meaningful locution. They are simply mentioned more often by the Polish leader than by the Pope. Thus *state* (17 and 12), *Church*, under different designations: *Church, Roman Catholic Church, episcopate, Holy See* (10 and 6), *society* and its constituents: *citizens, workers, men* (12 and 6). *The people* is also mentioned (5 times) unlike *soldier*, only referred to by General Jaruzelski.

But it is obvious that these actors are not moved by the same forces, and are not pointing in the same directions or inspired by the same values. *Freedom* (or *independence, sovereignty*) is indeed mentioned equally (6 and 5 times) as is *religion* (once each), but General Jaruzelski uses a whole series of words whose presence is no more neutral than is their absence from the Pope's utterances: *socialism* (2), *constitution, security, order, economy* (once). At the same time, the word *democracy* is employed only once, and then by John Paul II.

Both speakers refer to *peace*, but whereas the Pope uses the word 14 times, the general has only 6 references, hardly more than to *war* 5, which is virtually absent from John Paul II's speeches. On the other hand, General Jaruzelski mentions *history* twice as often as the Pope (8 and 4).

That explains why the overall tone of the general's speech is more sombre and solemn. One must confess that it strikes the reader as being self-justificatory and, on occasions, pleading:

> It is said that Poland is suffering, but who will place in the scale of the balance the infinite sufferings of the people, the torments and the tears we have been able to avoid? I wish in this residence to recall the memorable words of Tadeusz Kosciuszko: the time has come when much has to be sacrificed in order to save everything. We do not fear the judgement of posterity. It will be just, assuredly more balanced than many a contemporary judgement.[27]

Once again, the argument advanced is that of the *lesser evil*, the only possible justification for martial law. Since he here places himself in the position of the accused, it is hardly surprising that General Jaruzelski wants to be convincing, and that he uses all the resources of vocabulary in order to do so. Consequently his speech is far more diversified than that of the Pope: whereas the latter uses 60 different adjectives, 97 times, the Polish Party chief uses 104, 145 times. From these two speeches can be derived two main axes around which four logical series are grouped, which, when analysed, enable the trends already noted to be verified and supplemented – good and evil, time and space.

The first of these axes is by far the most important: 32 adjectives for the Pope, 50 for the general, making one-third of the total number studied. In both cases what is good and desirable has the advantage over what is bad and deplorable: 33 against 17 for the general, and 26 against 6 for the Pope. But the proportions are different and General Jaruzelski paints the negative pole in much richer, more sombre colours than does the Pope. Whereas the latter uses only 4 adjectives (*terrible*, twice, *difficult*, twice, *severe* and *critical*, the general employs 16 of them (*vain*, twice, *tragic*, *imploring*, *heavy*, *cruel*, *terrible*, *dangerous*, *critical*, *bloodstained*, *miserable*, *serious*, *difficult*, *unusual*, *unjust*, *guilty*, *dishonest*).

The same difference recurs in the description of the positive pole. There are 14 adjectives in the Pope's discourse (*good*, 6 times, *prosperous*, *serene*, *true*, 3 times each, *necessary*, *effective*, twice each, *elevated*, *loyal*, *constructive*, *fruitful*, *possible*, *capable*, *pacific*, *reasonable*) and 22 in the general's (*moral*, 5 times, *just*, 3 times, *sincere*, *good*, *valuable*, *fundamental*, *human*, twice each, *equitable*, *incontestable*, *humanitarian*, *legal*, *necessary*, *balanced*, *normal*, *pacific*, *better*, *elevated*, *constructive*, *interdependent*, *luminous*, *open*, *worthy*).

The claims of the head of the Polish Communist Party that he is not looking for 'facile justifications' and that 'it is not the government that has brought the country to the edge of catastrophe'[28] ring hollow, while his description of reality is intended to justify the use of force, just as his purpose in exalting the good is to prove that he has good intentions.

The second axis in order of importance concerns the representation of time and space: 28 adjectives for the Pope, 39 for the general. But whereas the Pope has more to say about time, the general attaches more importance to space. The fact is that while the 13 adjectives used by John Paul II to 'date' his speech have only an indicative function (*first*, *second*, *annual*, *current*, *contemporary* . . .), the 26 employed by General Jaruzelski acquire, in their diversity and their repetition, an almost incantatory dimension, which emphasizes and punctuates the different phases of his address. The man of 13 December makes his appeal to the past (*antique*, *ancient*, *traditional*), to the present (*new*, twice; *young*, *up to date*, *recent*, *contemporary*) and to the future, to the view that posterity will take of him (*historic*, 3 times; *memorable*). He even adopts locutions that one might rather expect to hear in the mouth of the Pope (*eternal*, twice; *infinite*), even going so far as to appoint a term to time (*irreversible*, *ultimate*).

As regards the representation of space, both speakers give more room to what is external than to what is internal, which they describe in the same terms and in more or less the same proportions. But their descriptions of the international environment differ widely. The Pope explicitly refers 7 times to the world (*international*, 3 times; *world*, 4 times), whereas the general makes only two references to it (*universal*, *international*). Furthermore, although John Paul II endeavours to give an uncoloured description, General Jaruzelski's description stresses the otherness of the world, an otherness not without a certain threatening quality (*external*, *foreign*, *enemy*). Lastly, it is hardly necessary to emphasize the prominent place in the Pope's vocabulary given to Europe, the West and America (*European*, twice; *Western*, *American*), while, as in a mirror image, Poland's powerful neighbour appears in the general's vocabulary (*Russian*).

Inside or outside these axes are adjectives that occupy a special position, in that they are repeated more often than the others (of course the analysis does not include adjectives such as *big*, *large*, *numerous*, which are meaningful only in their context). Adjectives used at least three times by General Jaruzelski are *moral* (5), *real* (4), *social* (4), *historic*, *current*, *just* (3). For the Pope, the list is: *good* (6), *social* (5), *worldwide* (4), *international*, *prosperous*, *serene*, *supreme* (3). Here we find, accentuated, the major themes of the Pope (7 references to the world) and of the Polish leader whose 8 references to the good, 6 to time, and 4 to *reality* are intended to underpin the thesis of the 'lesser evil', taking account of objective facts, and the fact that posterity will one day recognize . . .

His argumentation seems to be permanently based on an appropriation of reality, which he alone can decode and of which he is the embodiment. Moreover, it sometimes surfaces in rather unexpected places, as for example when the head of government states that 'nowadays *real* alliances contribute to the external security of the state'. It is difficult to grasp the meaning of such an adjective, unless the general intended to convey that it would be in illusion to suppose that Poland could jettison these alliances.

The Pope's response to this understanding of 'real' is his conception of the *true*: 'I shall continue to think of all the *truly* good things in my country as belonging to me',[29] which is one way of suggesting that there is a good that cannot be truly described as such.

Words do not hold the same meanings for the two speakers. This can be proved by studying the 'couplings', a simple exercise consisting of systematically recording the common noun that comes immediately before and immediately after a 'star' word, in the present case the two most frequently used common nouns, *state* and *nation*. The former is associated by General Jaruzelski with *security*, *alliances*, *anarchy*, *economy*, *work*, *efforts*, *initiatives*, *activities*, *constitution*, *law*, *approbation*, *(public) opinion*, *rank*, *relations*, *Church*, and by the Pope with *nation*, *sovereignty*, *authority*, *dialogue, country, Poland, people, vow*. For the Pope, the state has no meaning except to symbolize the sovereignty of the nation, whereas the head of the Polish Communist Party stresses the values of order and security.

This is confirmed by the words coupled with nation by the two men: *defence, peace, order, vices, (moral) health, law, civilization, state, history, oppression, future, people, friends* by General Jaruzelski, and *collaboration, meeting, Europe, Church, (extermination) camps, peace, gratitude* by the Pope.

Jasna-Gora: the theology of the nation

Analysed in the same way, the homily of the mass celebrated at Czestochowa on Sunday, 19 June 1983, was the highlight of John Paul II's journey to Poland. This text, about 18,000 signs or some 2,400 words long, spoken to a crowd estimated at 2 million, contained the core of the message that the Pope wished to deliver to the Poles. Besides being a veritable hymn to the nation, it was also intended to be a *programme*, making explicit the *political* design that John Paul II had for the whole of Sovietized Eastern Europe, and not for Poland alone.

For the Holy Father's speech is punctuated by the reference to the nation. Under different forms (*nation*, 20 times, *Poland*, 13 times, *fatherland*, 11 times, *Polish earth*, 4 times) it appears 48 times, an average of once every 50 words. In the first 5 sentences of the homily alone it is used 5 times.

John Paul II set the tone from the outset by saying: 'I have come on pilgrimage to render glory to the eternal God in this national sanctuary of my country.'[30] This emphasis on the official purpose of the visit, an obligatory passage at the beginning of the speech, was aimed at deflecting from the outset any criticism by the government. Here there is no question of politics; it is the act of a pastor making a pastoral visit at the invitation of the bishops. But taken in its religious sense the pilgrimage, as a quest, leads to a sanctuary, the specifically national character of which is emphasized by a redundancy. *Freedom* serves as a criterion and measure of this singularity. Ever since his first journey, made in 1979, John Paul II had emphasized this, as we have seen, by calling Czestochowa 'the place where we have always been free'.[31] Whether as counterpoint or definition, or even a synonym, freedom, under its various forms (*freedom*, 20 *sovereignty*, 6, *independence*, 4), is, with the nation, the leitmotiv of what John Paul II has to say.

This freedom is in the first place individual freedom. 'As children of God', said the Pope, 'we cannot be slaves. Our status as children of God carries within itself the heritage of freedom.'[32] But, for John Paul II, 'the proclamation of freedom at Jasna-Gora has yet another dimension – that of the freedom of the nation, of the free fatherland which has recovered the dignity of a sovereign state'.[33] What is true of the individual is true of the nation:

"Freedom is given to man as a measure of his dignity[34] and to the nation as a measure of the dignity of that which claims to embody it, the state, and which cannot do it effectively unless it is sovereign. Just as freedom avails to mediate between man and God, between man and what makes his dignity as a man, so the state has no other purpose than to assure the freedom of the nation. If it defaults on that duty, it is quite naturally disqualified. Hence the function assigned to it appears to be purely instrumental, and this should cause no surprise to a nation that has hardly ever been able to identify itself with a state, even when the state was not actively *against* it.

However, this conception of the state does not constitute a break with the traditional doctrine of the Church, introduced by the Polish Pope. It would be much truer to say that John Paul II's argument reinforces a movement that has a long history. Marcel Merle, concluding an analysis of the most outstanding actions of the Magisterium in the field of international relations, had already noted that 'the state becomes nothing more than a tool at the disposal of human groups who are the real incumbents of sovereignty, on the basis of their cultural identity or of the strength of common aspirations characterizing the activities of their members.'[35]

This is what John Paul II is emphasizing when he states:

> The nation is truly free when it can take the form of a community determined by unity of culture, language and history. The state is strengthened in its sovereignty when it governs society and at the same time serves the common good of the society and enables the nation to realize itself in its personality, its identity. This implies among other things creating conditions suitable for development, in the sphere of culture, of the economy and other sectors of the life of the social community. *The sovereignty of the state is profoundly linked with its capacity to promote the freedom of the nation*, that is to say, to develop conditions enabling the nation to express its special historical and cultural identity, or in other words to be sovereign though the medium of the state.[36]

These reflections, presented by the Pope as so many 'elementary moral truths',[37], are diametrically opposed to the ideas expressed by General Jaruzelski in the speech he made on 17 June: 'When the state weakens and falls into anarchy it is the people who suffer.'[38] He was explicitly referring to a definition of the state given by John Paul II himself during his first visit to Poland: 'The state, as an expression of sovereign self-determination of peoples and nations, constitutes a normal construct of the social order. Therein consists its moral authority.'[39] It is clear that in expressing satisfaction at this statement, 'in harmony with the traditional and current understanding of the essence of the state', the general was betraying a somewhat selective reading of the definition put forward by John Paul II. For who would seriously contend that the state he represents is 'the expression of the sovereign self-determination' of the Polish people? But, apart from this observation, it appears that whereas for the Pope the state is nothing more than an intermediary, for General Jaruzelski it is an end in itself. The stronger the state, the greater the individual guarantees it will be able to provide for its citizens. For John Paul II, on the contrary, the more freedom the nation has the more legitimate, and hence the stronger, will be the state with which it is provided. In the one case, the stronger the state the freer the nation; in the other case, exactly the opposite.

In the light of the foregoing, it is understandable that for John Paul II both *dignity* (3 mentions) and *power* (3), *law* and *greatness* (2 and 1), *morals* and the *economy*, *work*, *reform* or *duty* (2 then 1) are totally subordinated to freedom. *History* (12 mentions), *culture* (3) and *language* (1) have, however, a major role to play in defining and promoting this freedom. John Paul II said:

> We have a very difficult geopolitical situation. We have had a very difficult history, especially during the last few centuries. The painful experiences of history have sharpened our sensibility in the realm of basic human rights, and in particular the right to freedom, sovereignty, respect for freedom of conscience and religion and the rights of human labour.[40]

But history, culture and language cannot be dissociated from religion, for not only has 'the image of Jasna-Gora witnessed to the special presence of the Mother of God in the history of our nation',[41] but in addition, 'the experience of history shows . . . that Mary was given to us in her image at Jasna-Gora above all for the difficult times'.[42] The 'special link between the sanctuary of Jasna-Gora and the increasingly difficult history of the nation'[43] spoken of by John Paul II led him to establish a system of symbolic reverberations between the Virgin, queen of Poland, 'she who was given us for the defence of the Polish nation', freedom and the constitution of 3 May, the date of the festival of Mary. 'This constitution is an irrefutable evidence of the will to preserve the independence of the nation by the promulgation of necessary reforms.'[44] And it is at Czestochowa that 'the hope of the nation and the indefeasible longing for a return to independence'[45] are to be found. Thus the Pope's speech held up the Church simultaneously as the place, the symbol and the vehicle of freedom, giving it a central role in preserving and promoting the tradition of independence that is the foundation of the Polish nation.

The address to the plenary meeting of the episcopate: the Church in the service of the nation

And in fact, John Paul II, speaking to the Polish bishops gathered at Czestochowa on 19 June 1983 did pay tribute to the late primate, Cardinal Wyszynski, praising him as 'a singular example of love of country', adding that as such 'he should be counted among the greatest figures in its history',[46] thus stressing the *national* stature of the deceased prelate. In his address to the bishops the Pope kept the nation in the forefront of his discourse, just as much as when speaking to the government or the crowds. Once again, under different forms (*Poland*, 22 mentions; *fatherland*, 7; *nation* 6; *country*, 2), this was the term most often used. However, in contrast with his previous speeches, it did not overwhelm everything else. The word *man* occurred 28 times, *Church*, 27, *society*, 17, and *episcopate*, 14. Moreover, in general his vocabulary included some words seldom or never previously used (*classes, opponent, trade union, solidarity, economy, unity*). For unlike other texts, the address to the bishops was intended to do more than simply proclaim great principles. In it John Paul II painted a specific vision of the future and laid down a programme of work for the Polish Church, and he emphasized the importance of this task both to society and to the whole world (which was mentioned 11 times); 'Carry out this [evangelical] task in full view of Polish society, and of the world too. For the events of the last few years have concentrated the attention of wide circles of opinion on the Church in Poland,'[47] Nothing better illustrates the exemplary role in which John Paul II cast Poland, a role that he explained in greater detail in the encyclical *Slavorum Apostoli*.

Here the tone was hortatory. It was a directive more than counsel or prayer. And the 'pastoral plans' enumerated by John Paul II were all the more urgent for covering a period in which 'the Polish jubilee of Jasna-Gora partly coincides with the Year of Redemption, the extraordinary Jubilee of the universal Church. This jubilee is, as it were, a milestone of the Church along the road leading to the year 2000 since the birth of the Saviour. *For this reason it has something of the Advent about it*'.[48] So John Paul adopts the solemn language of a Messianic millenarianism.

The programme sketched out by John Paul II had several different facets. Besides being at the service of truth and love, the Church also had a duty towards freedom and to the nation: 'I feel that the declarations of the [episcopal] conference are a response to the need to listen to the truth, a need so sorely felt in society. The truth is the primary and fundamental condition of social renewal.'[49] This 'truth-speaking', nourished by culture and traditions, and linked to 'active love of neighbour',[50] enables the Church to defend freedom: 'From the Marial inspiration of our millenary, sustained by the figure of Saint Maximilian, must spring all that serves the freedom of the Church and, by that inspiration, the Church must serve true freedom of man and the nation.'[51] Clearly, neither the reference to Maximilian Kolbe nor the use of the adjective *true* was fortuitous. The 'truth-speaking' of the Church is first and foremost a response to the perversion of language on which every totalitarian regime is based. At the same time, the function of the Church as a mediator between the nation and its freedom is reaffirmed.

John Paul II was bound to refer to the problems in the world of labour. In fact, this word occurs 13 times in his text. Referring to the encyclical *Laborem Exercens*, the Pope uttered some observations on this subject which must have rejoiced the hearts of his hearers. The government had always contended that there was no connection between religion and work. Both the Church and Solidarity had resisted this claim, the former by its many interventions in this sphere, and the trade union by explicitly appealing to Christian principles in its programme. As for John Paul II, he expressed his 'conviction that the social teaching of the Church is not out of harmony with the real aspirations of the workers, indeed that it goes in the same direction'. And in case this message was not clear enough, he added: 'The Christian doctrine of work postulates on the one hand solidarity among workers, and on the other hand the need for a sincere solidarity between the workers.'[52] Later on he referred to the problems of the 'authentic form' of trade unions.[53]

Last but not least, the 28 mentions of the word *man* clearly indicate the importance attached to it by the Pope. 'The first and fundamental road of the Church', according to *Redemptor Hominis*, man is that towards which all things converge.

It was inevitable that the totality of what John Paul II was able to say in Poland in 1983 should arouse some reactions. In July 1983, for example, the weekly paper of the Czech Communist Party, *Tribuna*, devoted a centre page spread to an interpretation of the Pope's pilgrimage, signed by Miroslav Borovicka. This article denounced 'that not inconsiderable part of the hierarchy and of the clergy which openly carries on activities which, according to many opponents, have nothing to do with the religious mission or the charitable activities of the Church and which display an increasing tendency to become a sort of counterweight to the government'. The author also disputed what the Pope had said about the links between the faith and the national identity: 'Poland is a socialist state, a secular state, and such it will remain. It will continue to be a loyal ally of the Soviet Union, of Czechoslovakia and of the other socialist countries, a reliable member of the Warsaw Pact and of Comecon.' He ended by rejoicing that the second journey of John Paul II to Poland had not 'introduced fresh elements of disorder' and had not 'resulted in another political earthquake' in the country.

In the same vein, the Slovak Ondrej Danyi, in an article published by *Ucitelske Noviny* in Bratislava on 11 August 1983, expressed his indignation at the 'crusade' undertaken by John Paul II and warned against 'illusory atempts to unite the Slavs on the basis of a clerical panslavism intended as the pattern for the rechristianizing of Western Europe and the main plank in an anti-communist design for unifying Europe on Christian foundations'. Nearly two years early, the author launched into a critique which he might have repeated word for word in reviewing the encyclical *Slavorum Apostoli*.

Slavorum Apostoli

The encyclical letter *Slavorum Apostoli*, dated 2 July 1985, did more than pay tribute to Saint Cyril and Saint Methodius, who had already been proclaimed co-patron saints of Europe by an apostolic letter dated 30 December 1980. It set out a definite standpoint on contemporary events and contained a call and a programme for the future. It describes a Messianic undertaking, and the solemnity of the vehicle used bears witness to the importance attributed to it by the Pope: 'The first Pope called from Poland, and hence from the heart of the Slav nations, to occupy the chair of St Peter feels *specially* impelled to do so.'[54]

For surely the observation 'Sometimes God requires of the men whom he chooses that they leave their fatherland' contains a direct reference to the personal destiny of Karol Wojtyla. Especially as the word he uses (*fatherland*) is used only once in the text, and in his other speeches the Pope is wont to give it an individual, tender connotation (*Poland, my fatherland...*). John Paul II goes on to say, 'To accept [this separation] with faith in His promise is always a mysterious and fruitful condition of progress and growth for the People of God on earth.'[55]

The Pope's intention was 'to decipher from the life and the apostolic activity of Cyril and Methodius the lessons which the wisdom of divine providence has written therein, so that they may be revealed in a new plenitude *to our age* and may bear new fruit'.[56] Thus right from the outset the Pope was stressing the exemplary nature and the contemporary impact of the work of the two evangelists, precisely because this 'work... among the Slav peoples was destined to constitute an important link in the mission entrusted by the Saviour to the universal Church until the end of time'.[57]

Exemplariness, contemporaneity, lasting significance, those are all registers of time that John Paul II explores here, calling the past to witness, evoking and invoking the future in view of present emergencies, to answer its challenges and master its turbulence. For the mission of Cyril and Methodius was performed precisely in the context of 'troubled years', 'of years of crisis in which the fatal and bitter controversy between the Churches of East and West arose and began to deepen', whereas Cyril and Methodius were on the contrary aiming to promote 'unity between East and West'.[58]

Clearly, then, this extraordinarily rich text is not intended to be simply an exercise in hagiography. Nor, of course, is it neatly summarized by the interpretation we propose to give it here. It can be read at several levels, and the one we have selected, essentially political, is far from exhausting its meaning or meanings. But on the assumption that the situation described by John Paul II in his encyclical is not really about events that took place in the ninth century, but about the contemporary political scene, the exercise has the merit of revealing the objectives that the Pope has selected and the methods by which he proposes to attain them. For it is indeed a spiritual reconquest that John Paul II has in mind: 'The threats which are piling up on humanity in our time must bring to mind the prophetic intuition of Pope John XXIII who convened the council with the purpose and the conviction that he would be able to prepare and to begin a spring and a rebirth in the life of the Church.'[59] Here we are in the realm of *faith* and of *conviction*, with *intuition* as our support.

Who are the actors referred to by John Paul II? A systematic count gives a clear predominance to the *people* (cited 49 times), followed by *man* (36 mentions) and by the *nation* (32 mentions). *Society* is referred to only 7 times, the *country* twice, and the *state* only once.

The minuscule count of one for the last-named should cause no surprise, for, as we have already seen, the state has a purely instrumental role in the Pope's opinion as expressed in his speeches.

Nor is it surprising that *Europe*, with 17 mentions, takes precedence over *the world* with 13, in a text which, after all, is mainly about the Slavs. But the counts are not very different, and this doubtless reflects the link that John Paul II sees between what happens in Europe and the shape of future developments in the world. The project that receives its start in life at European level is clearly capable of effecting fundamental changes worldwide. Indeed, John Paul II himself made this quite clear when he wrote: 'Grant also to all Europe, O most holy Trinity, that by the intercession of the two brother saints . . . she may be for the whole world an example of living together in justice and peace, mutual respect and inviolable freedom.'[60]

Justice and peace, respect for the other and freedom – these are ideals towards which humanity should strive! In this quest certain instruments are available to it: *politics* (mentioned twice), *history*, especially for the lessons to be learned from it (7 mentions), and, above all, *culture* (mentioned 18 times). In fact, a whole chapter of the encyclical ('The gospel and culture') is devoted to this subject, which seems to occupy a central place in the Pope's thought. Both as a determinant and a foundation, culture appears in John Paul II's writings to be both instrumentalized, having an operational function, and instrumentalizing, deciding and organizing human behavioural patterns. As early as the *Talk to Young People* at Gniezno in 1979, the Pope took the opportunity of explaining his thinking on this subject:

> Culture is the expression of man. It is an affirmation of his humanity. Man creates it, and in so doing he creates himself. He creates himself with the effort of his mind within him; of his thought, of his will, of his heart. . . . Culture is the expression of communication between men, of a communion of thought and a communion of action between men. It is born in the service of the common good and becomes the most basic asset of the human community.

And although religion is not altogether the same thing as culture, nevertheless there are many points of contact between them: 'Not only culture, but also faith, requires a synthesis between culture and faith . . .' A faith that is not passed on into culture is an incomplete faith, not thought through and faithfully perceived.[61] That is why, 'because of the services rendered to all the Slav peoples and nations, the work of evangelization carried out by Cyril and Methodius is, in one sense, always present in history and in the life of these peoples and nations'.[62] For Catholicism is the bearer of the cultural values of Latinity whilst at the same time weaving indissoluble ties between the Slav world and the West. John Paul II had already enlarged on this point on 20 June 1983 at Poznan: 'Ever since the beginning, on this land of the Piast and throughout Poland, the Church has been united to Rome. To Rome not only as the See of Peter, but also as a centre of culture. That is why Polish culture possesses above all the characteristic marks of Western Europe.'[63]

That the Pope regarded culture as having a crucial part to play is also evident from the development of the terms he used, which become more and more inclusive: 'The Gospel does not result in impoverishing or effacing that which all men, peoples and nations, all cultures throughout history . . .'[64] This word order is not haphazard, for it is taken up again later: 'All men, all nations, all cultures and all civilizations have a part of their own to play and a special place in God's mysterious plan and in the universal history of salvation.'[65]

Culture both serves and shapes man, but it cannot be a substitute for him; man is still the foundation: everything depends on him and leads back to him. For the progression is not a hierarchy, but a complex chain of interactions: *man* is the unit which, added together, forms the *people*, an aggregate of individuals which only becomes a *nation* by the intermediary of a *culture*. As for the highest stage, *civilization*, it is not very clear whether this represents an addition of cultures, 'the immense quantity of multicoloured stones which make up the living mosaic of the Pantocrator',[66] or a selection of that in them which most illuminates and reveals man.

A special role is of course accorded to *language*, whether in the ordinary meaning of the word, in view of the specific contribution made by Saint Cyril and Saint Methodius, or figuratively, as a means of interpersonal communication. For the task of the two evangelists was 'to proclaim the word of God . . . in a way fully compatible with the particular mentality [of Slavs] and with the specific conditions is which they were living'.[67] It is obvious that the Pope is no longer speaking about history – or about Slavs. And in fact the next sentence deals with Vatican II which, 'twenty years ago faced above all the task of awakening the Church to self-awareness and, thanks to its renewal within, giving it a new missionary impulse'. At this point the problem is to find a language understandable by all whom the Pope is addressing, starting from the realities of their own situation and capable of elucidating its meaning and pointing to the future.

What message is this language intended to convey? John Paul II seems to formulate it in his text by means of three propositions:

1 Frontiers are temporary, but the Church's message is eternal: 'The annunciation of the eternal message of peace and goodwill between peoples and nations, beyond all the frontiers which still divide our planet which is destined to be a common dwelling place for all humanity.'[68]
2 The Church has an essential part to play and this is in accordance with its nature: 'The universality of the Church is most present when she welcomes, unifies and exalts in her own special way, with a mother's tender care, every true human value.'[69]
3 There is convergence between the task that the Church takes upon itself and man's legitimate expectations: 'The Church is catholic . . . because she is able to present in all human contexts the revealed truth, the divine content of which she preserves intact, in such a way that she makes contact with the noble thoughts and just expectations of each man and each nation.'[70]

Clearly, this function and this mission are of lasting validity: 'Such a vision of the catholicity of the church . . . fits in particularly well with the theological and pastoral vision which inspired the apostolic and missionary work of Constantine the Philosopher and Methodius and which was the principle of their mission in the Slav nations.'[71] But the reference to the past is also in tension with the future, seen in relation to 'the new missionary impulse'[72] of the Church.

A comprehensible language implies a credible model. Meeting people where they are entails a refusal to import a model from abroad: Cyril and Methodius 'did not try to impose on the peoples to whom they were sent to preach either the indisputable superiority of the Greek language and the Byzantine culture or the customs and behaviour of the more advanced society in which they had been brought up'.[73] Quite the reverse. 'Their wish was to become integrated with those peoples and fully to share their lot in life'.[74] Does not this involve a risk of division, all the sadder because the foreign model appears more attractive and more dynamic: 'It is understandable that . . . any diversity was in danger of being perceived as a threat to unity . . . and that the temptation to eliminate it by resorting to various forms of coercion could become strong.'[75] Not so, replies John Paul II, because in unity between East and West 'each party brings the benefit of his own gifts to the others and to the Church'.[76] That gave the Pope the opportunity to spell out what he calls *inculturation*, that is to say, 'the embodiment of the Gospel in indigenous cultures and at the same time the introduction of these cultures into the life of the Church'.⁷⁷ Conversely, 'the older churches can and must help the young churches and peoples to mature their own identity and to make progress towards it'.⁷⁸

There can be no disputing the importance of the task of living among peoples whom one is called to convert, inventing a language for so doing, creating a culture that shall both respect local traditions and enrich the whole world, and expressing and exalting by and for this culture the formative values of the nation. John Paul II did not conceal the difficulties of such a task; he referred to them on several occasions: 'Often situations of conflict supervened in all their ambiguous, painful complexity; but Constantine and Methodius did not on that account try to escape the trial: misunderstanding, evident bad faith and at the last, for Saint Methodius, chains accepted for the love of Christ, did not deflect either of them from their firm resolve to promote and serve the good of the Slav peoples and the unity of the universal church.'⁷⁹ Or again:

> Methodius, in particular, did not hesitate to face misunderstanding, opposition and even defamation and physical persecution rather than fail in his exemplary loyalty to the Church, and to remain faithful to his duties as a Christian and a bishop . . . towards . . . this Church growing on Slav soil which he thought of as his own and which he championed, convinced of the rightness of his cause, against the ecclesiastical and civil authorities.⁸⁰

What attitude should be adopted in the face of such difficulties? The Pope advocated only one: dialogue. 'Acting thus', he wrote about Methodius, 'he, like Constantine the Philosopher, always engaged in dialogue with those who were opposed to his ideas or his pastoral initiatives and who contested their legitimacy. Because of this, he will always be a master for all who, in any age, seek to smooth out differences with full consideration for the multiform plenitude of the Church which, in accordance with the will of its Founder Jesus Christ, must always be one, holy, catholic and apostolic.'⁸¹

But there must be no time-serving or surrender in this dialogue. It must not mean that the Church gives up her right to speak out about everything that concerns her, for the sake of avoiding tension:

> It was precisely for these reasons that they found it quite natural to take a definite line in all the conflicts which at that time were disturbing the Slav societies then coming into being, bearing the full weight of the difficulties and problems which inevitably arose for peoples who were fighting for their identity against the military and cultural pressure of the new Roman Germanic empire and trying to reject patterns of living that they considered as foreign.⁸²

Is not that an accurate description of the line followed by the Polish Church over against the government? Search for dialogue and repeated affirmation of the rights of the Church. One need only substitute *Soviet* for *Roman Germanic* to find in this text the justification of the attitude that, so the Pope believes, the Catholic Church should adopt towards the authorities.

To affirm the unity of Europe and to write that 'the heritage of the Salonika brothers is and remains for [Slavs] deeper and stronger than any division',[83] was bound to upset the rulers in the Kremlin. To say that the mission of the Church is to take part in the defence of a national identity is tantamount to throwing down the gauntlet to a Soviet-type government, and indeed to the USSR itself. But John Paul II went even further when he saw in the work of Cyril and Methodius 'a decisive contribution to the building of Europe, not only in the religious Christian community but also in the spheres of its political and cultural union',[84] and 'an outstanding contribution to the formation of the Christian roots which by their strength and vitality constitute an extremely firm foundation that cannot be ignored in *any serious attempt to recreate the unity of the continent in a new way, relevant to our times*'.[85] He was thereby underlining the efficacy of religion as a political instrument of destabilization and of reconstruction.

One objection might still be raised to the Pope's address – his support for the Polish tradition of resistance to arbitrary power and the explicit reference to a Messianic project in which the Polish Pope and the Slavs are given a specific role. These might be thought to carry some risk of becoming sidetracked and perverted into nationalism, chauvinism and a feeling of superiority. But John Paul II removed this prospect with a single sentence: 'Perfect communion in love preserves the Church from all forms of particularism and ethnic exclusivism or racial prejudice, and from all nationalist arrogance.'[86]

The collection of extracts presented here contains the outline of a veritable 'programme of spiritual resistance' meant for the faithful and for the societies of Sovietized Europe. In them John Paul II concentrates the main substance of what he had already stated on several occasions, not hesitating to adopt a solemn tone when the occasion required, as when speaking to young people at Czestochowa on 18 June 1983:

> It is good that we are met together here at the hour of the call of Jasna-Gora. In the midst of the trials of the present time, in the middle of the trial your generation is undergoing, this appeal of the Millenary continues to be a way forward. This appeal contains a fundamental possibility of an outcome. Because the outcome, in all the dimensions of the word – economic, social, political – must first come at the human level. *Man cannot live with unresolved problems.*

John Paul II's third journey

The third visit made by John Paul II to his native country, from 8 to 14 June 1987, seems to have aroused rather less interest in international public opinion than the preceding ones. Could this betray a certain satiety in regard to a country which for so long had been front-page news? Or was it perhaps that there was less mileage in an event which might appear in some sense a repetition, without the pulling power either of the first visit of a Pope to a country living under a Soviet-type regime, or of the visit he made after Solidarity had been crushed? Certainly this journey bore many similarities to the pilgrimages of 1979 and 1983: there were the same huge crowds around the Pope, the same exaltation of the freedom of the Polish nation on the occasion of John Paul II's visit. So onlookers might be forgiven for having a certain feeling of *déja vu*. And yet there were so many special facets to the Pope's third visit to Poland that it may not be an exaggeration to say that in many respects it was a major event, the significance and consequences of which will be with us for a long time.

John Paul II's first visit to his native country, undertaken almost immediately after his elevation to the Holy See, had provided the opportunity to tell the world about the power of the Polish Church and to summon the Poles to conquer their fear. The words he then spoke were those of a Father proud of his children. In 1983, in a Poland that was weary, the Pope had come to bring consolation and hope, purposes worthy of the example of Christ. In 1987, celebrating man's status as a subject (*podmiotowosc*), what John Paul accented was the Spirit, as if he were trying to tell the Poles that from then onwards they should draw the faith and courage they needed to change their life from within themselves. From this point of view, it is no surprise that although the Pope met all the groups of which Polish society is composed, he should have made a special place for the intellectuals. For example, most of the speech he gave on 9 June to graduates and undergraduates at Lublin was given over to 'subjectivity', which he described as 'a problem of such crucial importance for the whole nation', and said that it

> is found everywhere, in the various spheres of work in our native land. It challenges the industrial workplace and agriculture. It challenges each family and each person. Subjectivity is born of the very nature of personal being: it belongs above all to the dignity of the human person. It is the confirmation, the verification and at the same time the demand of this dignity, whether in personal or collective life.[87]

But, he added,

society expects of its universities the consolidation of its own subjectivity, it asks that they shall demonstrate the reasons that underpin it and the initiatives that serve it. Closely linked with this is the requirement of academic freedom, meaning that universities and faculties shall be truly independent. It is just this self-government in the service of truth known and handed on which is as it were the primordial condition of the whole of society within which the universities carry out their own task.[88]

Affirming that 'the university, by its very nature, is at the service of man and of the nation',[89] and, moreover, meeting the representatives of culture and art, the Pope also paid tribute, during his address of 13 June at Czestochowa, to the 'men of letters and of other creative milieux who, by sincere work in the field of the mass media and particularly of the press, have reached out to very wide circles in society, have broken down barriers of fear, egoism, bad conduct and easy acquiescence and have borne witness to the truth'.[90]

There can be no doubt that by addressing his remarks to scientists, university personnel, artists, writers and journalists, John Paul II was trying to stress the special responsibilities resting on their shoulders, simply because of the high expectations that society had of them.[91]

As in 1979 and 1983, the beatifications that were celebrated and the tributes that were paid had quite clearly a symbolic significance. From Karolina Kozka, a young country girl killed by a Russian soldier who wanted to rape her, to Michal Kozal, bishop of Wroclawek, executed by the Nazis at Dachau, not forgetting Father Jerzy Popieluszko, murdered by the police, at whose tomb the Pope went to pray on 14 June 1987, the reference to the nation's resistance to arbitrary power was at all times explicit. Moreover, John Paul II mentioned the stewardship of Saint Stanislas on three separate occasions during his journey, citing him on 8 June, holding him up as an example in the same category as Saint Maximilian Kolbe and Monsignor Kozal on 9 June, and on 10 June at Tarnow, saying of him that 'a priest shares the lot of his nation; a priest should be among us as a witness'.

As soon as he arrived in Poland, on 8 June 1987, the Pope, a priest first and foremost, said in his speech to the government authorities, 'pray without ceasing . . . for the nation of which I always feel myself to be a son',[92] a nation as constantly on the Pope's lips as during his previous journeys. In this speech, some 1,700 words long, the nation is explicitly mentioned 16 times. This is increased to 26 if we include the 6 mentions of *fatherland*, the 4 references to *Poland*, the 3 references to the *people* and the allusion to the *Republic*. Certainly, the *state* is mentioned 11 times, but it is always subordinated to the *nation*, which is the only entity described as *independent* and *sovereign*. On this occasion, the Pope added to what he had been able to say about the function of the state on his previous visits. 'The nation is not living authentically except when it experiences itself as a subject in the entire life of the state – when it finds itself to be mistress there, when it participates in decisions by its work, its contribution.'[93] At the bishops' conference the Pope went even further; he laid down conditions for the authenticity of the state: the state 'fulfils an ethical requirement only when it is the expression of the sovereignty of the nation. In other words, when society is the responsible entity and the authentic contriver of the common good.'[94]

This gives the measure of the extent of the Pope's opposition to General Jaruzelski who, in his speech of welcome, had said that he was 'open to any realistic initiative' as long as it took account of just one 'limit': 'Polish *raison d'etat*, the acceptance of the socialist principles of our state'.[95]

Such a limitation was not acceptable to the Pope; 'Man always comes first.'[96] And, in point of fact, *man* is mentioned 18 times, making it the most frequently mentioned word, even coming before *nation*. And John Paul countered General Jaruzelski, who stressed the *peace* that the regime had brought to Poland, with another conception of peace, which can only be 'the ripe fruit of social justice: *opus justitiae pax*, and he spoke of the "special challenge" constituted by "the struggle for peace, in our own country as well".[97] Without *dignity* (referred to 4 times), without *truth* and without *justice*, there could be no *authentic freedom* (2 mentions).

The word *challenge*, like the word *subjectivity*, was a leading theme in John Paul II's speeches. He spoke at length about them to the conference of bishops:

> The twentieth century has become, also in the history of the Church, and perhaps especially in Poland, the era of a fresh challenge. After a thousand years, Christianity in Poland has had to accept the challenge contained in the ideology of dialectical Marxism; which describes all religion as a factor of alienation for man. We know this challenge. I have had personal experience of it, in this country. And the Church is experiencing it just now in different parts of the world. It is not the only challenge, but it is a very penetrating challenge. According to materialist anthropology religion is a factor that deprives man of his full humanity. . . . This can be a destructive challenge. But, after years of experience, we are bound to acknowledge that it can also be a challenge that has thoroughly roused Christians to try to find new solutions. From this point of view the challenge becomes to a certain extent a creative one.[98]

So John Paul II is speaking of a threefold challenge: a challenge to peace, a challenge to justice, and a challenge to the Church. But pre-eminently a challenge to man, since the Pope profoundly believes that:

> God [and hence also religion] . . . is still the ultimate [and final] guarantor of human beings as subjects, of the freedom of the human spirit, above all in

conditions where this freedom and this subjectivity are threatened not only in a theoretical sense but even more in a practical one, through a system and a scale of values. Through the one-sidedly technocratic ethos [or anti-ethos]. Through the diffusion of a consumerist pattern of society. Through various forms of totalitarianism of the system.[99]

As was mentioned earlier, John Paul II believes that intellectuals have a special responsibility for meeting this challenge: 'Nothing can relieve the people who live here, especially the scientists, of their responsibility in relation to the final outcome of this process in this part of Europe! And of the world! I would say: in this place of a difficult challenge.'[100]

For John Paul II was pinning his hopes not only upon the intellectuals, but on the whole of Poland. 'I have sometimes said that Poland is the country of a difficult challenge. This challenge marks the course of our history. It is also responsible for Poland's special place in the great family of nations on the continent and throughout the whole world.'[101] This was a further appearance of the Messianic themes dear to the Pope, who loses no opportunity of hailing his 'pilgrim brethren of Hungary' or the 'Slovak, Czech and Moravian brothers',[102] or of speaking about 'our Lithuanian brethren, makers of our common history [who] are celebrating at Vilnius and throughout the country the 600th anniversary of the baptism of their nation'.[103]

For John Paul II, 'Lublin has not only a Polish but a European dimension, without doubt a universal one'.[104] And he added:

> [Lublin] possesses a historic eloquence. It is not only the eloquence of the 'Union of Lublin' [which in 1569 sealed the union of Poland and Lithuania] but of everything that goes to make up the historical, cultural, ethical and religious context of this union. All the great historical process of the encounter between West and East. Their mutual attraction and repulsion. Repulsion – but also attraction. This process is a part of our whole history – maybe of yesterday more than today; yet it is not possible to separate yesterday from today. At all times the nation is living its own history, and the Church in the nation as well: and this process has not ended.[105]

And so a threefold task of evangelization is laid upon Poland – first within herself, then in Eastern Europe, and lastly in the whole of Europe: 'The whole of the Church is missionary', said the Pope on 14 June in Warsaw in his homily for the beatification of Michal Kozal. 'The whole Church, everywhere. Those of you who do not take up service in the mission field, remember that our own country, Poland, is still in need of re-evangelization – as is the whole of Christian Europe. After centuries and millennia, always and afresh. The whole of Europe has become the continent of a huge new challenge for the Gospel.'[106] Yet again he speaks the word. 'Go', cries

John Paul II, 'and may missionary enthusiasm grow on Polish soil. . . . Go, and take to others the heritage of a thousand years on Polish soil, and share it with others.'[107]

We cannot doubt that the Pope addressed this summons first to himself. There is an inescapable parallel between Queen Jadwiga and Karol Wojtyla. When John Paul II addressed her, he said:

> You have not yet loved to the end. The term of your love is beyond, beyond the bounds of what your girl's heart bore here, in Wawel Castle, on the throne of Poland. The bound of your love goes beyond. God has placed you amidst peoples and nations. He has called you to embrace with your heart their destinies, their aspirations and their struggles. *To divine God's plans concerning Poland, Lithuania and the Russian lands.*[108]

The former archbishop of Cracow too had been called by God to occupy a throne 'amidst peoples and nations'. And confessing 'the truth about the Eucharist', the Pope declared himself to be in union with 'The Church that is at Rome and Antioch and at Jerusalem and at Alexandria and at Constantinople', and immediately thereafter with the Church 'which is in Lithuania and Byelorussia, in the Ukraine and at Kiev, and in the territories of Great Russia and of our Slav (and also non-Slav) brothers to the south of the lands visited in the past by the holy brothers Cyril and Methodius'.[109] John Paul II devoted less space to enumerating Europe, North and South America, Africa, Australia and Asia . . .

The Pope and the general (continued)

One of the high points of John Paul II's third visit to Poland will indisputably have been his meetings, both private and official, with General Jaruzelski.[110] All observers agree that the latter showed far more assurance than he had been able to muster in 1983. At that time, writes Jan Krauze:

> in uniform, but with his legs trembling uncontrollably, [he] was bent on justifying himself to the Pope, on explaining why he had imposed martial law on his country. . . . This time the general wore civilian dress; only his hands trembled a little, but the tone was that of a self-confident man, assuming not only his role as head of state but also the essential role of head of the Party and voicing ideological themes without embarrassment.[111]

In contrast to 1983, General Jaruzelski had no hesitation in resorting to cynicism. Thus, in his speech of welcome, he said to John Paul II that 'in visiting Gdansk and Szczecin, His Holiness will not be in a foreign country but in the land of his birth. It was the people's Poland that recovered wide access to the Baltic.'[112] Or when in his farewell speech on 14 June he tried to appropriate for himself the term 'subjectivity' so often used by John Paul II: 'In the last few days [Poland] has been, as is often the case, the victim of foreign manipulations which have wronged the good sense of our nation. We have our own way, a way of renewal, of democratization, of reform, reinforcing man's subjectivity, which is in line with the far-reaching changes in the world of socialism.'[113] But the Polish leader overstepped the bounds of good taste when, in the same speech, he tried to turn the word *solidarity* to his own advantage: 'May the word "solidarity" be wafted from our Polish soil to all the masses of people who are still suffering from racism and neo-colonialism, violence and unemployment, exploitation and intolerance.'[114]

General Jaruzelski had, it is true, every reason to be touchy, for besides avoiding the traps so carefully laid for him, the Pope had adopted a high profile, speaking out on many occasions more clearly than ever before about the internal situation in Poland and taking a stand in terms that may very well have jolted even some members of the episcopal hierarchy. We are of course referring here to the two speeches given on 11 and 12 June 1987 at Gdynia and Gdansk respectively, on the Baltic coast where the movements of 1970 and 1980 had had their origin. At Gdynia, for example, the Pope proclaimed loud and clear: 'In the name of the future of man and of humanity it was necessary to pronounce this word solidarity. Today this word is breaking like a great wave across the world.'[115]

If we analyse the farewell speeches of General Jaruzelski and John Paul II in June 1987 in the same way as the 1983 speeches, we find they contain a number of constants. Just as in the earlier journey, Poland acquired a more affective dimension in the mouth of the Pope, well expressed by the phrase 'my native land'. John Paul II never used the official designation 'People's Republic of Poland'. In the same way, General Jaruzelski was always at pains to distance the Pope as far as possible from the *real* Poland. 'In a few moments Your Holiness will say his farewells to the fatherland and will carry its likeness in your heart. But you cannot take with you our real problems. The nation remains here, between the Bug and the Oder,'[116] the implication being: and I'm responsible for it. And a systematic listing of the names used by the two protagonists shows how hard the head of the Polish Communist Party tried to monopolize the reality. The two main logical series that can be extracted from the vocabulary he employed are, first, an enumeration of the values of order and, second, a thorough description of an extremely depressing reality. Conversely, the two logical series that preponderated in the Pope's speeches were the expression of a considerable straining towards the future and consequently the recital of the values of movement, and a stress laid on the factors that could bring about this movement.

Thus, General Jaruzelski made use of a whole range of words to paint reality (*misfortune, injustice, scorn, violence, fear, intolerance, exploitation, spoliation, unemployment, racism, neo-colonialism*), whereas the Pope employed only two, and these were much more neutral (*problem*, *difficulty*). And he countered the head of state, who stressed *security* (2 mentions), *responsibility* (2 mentions) and then, pell-mell, *authority*, *morality*, *maturity*, *stabilization*, *work*, by affirming his faith in *progress* (8 mentions) and his expectations for the future (*aspirations*, *energy*, *courage*, *perseverance*). Lastly, the Pope replied to General Jaruzelski's use of the words *socialism* (twice), *truth* (3 times), *good sense*, *development*, *renewal* and *reform* with the words *truth* (3 mentions), *dignity*, *humanity*, *freedom*, *beauty*, *justice*, *love*, *peace*. Thus it is hardly surprising that the word that recurs most frequently as such in the Pope's discourse should be the word *man* (referred to 16 times as against General Jaruzelski's 4), and that the Pope made no use whatever of the word *state*, which is one of the 7 words most frequently used by General Jaruzelski. We see, then, that, as in 1983, the Pope used two words, *fundamental* (twice) and *true* against General Jaruzelski's *real* (used 3 times) and *necessary* (3 times) (to which we might add *important*, *superior*, *constructive*, *vital*, etc.). The Pope did not hesitate to lecture the state when he felt it necessary, in particular as regards alcoholism: 'One cannot "sell" man for an immediate, base profit, obtained by speculating on man's weaknesses and his vices. It is impermissible to exploit and increase human weakness. It is impermissible to permit the degradation of man, the family or society when we have a responsibility before history concerning them!'[117]

But John Paul II was chiefly concerned to call into question in the name of truth the official doctrine of 'security before all things',[118] by confronting it with an analysis based on the duties of the state towards man:

> Man is not alone, he lives with others, by means of others, for others. All human existence has a communal dimension of its own, and a social dimension. It cannot signify a limitation of the human person, of his talents, his potentialities, his tasks. It is in the interest of the social community itself that each person should have an adequate area of personal freedom. *One of the fundamental tasks of the state is to create this space*, so that each person may, through the medium of work, develop himself, develop his personality and his vocation. This development of the person, this space for the person in the life of society is at the same time the condition of the common good. *If man is deprived of these possibilities, if the organization of the collective life contains excessively strict constraints on human potentialities and initiatives – even if this is done in the name of some social motivation – well, that is, alas, against society. Against its good, against the common good!*[119]

John Paul II maintained that these problems were nowhere more meaningful than in the relationship of man and society to work:

> Work must not be treated – anywhere at any time – as nothing more than a commodity, for man cannot be a commodity for man; he must be a subject. He

enters into work through all his humanity and all his subjectivity. In the life of a society, work manifests the whole dimension of man's subjectivity, and also the subjectivity of society itself, made up of workers. It is therefore important to see all human rights in relation to human work, and to satisfy them all.[120]

Consequently, John Paul II lost no opportunity of reminding his hearers that 'man always comes first' and that the state cannot subordinate his rights to any 'higher interests'. Speaking to the conference of bishops, he said:

Man is a person and the subject of his own actions; the subject of morals, the subject of history. He is not simply the 'reflection of existing socioeconomic relationships', nor is he only an epiphenomenon of the economy. Even in relation to the economy he is a subject and a creator, unless we wish to deprive him of his subjectivity and his creative initiative, in an area so important to the life of men, societies and nations.[121]

It comes as no surprise that John Paul II formed a very favourable impression of the workers' movement of 1980: 'The Gdansk agreements will go down in the history of Poland as the very expression of this growing awareness among working men of the whole of the social and moral order on Polish soil. They were first conceived in the tragic month of December 1970. And today they still remain a task to be accomplished.'[122] But the Pope did more than simply pay this tribute to an organization that was now officially dissolved. He solemnly reaffirmed the legitimacy of the action that had led to the formation of the trade union: '[Man] has the right, as a worker, to be self-governing. One function of trade unions is to be an expression of this right – to be "independent, self-governing" trade unions, as was underscored at Gdansk.'[123]

But John Paul II's main concern was to ensure the long-term viability of this action by enunciating a 'philosophy of solidarity' embracing much more than just the problems of work:

Solidarity means a way of existing in the human plurality, for example within a nation, in unity, respecting all differences, all divergences such as exist between men. Hence it is unity in plurality, in other words pluralism. All of this is involved in the concept of solidarity. It is a way in which the human plurality, larger or smaller, can exist for all of humanity, for a particular nation. A way of existing in a unity worthy of man.[124]

To make matters even clearer, and still in his challenging mode, John Paul II recalled that solidarity has to be won:

Solidarity must come before struggle. I add: solidarity is also a call to fight – but never against fellow men. It is not a fight that treats the other as an enemy, an adversary, and does its best to destroy him. It is a fight for man, for his rights, for his true progress: a fight for a more adult form of human life. The fact is that human life on earth becomes more human when there is government with truth, freedom, justice and love.[125]

It was on these same four words that the Pope concluded his third pilgrimage to Poland, when he said:

> ... [the] four fundamental human rights, which are the basis of real peace on earth. They are: the right to the truth, the right to freedom, the right to justice and the right to love. Each of these rights speaks to a deep-seated need in human nature and to the dignity of the human person. Each is a condition of true progress, not only of the person, but also of society. And not only spiritual progress, but also material and economic progress.[126]

Conclusion

> What would happen if one day – one fine day – Poland were to recover the freedom of its political life? Would its marvellous spritual tension still persist . . .? Would the churches be deserted? . . . What we have succeeded in saving, in preserving from destruction and annihilation, and even in raising above the threat like a great, beautiful wall, that which was born in response to the dangerous challenge of totalitarianism, would all that cease to exist on the day when the threat was lifted?[1]

These questions, raised by Adam Zagajewski, are by no means only theoretical ones. Georges Mink, summing up the results of surveys, pointed out that no increase in religious observance had been noted, but that civil society's recourse to religious symbols strengthened the position of the clergy. This brings us to an apparent paradox: the Church is becoming secularized and is losing something of that which used to distinguish it, while at the same time becoming a more potent symbol. Mink says that, 'The Church has moved closer to the nation, the nation has not been absorbed by the church.'[2] Indeed, one may wonder whether the ambiguities in the status of Catholicism in Polish society, and more generally in the context of a Soviet-type political regime, do not turn it into a *civil religion*, in the meaning attributed to the term by Robert Bellah in his well-known essay published in 1967;[3] that is to say, a series of politico-religious symbols and rituals related to the history and the future of the nation. That at least is what Ewa Morawska believes. She has no hesitation in writing that, 'the romantic faith of Poland is a civil religion, constituted and reconstituted through the prolonged conflict between a civil society persistently coming to new birth and a regime imposed from abroad'.[4]

These observations would appear to support what Marcel Gauchet writes in his *Désenchantement du monde* that, 'supposing that by a miracle the Polish people should shortly be liberated from Soviet oppression, it is reasonable to suppose that Catholicism, by reason of its role in safeguarding the identity of the nation, would have a preponderance of spiritual power with the government. . . . Nonetheless this would be *an atheist society* composed of and governed by a *majority of believers*'.[5]

For there is a striking overall resemblance between the broad trends in the development of Christianity in Eastern and East-Central Europe and those that are observable in Western Europe. There is the same interiorization and intellectualization of the faith, the same striving towards a community Church, the same distancing from the moral teaching of the Church, the same preference given to religion lived in small groups. This being so, what is peculiar to Christianity in Eastern Europe has to be sought in its relationship to the political and social system, and its socially animating character may be explained by the fact that it is called upon to put forward an alternative to this system.[6]

There would appear to be a dialectical link between the social movements in East-Central Europe and the 'breeding grounds' of these movements, veritable informal networks enabling the original ones to be reproduced over time, to withstand repressive measures, and in fact to reproduce themselves cyclically. Clearly, the religious language and symbols used by these movements express both processes proper to the field of religion and also needs and tensions of a political nature. If, as empirical research would seem to indicate (Tomka in Hungary, Jerschina and Ulasinski in Poland), religion means freedom to identify and hence the social construction of enclaves in society recognizing such belonging, it is then evident that the function of religion is to produce socially a parallel democratic society within totalitarian political systems. The collective movements appear as indicators of inconsistencies and diffuse, underground social trends, as it were assembly areas; that is to say, like a submerged network of groups, circles, solidarity circuits, formal and informal structures. Furthermore, it is above all among the new generations that the socio-religious groups provide the opportunity of religious experience, the result of a personal choice, lived as authentic, directed towards the community and committed to creating a new order in society, founded on a new ethic advanced as an alternative to the dominant political order. In the light of these stirrings it is not difficult to understand the intensification of ideological propaganda and the adoption of measures for promoting atheism: Soviet-type power does not conceal its disquiet at the prospect of a religious renewal, the signs of which are all around. At the conclusion of the 17th congress of the Czechoslovak Communist Party at the end of March 1986, the militants were urged 'to intensify their propaganda campaign based on scientific atheism'. As for the Polish authorities, they did not hesitate to introduce into the school curricula a course[7] dealing with the 'science of religion' (*religioznawstwo*). In the Soviet Union, at the 27th congress, although Mr Gorbachev referred to 'reactionary nationalist and religious survivals', the main anti-religious (especially anti-Islam) oration was given by I.B. Usmankhodzaev, general secretary of the Uzbekistan Communist Party. A few months later, on 28 September 1986, *Pravda* published an article that aroused a good deal of comment, on the need to reinforce atheist propaganda and to develop socialist ceremonies; this article prepared the ground for an address by E.K. Ligachev to professors in the humanities, in which he earnestly bade them combat Islam, Catholicism and the Ukrainian Greek Catholic Church; the latter Church was particularly violently criticized in 1986 when the Orthodox Church was celebrating the fortieth anniversary of the merger of the Uniate Church with the Russian Orthodox Church. Similarly, in Bulgaria on 20 February 1986 the plenum of the central committee of the CPB put forward measures for consolidating atheist propaganda, and these were ratified at the 13th congress of the Party on 2 April 1986; furthermore, the politburo document on atheism, which first appeared in 1957, was republished in full in 1986 in *Ateistichna Tribuna* (1986, no. 1).

This hardening of Soviet-type government has at least the advantage of showing its true colours. As Alain Besançon wrote, 'We may even say that atheism is probably the best – or the least bad – thing about Leninism, for it is the only point at which it is not lying.' However, this statement is followed by an expression of disquietude:

> Until now Leninist communism has not claimed to be Christian. But it might discover that it is to its advantage to give up this costly openness and to integrate Christianity as it already claims to integrate science and philosophy. . . . It would be wise for the Church to keep a careful watch on these so-called 'dialogues' between communists and Christians which have no prospects except this decisive progress of the ideology which it can no longer achieve under its own power, although many religious zealots are trying to help it to do so.[8]

For there is a danger that Marxism and Catholicism might plunge into an identity crisis from which they will undoubtedly emerge transformed into 'vague forms, characteristic of ideological disintegrations', to borrow the phrase of the Yugoslav sociologist Jakov Jukic.[9]

Nowhere is this danger clearer than in Hungary, because of the strategies for which both Church and state have opted. And it is no accident that Budapest was chosen as the venue for the meeting organized from 8 to 10 October 1986 between fifteen Catholic theologians and philosophers and fifteen Marxist intellectuals, most of whom came from East European countries. Nevertheless, Father Jean-Yves Calvez, writing about this gathering, said that, 'nowadays there is not the slightest misunderstanding about the nature and development of Marxism or of Christianity', adding,

'At Budapest, we were looking at men who had lost some of their assurance.'[10]

How could it be otherwise? True, the cardinal-primate of Czechoslovakia, Monsigner Tomasek, deplored during 1986 that 70 per cent of Catholic priests were forbidden to practise their profession or had been arrested. Despite that, more than 100,000 people took part in the pilgrimage to Levoca in Slovakia in July.[11] Moreover, statements by the primate are published in the opposition press,[12] and the attitude of believers shows less fear in the face of repression. For example, in May 1986 a letter drawn up on behalf of Slovak Catholic youth demanding the cessation of measures against the Church was sent to Gustav Husak, at that time head of state and of the Party.

Nor is Czechoslovakia an isolated case. A similar development is observable in Eastern Europe, though its size and importance naturally differ from country to country.[13] In an open letter written from prison and addressed to the Party leaders on the eve of the Party congress, Adam Michnik wrote a letter entitled: 'Do not make religion into a synonym for opposition.' In it he said:

> It is not hard to foresee the consequences of this state of affairs. They are: the disappearance of the separation between the sacred and the secular, an increase in passion and intolerance on both sides, and the destruction of even the slimmest chance of a dialogue. For, remember, the present conflict can be transformed into a dialogue, since politics by its very nature is an area of compromise. But a religious conflict is a place of moral witness, making compromise hard to achieve.[14]

For as soon as religion can no longer be confined, localized in a place acknowledged to be its own, it acquires an autonomy that enables it to be the bearer of directly political aspirations or demands, or to associate itself with them. In these circumstances the observation made by Michnik in *Kosciol, Lewica, Dialog* ('The Church and the Left – the Polish Dialogue'),[15] that religious freedom is inseparable from freedom as such, is fully vindicated. Religion becomes a synonym for freedom, since fighting for religious freedom becomes a fight for all freedoms.

In an article that was widely read in Poland, Jerzy Turowicz set out to define the limits of the Church's involvement in politics:

> The Church in its concern for the true good of man cannot confine itself to proclaiming its doctrine and communicating it to the faithful. It also has the right and the duty to react to events and situations, to judge and condemn injustice and violence, to stand up for the offended and oppressed, to call for justice and respect for human dignity and human rights, in particular man's right to be a subject, to be able to forge his own destiny. . . . The Church will never give up this critical function with respect to secular society, because it is of the very

essence of its mission in the world. In the exercise of this function, the Church has the right and the duty to express its opinion about the problems of political life, to issue requests, to protest or even condemn or denounce.[16]

Here Turowicz is repeating some of the things on which Patocka laid stress, when he tries to show that although the Church cannot wash its hands of events in the field of politics, this does not necessarily mean that it must take part in politics. Its role, as guarantor and guardian of values that are obligatory for all people, is to point out where the boundary comes, where politics must stop. The violent attacks on this thesis in official circles in Poland or Czechoslovakia are proof of how impossible governments find it to accept that there may be an autonomous area in which its writ does not run, or values to which it must yield place. This being so, it is clear that it is not the Church that introduces the confusion between the religious and the political areas of life, but the state. It is the state that, by refusing to leave the Church alone and make a clear distinction between religion and the secular world, compels the Church to enter the ground of compromise, a step which, as Michnik observed, is certainly not part of the Church's vocation. At that point religious questions are bound to become a political problem as well, for there is no longer a specifically religious field. When it forms part of an overall field of force which embraces both political and social, economic and cultural questions, religion appears both as a potential agent of opposition and a place where this opposition may find expression and grow.[17] Moreover, as we have said, religion may even be turned against the Church itself, caught in the play of very complex interactions, in which it advances and retreats, fights against the government and treats with it, utilizes civil society and is utilized by that society, provides symbols, which in the end partially escape from it, contests the system in the name of religious values, supports it in the interest of its own survival, and to ensure the triumph of these values in the future is challenged in the name of those same values.

Forty years after a Soviet-type regime came to power in East-Central Europe, it would appear obvious that all the dreams of annihilating or manipulating religion cherished by the government are as far from realization as ever. Religion has manifested too great a flexibility and an astonishing aptitude for springing up again where least expected. In a recent book, Raymond Boudon noted that:

> The purportedly comprehensive syntheses emanating from science are characterized by great rigidity and by the fact that by their very nature they cannot easily escape being negated by reality. . . . That is probably one of the reasons why none of them has survived, except Marxism. Extrapolating some remarks by Robert Bellah, one might on the contrary suggest that religious syntheses, by the very nature of the language games they use, and in particular

by the fact that these introduce supernatural elements, have greater capacities for transformation and adaptation.[18]

This may lead on to speculation about the deeper motivations of Soviet-type government. Would it not be simpler for it to give up all desire to repress religion and the Church? In his open letter, Michnik posed this question and suggested a reply:

> What are the professional anti-clericals up to? Lies make no difference: they are out to bring back the forms of extreme oppression of the totalitarian dictatorship – to transform the political conflict between the totalitarian apparatus of power and society into a conflict between the state and the Church; to give social and political conflicts the external forms and the illusion of being religious conflicts. They are seeking a pretext for launching a police attack against the only independent institution in Poland.[19]

Naturally the police are not the only instrument available to the government, for which the ideal would certainly still be to place a strict control on the Church while preserving the appearance of full self-government. This is clear from the situation in Hungary where the succession of Cardinal Lekai, who died on 30 June 1986, partly hinged on the independence of the Church *vis-à-vis* the goverment, which was trying to impose a candidate who would enable it to retain the Josephist system it had managed to install more than a decade previously. As for the Vatican, moved by the criticisms from the mass of believers, in particular by the 'base communities',[20] it would doubtless have preferred the new primate to have a more 'combative' image.

But the management by the Vatican of a situation as complex and diversified as that of Eastern and East-Central Europe cannot be described as homogeneous. Caught between the constraints of normalizing diplomacy and the demands of the spiritual offensive carried on by John Paul II, the attitude of Rome is not easily grasped at first glance. There are various hints suggesting that a wide-ranging process of rethinking is under way, covering both the succession of the primate of Hungary and the official visit of the Pope to Poland in June 1987,[21] or the visit that the Pope has long wished to pay to the Soviet Union.[22] The invitation received by the primate of Poland to go to Moscow and the publication in the *Literaturnaya Gazeta*[23] of an interview that he gave would lend credence to this hypothesis.

Obviously no firm conclusions are in order. Too many factors would be involved, and too many situations are still developing, for such an attempt to be possible. Nevertheless, it is hard to visualize a government of the Soviet type giving up its design to eradicate religion; consequently, the main lines of analysis enumerated here are likely to retain their validity for some considerable time.

Conclusion 177

In a report submitted to the International Conference on the Sociology of Religions, Srdan Vrcan, a professor at Split University, rehearsed three possible ways in which religion might develop in socialist societies: a Bulgarian scenario, which does not call for extended treatment here,[24] a Hungarian scenario, which the author describes as a certain desecularization of social life without immediate or direct political consequences (or without any increase in the politicization of religion), and a Polish scenario, of which he said that 'the obvious and direct politicization of religion [there] was not simply a distant consequence of the religious renewal, or purely coincident with it; it has been an essential part of it'.[25]

This redeployment of religion far beyond the recognized area traditionally assigned to it can be easily explained. The enterprise announced by John Paul II is political *because* it is Messianic, because it advances a global alternative whose power of attraction is drawn both from the *sign* that the circumstances of Karol Wojtyla's birth constitute and from actual developments in the societies of East-Central Europe. It is clear, as Michel de Certeau observed in a discussion of the book by Maria-Isaura Pereira de Queiroz on Messianic movements in Latin America,[26] that:

> religion provides an overall symbolization of their sickness to dispersed people, all the more separated from one another because their common references are broken and they have reacted to the pressure of a foreign culture without order, without common resources, and without any means of compensating for the anomie and disintegration. Whether it be egalitarian, eschatological or revolutionary, a new use of religion has to do with the totality of human experience. Religious language provides a disarray (which has often remained subconscious) with an outlet and, as it were, a light which illuminates the nature of the problem experienced; it is a question of the whole.[27]

There is no doubt that in this process of recombining a broken wholeness, religion enables a fresh integration to be achieved. It enables the differences that have emerged from the historical process to be transcended, and the breaks *incidentalized* by incorporating them into a continuity that is indeed deeper but, above all, coherent, instrumentalized and marked out with guiding values.

At this point religion is both a radical critique of the present, a reminder of a historic past pregnant with the imagined meaning of the national history, and the agent of a social enterprise that is proclaimed and produced by its means. First of all it does something to time, for Messianism always proclaims itself to be a return to *archaic* values, so as to distance itself from the present, and to project itself into the future, with the object of defining a solution to the questions that have been raised.

In his autobiography, Lech Walesa provides a fascinating illustration of this process, in a passage that is worth quoting at length, for the Nobel Peace Prize, starting with the

> feeling that what was now happening was not simply a *historical necessity* but a *chance of revolution*, we found a new formula, the resultant of the fusion of several elements: religion, patriotism, stereotype of the 'working class – yes, that tradition as well. . . . It was a kind of 'revolution on the knees' with prayer, chaplet and mass. Prayer protected us, but we increased its importance; it had ceased to have anything to do with devotion. When we sang *Kiedy ranne wstaja zorze* ('When dawn breaks') we were thinking of the Poland of yesteryear, of this country of good people who cared for their country, we were expressing nostalgia, the wish to be like them, to show ourselves devoted to this earth, to stand up for her. . . . We changed Poland then. Since that time it has become a country in which is sung *Boze cos Polske* ('Lord, who hast saved Poland') not only in the churches but everywhere else, even in the factories and offices where it has been possible to say mass. We have brought the Church out of the museum to which propaganda had relegated it, and in this way we have shown that we are not just tenants but co-proprietors. That too happened, nothing was able to halt it; they could do nothing against that.[28]

Everything in this extremely complex text is worth underlining – the idealization of the past, to be understood as indicated above, or the instrumentalization of religion, utilized as a sign, a way of distancing and a vehicle in which to return to the assault. But the main point appears to be the realization by the Solidarity leader that the desovietization of Poland was irreversible; in other words, that civil society (the main actor here, make no mistake) had reoccupied the political field once and for all. Lech Walesa, whom nobody would suspect of hostility to the Church, even concealed hostility, had no hesitation in writing: 'We brought the Church out . . .' And it was through this action that the reality of a Poland defined as *ours* was forged.

This is a far cry from what 'consensualist' thinkers would describe as a transaction system between the necessary monism of the state and the real pluralism of society. Such a presentation errs by reductionism, in that it freezes once and for all the give and take between government and society and locates both of them, not to say the Church as well, in places wrongly regarded as fixed.

Moreover, Walesa is very explicit on this point, when he says: 'These were the problems that faced us: which Poland do we need? Which one is possible?' And when he says that the situation was

> the first confrontation with totalitarianism that had reached a certain stage in its development, but a totalitarianism limited by the existence of the Church, the existence of private individual farms, by the historical consciousness of the

population, and by the presence in the Vatican of a Polish Pope and by his explicit reminder that Poland is a part of Europe and its Christian heritage.²⁹

Here again, the Church is both a sign and an instrument, at the heart of a system of multiple transactions, in which each partner, in search of an identity in constant flux because it was never *self*-defined but always *in relation to* another, pursues its own interests, it being understood that this process is not linear, that it may make common cause with other similar processes, or oppose them, and finally that there is no end to the process. We can then understand how Walesa could say:

> We simply are not interested in politics as practised by the parties. Take power, re-establish order by a new government installed by us? No! Better a profound change in the present government, because there is no guarantee that another one would be better and we have already had experience of similar situations. What had to be done was to compel the authorities to take account of the aspirations of the people, to create protective machinery such as to forestall the degenerescence of the government, to prevent it from ignoring people's existence, especially that of the underdog.³⁰

Such a scheme is undeniably an application of what Walesa calls the 'wisdom of the Church', which:

> accepting the rules laid down for the game, fills them with its own content and thus gains some ground, even if at the outset this seems to be nothing but quagmire: the land is ceded for the preservation of the Holy Peace, in the belief that nothing can ever be built on it. That is how the Polish Church has proceeded since the end of the war: such was the line of Stefan Wyszynski. He took slanted promises and agreements as if they were good money and, starting from there, erected strong buildings.³¹

But apart from a pure question of method, the bonds between Solidarity as a social movement and the Church are quite understandable, since the very ambivalence of a Messianic message makes it possible to incorporate what other sources are saying. Clearly the Church's objective in reinterpreting the Catholic tradition is to consolidate its positions or to gain fresh ground. From this point of view, its objective alliance with the secular opposition could have been interpreted by the latter as mere opportunism. In the same way, the Church would be and is justified in querying the motivations and real intentions of some of its 'travelling companions', who only refrain from criticizing it for tactical reasons. And yet that is probably not the important point. The ambivalence referred to is primarily an affirmation of the necessarily dominant nature of spiritual things.

The word *necessarily* is employed deliberately here. For as we see it, the problem is not, in East-Central Europe, to take the measure of an alleged 'religious renewal', of a 're-enchantment of the world'; far from that, it is to explain the felt need of a desacralization, or, more accurately, a postponement of politics. That is certainly nothing new, in a part of the continent in which membership of a nation was much more a matter of a *destiny*, in the words of Adam Mickiewicz already quoted, than the exercise of civic rights. The idea, widely held in Eastern Europe, that the only political struggle to be carried on in a Soviet-type system is the defence of human rights may appear to be a throwback to this tradition. Indeed, in an analysis of the nineteenth century Norman Davies was able to write:

> What the romantic patriot and the pious Catholic had in common was without doubt belief in the primacy of things spiritual. . . . Those who were more patriot than Catholic demanded action; their brothers and sisters, perhaps more Catholic and less patriot, preached moderation. But all unhesitatingly accepted the idea that the key to the future of the country and the object of their life lay in the exercise of spiritual mastery.[32]

No doubt we have moved on since then: any enterprise embodying a new pattern is bound to place that pattern at the summit of the hierarchy of existing patterns, and furthermore, Solidarity has made it quite clear that the establishment of a Western-style socioeconomic system was for Poles neither a panacea nor even a prospect that would be unreservedly welcomed.

Hence at this point Messianism, whether purely ecclesiastical or clearly laicized, as in the case of Solidarity, is aiming more or less explicitly at *inventing* what might be called a 'third way', if the term did not already have historical connotations. In any event, it is quite clear that neither the West nor the East are seen as models by John Paul II, though he does not place them on an equal footing. But the Pope would no doubt agree with the remark made by Jung at the end of the 1950s:

> What [Western man] does not see is that it is his own vices, which he has disguised under the mask of good manners at the international level, which the communist world is flinging back in his face shamelessly and methodically. What the West has tolerated, though secretly, with a slight feeling of shame (diplomatic falsehoods, systematic trickery and veiled threats) is dished out to it openly in large helpings by the East, causing our hackles to rise. It is the grimacing face of his own 'shadow' that Western man sees leering at him from the other side of the iron curtain.[33]

It was in line with this train of thought that Gyorgy Konrad suggested that the East–West conflict should be bypassed by the *mediation-invention* of Europe, a process whereby the old continent should (re)discover its identity, beyond the scission that followed the Second World War, in the very act of implementing this identity:[34]

> If there is a Soviet ideology and an American ideology, why could there not be a European ideology? Nobody else has a better prospect of exercising influence over the two superpowers. It is for Europe to induce them to engage in an intelligent dialogue, to bring the Russian and American élites together, and to help influential people in Russia and America to learn to talk to each other without the prejudgements caused by propaganda, without the wild talk of demagoguery, and without this primitive yen to score points off the other side.[35]

Naturally this process would be a minefield of ambiguities. For surely religious renewal actually depends upon politicization of religion, inasmuch as religion generates a *mission* or is linked to one. That, at any rate, was what Michel de Certeau suggested when he stated that 'the use of religious language would be characterized by misunderstanding; it would work in a different way from the purported way; it would conceal a different reality from the reality it proclaimed; it would have a dual meaning, either political or else made up of a different religious experience, and this implicit meaning would not be the same as that which it explicitly affirmed'.[36]

However obvious the remark may seem, this would make it extremely difficult to determine what was in the religious sphere, and what in the political. This is true, incidentally, of other sociopolitical contexts: Otto Maduro's[37] writings on liberation theology in Central America or Latin America show that the way in which Christian base communities develop is closely related to the extent to which the existing government practises suppression. For instance, such communities have not spread as much in Mexico, Costa Rica or Venezuela as they have in other countries too numerous to mention here.

The parallel can be taken even further: without forgetting what sets the Catholic Church quite apart from other Churches, namely the existence of the Vatican, but with all other things being equal, some of the observations made here concerning the relations between politics and religion seem susceptible of adaptation to situations pertaining in Islamic countries. For example, many observers have claimed to detect some similarities between the revolution in Iran and Solidarity. In both cases, religion constituted a symbolic vehicle for expressing the aspirations and the differing, heterogeneous and at times opposed interests of social groups which, though disparate, were all animated by a profound unease about a regime seen as illegitimate, or at least as representing values with which civil society did not identify. This search for an identity did not, of course, eventuate in the same way, and furthermore it is certain that Cardinal Wyszynski had no plan to take power himself in the way that Imam Khomeini did. But whether we are thinking of Poland or of Turkey, about which Olivier Carré speaks, it was agreed 'with regard to religious matters and religions, that secularization, not to mention irreligion and atheism, is always involved in modernization. It is even this uncontested necessary condition which allows the big misinterpretation . . . about Ibn Khaldoun: it was thought that the *rational* is inevitably opposed to the religious'. The author goes on:

> Let us not dwell on this, except to support what Turner said about secularization in Turkey during the twenties and thirties: contrary to what most writers on politics think, the example of modernization in Turkey under Mustafa Kemal Ataturk does not prove that Weber's idea that secularization, which is the necessary social product of modern capitalism and of the Protestant work ethic for this world, also necessarily always applies completely and worldwide to this *Brave New World* with its well-known motto: "Community, identity, stability".[38]

The work done by Zbigniew Wierzbicki with regard to the village of Zmiaca in the south of Poland has shown the symbolic link existing for peasants between the fight against secularization of schools imposed by the government and the defence of private ownership of land. The author demonstrates the integrating effect of the conflict between the village community and the authorities in the 1950s on the dual question of religion in schools and land collectivization, and 'the considerable influence of the curé, who was the local authority in religious and moral matters.[39] This influence was of course all the greater because the priest himself was no longer seen as a landowner, owing to government action taken against Church property, and because he was the target of open hostility from the government. It is astonishing to see the extent to which the conclusions arrived at by Olivier Roy from his researches in Afghanistan could be applied to the case of the Polish village without a great effort of transposition. In fact, he observes:

> The appeal to Islam as a counterweight to arbitrary state action has long been known, but it has once more assumed great importance since the state commenced a process of secularization in 1924, and the two are identified. The marginalization of the *ulema* drives them away from the seats of power, and hence of corruption, and gives them an aura of honesty that not all of them would have assumed if they had held public office. Moreover, decisions of the state are perceived as tyrannical, because they take away from the peasant the control of all his activities. Intellectuals explain the rejection of reforms by the peasants as a consequence of their alienation, whereas strictly speaking the peasant feels himself alienated by the state's determination to rethink the relationship of the peasant to the productive process.[40]

Similarly, there is an obvious parallel between the Islamic plan, as given out and tried in the Maghreb, for example, and that of the underground Church in Czechoslovakia, for example, when one reads what Bruno Etienne says, that it:

> is certain that at the present time in the Maghreb there is a coincidence between the *Da'wa* [the call (preaching)], a political plan, and the *Da'wa*, the duty of every committed *'Alim* [preacher]. The Islamist *Da'wa*, which is the preliminary to an embryonic project of the restructuring of society, promotes the development among the faithful of a demand for committed Alim, just as the circles animated by the free preachers in turn supply the Islamist movement with new converts.[41]

These considerations naturally counsel great caution in formulating conclusions. As Jacques Zylberberg emphasized:

> The historic churches are only one of the bearers of the sacred, which will continue to be manifested both within them, on their fringes, and outside them. Therefore sociology must perforce content itself synchronically with limited investigations, either comprehensively of small homogeneous groups observed at close quarters, or by long range study of populations observed in multiple transactions, of opposed socializations and of both synthetic and fragmented feedback. In short, sociologists when studying socialization are compelled to cease studying the confessional as a monopolistic instance of socialization. The Church is not the centre of the world, it is a power centre; the harmony of the divine order, its continuity and its eternity are central to our vision. It is therefore an object of research but it is not the paradigm of our researches.[42]

Talking about the millennium a former Polish Stalinist leader, Stefan Staszewski, told how,' The Black Virgin of Czestochowa which was carried into churches throughout Poland . . . had the police after it. The Party faithful were mobilized, force was used. One day, the Virgin was even arrested.'[43] Some fifteen years later, the same image of Our Lady of Czestochowa symbolized the fight of the Polish nation and was used as a standard by Solidarity. No doubt it is in this sense that Father Vaclav Maly, a signatory of Charter 77, acknowledged that, 'prison may, it is true, be a salutary test of one's own faith'. But he added, 'I'm not saying I want to go back there.'[44]

It would doubtless be an exaggeration to claim that the struggle for freedom now taking place in East-Central Europe can be categorized as a struggle between good and evil. There are many in Eastern Europe who have drawn comfort from identifying evil with the countenance of the government alone. The fight is primarily a struggle for meaning, so as to reintegrate it into a universe that seems to have lost any idea of what that is. It also depends upon the West, on a West of which Kundera says that he no longer believes in Europe, that this fight should be brought to a conclusion. As Vaclav Havel wrote, in his acceptance speech as recipient of the Erasmus prize in 1986. 'There is only one Europe, a Europe politically divided, it is true, but which is not and cannot be divided on the spiritual plane.'[45]

Postscript to the English Edition

Three theoretical conceptions of the relationship between politics and religion in Central Europe under the Soviets

Because of the revolutions that occurred in 1989 and 1990, Central Europe and its religious development are now subjects of topical interest. The destruction of the Berlin Wall and the 'return to history' spoken of by Vaclav Havel are some of the results of the slow process of desovietization described throughout this book as evinced by the specific case of the part played by religion as a symbolic vector challenging the legitimacy of the system, as a means whereby society is reconstituted, and as a major force in the redefinition of politics.

Does this justify the contention that there is a type of religiousness peculiar to this part of the continent? While there is no doubt that forty years of sovietization have indirectly resulted in a process of homogenization in this respect, it has to be said that the churches seem to have been more concerned to legitimize the nation state than to encourage societies to transcend national differences. And the democratization now taking place seems actually to be accompanied by a strengthening of this tendency.

The areas under discussion do, however, appear to have one point in common. In this part of Europe, where the definition of a national identity has never been something to be taken for granted, the passionate questioning to which this uncertainty has given rise has led to a permanent activation of the order of ultimate purposes that is needed in order to give a meaning to history. This theme of *election* reappears even in the Pope's speeches. Thus, if communism has been placed in the position of christianizing Poland, it appears to have been in order to serve the spiritual reconquest of a Europe that has been cut off from its roots.

In any event a page has been turned, a chapter closed. The holding of free elections in every one of the countries of Central and Eastern Europe in 1990 is the end of an epoch. It makes it possible to think about the years 1945–89 as a coherent whole, and to try to apprehend them in a theoretical perspective that seeks to reveal the ways in which politics and religion have been engaged in a dialectic of mutual reinforcement. From this viewpoint we can see, as in a laboratory, over less than half a century, three distinct conceptual types of the relationship between politics and religion: persecution, compromise and conflictualization.

It is clear that in the process of moving forward towards a meaning initiated by religion and politics, their interrelationship is never left to chance; indeed, it forms a major constituent of the arrangement adopted, whatever that may be. But soviet-type systems, by the peculiar nature of the relationship they claim to establish between ideology and reality, compel us to think *differently* about movement and continuity, inclusion and exclusion.

Religion counters the drive towards totalitarianism with its radical specificity, claiming to speak for the One Who alone, in terms of legitimacy, is beyond all questioning. By affirming that the manifestations of Meaning are a part of the divine plan, by which alone they are explicable, and that therefore earthly travail, disarray or suffering are in the last resort merely a sign of incomprehension, religion, disavowing any need for *recognition*, claimed to possess what can only be called 'absolute legitimacy'. That is the source of the dual nature of religion, on which of course the Church relies: it is at the same time in the world and out of the world. This second part is from the outset posited as inaccessible to human reason, in other words not amenable to confrontation with reality. Religion, which is by definition less subject to the pressure of sense, exhibits a tremendous ability to re-form without being injured by the apparent contradictions existing between its old and new forms, to stage the organization of forgetfulness of what it might have represented, whereas the soviet-type system with its scientific outlook could not avoid a confrontation with reality.

It is the 'extramundane' part that provides grounds for arguing that religion is autonomous. Whatever disputes may surround the part that is in the world, the other part is always and by definition immune to any attempt to challenge it.

The Church has always known how to deploy this ambivalence, claiming both to be 'of the world' and 'outside' it, precisely because it had the sole prerogative of defining the boundaries between the two spheres in which it moved. It is by appealing to and standing on its extramundane part that religion contrives to in-form politics. This is a twofold process: of charting a route intended to bring the course of worldly events closer to divine plan, and also of trying to wrest from politics the autonomy it attempts to claim – in other words of changing the shape it assumes and diluting this shape into a larger entity of which the outlines are necessarily vague, since they merge ineluctably with the transcendent. Faced with this endeavour to outstrip it by engulfing it; soviet-type government, whose ideology forbade it either to return the compliment or by excluding things religious to ensure their real independence, was unable to offer any other rejoinder than to make a show of exclusion aimed ultimately at a legitimating inclusion. This interactive meeting of ideologies manoeuvring in one and the same field 'produces' simultaneously displacement and sedimentation, movement and institutionalization. First because this meeting, which is never fortuitous, is subject to pre-existent rules, forged by history, custom, etc., which it tends to adapt and transform, and secondly because at this point religion is instrumentalized as a vector for defining an identity, and this definition is necessarily founded upon a progession towards differentiation, which in turn naturally leads to the adoption of autonomy. But in the calling into question that which it presupposes and generates, and which it compels the protagonists to take upon themselves, this search may be productive of a demand for linkage, more or less explicitly formulated. Hence the process of becoming independent ends in the paradoxical result of recreating a bond as it also brings about independence. This coupling of independence with linkage, of which the combination and the amount are constantly being adjusted over time, enables religion to be brought into play in two senses here as a political category. It can be both an affirmation of the absolute irreducibility of the individual to the group – that is to say as a decisive potential challenge to a social order that is perceived as being unjust, irrational or simply unsatisfactory – and also the affirmation of a continuity, backed by a tradition in which it is rooted – that is to say as a crucial element in the stability of the governmental sphere. This outline could be modified and filled in, according to the values the government claims to represent and defend. If it boasts of movement, the recall to a tradition immediately takes on a different meaning: it changes into a radical critique and becomes objectively destabilizing.

Thus the delegitimation of the state by the Church in a soviet-type system is first of all a process of restoring a continuity, of which religion is both the sign and the means; if the breaks are not being denied, their importance is at least being diminished within an overall historical process. In short, an a-historical stance is being adopted in order to claim mastery of historical time.

But when religion is accorded (or claims sole rights to) a relationship to time that combines as harmoniously as possible movement and continuity, this gives rise to a great number of misunderstandings. Whether conscious or unconscious, these misunderstandings are in the last resort necessary. Religious language, more than any other, is characterized by its very great polysemy; it is capable of saying what it does not say, or of leaving the impression that it is doing so.[1] As was said earlier, the greater the need to clear up these misunderstandings, the weaker will be the Church's influence, as an institution that manages the link and autonomy, and a self-proclaimed depository of religious legitimacy. The more these musunderstandings have to be maintained, whether simply for tactical reasons or because such an attitude springs from a more complex combination of factors, the greater the Church's influence on society will be.

Persecution as a reinforcer of legitimacy

Persecution, a perverted mode of institutionalizing movement, is a complex undertaking, both a consequence and an epitome of the totalitarian design, a means of concretizing this design and of revealing its very contradictions. Evincing a will to hijack meaning, it inevitably places its instigators in the position of squatters; they claim to occupy a totality of which they are not the owners, and in the final analysis the aim of perpetual institutionalized movement is to obscure the illegitimacy of such a claim.

But 'pursuit' (per-secution) can perpetuate itself as mobility only if it never catches up with its quarry – never gains the response allegedly sought from the persecutee. Were the quarry to be caught, it would cease to provide justification for the movement.

There is also ambiguity in the way a church reacts to persecution. It is good to have martyrs, pledges of legitimacy, provided that their memory can be perpetuated; but a course set for institutional reproduction runs counter to one aimed at harvesting the gains of persecution.

Nevertheless, persecution gives a meaning to the persecuted object. More than that, by naming it as the Enemy, it gives it the power to produce meaning. By setting out to destroy it, in order to make progress towards the non-differentiation at which it aims and of which it is the instrument, it helps to individuate it; it enables its victim to redefine himself, in the very confrontation it is bent on staging. By identifying him it sacralizes him.

For, as was said earlier, it needs him. How can the maintenance of a design for total control of society be justified if the need for it is not attested by the existence of a threat, whether real, imagined or fabricated, against which it is supposed to protect society? What would become of the persecution apparatus if the object which it has pledged itself to destroy, which it bodies forth and battens upon, were actually to disappear? Suppose it completed its task! It would no longer have a reason for existing; its own identity would be gone. Thus, Jacques Zylberberg has laid bare the complex relationship existing in the East between the administrations that have the task of monitoring the activity of the churches and the churches themselves, reminding his readers that the leaders of the Russian Orthodox Church had noted with satisfaction the creation or re-establishment from 1931 onwards of government bodies responsible for supervising them.[2]

Persecution results in making religion autonomous, even if the way in which the government apparatus works cloaks this independence in the shape of apparent marginalization. The criminalization of religion, which is the logical consequence of the deviance it supposedly constitutes, is tantamount to pushing it to the periphery of the proclaimed social order. The new status of 'without a fixed address' confers on religious life the characteristic of being no longer easy to locate in the space of society. Once marginalized and criminalized, religion straight away compensates for the loss of the space traditionally assigned to it by its speed of movement and the tactical surprises of its reappearances: and from then onwards its own logic is deployed in the recesses of the existing social order, in its silences, or rather in the divergence between what is said and what is not said, the explicit and the implicit, in the recess of an *elaborated* meaning, that it questions and tranforms, where fundamentally the difference never amounts to more than interstices in what is central. Zinoviev, in *L'Avenir radieux*, well illustrates the point, when describing this wasteland sociability welling up, well fortified by vodka, right under a huge government propaganda poster, in front of a hoarding that, fragile frontier that it was, still served to separate the sphere of meaning from that of meaninglessness. For all that, this frontier is far from being impenetrable . . . But what matters here is what the interval says and what is said in the interval, what is placed in position where the totality meets the specific, in this reciprocating movement that is both search and confrontation.

It is not only that religion is becoming independent; it is being reworked, and this reworking takes the form of a utopianization (or counter-utopianization). The object of the enterprise is a reapprehension. The problem is to effect a redistribution of time in order to vindicate a utopia that aims at combating another utopia. More accurately, since the official utopia was built in the very pattern of the Christian utopia that justified the old order, the Christian utopia that opposes the new order, the official counter-utopia, itself becomes a counter-utopia. Its positivity is built upon a double negation – negation of that which, in itself, has produced and provided a reason for the counter-utopia that is using violence against it, and negation of the justice of this violence. Its operational power is in direct proportion to its ability to reorganize the whole of the relationship that might exist between the registers of time. As in pristine Christianity, the state will not be glorified, but theologically justified and integrated into God's design.

This construction takes place in a constant reference to universality, which is assuredly displayed by one of religion's most extraordinary ambivalences: its efficacy in the search for identity is unrivalled; it is both the sign and the means of social cohesion and at the same time – its first function depends on this – a striving towards the universal. Affirmation of the universal provides both a referent for the individual seeking his identity and a foundation for his existence. Without claiming to embrace the universal, by means of a reinterpretation, a translation enabling it to be apprehended in the categories on which the individual's quest for identity is based, the striving for individuation would be no longer meaningful and certainly devoid of prospects.

This complex relationship between the universal and the particular is the source of most of the conflicts and misunderstandings that beset the relationship between messianism and nationalism.[3] There is no messianism without definition of a role both specific and universal assigned to a particular community, group, class or nation. This being so, it is pertinent to ask in what order of priority the objects aimed at are really placed. Is not nationalism here only the necessary concentration of energy indispensable to a community in order to serve aims that transcend it? And conversely, might not messianism be in the final analysis the alibi of a search for identity that ought to involve the universal in order to be legitimate? However this question is answered, one is bound to note that we are faced with a double instrumentalization of politics and religion, each endeavouring to justify and serve the other.

This mutual reinforcement of religion and politics inevitably breaks down into the definition of a new relationship to time seeking to reappropriate the present, conferring meaning upon the path already traversed and hitherto experienced more as wandering than following a settled itinerary. The present becomes a stage in a process of initiation, a resting place along a pilgrim road, where the individual endeavours to rediscover himself in the act of immersion within a society that he forms and that forms him.

However, at this point it would be necessary to establish why the religious appears as a higher authority than the others in terms of its ability to move to action. Although this explanation is not the only one, the specific role of communist-type government and the nature of the design inspiring it have naturally to be emphasized in the case of soviet-type systems in Europe. Countless analyses have stressed the similarities between the Christian design and that of communism. But the problem here is that, claiming to be based on reason, communism could not avoid a confrontation with reality, even in the context of a messianic design, and was consequently playing a losing game from the start, almost by definition, when faced by religious synthesis. The energy it unleashed to overcome this handicap, far from enabling it to do so, merely increased the handicap. In the Polish situation, when the government attacked the Church and sought to compromise it or force it to compromise, it merely helped the Church to gain in influence. Its only hope would have been to claim to incorporate the Church, and that was the one thing its own ideology forbade it to do. This 'self-censorship' did much to render the Church's actions effective. For messianism aims at ejecting the Church from the differentiated, a-historical space it occupies and bringing it back into history and into the city. The object was to end its extraterritorial status and, as it were, to celebrate the mass not inside the cathedral but on the square in front of it, or in the street. Among the common people of Poland, the government's claim to a monopoly of the public domain coupled with its refusal to penetrate the Church's space which, though institutionally useful, was ideologically unattainable, led to the paradoxical result that the Church became society's public space while the space outside it was abandoned to the government, as if marginalized. The cathedral swallowed its parvis; or, more accurately, since no parvis was available, the nave did duty for a parvis. And the final twist, one which incidentally could give rise to misunderstandings, is that the said interiorization was a complex matter: it gave the Church the privilege of being the place where the freedom of the nation was proclaimed and worked out, but that did not necessarily mean that this nation identified itself with the Church. The phenomenon was what Michel Maslowski, after Kazimierz Brodzinski, calls 'a copernican reversal': 'The institutional individualistic religion of tradition becomes the religion of prophetic social dynamism embodied in History and of individual charismatic missions emanating from collective tasks',[4] since the 'messianic model' has the advantage over the 'heroic model' of making the same kind of witness (refusal of reality as it is), without necessarily exposing those who espouse it to the same risks. But in that event, is the question still about the meaning of instrumentalization between messianism and nationalism? For are not both in the final analysis raised up and utilized by society itself, as so many means of affirmation available to it? For though messianism is an urge towards linking a design to reality, it is first of all the recognition of an inability to change the present while leaving intact the intellectual edifice upon which it is built. It is the expression of a disquietude, a sense of man's inability to apprehend more than the fragments of a whole, and its aim is to reconstruct from an idealized future a past that will make sense of a meaningless present. Before reinventing anything, it gives man the opportunity of telling himself everything by saying it. Working upon time, it leads to recomposition of human space, by assigning to each and everyone a new place, by simply defining the outlines of a new task to be performed in an old place. More an outcome than an undertaking, messianism is the concentrate of a weakness that feels it is becoming strength. It is a way of reintroducing meaning into a universe that was without meaning, it is the charting of a course whereby man may relocate his wanderings, where the exile may return home, where the weak is at liberty, if he so desires, to make a show of strength. Messianism is an attempt to change the rules of the game, made by those who hitherto had been always the losers because the rules were weighted against them.

Revitalizing politics

In regaining its independence, religion became reactivated. As the basis and symbol of a refusal, it responded to the attempt to expel it by regrouping throughout a social sphere which it impregnated with moral values. After seizing power, the communists had tried to make use of a certain conception of Good and Evil to their own advantage, one partly derived from the Gospel. They claimed to be responsible for the common good, against private interests, which were denigrated. But the progressive discrediting of the regime resulted in a reversal of this approach: the sphere in which morality was exercised came to be that of private life, while the public sphere, in which all the compromises had to be made, all the lies told and all the accommodations effected, became the hunting ground of evil.

Of course this reversal, amounting to a redistribution of religious values, was inevitably bound up with a parallel redistribution in the political sphere, in which things religious had played a leading part: by providing the materials necessary to assign limits to politics, by compelling it to be subject to ethical standards and by bringing it once more within an axiological hierarchy. Confronted with the contrast between the breadth of the state sphere and that of legitimation, the state had no option but to take up the challenge offered to it: to change in order to survive. Consequently it is not surprising that the rationalization it undertook, which of necessity was also an attempt to recreate the social bond and to make it independent, at least in appearance, should have teken the form of a feigned intention to break off the engagement.

But this was no true disengagement. Ideologically committed to renounce any attitude of neutrality with regard to religion, the Party was obliged to go on proclaiming the illegitimacy of religion as an article of faith. At the same time, as its isolation increased, the very weakness it evinced on the ground of a legitimacy which it was constantly forced to patch up and display, drove it to a more or less open confession of its failure. So it had to give up its utopia and compromise with reality, a change of attitude not necessarily resulting from new thinking and a strategy. It was more like a series of compromises with reality, not necessarily dictated from the centre. A simple economic cost/benefit calculation clearly showed the increasing loss of legitimacy that would have followed the pursuit of a policy of persecution. Consequently it was becoming urgent to mount an effort to recover the 'legitimacy gains' from religion, yet without losing sight of the ideological objective that could not be abandoned without loss of identity. In short, the object was still to destroy the legitimacy of religion, and the only means of achieving this was to compromise it by instrumentalizing it under the pretence of making it independent.

Moreover this so-called grant of independence was all the more necessary, since the failure of the government to promote a 'secular' morality had caused an enormous need for a system of rules, or more accurately a credible source of standards, to surface; this explains the attempts made by some governments in the East to bring about a rapprochement with the Church on specific subjects such as morals, alcoholism, etc. This situation further complicated the challenge mentioned earlier; the very core of the object in view was to change the methods of the apparatus employed, in terms of social control, in order not to do so.

Faced by this new situation, religion reacted by demonstrating its ability to do two apparently contradictory things at once, by legitimating and delegitimating the political system,[5] the contradiction in this case being resolved by the difference that existed between the registers in which this work was situated and conducted.

The new policy of state regulation of religion by way of an institutional compromise between the Party and the Church, once the government had understood that religion was politically and socially less dangerous if it was framed by a more or less representative institution, was inseparable from the attempt by the system to endow itself with operational legitimacy, based on an effort to satisfy the consumerist needs of the population. The real objective was to buy acquiescence rather than to canvas for acceptance – to bring in a legitimacy of appearances or of conformity. For what did disapproval matter as long as it remained silent and did not lead to open opposition? Hence the importance of frittering, disconnection and atomization that are inseparable from the use of consumerism as a means of maintaining the system in power.

It is from this perspective that the election of Karol Wojtyla to the Papacy, followed by his journey to Poland in 1979, should be analysed. Coming at a time when the economic and social crisis created by the failure of Gierka's plan for a 'Second Poland' had been exacerbated, the presence of massive crowds on the Pope's itinerary underscored the government's failure to mount its programme, both as regards the control of society and in terms of the countervailing satisfactions to be provided for the people's material needs.

The course of events described here had been a long time preparing. The Church's takeover of the fundamental interests of the nation, explicitly affirmed with the *Letter to the German bishops* of 1965, forerunner to the celebration of the *Millennium*, was strengthened in the mid-seventies by the association of religious rights with human rights. In 1975 Cardinal Wojtyla, while still Archbishop of Cracow, said to Jean-Marie Domenach, at that time director of the review *Esprit*, that the Church's first duty in Poland was to defend human rights. The paradoxes inherent in this intention need no emphasis, for in the modern period the Catholic Church was built upon the refusal to go along with developments incorporating these very human rights. And what exactly do these rights mean? How far was and is the Church in Poland ready to fight for the upholding of the rights of non-believers? A reply to these questions was not exactly a burning issue during the seventies and eighties.[6] The Church was playing too important a role as a symbolic vehicle in Poland for the systematic disparity between its own interests as an institution and objectives pursued by the opposition, where differences were sunk in a common cause, to be usefully highlighted. For the time being politics had to take a back seat, being subordinated to ethics.

From then onwards, the delegitimation of government by religion could be likened to a *modus operandi*, a complex system of combining the different registers (human rights, history, culture, tradition, social and economic concerns, etc.) with the aim of making reality and the good coincide. There, in the final analysis, legitimacy becomes an ethical concept. What is legitimate is necessarily turned towards the good. This does not mean that it is wholly identical with good: it may be legitimate to do evil, provided that it is done in pursuit of what is believed to be a further higher good (this was the register played by General Jaruzelski to justify 13 December 1981 – the excuse of the *lesser* evil). As ethics energized, legitimacy is an ethic always straining towards practical application. Both the legitimacy of a government and that of a revolt against that government are always governed by an understanding of what is good and what is evil at the given time.

In a situation which, although governed by a series of compromises, is nevertheless characterized by the absence of a 'social contract' as a basis for the political organization, there is no legitimation emanating from the subjects; at most there is an acceptance, tacit or explicit, born of fear (the respect naturally inspired by power), indifference (the feeling of belonging to a sphere that has no connection with the place where domination is presumed to be exercised, of having nothing to do with 'that'), or of relative satisfaction (access to material or symbolic goods of which the government is seen as the guarantor).

Hence it is not surprising to observe how, in Poland, both state and Church became perceptibly convinced at the same time that practical influence was tantamount to legitimacy. This raises the complex problem of the management of the influence of religion on society, with reference to the Helsinki agreements and the 'religion of human rights', and against the background of institutional compromise, and of double instrumentalization – of the Church by the opposition, and of the opposition by the Church. It has been said that for the Church this management was effected by defining an ideal threshold of combination between normalization-institutionalization and non-normalization-non-institutionalization, in time and with reference to a given context, in a blend of social demand, offer of power, constraints and its own objectives.

That refers back to the hypothesis of the 'necessary ambiguity' advanced earlier. It also means that the analysis most not be confined to institution-to-institution relationships between the Church and the state. In its dealings with the soviet-type system, the Church has employed three kinds of strategies that could be used in various combinations, and all aimed at revealing that the government lacked legitimacy. Of course this unswerving aim served the interests of the Church as an institution. Each of these strategies suggests a priority: *survival*, which implies a compromise, or an overt will to compromise; *resistance*, which makes the Church the place of a moral testimony, whether self-chosen or imposed; and the *offensive*, which is often evoked when the government is weak and unable to hide the fact. But merely to describe these three attitudes, the relationships of meaning and of the networks of relationships of meaning that underlie them, the compromises into which Church and state enter, does not exhaust the complexity of an overall relationship between politics and religion that defies any hasty categorization. For the objective sought could not possibly be achieved, the strategies adopted could not be effective, except in so far as they were consonant with the overarching aspirations of the societies concerned. In Bohemia, for example, it seems that the government managed to achieve the prodigious feat of reconciling, at least for a time, Catholicism and the 'meaning of Czech history', as demonstrated by the way in which the primate Cardinal Tomasek gradually came to be regarded in society. Moreover this change of perception was strongly nourished, in a very 'Hussite' way, from grass-roots level. And even in ultra-Catholic Poland, the Church, though remaining impregnable, both as a symbolic vehicle of the affirmation of an identity and as an indispensable area of freedom, began to attact criticism for the political game it was seen as having played and as playing.

Towards conflictualization

Confronted by the impossible, caught in the major contradiction of being unable to be and unable not to be, religion was for long reduced merely to making pronouncements. It had to build up a purely temporary fiction, with the sole aim of structuring *differently* a field crowded with constraints and plastered with prohibitions. Reality had to be challenged and then reorganized from and in a stance of the imagination. In this way subjectivity becomes the first factor of legitimation, from which all coherence derives and to which all coherence is referred. This subjectivity, with the dual ability to describe the universe while describing one's own universe, can integrate anything whatsoever. And in the last resort, integration is all.

This discourse of subjectivity, born of the heart of an impossibility, aimed at restructuring it so as to make it habitable. It was designed to operate in the restricted space created by the existence of constraints both insurmountable and contradictory. To escape suffocation it was necessary to contrive an opening. Since the walls did not allow this, only the ceiling was left. The opening thus made accentuated the already clear gap between the discourse thus instituted and the cultural universe trying to affirm itself and to restructure itself at the same time. And because of this the discourse of subjectivity began to operate in a field for which it was not designed. It is in this field that it *really* started operating. It began as just a palliative, an imaginary escape, but it changed into a very effective instrument for changing the shape of the political arena. But it is not possible to think, speak or live in a vacuum. Just as the adversary in power had come under the influence of religion, from which it had drawn its symbols, so subjectivity, defined on the basis of religion, leads to a relativity of thought which, in turn, results in a questioning of the category that gave rise to it.

In fact this causal chain signals the impossibility of utopia, which carries its own end within itself, namely compromise, and is itself challenged by the new utopia created by the compromise. On this reasoning conflictualization leads to a different, new configuration in as much as none of the 'axiological nodes' present can, by definition, claim to exhaust the whole. At that point compromise ceases to be the instrument of a strategy and becomes a rule of the game.

However, this chain of events has without doubt profoundly affected the situation, so much so that the appearance of the 'process of reconstitution of the social fabric' given by a country like Poland over the past decade is in need of correction. For the dominant element in this process is the emergence of social identities, in which the moral demand resulting from the action of religion acts as a cement. Does the sum of these social identities yet constitute a social identity? There is no denying that the advent of political pluralism has resulted in a curious expansion of space and that this process of enlargement and rearrangement of the landscape brings with it a muted disquiet or even panic fear.

Moreover, it is by no means certain that the successes achieved by the Church in its long fight against totalitarianism are without their negative aspect. Communism has rendered the Church the signal service of sparing it the necessity of undertaking the difficult task of coming to terms with the modern world that has been thrust upon the churches of the West. Now that pluralism has been firmly established and a 'competitive market of values' opened in the East, there is a strong likelihood that this argument might surface again. This might well turn out to be a fresh challenge, and there is no assurance that it would prove easier for the Church to accept than the challenge it once faced from totalitarianism.

Appendix

I Person and life of Christ

Table 1 Summary of cult buildings

	Churches		Chapels		Oratories	Niches
	1st title	2nd title	1st title	2nd title		
Christ the King	1		1			
Christ with Orb					1	
Christ			1	1	1	6
Ascension			1			
Sacred Heart	2		1	1	2	4
Jesus of Nazareth					12	
Chrystus Frasobliwy					3	3
Christ scourged			1		1	
Ecce Homo			2			1
Christ bowed			9		9	
Holy Trinity			1	1	2	
Holy Family						1

Table 2 Appearance of cults revealed by the appearance of buildings (churches, chapels and oratories)

	16th	17th	18th	19th	20th
Christ the King				1	1
Christ with Orb			1		
Christ			2	2	
Ascension					1
Sacred Heart				2	5
Jesus of Nazareth			3	14	1
Chrystus Frasobliwy				3	
Christ scourged				2	
Ecce Homo				2	
Christ bowed		1	2	13	2
Holy Trinity				3	1

II The virgin

Table 1 Summary of cult buildings

	Churches		Chapels		Oratories	Niches
	1st title	2nd title	1st title	2nd title		
Liturgical titles:						
Annunciation	2					
Assumption	1		1			
Czestochowa	3	1	23	2	17	17
Imienia NMP		1				
Immaculate Conception				1	3	1
Our Lady of Loreto			1			
Our Lady of the Angels	1	1	1			
Our Lady of the Rosary	1	1	4		2	1
Matka Boska			20	1	34	45
Our Lady of Perpetual Succour	1	1	1			
Our Lady who aids Believers	1					
Our Lady of Consolation			1			
Virgin with Child					7	1
Virgin Weeping			1			
Sacred Heart of Mary	1		2			
Mary Queen of Poland	1					
Mary Queen of the World		1	1			

Table 2 Appearance of cults revealed by the appearance of buildings (churches, chapels and oratories)

	16th	17th	18th	19th	20th
Annunciation				1	1
Assumption		1		1	
Czestochowa		1	6	18	20
Imienia NMP					1
Immaculate Conception			1	1	1
Our Lady of Loreto			1		
Our Lady of the Angels				1	2
Our Lady of the Rosary	1		1	1	5
Matka Boska			4	32	14
Our Lady of Perpetual Succour					3
Our Lady who aids Believers				1	
Our Lady of Consolation				1	
Virgin with Child			1	3	3
Virgin Weeping				1	
Sacred Heart of Mary					4
Mary Queen of Poland				1	
Mary Queen of the World				1	1

Appendix

III Saints

Table 1 Summary of cult buildings

	Churches		Chapels		Oratories	Niches
	1st title	2nd title	1st title	2nd title		
Traditional Saints:						
Andrew	1				1	
Anthony of Padua		1	2		2	7
Bartholomew	1					
Florian	1		1			1
Francis of Assisi						1
Stigmata of Francis		1				
John the Baptist			1			
John the Evangelist				1		
Martin	1					
Archangel Michael	2				1	
Nicholas	1				1	
Onufrius			1			
Peter						1
Peter and Paul		2				
Simon and Judas Thaddaeus	1					
Wawrzyniec (Lawrence)	1				1	
Local saints:						
Felix						1
Jan Kanty		1				
Kazimierz Wielki		1				
Stanislas		1				1
Szczepan or Zygmunt				1		
Wojciech	1					
Saints of the Counter Reformation:						
John of Nepomuk			1	1	5	
Karol Boromeusz	1					
Saints of contemporary devotion:						
Joseph the Worker	1					
Maximilian Kolbe	1					
All Saints	1					

Appendix

Table 2 Appearance of cults revealed by appearance of buildings (churches, chapels and oratories)

	16th	17th	18th	19th	20th
Andrew	1		1		
Anthony of Padua				4	1
Bartholomew	1				
Florian				1	1
Stigmata of Francis				1	
Jan Kanty					1
John the Baptist				1	
John the Evangelist					1
John of Nepomuk			5	2	
Joseph of Worker					1
Karol Boromeusz				1	
Kazimierz Wielki		1			
Martin	1				
Maximilian Kolbe					1
Archangel Michael	1			1	1
Nicholas	1				1
Onufrius				1	
Peter and Paul	2				
Simon and Judas Tadeusz		1			
Stanislas					1
Szczepan (or Zygmunt)				1	
All Saints					1
Wawrzyniec		1			
Wojciech	1				

IV Saints

Table 1 Summary of cult buildings

	Churches		Chapels		Oratories	Niches
	1st title	2nd title	1st title	2nd title		
Anne		2	2			
Bernadette			1			
Catherine	1					
Elisabeth			1			
Helen						1
Jadwiga					1	
Veronica			1	1	2	
Woman at the Tomb of Christ					1	

Table 2 Appearance of cults revealed by appearance of buildings (churches, chapels and oratories)

	16th	17th	18th	19th	20th
Anne	1	1		2	
Bernadette					1
Catherine	1				
Elisabeth					1
Jadwiga					1
Veronica			1	3	
Women at the Tomb of Christ				1	

Notes

Introduction

1 Juan Miguel Garrigues, *L'Eglise, la société libre et le communisme*, Commentaire Julliard, Paris, 1984.
2 Quoted by Alexander Tomski, 'Modus moriendi: L'Eglise catholique en Tchéchoslovaquie', *Communio*, VII, no. 5, September–October 1982, p. 82.
3 Alain Besançon, *La confusion des langues – La crise idéologique de l'Eglise*, Calmann-Lévy, Paris, 1978, p. 83.
4 In *Le Monde*, Paris, 7 November 1978.
5 O. V. Borisov, 'Sojuz novogo tipa' ('A new type of union'), *Voprosy istorii KPPS*, Moscow, no. 4, 1984, pp. 34–9.
6 In *Le Monde*, Paris, 26 November 1986.
7 Cardinal Ratzinger, in collaboration with Vittorio Messori, *Entretiens sur la foi*, Fayard, Paris, 1985, p. 234.
8 Quoted by Pierre Daix, *Ce que je sais du xxe siècle*, Calmann-Lévy, Paris, 1985, p. 129.
9 During an interview he granted us at Budapest in June 1983.
10 Émile Poulat, *L'Eglise, c'est un monde*, Le Cerf, Paris, 1986.
11 Bruno Étienne, *L'Islamisme radical*, Hachette, Paris, 1987, p. 10.
12 Zdenek Strmiska, 'Nations de l'Europe centrale et identité culturelle: remarques épistemologiques marginales', *Groupe de travail sur l'Europe centrale et orientale - Bulletin d'information*, no. 3, M.S.H, Paris, July 1980, p. 143.
13 Milan Kundera, 'L'Occident kidnappé', in *Le Débat*, no. 27, Gallimard, Paris, November 1983, pp. 3–27.
14 T. H. Rigby, 'How communist states deal with the problem of religion?', in R. F. Miller and T. H. Rigby (eds), *Religion and Politics in Communist States*, Occasional Paper no. 19, Department of Political Science, Research School of Social Sciences, Australian National University, Canberra, 1986, pp. 136–7.
15 The example of Father Maximilian Kolbe is symbolic from this point of views. More generally, 'according to incomplete statistics, the overall losses of clergy in occupied Poland amount to 6 bishops, 1,863 diocesan priests, 63 seminarists, 580 religious of whom 289 were priests and 289 Nuns, killed by the occupying power. These figures are incomplete. Many have suffered prison and concentration camps. Many died after

Notes to pp. 7–9   203

being liberated. Others remained at liberty but were deprived of their pastoral functions. It should be emphasized that obviously pastoral work was disorganized. In comparison with the losses of Polish society as a whole (more than 6 million Polish citizens died, 3 million of these being Catholics of the Latin rite), the clergy losses were particularly high. This was the result of the policy of the occupying power, whose primary objective was completely to destroy the intelligentsia of Poland' (Lidia Müller, 'L'Eglise de Pologne en 1939–1945 – Géographie et statistiques', in *Miscellanea Historiae Ecclesiasticae (IX), Congrès de Varsovie (25 juin-ler juillet 1978)*, Section IV: Les Eglises chrétiennes dans l'Europe dominée par le III e Reich, Bibliothèque de la revue d'histoire ecclésiastique, fascicule 70, Ossolineum (Wroclaw), Ed. Nauwelaerts (Brussels), 1984, p. 276).

16 René Rémond, 'Les transformations de la vie religieuse dans l'Europe dominée par le III e Reich (1939–45)', in *Miscellanea Historiae Ecclesiasticae*, p. 527.

17 Where is in fact the point of difference between the Protestant Bozena Komarkova and the Catholic Josef Zverina, both of whom signed Charter 77, when the former entitled her work *La Difficulté d'être Eglise* while the latter called his *Le Courage d'être Eglise*? From the same point of view, it is not without significance that *Tygodnik Powszechny*, the prestigious Polish Catholic weekly, independent of the state and very close to John Paul II, should have published on the front page of its issue of 9 February 1986 an article signed by Stefan Swiezawski entitled 'Jan Hus, heretyk czy prekursor Vaticunum secundum?' ('John Hus, heretic or precursor of Vatican II?')

18 One realizes that such a statement calls for extensive qualification, since the 'Russophile' Czech was in part cleverly (re)constructed shortly after the Second World War. After the insurrections of 1830 and 1863 in Poland, Czech opinion became divided between two camps, one supporting the Poles while the other supported the Russians. But in 1867, shortly after the conclusion of the compromise between Austria and Hungary, the Czechs turned clearly towards Russia, as is shown by Rieger's speech to the Slav Congress in Moscow in April 1867 (on which see Jean-Paul Bled, *François-Joseph*, Fayard, Paris, 1987, pp. 361–7).

19 Zdenek Strmiska, 'Intervention at the discussion organized on 16 March 1979 M.S.H.-E.H.E.S.S.: Religion and cultural identities in Central and Eastern Europe – The case of Catholicism and Protestantism', *Groupe de travail sur l'Europe Centrale et Orientale – Bulletin d'information*, no. 3, M.S.H., Paris, July 1980, pp. 89–90.

20 Tomas Guarrigue Masaryk, *Ceska otazka. Snahy a tuzby Narodniho obrozeni* ('La question tchèque, Efforts et espoirs de la renaissance nationale'), Prague, Melantrich, 1969, trans. by Marie-Elisabeth Ducreux, in *Groupe de Travail sur l'Europe Centrale et Orientale – Bulletin d'information*, no. 3, p. 102. Jan Kollar (1793–1852) of Slovak origin, inspired by Herder; Pavel Safarik (1795–1861), also of Slovak origin; Frantisek Palacky (1798–1876), Czech politician and historian, 'father of the fatherland' and author of *l'histoire de la nation tchéque*; Josef Dobrovsky (1753–1829), linguist and grammarian, one of the first representatives of the Czech national renaissance.

21 ibid., p. 103. We are aware that Masaryk's ideas have been criticized. In particular, Josef Pekar has accused him of romanticism and of 'idealizing' the past (on this subject, see Bernard Michel, *La Mémoire de Prague*, Perrin, Paris, 1986, pp. 110–15). But the current influence of Masaryk's thought in Bohemia justifies ample reference to it today (as does Vaclav Havel in an interview given to the *Times Literary Supplement* for 23 January 1987).

22 ibid., p. 103.

23 Stefan Smalik, in a text that savours more of *pro domo* pleading than of a scientific article ('L'Eglise catholique en Slovaquie dans les années 1939–44', in *Miscellanea Historiae Ecclesiasticae*, pp. 262–3 for the extract cited below), recalls that 'in the struggle for recognition of the rights of the Slovak nation, according to Dr Gustav Husak, Catholicism was the first to take part, and did so with the greatest vigour'. But he has to admit that 'independence was attained, it is true, at the cost of some collaboration with German National Socialism.'
24 A detailed chronology is given at the end of the book.
25 See the Bibliography at the end of the book.
26 Moshe Lewin, *La formation du système soviétique*, Gallimard, 'Bibliothèque des Histoires', Paris, 1987, p. 11.
27 We refer here to the following works, without taking account of studies on the *Ostpolitik* of the Vatican, which naturally adopt a somewhat special view of the problems: Gabriel Adrianyi, *Die Führung der Kirche in den Sozialistischen Staaten Europas*, Johannes-Berchmans Verlag, Munich, 1979, Trevor Beeson, *Prudence and Courage – The Religious Situation in Russian and Eastern Europe*, Collins, London. 1974; Bohdan Bociurkiw and John Strong (eds), *Religion and Atheism in the USSR and Eastern Europe*, Macmillan, London, 1975; Richard De George and James Patrick Scanlon (eds), *Marxism and Religion in Eastern Europe* (Papers presented at the Banff International Slavic Conference, 4–7 September 1974), Sovietica, D. Reidel, Dordrecht-Holland and Boston, 1976, Pedro Ramet (ed.), *Religion and Nationalism in Soviet and East European Politics*, Duke University Press, Durham, N.C., 1984, and R.F. Miller and T.H. Rigby (eds), *Religion and Politics in Communist States*, Occasional paper no. 19, Department of Political Science, Research School of Social Sciences, Australian National University, Canberra, 1986. All these works consist of a number of chapters, each one of which deals, sometimes in a remarkable way, with a particular country. An attempt is made in an introduction and/or a conclusion to draw out any similarities and differences. This procedure, which was adopted in the 1950s (Vladimir Gsovsky (ed.), *Church and State behind the Iron Curtain, Czechoslovakia, Hungary, Poland, Romania and an Introduction on the Soviet Union*, Praeger, New York, 1955), still has value today, as witness the symposium organized on the subject in 1985 in Paris, under the auspices of the Fondation Saint-Simon, during which Krzysztof Pomian, Istvan Kemeny, Margaret Manale, Steven K. Pavowitch and Jacques Rupnik spoke.

Special mention should be made of the work of Bohdan Cywinski, *Ogniem Probowanie* (*Trial by Fire*), Papieski Instytut Studiow Koscielnych, Rome, 1982, though it should be emphasized that it adopts a different historical perspective from ours here.

Lastly, in Eastern Europe itself, the only works dealing with the question approach it mainly from the legal aspects of relations between Church and state, as, for example, M.T. Staszewski, *Stosunki miedzy Panstwem i Kosciolem w europejskich krajach socjalistycznych (Relations between Church and State in the Socialist Countries of Europe)*, Warsaw, 1976.
28 Kundera, 'L'Occident kidnappé'.
29 In preface to Jeno Szucs, *Les Trois Europes*, L'Harmattan, Paris, 1985, p. 6.
30 Istvan Bibo, *Misère des petits Etats d'Europe de L'est*, L'Harmattan, Paris, 1986.
31 Szucs, *Les Trois Europes*.
32 One thinks here especially of the research project on the crises of Soviet-type systems directed by Zdenek Mlynar, and in particular of study no. 1 by Wlodzimierz Brus,

Pierre Kende and Zdenek Mlynar, *Processus de normalisation en Europe centrale sovietisée - Hongrie, Tchécoslovaquie, Pologne*, Index, Cologne, 1983.

33 Timothy Garton Ash, 'L'Europe centrale existe-t-elle?', *Lettre Internationale*, no. 10, Paris, Autumn 1986, pp. 5-6.

34 'In the main', Imre Miklos told me during an interview in Budapest in June 1983, 'the situation as regards relations between the state and each of the confessions is exactly the same. Formerly this was not so, as there were considerable differences between the Protestant Churches and the Roman Catholic Church. The latter is international, whereas the Protestant Churches are national Churches. For the Catholic Church it meant a change of direction. Furthermore, the Catholic Church, because of its feudal past, is slower in developing: it grasped the extent of the social revolution later than the other Churches. But the fundamental differences that existed at the liberation have disappeared owing to the profound change that occurred in the middle of the seventies.'

35 See, *inter alia*, Rudolf Otto, *The Idea of the Holy*, 2nd edn, OUP, Oxford, 1950; and Mircea Eliade, *Le Sacré et le Profane*, Gallimard, Paris, 1965.

36 Peter Berger, *La Religion dans la conscience Moderne*, Ed du Centurion, Paris, 1971.

37 Barrington Moore, *Social Origins of Dictatorship and Democracy - Lord and Peasant in the Making of the Modern World*, Beacon Press, Boston, 1966, pp. 522-3.

38 P. Bourdieu, *Choses dites*, Editions de Minuit, Paris, 1987, p. 118.

39 Daniel Beauvois, 'Contribution to the discussion organized on 16 March 1979 at the M.S.H.: Religions and cultural identities in Central and Eastern Europe. The case of Catholicism and Protestantism', in *Groupe de travail sur l'Europe centrale et orientale - Bulletin d'information*, no. 3, M.S.H., Paris, July 1980, p. 97.

40 Étienne, *L'Islamisme radical*, p. 24.

41 This concept is used in the sense given to it by Pierre Bourdieu: 'The actors who are competing in the field of symbolic manipulation have this in common: they carry out a symbolic action. They are people who try to manipulate the way the world is seen (and hence to change courses of action) by manipulating the structure of perception of the world of nature and society, by manipulating words and, through words, the principles of the construction of social reality.' And Bordieu adds: 'The so-called Sapir-Worf or Humbold-Cassirer theory which says that reality is constructed via verbal structures, is absolutely true in respect of the world of society' (in *Choses dites*, p. 119).

42 Gilles Deleuze, *Foucault*, Editions de Minuit, Paris, 1986, p. 78.

43 From this point of view it is significant that when speaking about the possible reestablishment of diplomatic relations between Poland and the Vatican, John Paul II emphasized that 'relations [would have] an international character, not an inter-state one. Here - said the Pope - the subject is not the Vatican state but the Apostolic See. By this he meant the totality of the services provided by the Bishop of Rome in relation to all the local churches' (in 'Discours du 14 juin 1987 à la Conférence épiscopale polonaise', *La Documentation Catholique*, no. 1944, Paris, 19 July 1987, p. 757).

44 In *L'URSS et l'Europe de l'Est (Edition, 1986)*, Notes et Etudes Documentaires, no. 4817, La Documentation Française, Paris, 1986, pp. 13-30.

45 Fayard, Paris.

1 Concerning Time and Space

1 Constitution of the USSR, in supplement no. 4 of *Etudes Sovietiques*, no. 356, Paris, November 1977 (official translation).

2 *Konstytucja Polskiej Rzeczypospolitej Ludoej* (constitution of the People's Republic of Poland), Warsaw, 1976. Similarly, article 39 of the constitution of the GDR states that 'every citizen is entitled to freedom of conscience and the free practice of the worship of his choice' (constitution of the GDR dated 6 April 1968, as amended by the law of 7 October 1974, supplementing and amending the constitution, jointly published by the Staatsverlag der Deutschen Demokratischen Republik and Verlag Zeit im Bild, Dresden, 1974).

3 Provisions identical for example to those of article 46, section 4, of the Yugoslav constitution of 7 April 1963 which provides that 'the misuse of religion and religious activities for political ends is against the constitution' (in *Constitutions et documents politiques*, PUF, Paris, 1971, p. 686). In actual fact, Albania is the only exception. In that country, article 55 of the constitution of 28 December 1976 forbids the formation of all organizations and all religious propaganda. Furthermore, under article 37 the state supports and promotes atheist propaganda.

4 V.I. Lenin, 'Socialism and religion' (text published in *Novaja Zizn*, no. 28, 16 December 1905) in *Lénine et la Religion*, Editions Sociales, Paris, 1949, pp. 26–7.

5 With the notable exception of Albania, referred to above.

6 Cardinal Stefan Wyszynski, *Zapiski wiezienne* (Notes from prison), Editions du Dialogue, Paris, 1982, p. 23.

7 Cardinal Mindszenty, *Mémoires*, Table Ronde, Paris, 1974, p. 45.

8 Wyszynski, *Zapiski wiezienne*, pp. 20–1.

9 Mindszenty, *Mémoires*, p. 135.

10 ibid., p. 57.

11 Wyszynski, *Zapiski wiezienne*, p. 21.

12 Mindszenty, *Mémoires*, p. 27.

13 ibid., p. 388.

14 Quoted by Alain Woodrow, 'Les croyants en Hongrie', *Le Monde*, Paris, 17 October 1979.

15 Quoted by Bernard Michel, *La Mémoire de Prague*, Perrin, Paris, 1986, p. 60.

16 A reading of the book by the Hungarian peasant girl Margit Gari, *Le Vinaigre et le fiel* ('Terre Humaine', Plon, Paris, 1983), is very revealing in this connection. Class consciousness seems to be an indelible trait – understandably so in one so poor. For instance, when Margit Gari is describing what she considers to be the main change that has taken place in religious life since the Second World War: 'Then, [dawn masses during advent] the first ones to go up to the Holy Table were the womenfolk of the notables, but after the new regime came in they had disappeared and thereafter there was nobody left but us, the poor tertiaries' (p. 200); or when she talks about going before the 'Agrarian reform committee': 'The committee was composed of former summas [seasonal workers] just like the signals which govern the arrivals and departures of trains at stations. As soon as the new regime had been installed they showed their other side; from the green of the Nazis they had, as if by a miracle, changed to red. . . . They immediately found a good argument for getting rid of us, poor among the poor – to make suspects of us! "Dear Pesta, excuse us! but you would be better advised to apply to the curés!" All that because my sister Erzsa was a servant in the parish and because I went to church – like everybody else had in the past. Never mind that it was from the curés that the land had been taken – the very land they were now dividing out! Too bad! There wasn't any more for us! As I had never in my life asked the priests for anything, nor given anything (except the mite for the collection) what crime had I committed by singing canticles and praying for my family to survive?' (pp. 322–3). On

the relationship between country people, national identities and class consciousness, see *Paysans et Nations d'Europe centrale et balkanique* a compilation by the RCP of the CNRS, Maisonneuve et Larose, Paris, 1985.

17 We are not speaking here about the experiments in Christian democracy carried out before the First World War and between the wars. Nevertheless, it has to be admitted that a party such as the Czech Christian Social Party, founded in 1894 under the inspiration of *Rerum Novarum* is not entirely innocent of the accusation of anti-Semitism that has been brought against it. . . . It is, however, only one example among others.

18 This statement, too, is in need of extensive qualification. It is much truer of Hungary and Poland than of Bohemia or Slovakia. In fact, in Bohemia after the battle of the White Mountain on 8 November 1620, 'Czech society lost practically all its nobility, for most of the nobles who had not been executed after the revolt of the States had been crushed and those who did not emigrate, allowed themselves to be carried away by the current of Germanization and lost all thought of sharing the fate of the Czech population' (Josef Macek, *Histoire de la Bohème (Des origines à 1918)*, Fayard, Paris, 1984, p. 215). In Slovakia it was in the main the Church that did duty for a nobility vis-à-vis the nation.

19 Michel, *La Mémoire de Prague*, p. 91.

20 This national culture began of course with the language (in Bohemia it was Josef Dobrovsky (1753–1829) who laid the foundations of modern Czech philology) and with history (the first volume of Frantisek Palacky's history of the Czech nation appeared (in German) in 1836).

21 This is not a superannuated problem. In Sovietized East-Central Europe the intelligentsia still to a large degree enjoys the prestige historically attaching to a group which feels, and up to a point is accorded, a special responsibility in respect of the nation. At the same time, this group is often resented as a privileged one, in status and social position, and this carries the risk of isolating it from the rest of the population, whose immediate preoccupations are not necessarily the same as its own. The events of 1968 in Poland are a good example of this, as are the discussions about the place and role of experts within Solidarity (on this see, in particular, Jerzy Holzer, *Solidarnosc* (1980–1), Kultura, Paris, 1984, and Jadwiga Staniszkis, *La révolution auto-limiée*, PUF, Paris, 1982.

22 Istvan Bibo, *Misère des petits Etats d'Europe de l'Est*, L'Harmattan, Paris, 1986, p. 164. This exaltation of nationalism, by a group moreover very much influenced by the aristocratic values of which it felt itself to be the heir (the 'Sarmatian culture' in Poland) did have some effects – a sometimes very exaggerated national and personal vanity, chauvinism, etc. It would be unjust to claim that these tendencies are the norm; many Poles, Czechs and Hungarians fight against them, but it would be absurd to deny that they exist. As Bibo has also written: 'Under the effect of the violent shocks they have sustained, the three nations of Eastern Europe have acquired a creditor-mentality; they think the world owes them everything and they owe the world nothing' (p. 157).

23 For example, we heard a peasant in the south of Poland saying he was glad he had 'punished' his curé, who he thought was rather too interested in collecting his church offering, by sticking the banknotes to the kitchen table before being visited by the priest on his rounds. He was crowing over the priest's surprise when he first tried to pick up the notes, not realizing that they were not simply laid on the table.

24 Here, as regards Poland, see Jerzy Kloczowski (ed.) *Histoire religieuse de Pologne*, Le

Centurion, Paris, 1987, and for Bohemia, Slovakia, Hungary and Galicia, Adam Wandruszka and Peter Urbanitsch (eds), *Die Habsburgermonarchie*, vol. 4: *The Confessions*, Verlag der österreichischen akademischen Wissenschaften, Vienna, 1985.

25 As Professor Kloczowski told us during a conversation in Paris in June 1987.
26 This refers of course to the Polish Church, not that of Rome.
27 In this connection it is not surprising that the stereotype 'Polish-Catholic' should appear with the Swedish wars of the seventeenth century, or that legends such as that of Mount Blanik should have arisen, in the depths of which the Hussite army is supposed to be sleeping, ready to emerge if the country is in serious danger, so as to liberate the Kingdom of Bohemia.
28 Bibo, *Misère des petits Etats d'Europe de l'Est*, p. 169.
29 In 1960 Cardinal Ottaviani, Secretary of the Holy Office, did not hesitate to declare: 'The times of Tamerlane have returned to history! In the mid-twentieth century we have had to deplore genocides, mass deportations, mass murders like that of the Katyn pit and massacres like those in Budapest. And that's not enough! Nobody now minds shaking hands with the new antichrists. On the contrary, they try to be the first to shake hands and exchange friendly smiles with them.' And the cardinal concluded: 'But can a Christian smile at a man who massacres Christians, at a man who, not content with denying God, insults Him and scourges by a cruel challenge His servants and His children? . . . Can one take satisfaction from any détente when there is no détente without the most elementary respect for consciences, for our faith and for the countenance of Christ, once again covered with spittle, crowned with thorns and buffeted? Can one hold out one's hand to the person who does that?' (quoted by Ernest Milcent, *A l'Est du Vatican – La papauté et les démocraties populaires*, Ed. du Cerf, Paris, 1980, pp. 8–9). In *Pacem in Terris* John XXIII writes: 'It is right always to distinguish between error and those who commit it, even in the case of men whose false ideas or inadequate ideas involve religion or morals. A man wandering in error is still a human being and retains his dignity as a person, which must always be respected. Nor does a human being ever lose the power of becoming freed from error and making his way towards the truth. And to help him to do so, the providential power of God is never lacking. Therefore it is possible that a man who today is deprived of the light of faith or wandering in error may tomorrow, thanks to the divine light, be capable of accepting the truth. If in order to perform temporal tasks believers have dealings with men prevented by erroneous ideas from believing or having full faith, such contacts may be the occasion or the incentive to a movement which may lead such men to the truth.'
30 *Le Monde*, Paris, 17–18 August 1986.
31 *Kurier*, Vienna, 30 July 1986.
32 During a conversation with the author in Budapest in June 1983.
33 In Bernard Lecomte, 'Catholiques de Hongrie: une relative liberté', *La Croix*, Paris, 14–15 July 1983.
34 According to ecclesiastical circles, the percentage of practising Catholics is around 20 per cent.
35 Quoted by Alain Woodrow, 'Les croyants en Hongrie', *Le Monde*, 17–18 October 1979.
36 Conversation with the author in Budapest on 28 June 1983.
37 Six hundred others are doing the courses by correspondence. It should, however, be said that the bishops who are members of the pro-government majority have only the status of apostolic administrators. The members of the minority are auxiliary bishops,

often at the same time in charge of a parish. Gellert Belon, auxiliary bishop of Pecs, appointed by John XXIII in 1959 – which nomination was made official by the state in 1982 – is a parish priest in another diocese; Izidor Marosi, auxiliary bishop of Vac, is also a parish priest at Kecskemet.

38 It should be borne in mind that 60 per cent of the Church finances are met by the contributions and gifts of the faithful, 15 per cent by gifts from abroad, and only 25 per cent by state subsidies.
39 Conversation with the author in Budapest in June 1983.
40 *Le Monde*, 21 January 1983.
41 Miklos Tomka, 'A Balance of Secularization in Hungary', *Social Compass*, Louvain XXVIII, 1981/1, p. 25 (published in Hungarian under the title 'A szekularizacio merlege', *Valosag*, Budapest, 1979/7, pp. 60–70).
42 Thus about 15 per cent (367) of the parish posts are vacant. In 1984 only 35 new priests were ordained. But what most calls for comment is the religious press and teaching. The Catholic press labours under restrictions caused by paper rationing. Without this constraint, *Uj Ember*, a weekly with a print run of 90,000 copies, which from its own profits finances several Catholic organizations, *Vigilia*, a monthly with a print run of 15,000 copies, *Teologia*, a quarterly, and *Katolikus Szo*, a fortnightly journal of the movement of Priests for Peace, which is government-inspired, could easily increase their circulation.

Above all, normalization does not extend to the sphere of education. Although religious instruction is officially supposed to be given in schools, the state has never ceased pressuring parents, most of whom prefer to send their children directly to the Church. 'In the case of students in the higher classes, the young people are personally interviewed and told that if they continue to attend religious education they will not be given a passport to travel abroad or that they may lose their study scholarships. Others are not allowed to join the youth movements; and still others, especially small children, are ridiculed in front of the class. Some teachers give lower marks to children who have been seen at catechism' (Paul G. Bozsoky o.f.m., 'Christians in Hungary', *Etudes*, Paris, March 1977, p. 412).
43 Quoted by Woodrow, 'Les croyants en Hongrie'.
44 In Trevor Beeson, *Prudence and Courage – The religious situation in Russia and Eastern Europe*, London, Collins, 1974.
45 Robert Aigner, 'Czechoslovakia', in *Notes et Etudes documentaires: Les problèmes religieux en Europe Orientale (1945–70)*, La Docuentation Française, no. 3790–1, Paris, May 1971, p. 47.
46 Alexander Tomski, 'Modus Morendi: L'Eglise catholique en Tchécoslovaquie', *Communio*, VII, no. 5, September–October 1982, p. 80.
47 In 'L'association *Pacem in Terris* – Un aspect des relations Eglise/Etat en Tchécoslovaquie', *Etudes*, Paris, January 1978, p. 37.
48 In *Le Monde*, 3 November 1979.
49 According to diplomats en poste in Prague, the actual percentage of resignations is over 80 per cent. Pacem in Terris had about half the Czechoslovak priests as members.
50 See on this subject, A. Heneka et al. (eds), *A Besieged Culture – Czechoslovakia Ten Years after Helsinki*, The Charter 77 Foundation and International Helsinki Federation for Human Rights, Stockholm–Vienna, 1985.
51 See *Le Monde*, 13 July 1984 and 26 September 1985.
52 For comparison, the secretary general of the PZPR (Polish Unified Workers' Party) was mentioned by only 4 per cent of respondents.

53 For example, it was the Polish bishops who, in a letter sent to the bishops in West Germany, called for reconciliation between the two peoples in 1965, immediately provoking the government to anger.
54 Adam Michnik's work *L'Eglise et la Gauche – Le dialogue Polonais*, Le Seuil, Paris, 1979, is essential reading for a recital of the development of relations between the Church and the secular opposition, and an analysis of how they drew closer to each other.
55 This word 'secularization', even when watered down by its adjective, has been queried, not to say criticized, in Poland. To avoid any misunderstanding we think it important to make it clear that is not intended to suggest that the existence of the Church has at any time ceased to appear as beneficial to the country because Solidarity came into being. But what the word does seem to us to cover is that initiatives coming from the grassroots, which before August 1980 had no other possible channel than the Church for making their appearance, found in Solidarity a vehicle and a locus which made it less urgent and indispensable to have recourse to the Church.

Moreover, the feeling of real unease that seized some leading Catholics while Solidarity lasted is sufficient testimony to the reality of this process. The logic of the movement required that the Church, after having played a leading part in bringing it to birth, should retire from the front of the stage. Moreover, other things being equal, this feeling of having lost control of a situation, and of being marginalized, was in a certain way also experienced by the members of the secular opposition who had been committed to the struggle for several years, though their feelings were expressed at other levels and in different ways. As Seweryn Blumsztajn, a member of KOR, wrote: 'Many veteran membes of the opposition felt lost in the wave that was washing over them, members of KOR in particular. They all felt themselves to be fathers of the movement. At the same time, many of them had lost their jobs and were living from hand to mouth by working underground. Therefore on a strict reading of the rules of the trade union, they were not eligible. They could not even become members of Solidarity' (in *Je rentre au pays*, Calmann-Lévy, Paris, 1985, pp. 128–9). Needless to say, both the Church and KOR regarded Solidarity as a huge success which they were proud and glad to see. All the same, it seems to us that they experienced some difficulty in finding *their* place in relation to the movement, and even within it.
56 As Bronislaw Geremek, one of Lech Walesa's principal advisers, said to us in February 1983: 'Nowadays the Church is the one place where one can feel safe, besides home. And even at home there is television – and television is the intrusion of lies. And it's not always easy to switch that off.'
57 Homily of 13 December 1981.
58 This opinion was also expressed outside the frontiers of Poland. For example, Alain Besançon in a comment on Monsignor Glemp's homily wrote: 'I would not dream of reproaching the primate for the *political* decision not to resist with force. Like any political decision, this one is a matter of opinion which awaits the verdict of history. I do not judge it. The primate had the right in his pastoral discretion to exhort his people not to mount an uprising, with the object of avoiding a massacre. But he did not have the right as a bishop to back up this statement by affirming as a Christian principle *that human life is the supreme value*. For although scripture teaches that human life is a great good, it also teaches that it can and should be sacrificed to still higher goods, such as the salvation of the soul and the worship of the true God. . . . The church has never condemned armed struggle *pro aris et focis*, an armed, violent fight to the death to save honour, justice and a minimum of freedom, without which there is no human life

Notes to pp. 44–46   211

worthy the name. It is just to fight against annihilation or the perversion of created nature because that nature is good' (in preface to Juan Miguel Garrigues, *L'Eglise, la société libre et le communisme*, 'Commentaire', Julliard, Paris, 1984, p. 22).

59 In particular during a meeting with 300 priests from Warsaw diocese in December 1982.
60 *Le Monde*, 17 February 1984.
61 *Le Monde*, 20 March 1984.
62 *Le Monde*, 17–18 August 1986.
63 *Le Monde*, 18–19 March 1984.
64 In the words of Colonel Wiskicki, the military commissioner responsible for controlling radio and television personnel during the martial law, in a secretly recorded statement: 'In the hierarchy of the Church there are divergences of opinion. The most docile, let us say, is Glemp who accepts a certain dialogue with the government. . . . Macharski [cardinal-archbishop of Cracow], takes a harder, though not extrimist, line. As regards – hm! – what's his name, Gulbinowicz [archbishop of Wroclawl], he represents the most extremist wing of the Church. . . . It's not by chance that those three have gone to see the Pope. . . . As for the lower clergy, most of the time their activities are resolutely hostile to the state' (quoted by Norman Davies, *History of Poland*, Clarendon Press, Oxford, 1982).
65 This is dealt with in our work (Patrick Michel and Georges Mink) *Mort d'un Prêtre – L'Affaire Popieluszko: Analyse d'une logique normalisatrice*, Fayard, Paris, 1985.
66 There are in the Polish church 27 dioceses, 6,790 parishes, 85 bishops (1983), 26,000 priests and 30,000 Nuns, 24 dioceses seminaries and 23 monastic seminaries. The Church has a university (the Catholic University of Lublin), as well as the Warsaw Theological Academy and the Cracow Pontifical Academy, detached from the Jagellon University, as well as 10 general secondary and trade schools. In 1980 there were 70 Catholic periodicals, with a total print run of some 720,000.
67 These were seven important leaders of Solidarity, who included Andrzej Gwiazda, Karol Modzelewski and four KOR militants including Jacek Kuron and Adam Michnik who, after having been interned on 1 December 1981, spent more than two years in prison awaiting a trial that the government had the greatest difficulty in organizing. They were amnestied after a great deal of negotiating, which went as far as the intervention of the secretary general of the United Nations, had confirmed that they were desperately seeking to avoid embarrassing trials. The accused resolutely refused offers of exile or freedom made to them on condition that they gave up all political activity.
68 *Le Monde*, 27 December 1977.
69 On this subject, see *Mort d'un Prêtre – L'Affaire Popieluszko*.
70 One of the major risks of normalization is wealth. As the Yugoslav sociologist Jakov Jukic stressed: 'It is unlikely that the Church will ever become as rich in a socialist society as it is in Western countries. It is sociologically forced to be a poor Church, and that only involves a wish in accordance with its doctrine to be a Church of the poor. In terms of its moral mission, this witness is of fundamental importance. Over against a pattern of unconstrained consumerism in certain parts of society, the Church by its very poverty takes upon itself to criticize these deviations, and also points out the real possibilities of living in a society of well-being. And the problem of abundance – material as well as spiritual – is always a moral problem with which every modern society must sooner or later be confronted in a life or death conflict. The religious community, however, already anticipates this confrontation in paradigmatic

form, not indeed because it would choose to do so, but as a consequence of historical developments and of the appearance of new social relationships' ('La religion et les sécularismes dans les sociétés socialistes', *Social Compass*, Louvain, XXVIII, 1981/1, pp. 23–4).
71 This is obviously the contingent ideal of a government that has renounced total elimination of the Church in the short or medium term. Quite obviously, the absolute ideal would be that there should be no religion, no Church, and no religious longings within society.
72 Quoted by Nicholas Bethell, *Gomulka, His Poland and His Communism*, Penguin, Harmondsworth, 1972, p. 245.
73 In *Istina*, Paris, no. 3–4, 1977, pp. 332–7.
74 See *Le Monde*, 5 September 1986.

2 Religion and Scientific Socialism: A Sociological Analysis

1 We are not here discussing events in East Germany in 1953, which had quite a different motivation.
2 For examle, a *Report on the ecclesiastico-political situation* had been submitted to the central committee of the Slovak Communist Party on 9 September 1969, resulting in a *Draft of measures for the process to be followed in the field of ecclesiastical policy in Slovakia*.
3 See his press conference in *Istina*, Paris, no. 3–4/1977, pp. 332–7.
4 It should also be stressed that from 1960 onwards some writers – here the Hungarian J. Lukacs – were talking about 'personal solitude' as an essential factor in the maintenance of religion in a socialist country. He contended that even if the government creates the superstructures promoting the flourishing of the individual in society, subjective factors may oppose this blossoming and hence help to maintain archaisms – that is to say, mental structures in which subjectivity overpowers objectivity.
5 Miklos Tonka, 'A Selected Bibliography of Sociological Studies on Religion in Hungary (1945–79)', *Social Compass*, Louvain, XXVIII, 1981/1, pp. 125–41.
6 In this connection see the revelations that emerged in the trial of the policemen found guilty of the murder of Father Popieluszko in Patrick Michel and Georges Mink, *Mort d'un Prêtre – L'Affaire Popieluszko: Analyse d'une logique normalisatrice*, Fayard, Paris, 1985, and, by the same authors, 'La police polonaise comme instrument de normalisation', study for the research project *Les crises des systèmes de type soviétique*, directed by Z. Mlynar, no. 12, Cologne, Index, 1986.
7 Jaroslav Krejci, 'Religion and anti-religion: experience of a transition', *Sociological Analysis*, vol. 36, no. 2, Fisk University, Nashville, Tennessee, 1975, p. 114.
8 Istvan Kiss, 'A vallasos gondolkodas es magatartas nehany szerkezeti sajatossaga a tsz tagsag köreben' ('Some structural characteristics of the religious thinking and behaviour of peasants members of cooperatives'), *Tajekoztato*, no. 3, 1977, pp. 91–103.
9 Laszlo Nemeth, 'A vallasi szekularizacio es a szektak' ('Secularization and sects'), *Hevesti Szemle*, no. 1, 1978, pp. 43–6.
10 See, for example, Josef Poor, 'Az atheista propaganda es a vallasos vilagnezet' ('Atheist propaganda and religious ideology'), *Partelet*, no. 6, 1978, pp. 42–8.

11 Mihaly Muranyi and Zsuzsa Dömök, 'Vallasossag, hitkozöny, ateizmus?' ('Faith, indifference, atheism? Characteristics of the ideological orientations of young people of Budapest'), *Vilagossag*, nos 8–9, 1976.
12 J. Bango, 'L'influence des facteurs politiques et socioculturels sur la religiosité de la jeunesse hongroise', *Revue des pays de l'Est*, Institute of Sociology of Brussels Free University, 19th year no. 1, 1978, pp. 63–83. Table 2.3 is taken from that publication.
13 Bela Hegyi, 'A Vaallasgyakorlas szociologiaja' ('The sociology of religious practice'). *Teologia*, Budapest, no. 1. 1969, p. 44.
14 This survey, which is quite representative despite some over-representation of the large cities (Prague, Brno and Bratislava), and under-representation of peasants and Party members (8 per cent instead of 14 per cent) was presented at the Ecole des Hautes Etudes en Sciences Sociales, Paris, on 21 April 1986, in the course of a seminar originated by Georges Mink and the author. An article about it was written in Czech, 'Vysledky pruzkumu', in *Svedectvi*, XX, 78, Paris, 1986, pp. 265–334, the main parts of which were reprinted in 'Tchécoslovaquie: enquête sur l'opinion', *L'Autre Europe*, no. 13, l'Age d'Homme, Paris, 1987, pp. 85–108.
15 Andrzej Swiecicki (in collaboration with Andrzej Potocki, Janina Slonimska and Witold Zdaniewicz), 'Situation de la sociologie des religions in Pologne comparée à celle des autres pays socialistes d'Europe', *Actes de la 14e*, CISR (Strasbourg, 1977), Lille, 1977, p. 411.
16 ibid., p. 421. Our emphasis.
17 ibid.
18 Leonard J. Pelka, 'Rozwoj badan nad demonologia ludowa w Polsce w latach 1918–78' ('The development of the study of popular demonology in Poland from 1918 to 1978') *Studia Religiologica*, zeszyt 3, Zeszyty naukowe Uniwersytetu Jagiellonskiego, DXXIII, Panstwowe Wydawnictwo Naukowe, Warsaw, 1978, pp. 73–82.
19 Emilia Przywara, 'Obraz Religijnosci w przyslowiach polskich' ('Religious belief reflected in Polish proverbs'), ibid., pp. 99–122.
20 Piotr Szydlowski, 'Walka polskiej filizofii katolickiej (1918–39) z kultura swiecka' ('The fight of Catholic philosophy against secular culture (1918–39)'), ibid., pp. 43–72.
21 R. Ludwikowski, 'Poliyczny rodowod stereotypu ''Polaka-katolicka'' ' ('The political origin of the stereotype: Polish-Catholic'), ibid., pp. 19–42.
22 Jan Pawlicka, 'Pojecie i przedmiot swiatopogladu' ('Formation and object of a worldview'), ibid., pp. 9–18.
23 Beata Witkowska, 'Stosunek Episkopata Polski do niektorych zalozen ustrojowych Polski Ludowej' ('The attitude of the Polish episcopate regarding some principles of the political system of the People's Republic of Poland'), ibid., pp. 83–98.
24 Stanislaw Gebethner, 'La Pologne 1980–85 – La société bipolarisée ou coupée en trois', paper read at the Franco-Polish colloquium *Etat et société en France et en Pologne (1980–85)*, Paris, 15 and 16 July 1985, directed by Professor Duverger and Professor Suchecki, typewritten manuscript in the author's possession, appendix VIII, table 40, p. xii.
25 ibid., appendix IX, table 41, p. xiii.
26 It will however, be observed that only 37 per cent of respondents said they had confidence in the Party, against 42.9 per cent who had not, 19.6 per cent don't knows and 0.4 per cent who gave no reply.
27 ibid., p. 21.

28 In connection with his paper read at the above Franco-Polish colloquy, 'L'Eglise catholique de Pologne entre la société et le pouvoir'.
29 Gebethner, 'La Pologne 1980–85', pp. 21–2.
30 This does not take account of the special case of Yugoslavia, which does not in fact belong to Sovietized Europe, or of the presence in an individual capacity of some sociologists from the East, such as Tomka, at the CISR.
31 We tried to describe some of the trends in Polish sociological production in our work *L'Eglise de Pologne et l'avenir de la Nation*, Le Centurion, Paris, 1981, especially pp. 37–54. For a study in greater depth, see Maciej Pomian-Srzednicki, *Religious Change in Contemporary Poland: Secularization and Politics*, Routledge & Kegan Paul, London, 1982, and Wladyslaw Piwowarski, 'Les orientations, les méthodes et la problématique dans la sociologie de la religion en Pologne (1957–77)', in *Religiousness in the Polish Society Life (Chosen Problems)*, Studia socjologiczno-religijne, no. 3, The Sociological Research Institute of Religion, Pallottinum, Warsaw, 1982, pp. 5–33.
32 Besides these centres, independent researchers should also be mentioned. Especially during the Solidarity period, a great number of studies were carried out on religion. Most of these were micro-surveys, carried out within a single parish. Obviously not all such surveys are equally valuable – and few of them have been published.
33 Wladyslaw Piwowarski, 'Les orientations, les méthodes et la problématique dans la sociologie de la religion en Pologne (1957–77)', in *Religiousness in the Polish Society Life (Chosen Problems)*. See also Wladyslaw Piwowarski and Witold Zdaniewicz, 'Z badan nad religijnoscia Polska – Studia i materialy' ('Research on Polish religious sentiment – studies and data'), Studia socjogiczno-religijne, Pallottinum, Poznan-Warsaw, 1986.
34 We should also mention here the contribution made by the other social sciences, in particular by history and ethnology; that of political science has already been mentioned. For example, the work done by the team of researchers from the Institute of Historical Cartography of Lublin Catholic University under the direction of Professor Jerzy Kloczowski has already resulted in the publication of a joint paper on the history of Christianity in Poland, published in Polish but also in Italian and French (*Histoire religieuse de la Pologne*, Le Centurion, Paris, 1987) and containing in French a chapter on the period subsequent to the Second World War, which borrows extensively from sociographical and sociological works.

Ethnologists like Dobrowolski or Anna Kunczynska, among others, have investigated the problems of religion and a publication as important as *Etnografia Polska – Przemiany kultury Iudowej*, vol. II, Polska Akademia Nauk, Instytut historii kultury materialnej, Warsaw, 1981, carries, for example, an article by Ryszard Tomicki on popular religiousness. On the basis of the works of Thomas and Znaniecki, Poniatowski, Bystron, Czarnowski and Moszynski, the author deals mainly with three aspects of popular religion – beliefs, religious and magical practices, and relations between the priest, representing the official Church, and the community of believers. On the latter point the analysis deals with the factors conditioning the formation of the priest's authority and the complex relationship that exists between the canonically defined functions of the priest and what the people actually expect of him.
35 See on this subject the reports of Andrzej Nowicki, 'The Development of the Socialist Secular Culture in Poland', Arkadiusz Sikorski, 'The Role of the Society for the Popularization of the Secular Culture in Forming the Secular Educational Program in the Polish People's Republic', and Jan Jerschina, Halina Moszczynska and Jan Pawlica, 'Methodological Problems of Research on the Science of Religion', presented at the

Notes to pp. 66–69   215

meeting of researchers on the sciences of religions (*religioznawstwo*) of member countries of the Council of Mutual Economic Aid (COMECON) at the Institute of the Sciences of Religions (Cracow, 15–17 December 1977) and published in *Studia Religiologica - Zeszyty naukowe Uniwersytetu Jagiellonskiego*, DXXIII, Panstwowe Wydawnictwo Naukowe, Warsaw, 1978, pp. 157–77.

36 Piwowarski, 'Les orientations', p. 9.
37 Jerzy Goldlewski, 'Wspolczesne problemy laicyzacji' ('Contemporary problems connected with secularization') in W. Myslek and M. T Staszewski (eds), *Polityka wyznaniowa* (*The Politics of Religious Affairs*), Warsaw, 1975, p. 235.
38 Edward Ciupak, 'Marksowska socjologia religii' ('Marxist sociology of religion'), *Argumenty*, Warsaw, 3 December 1972.
39 There is a striking illustration of this in the (confidential) report by an eminent Catholic intellectual dealing with 'a review of pastoral activities in Poland' (typescript in the author's possession, 1986). The writer constantly refers back and forth from sociological and sociographic studies carried out by 'various ecclesiastical and lay centres', to the attitudes adopted in pastoral work, with the latter based on and attested by the former.
40 Andrzej Potocki, 'Conditionnements philosophiques de la sociology des religions en Pologne', in *Religiousness in the Polish Society Life (Chosen Problems)*, pp. 71–2.
41 A large amount of sociological writing on this subject has been published. Here we will mention only: Jan Jerschina, *Mlodziez i procesy laicyzacji swiadomosci spolecznej* (*Youth and the Secularization Process in Social Conciousness*), Prace socjologiczne, zeszyt 4, Zeszyty naukowe Uniwersytetu Jagellionskiego, CCCLXXXIV, Panstwowe Wydawnictwo Naukowe, Warsaw, 1978, 121 pp.; Hubert Domagala and Halina Grzymala-Moszczynska, 'Postawy wobec religii a niektore sposoby i warunki spolecznego funkcjonowania mlodziezy' ('Attitudes with regard to religion according to certain parameters and modes of social functioning by young people'), *Studia Religiologica*, zeszyt 4, Zeszyty naukowe Uniwersytetu Jagellionskiego, DXXVII, Panstwowe Wydawnictwo Naukowe, Warsaw, 1979, pp. 37–82; Joanna Blachnicka, 'Proba analizy spojnosci postaw religiinych mlodziezy' ('A tentative analysis of the coherence of the attitudes of youth with regard to religion'), ibid., pp. 83–106.
42 Maciej Pomian-Srzednicki, *Religious Change in Contemporary Poland: Secularization and Politics*, Routledge & Kegan Paul, London, 1982, p. 198.
43 Edward Ciupak, 'Marksowska krytyka "nieba" ' ('The Marxist critique of "heaven" '), *Argumenty*, Warsaw, 19 June 1978.
44 Wladyslaw Piwowarski, 'Popular religion in Poland: continuity and change', *Concilium*, no. 151, 1979, p. 80.
45 See Stefan Nowak, 'Wartosci i postawy spoleczne' ('Values and social behaviour'), in *Systemy swartosci a wzory konsumpcii spoleczenstwa polskiego* ('Value systems and consumption models of Polish society'), Warsaw, 1980, p. 295, and M. Misztal, 'Wielowymiarowa analiza wartosci' ('Multidimensional analysis of values'), *Studia Socjologiczne*, no. 1–2, Warsaw, 1982, p. 289.
46 Wladislaw Piwowarski, 'Przemiany religijnosci ludowej w srodowisku wiejskim' ('Changes in popular religion in the countryside'), *Kultura i Spoleczenstwo*, XXVIII, no. 3, Warsaw, 1984, p. 40.
47 Kazimierz Sopuch, 'Zroznicowanie stosunka do religii w zaleznosci od niektorych zmiennych struktury spolecznej' ('Differentiation of the attitude to religion in relation to certain variables in the social structure'), *Kultura i Spoleczenstwo*, XXVII, no. 3, Warsaw, 1984, pp. 202–3.
48 Franciszek Adamski, 'Sekularyzacja malzenstwa i rodziny' ('Secularization of marriage

and the family'), *Kultura i Spoleczenstwo*, XXVIII, no. 3, Warsaw, 1984, p. 212–13.
49 Zenon Kawecki, 'Postawy robotnikov wobec religii' ('The attitude of workers to religion'), *Czlowiek i Swiatopoglad*, Warsaw, no. 1, 1976.
50 Potocki, 'Conditionnements philosophiques'.
51 In particular the research of Krysztof Kosela, of the Institute of Sociology at Warsaw University, who holds that in matters of religion the respondents opt for the identification that would entail the minimum of social obligations (in 'The Puzzle of the Poles' Religious Identity', a paper presented at the 19th International Conference of the Sociology of Religion on 20 August 1987 at Tübingen, West Germany, manuscript in the author's possession).

3 Religion and Society: The Meaning of Modernity

1 In Alain Woodrow, 'Les Croyants en Hongrie', *Le Monde*, 17 October 1979.
2 Thus a Prague priest had his work permit withdrawn because he was attracting *too many* children to the catechism. He was basing his teaching on the use of audiovisual aids such as the projection of transparencies.
3 Miklos Tomka, 'A Balance of Secularization', *Social Compass*, Louvain, XXVIII, 1980/1, p. 25.
4 Laszlo Paskai, 'La vie religieuse des catholiques de Hongrie', *Conscience et liberté*, Berne, no. 28, 1984, pp. 94–5.
5 ibid., p. 96.
6 The material in this section was first published in *Social Compass*, Louvain, XXXII/4, 1985, *Archives de Sciences Sociales de Religions*, Paris, no. 62/1, 1986, and *Revue d'Etudes comparative Est-Ouest*, Paris, no. 14/1, 1983. It is reproduced by kind permission of these reviews.
7 Cardinal Stefan Wyszynski, 'Aux étudiants', an address given on 28 January 1963. French readers can refer to: Cardinal Stefan Wyszynski, *Un évêque au service du peuple de Dieu*, Ed. Saint-Paul, Paris-Fribourg, 1970, p. 51.
8 Title of an article by Henri Tincq in *Le Monde*, 15 October 1985. Reporting on a bishops' symposium held in Rome from 7 to 11 October, the author writes: 'The bishops from Eastern Europe almost think that the West, although it lives under a regime of freedom, is in process of losing its faith whereas the East, subject to ideological and political dictatorship, has been able to retain a deep sense of God.'
9 Dionizy Tanalski, *Katolicyzm – Ewolucja ideologii*, PWN, Biblioteka Problemow, Warsaw, 1978, p. 168.
10 ibid.
11 In *Prymas tysiaclecia*, special issue of *Nasza Rodzina*, Ed. du Dialogue, Paris, 1982, p. 131.
12 Wyszynski, *Un évêque*, pp. 78–9.
13 K. Kakol, president of the Office of Religious Affairs, at a press conference held in Warsaw on 19 May 1976, in *Istina*, no. 3–4, Paris, 1977, pp. 332–7.
14 Wyszynski, *Un évêque*, p. 80.
15 ibid., p. 80.
16 'The best field of battle for overcoming the Church is at the cultural level of a more properous, more comfortable life. With a consumer society, we shall have conditions comparable with those in the West so as to hasten the withering away of the Church', press conference by Kakol (see note 13).

17 In *Listy pasterskie Prymasa Polski*, Ed. du Dialogue, Paris, 1975, p. 616.
18 Adam Boniecki, 'Etre prêtre en Pologne', in *Nous, Chrétiens de Pologne*, Ed. Cana, Paris, 1979, p. 133.
19 Adam Michnik, *L'Eglise et la Gauche - Le dialogue polonais*, Le Seuil, Paris, 1979 (esp. pp. 136ff).
20 Adam Lopatka, in *Nowe Drogi*, theoretical monthly of the central committee of the PZPR, June 1983.
21 On this matter see Daniel Olszewski, 'W okresie ucisku i glebokich przemian spolecznych (1864-1914)', in *Chrzescijanstwo w Polsce*, Lublin, 1980, pp. 243-70.
22 ibid.
23 Jerzy Zawieyski, *Droga katechumena*, Wiez library, Warsaw, p. 35.
24 *Hebdomadaire universel*, published at Cracow, close to the Pope; *Le Lien*, monthly of the Warsaw Club of Catholic intellectuals.
25 Michnik, *L'Eglise et la Gauche*, pp. 112-13.
26 Cardinal Macharski, 'La vie chrétienne dans les temps difficiles', in *Les Quatre Fleuves*, no. 13 of series, Beauchesne, Paris, 1981, p. 12.
27 Boniecki, 'Etre prêtre en Pologne', p. 138.
28 The minutes of this meeting, 'Spotkanie Prymasa z ksiezmi Archidiecezji Warszawskei - 7 gruddna 1982', are published in *Zeszyty Historyczne*, no. 64, Instytut Literacki, Paris, 1983, pp. 206-18.
29 Boniecki, 'Etre prêtre en Pologne', p. 139.
30 In *Le Monde*, 13 June 1979.
31 Stefan Wilkanowicz, 'La signification de la Pologne pour les chrétiens d'Europe', in *Les Quatre Fleuves*, p. 18.
32 Cardinal Wyszynski, 'O zadaniach posoborowych Kosciola i o jego polozeniu w Polsce', in *Listy Pasterskie episkopatu Polski*, Ed. du Dialogue, Paris, 1975, pp. 460-1.
33 ibid.
34 Wyszynski, address of 20 February 1966, in *Un évêque*, p. 97.
35 Regarding them, Father Boniecki asks: 'A certain fanaticism and an attitude of superiority or the only way in which Catholicism in Poland can be renewed and deepened?'
36 Wyszynski, address of 4 January 1963, Gniezno, in *Un évêque*, p. 42.
37 Jerzy Lewandowski, *L'Eglise et la Nation polonaise selon le cardinal Wyszynski*, Ed. Peter Lang, Berne, 1982.
38 In *Prymas tysiaclecia*, pp. 182-3.
39 Jerzy Mirewicz, 'Jean-Paul II dans le drame du catholicisme polonais', in *Les Quatre Fleuves*, no. 13, Beauchesne, Paris, 1981, pp. 23-8.
40 Adam Michnik, *L'Eglise et la Gauche - Le dialogue polonais*, p. 124.
41 Mirewicz, 'Jean-Paul II'.
42 Cardinal Stefan Wyszynski, 'O Zadaniach posoborowych Kosciola i o jego polozeniu v Polsce', in *Listy Pasterskie episkopatu Polski*, Ed. du Dialogue, Paris, 1975, p. 469.
43 Jean-Marie Domenach, 'Société et Eglise en Pologne', *Esprit*, no. 10, Paris, October 1976, p. 345.
44 Biuro Prasowe Sekretariu Episkopatu Polski, 15 February 1978, published by *La Documentation catholique*, Paris, no. 1739, 2 April 1978, p. 323.
45 Alain Touraine et al., *Solidarity, Analyse d'un mouvement social, Pologne 1980-81*, Fayard, Paris, 1982, pp. 88-9.
46 Pastoral letter of Cardinal Wyszynski, *La Documentation catholique*, Paris, no 1739, 2 April 1978.
47 Statement by Cardinal Wyszynski at the Conference of Polish Conventual friars at

Notes to pp. 89–95

Warsaw on 11 May 1977, in *Prymas Tysiaclecia*, special number of *Nasza Rodzina*, Paris, 1982, p. 226.
48 Quoted by Trevor Beeson, *Prudence and Courage*, Collins, London, 1974.
49 Speech by Cardinal Wyszynski at Warsaw on 6 January 1978, in *Prymas tysiaclecia*, p. 143.
50 Press release from the 171st plenary conference of the Polish episcopate held on 13 and 14 December 1979, in *Raport o stanie Narodu i P.R.L.* (*Report on the State of the Nation and the People's Republic of Poland*), Instytut Literacki, Biblioteka Kultury, no. 313, Paris, 1980, p. 220.
51 Speech by Cardinal Wyszynski at Gniezno on 2 February 1978, in *Prymas tsiaclecia*, p. 144.
52 *La Réforme économique en Pologne – Prémisses, principes généraux, état de réalisation*, Government Press Office, Ministry of Foreign Affairs, translation by the Polish agency Interpress, Warsaw, 1982, p. 4.
53 ibid., p. 3.
54 In *Prymas tysiaclecia*, p. 191.
55 In Touraine et al., *Solidarity*, pp. 193–4.
56 Cardinal Wyszynski, speaking at the conference of Conventual friars at Warsaw on 11 May 1977, in *Prymas tysiaclecia*, p. 27.
57 Cardinal Wyszynski, homily delivered at Warsaw on 6 January 1978, in *La Documentation catholique*, no. 1739, Paris, April 1978, p. 323.
58 Cardinal Wyszynski, speech at Gniezno on 2 February 1981, in *Prymas tysiaclecia*, p. 192.
59 Cardinal Wyszynski, speech at the inauguration of the university year at the Catholic University of Lublin on 21 October 1979, ibid., pp. 185–6.
60 Cardinal Wyszynski, letters written in August 1977, ibid., pp. 141–2.
61 Cardinal Wyszynski, speech at pastoral conference in September 1980, ibid.
62 Cardinal Wyszynski, sermon at Christmas 1980, ibid., p. 234.
63 Cardinal Wyszynski, speech on 7 October 1979, ibid., p. 227.
64 Cardinal Wyszynski, homily delivered at Warsaw on 6 January 1978, p. 323.
65 Cardinal Wyszynski, pastoral letter 'O spolecznej krucjacie milosci' ('The social crusade of love'), in *Listy pasterskie episkopatu Polski*, Ed. du Dialogue, Paris, 1975, p. 551.
66 ibid.
67 Pastoral letter of the Polish episcopate, 'Wezwanie do trzezwosci' ('Call to sobriety'), in *Listy pasterskie episkopatu Polski*, p. 387.
68 In 'Appel de la commission episcopale sur la sobriété ('Chronique du diocèse de Sandomierz' nos 1–2), cited by Krzystof Pomian, 'La censure mise à nu', *Libre*, no. 79–6, Payot, Paris, 1979, p. 17.
69 In *Raport o stanie naroda i PRL*, Instytut Literacki, Biblioteka Kultury, no. 313, Paris, 1980, p. 94.
70 On this subject, see *Czarna ksiega censury PRL* (*Black book of censorship in the People's Republic of Poland*), Aneks, London, 1977.
71 Pastoral letter of the Polish episcopate 'O pijanstwie' ('Alcoholism') in *Listy pasterskie episkopatu Polski*, p. 49.
72 ibid., p. 50.
73 In *Raport o stanie narodu i PRL*, p. 219.
74 Stefan Nowak, 'Valeurs et attitudes du peuple polonais', *Pour la Science*, Paris, no. 47, 1981, p. 23.

75 In fact, Durkheim holds that religion is a social creation, reflecting a given state of development. For the author of the *Formes élémentaires de la vie religieuse*, religion expresses man's relationship to the sacred. Giving an ideal image of society, it forms a basis for integrating society and provides a bond of submission to the rules of society. It will disappear as society develops.

Max Weber's work gives rise to another broad line of explanation. Whereas Emile Durkheim was primarily interested in religion as a social phenomenon, its origin and functions, Weber did not seek to arrive at an overall definition of religion or to analyse its origins, but to list the consequences of the presence of a given religious system in a given society. Thus he emphasized the causal relations of the influence of religion (values, value systems, ideology) in the production of certain socioeconomic forms of collective life.

Marxism sees religion as a product of the infrastructure, that is to say, of the historically determined level of productive relationships in society. Its place is in the superstructure, this group of ideologies, beliefs, technical and literary knowledge that thinkers adopting this approach superimpose upon the true state of society and its economic relationships, most often as a misshapen representation, a reflection of man's alienation. Consequently, the more man dominates nature, understands the true state of productive relationships and is able to break free from false conceptions, the more will religion tend to disappear. In any event, this approach interprets religion as a product of socioeconomic structures.

The fourth great explanatory tradition has its roots in the work of the psychoanalysts. As a gross simplification, it seems that for a Freud or a Fromm, the individual produces

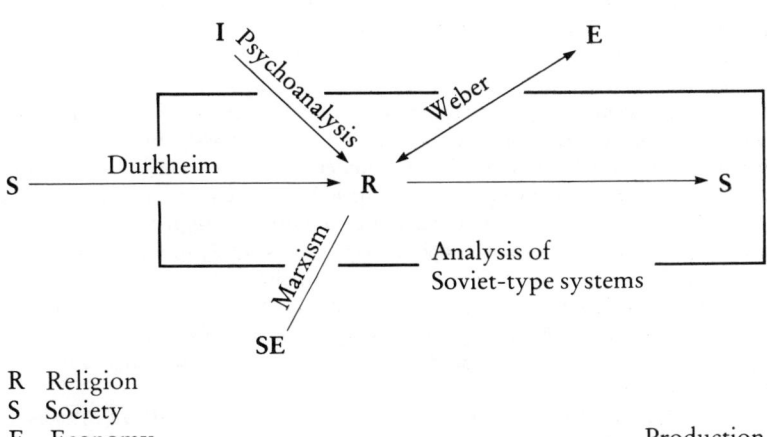

R Religion
S Society
E Economy
I Individual/Personality

⎯⎯⎯⎯⎯→ Production
←⎯⎯⎯⎯⎯ Influence

religion, finding in it a support against the threats contained in the incomprehensible forces of nature and those of instinct within. It provides a guidance system for better self-understanding. So the religious is an elaborate form of defence of the individual.

These four traditional approaches, here simplified to the point of caricature (and there are many other varieties of analysis, including those of Simmel or de Tocqueville, or those majoring in ethnology or anthropology), still influence studies of religion in relation to politics, economics or sociology. Each one, in its pure form, favours a determinist pattern. The following diagram is an attempt to illustrate this:

Naturally the case of the religious as producer of a social form which is threatened with absorption as soon as it appeared does not appear in the traditional approaches listed here.

76 Wladyslaw Piwowarski, 'Operacjonalizacja pojecia religijnosc' ('Operationalization of the concept of religiosity'), *Studia Sociologiczne*, no. 4, Warsaw, 1975, p. 155.
77 Quotations extracted from interviews held in Prague in December 1982 and January 1983.
78 Niklos Tomka, 'A szekularizacio merlege', *Valosag*, no. 7, Budapest, 1979, pp. 60–70 (article reprinted under the title 'A balance of secularization', in *Social Compass*, XXVIII, Louvain, 1981/1, p. 25).
79 J. Jerschina and C. Ulasinski, 'Kierunki przemian religijnosci mlodziezy polskie' ('Trends towards change in the religious attitudes of Polish youth'), *Kultura i Spoleczenstwo*, Warsaw, no. 4, 1985, p. 153.

4 Religion and Politics: Symbolism, Catacombs and Opposition

1 Peter Berger, *The Social Reality of Religion*, Faber, London, 1969.
2 The open letter published on 13 January 1977 by Maria Rut Krizkova giving her reasons for joining the Charter is an exemplary witness of this course of action. It included the words: 'I have begun to understand more deeply the meaning and the price of my conversion. . . . Before it was a hopeless desert of empty life, of life without God and without an aim, a life whose only foundation was my search for the truth' (in *Istina*, XXII, no. 2, Paris, 1977, pp. 196–7).
3 Berger, *The Social Reality of Religion*, p. 160.
4 For these problems, see Jean-François Bayard, 'L'Enonciation du politique', *Revue Française de Science Politique*, vol. 35, no. 3, Paris, June 1985, pp. 343–73.
5 We are aware of the limitations of such an undertaking. Michel de Certeau puts it very well: 'Must not any attempt at typology ultimately fail, even if it is useful . . .; because it is global? It would assert both the necessity and the impossibility of recapturing the whole' (in *Absent de l'histoire*, Repères-Mame, Paris, 1973, p. 142).
6 For this concept, see Bayard, 'L' Enonciation du politique'.
7 This study was first published in the *Archives de Sciences Sociales des Religions*, no. 51/1, 1981. It is reproduced here by kind permission of the review.
8 In *Anthropologie structurale*, Plon, Paris, Coll. 'Agora', 1985, see esp. chapters IX and X, pp. 191–234.
9 We have developed this example in our work, *Eglise de Pologne et l'Avenir de la nation*, Le Centurion, Paris, 1981, pp. 19–21.
10 This list was published under the title 'Espace sacré et espace social; l'exemple de

Zywiec (Pologne)' in *Richerche di storia sociale e religiosa*, Ed. di storia e letteratura, Rome, nos 19–20, 1981, pp. 265–308.

11 For example, we were assured at Zywiec that there had never been any Protestants in the district, but on examining documents in ecclesial archives we became convinced that some Hussites exiled from nearby Bohemia had settled at Zywiec, where they had obtained the right to use the so-called 'Three Crosses' church. Nobody at Zywiec seems to remember this.

12 During two lectures given at the Collège de France on 18 and 25 May 1977.

13 In *Istina*, Paris, XXVIII, no. 1, 1983, pp. 95–6.

14 In *L'Alternative*, no. 9, Paris, March–April 1981, p. 11.

15 'Les croyants en Hongrie', *Le Monde*, 17–18 October 1979.

16 'Catholiques de Hongrie: une liberté relative', *La Croix*, 14–15 July 1982. The reproach is by no means a new one. Margit Gari, a poor peasant girl of Nezökövesd, tells how (before the war): 'At the time we were working on an estate belonging to a religious order. But it was no use attending church assiduously, there were never any great priests. Yet we met them more frequently in the vineyards. . . . I recall very, very well all these important personages who passed very close to us while we were pegging away with the hoe. They sat round in a circle without deigning to glance at us and started to turn their spits. . . . As they rested them on forked branches, I couldn't help muttering to myself: "Oh, dear Lord, their hands can't even hold up the spits when ours would do it so gladly if only we had something to grill on it each morning" ' in *Le Vinaigre et le Fiel*, Plon, Paris, 1983, p. 217).

17 P. G. Boszoky, o.f.m., 'Chrétiens en Hongrie', *Etudes*, Paris, March 1977, p. 410.

18 Michèle Bertrand, *Le statue de la religion chez Marx et Engels*, Ed. Sociales, Paris, 1979, p. 138.

19 Unless otherwise stated, the quotations from Bulanyi are taken from an interview that took place in Budapest in June 1983.

20 In 'Les croyants en Hongrie'.

21 Bulyani's writings had already been submitted to the Congrégation pour la Doctrine de la Foi in 1978 by the vicar-general of the Piarists, who wished to end the growing tension between the episcopate and Bulanyi. In 1980 the Congrégration had stated that it found nothing heretical in the texts that had been sent to it for scrutiny.

22 Some of these priests explained their conduct in letters sent to the primate. Some of these texts, as it happens letters from Bulanyi, Barna Barcza, Ferenc Dombi, curé of Patka, and Laszlo Kovacs, curé of Annavölgy, are reproduced, on pp. 46–9, in a manuscript without title, date or signature but committing all the Hungarian base communities, and claiming to be an open letter to John Paul II (manuscript in the author's possession, 99pp. – we thank Istvan Niko for having sent us this text).

23 There are other Catholic basic communities, which cause fewer problems to the hierarchy and the government. The sociologist Szusa Horvath has carried out a complete study of this phenomenon, in a text of which the French title is *Le Ferment de l'Eglise: le mouvement des communautés de Base en Hongrie* (manuscript in the author's possession).

24 Quoted by Clifford Longley, 'Vatican Dilemma on Hungary', *The Times*, London, 11 April 1983. We may, however, recall in passing that twenty years ago Vatican II came out in favour of the necessary respect by states for individual conscience, implying that it was legitimate for a believer to choose conscientious objection.

25 It is in fact well known that the Hungarian government has approached the Vatican to

take steps against Bulyani, for example when Imre Niklos visited Rome early in 1983.
26 Noted down during an interview in Budapest in June 1983.
27 Manuscript cited *supra*, p. 33.
28 ibid., p. 37. There is a striking similarity between the terms employed here and those used by Father Yakounine in 1965 in his celebrated 'open letter to the Patriarch Alexis': 'At the present time the situation of the Church in Russia is such that it is subjected to interference by the government and the executives of this Council (for the affairs of the Orthodox Church) the object of which is the destruction of the church. . . . Driven by the imperative demands of Christian conscience, we consider it our duty to say that this situation could not have arisen in the Church but for culpable tolerance on the part of the highest authority of the Church, which has not fulfilled its obligations towards Christ and the Church, and by thus violating the Apostle's precept it has clearly "conformed to this world" (Rom. XII.2).' Further on, Gleb Yakounine expressed his indignation at the fact that the Church authorities obeyed 'without reserve' the directives of the civil power, (Gleb Yakounine, *Un prêtre seul au pays des soviets*, Ed. Criterion, Paris, 1984, introduction by François Rouleau and foreword by Olivier Clément, p. 41).
29 ibid., p. 99.
30 Ladislas Hejdanek, 'Le sens et la place du christianisme dans la société actuelle', *Istina*, XXVIII, no. 1, Paris, 1983, p. 66.
31 Jakub S. Trojan, 'En quoi l'Eglise est-elle irremplaçable?', *Istina*, XXVIII, no. 1, Paris, 1983, pp. 63–4.
32 Jan Patocka, 'Ce qu'est la Charte 77 et ce qu'elle n'est pas–Pourquoi le droit se trouve du côté des signataires et pourquoi des mesures répressives ne sauraient en venir à bout', *Istina*, XXII, no. 2, Paris, 1977, pp. 199–200, for the extracts cited here.
33 Quoted by Bernard Michel, in *La mémoire de Prague*, Perrin, Paris, 1986, p. 93. The author also quotes Masaryk (p. 105): 'The Czech question was and is a religious question. Just as the nation has undergone economic, social, political, scientific and artistic development, so also it has undergone moral and religious development. It is true that today many people do not see this. Most people's attention is drawn to national and social problems but whoever looks more deeply will see that a moral and hence also a religious question is involved as well.'
34 In *Listy*, XIII, no. 6, Rome, 1983, pp. 10–17.
35 Some people divined at a very early stage that only if it acted in this way would the Church be able to surmount the trial forced upon it by confrontation with the Soviet-type system. For example, in December 1949 Father Jean Boulier wrote in the December issue of the review *l'Europe*: 'Religion in a communist regime is destined to die by withering away;. . . . Under a Marxist regime the survival of the Church depends only upon itself, on its inner vitality, faith, hope and love, not on the crutches offered to it by the government. It is a wonderful trial, not of power, diplomacy, intimidation or cunning, but simply of health. The Church is not under threat because Marxism is strong: all that threatens the Church is its own weakness, or rather ignorance, the lack of true historical culture, an uncritical theology, laymen without initiative, a clergy which administers but has lost the sense of living witness, which would perhaps die bravely for the faith but which does not see in the faith reasons why its people should live.'
36 Trojan, 'En quoi l'Eglise est-elle irremplaçable?', p. 62.
37 For Max Weber, 'The life of the saint was exclusively directed towards a transcendental end: salvation. Precisely for this reason, it was totally *rationalized* in this world, and

dominated entirely by this single aim – to increase on earth the glory of God. Never had the precept *omnia in maiorem Dei gloriam* been understood with more rigour. Only a life directed by a constant thought could effectively transcend the *status naturalis* (in *l'Ethique Protestant et l'esprit du capitalisme*, Plon, Paris, 1964, p. 146).

38 The term is used here in the sense given to it by Albert Hirschman in his *Exit, Voice and Loyalty*, Harvard University Press, Cambridge, 1970.

39 Trojan, 'En quoi l'Eglise est-elle irremplaçable?', p. 46.

40 Cardinal-primate Tomasek, for example, never concealed in private the esteem in which he held the most radical priests and theologians, even if in the past he had had to criticize or even condemn them officially.

41 Josef Zverina, *Odvaha byt Cirkvi (The Courage to be the Church)*, Opus Bonum, Munich, 1981, p. 178. For more complete documentation on anti-religious persecution and the links between Christians and Charter 77, see *Krestane a Charta 77 (Christians and Charter 77)*, Index, no. 7, Opus Bonum, Munish, 1980. p. 320.

42 Patocka, 'Ce qu'est la Charte 77', p. 200. This quotation is all the more poignant since Jan Patocka, exhausted by the repeated interrogations to which he was subjected by the police, suffered a cerebral haemorrhage on 11 March 1977 and died two days later. Bernard Dupuy wrote, in a tribute published in *Istina* (XXII, no. 2, Paris, 1977, pp. 113–15): 'Jan Patocka, heir of Comenius and of Masaryk, like them a great European and a universal intellect, will in his death have brought a message of hope to a world more and more closely bound up in its interests and its conflicts, but which glimpsed in him, at least for a moment, the spirit of the prophets passing by.'

43 In *Informace o Cirkvi (Information on the Church)*, no. 6, 1981. The French translation reproduced here was published in *Istina*, XXVIII, no. 2, Paris, 1983, pp. 184–8.

44 In *Istina*, ibid., pp. 186–7. Early in 1983 a rumour was circulating in Prague that Soviet specialists in anti-religious persecution had been in the country since the previous autumn to share their experience with their Czech colleagues. In matters little whether this rumour was soundly based or not: its very existence says much.

45 For example, in a list published on 15 November 1983 of persecutees sponsored by VONS (Committee for the defence of persons unjustly proceeded against) there were twenty-two Catholics, priests or laymen, out of a total of forty-seven names (in *Listy*, XIV, no. 1, Rome, 1984, pp. 42–7).

46 In *Istina*, XXVIII, no. 2, Paris, 1983, p. 169.

47 In *Istina*, ibid., p. 200.

48 Patocka, 'Ce qu'est la charte 77'.

49 Pierre Bourdieu, 'Sur le pouvoir symbolique', *Annales ESC*, Paris, May–June 1977, p. 409.

50 Gyorgy Konrad, *Antipolitics*, Harcourt Brace Jovanovich, San Diego; New York; London, 1984, p. 223.

51 Vaclav Havel, 'Doing without Utopias', *Times Literary Supplement*, 23 January 1987. In this interview Havel mentions the thinking done by his compatriot Vaclav Belohradsky, particularly his 'eschatology of the impersonal'.

52 Eva Kanturkova, *Douze femmes à Prague*, Ed. Naspero, Paris, 1981, p. 188.

53 ibid., p. 210. Compare this with what Masaryk said about Hus's topicality: 'That means getting away from Rome, but spiritually, really, not nominally, each of us must triumph over Rome within himself' (quoted by Michel, *La mémoire de Prague* p. 109).

5 Slavorum Apostolus

1. Jerzy Turowicz, 'Ciaglosc i zmiznz – 20 lat po soborze Watikanskim II' *Tygodnik Powszechny Cracow*, 24 November 1985.
2. Quoted by Andrzej Walicki, *Philosophy and Romantic Nationalism – The Case of Poland*, Clarendon Press, Oxford, 1982, p. 289.
3. Cardinal Wyszynski is here referring to the violent attacks directed against the Catholic Church after the letter sent by the Polish bishops to the German bishops and during the celebration of the millennnium of Catholic Poland.
4. Statement by the primate of Poland on the occasion of the fiftieth anniversary of the 'Miracle on the Vistula', Warsaw, 3 September 1970.
5. Jerzy Lewandowski, *L'Eglise et la Nation polonaise selon le cardinal Stefan Wyszynski*, Peter Land, Berne-Frankfurt/Main, 1982, p. 158.
6. John Paul II, *Encyclical letter 'Slavorum Apostoli'*, Documents d'Eglise, Editions du Centurion, Paris, 1985, p. 6.
7. ibid., p. 41.
8. in *Znak*, no. 303, Cracow, September 1979.
9. In *Le Monde*, Paris, 5 June 1979.
10. In *Le Monde*, Paris, 7 November 1978.
11. In *Le Monde*, Paris, 5 June 1979.
12. ibid.
13. Agence France–Presse dispatch, 8 June 1979.
14. In *Le Figaro*, Paris, 12 June 1979.
15. In *Le Monde*, Paris, 10–11 June 1979.
16. Bearing in mind the general tone of Cardinal Lekai's speech, one is almost tempted to take the adjective in its literal meaning . . .
17. In *Le Monde*, Paris, 3 November 1978.
18. 'Bede Blogoslawii pana po wiecne czasy' ('Homily for the beatification of Urszula Ledochowska'), Pozman, 20 June 1983, in *Znak*, XXXV, no. 348–9, Cracow, November–December 1983, p. 1779.
19. The Cracow review *Znak* devoted a special number, 'Pokoj tobie Polsko! Ojcyzno moja!' ('Peace to you, Poland, my country!' nos 348–9, November–December 1983) to the Pope's journey, containing all the homilies and speeches given by John Paul II in full. The address given at the Belvedere is on pp. 1686–91. This is the publication referred to below. As regards General Jaruzelski's speech, French readers can refer to the official translation of the text in *La Documentation Catholique*, no. 1857, Paris, 7–21 August 1983, pp. 771–3.
20. In *La Documentation Catholique*, ibid., p. 771.
21. In *Znak*, p. 1690.
22. In *La Documentation Catholique*, p. 771.
23. ibid.
24. In *Znak*, p. 1687.
25. ibid.
26. 'On the pilgrim way of Your Holiness there are, like an eternal remembrance, innumerable tombs of soldiers, and many of them contain the ashes – as the poet says – of the "Russian brothers". Thousands, hundreds of thousands of them, gave up their young lives in bringing us deliverance.'
27. In *La Documentation Catholique*, p. 771.

Notes to pp. 149–158 225

28 ibid., p. 772.
29 In *Znak*, p. 1690.
30 'Tys wielka chluba naszego narodu' ('Homily at the Solemn Closing Mass of the 600th Anniversary'), *Znak*, no. 348–9, p. 1742.
31 'Na Jasnej Gorze, tu zawsze bylismy wolni', homily at Czestochowa, 4 June 1979.
32 In *Znak*, p. 1744.
33 ibid., p. 1745.
34 ibid., p. 1744.
35 Marcel Merle, 'Droits de l'Etat, droits de l'Homme, droits des peuples, droits des nations? Discours d'Eglise et discours profane', in *Pro Fide et Justitia – Festschrift für Agostino Kardinal Casaroli zum 70 Geburtstag*, Duncker & Humblot, Berlin, 1984, p. 770.
36 In *Znak*, pp. 1745–6.
37 ibid.
38 In *La Documentation Catholique*, pp. 771–2.
39 ibid.
40 In *Znak*, p. 1747.
41 In *Znak*, no. 348–9, pp. 1646–7.
42 ibid.
43 ibid.
44 ibid.
45 ibid.
46 'Kolegialna jednosc konferencji episkopatu – Wsparciem dla kazdego biskupa – Plenarna Konferencja Episkopatu Polski, 19 czerwca 1983 r.', *Znak*, p. 1759.
47 ibid., p. 1763.
48 ibid., p. 1767.
49 ibid., p. 1764.
50 'There is a need to be concerned about every man, to stand up for every compatriot, to protect every life, to prevent woundings which are caused so quickly when blows are received, especially by young and weak bodies. Similar care is needed towards old people, and the lonely, abandoned, sick. . . . The Church in Poland has its hands quite full with the work of love' (ibid., p. 1765).
51 ibid., p. 1765.
52 ibid., p. 1766.
53 ibid., p. 1767.
54 John Paul II, *Encyclical letter 'Slavorum Apostoli'*, Documents d'Eglise, Editions du Centurion, Paris, 1985, p. 6.
55 ibid., p. 14.
56 ibid., p. 7.
57 ibid., p. 16.
58 ibid., p. 26 and p. 24.
59 John Paul II, p. 29.
60 John Paul II, p. 49.
61 John Paul II, *Discours aux participants au Congrès des Associations Italiennes travaillant dans le domaine culturel*, Rome, 16 January 1982, quoted by Janusz Ziolkowski, 'Jan-Pawel II, czlowiek, narod, kultura' ('John Paul II, man, nation, culture') *Tygodnik Powszechny*, Cracow, 2 January 1983. The thoughts of John Paul II on the relations between nation and culture have aroused much reflection in

Poland. See, for example, Stanislaw Grygiel, 'Narod i kultura', *Znak* no. 329, Cracow, April 1982.
62 John Paul II, *Slavorum Apostoli*, p. 37.
63 John Paul II, 'Homily for the beatification of Urszula Ledochowska', Poznan, 20 June 1983, in *La Documentation Catholique*, Paris, no. 1857, 7–21 August 1983, p. 794.
64 John Paul II, *Slavorum Apostoli*, p. 32.
65 ibid., p. 33.
66 ibid., p. 32.
67 ibid., p. 28.
68 ibid., p. 49.
69 ibid., p. 33.
70 ibid., p. 31-2.
71 ibid., p. 30.
72 ibid., p. 29.
73 ibid., p. 23.
74 ibid., p. 17.
75 ibid., p. 23.
76 ibid., p. 29.
77 ibid., p. 35-6.
78 ibid., p. 42.
79 ibid., p. 18.
80 ibid., p. 27.
81 ibid., p. 27-8.
82 ibid., p. 17.
83 ibid., p. 40.
84 ibid., p. 43. As Timothy Garton Ash notes, 'When Pope John Paul II speaks about Europe, his look of an exiled visionary reaches beyond this artificial, synthetic, truncated Europe that is called the EEC, further than Prague or Budapest, or his beloved Cracow. Beyond the Pripet Marshes, he has in view the historical boundaries of Eastern Europe, the Ukraine, Byelorussia and even the bulbous domes of Zagorsk; and when he preaches in Polish a wholly European vision of things, he rolls his "l" almost as a Lithuanian would do' (in 'L'Europe centrale existe-t-elle?', *Lettre Internationale*, no. 10, Paris, autumn 1986, p. 5).
85 ibid., p. 40.
86 ibid., p. 20.
87 John Paul II, 'Speech of 9 June 1987 to Polish intellectuals', Lublin, Polish text in *Osservatore Romano* of 11 June 1987, French translation in *La Documentation Catholique*, no. 1944, Paris, 19 July 1987, p. 736.
88 ibid., p. 736.
89 ibid., p. 736.
90 John Paul II, 'Czestochowa address', Polish text in the *Osservatore Romano* for 15 June 1987, French translation in *La Documentation Catholique*, p. 751.
91 For example, J. Szczepanski mentions the value of education and the emphasis placed upon intellectual and artistic creativity as two of the seven traditional values of Polish national culture (*Polish Society*, Random House, New York, 1970).
92 John Paul II, 'Speech of 8 June 1987 to the Polish state authorities', Warsaw, Polish text in *Osservatore Romano* for 10 June 1987, French translation in *La Documentation Catholique*, p. 735.
93 ibid., p. 734.

94 John Paul II, 'Address to the bishops' conference of 14 June 1987', Polish text in the *Osservatore Romano* for 17 June 1987, French translation in *La Documentation Catholique*, p. 758.
95 General Jaruzelski, 'Speech of welcome on 8 June 1987', Polish text in the *Osservatore Romano* for 10 June 1987, French translation in *La Documentation Catholique*, p. 733.
96 ibid., p. 735.
97 John Paul II, p. 734.
98 John Paul II, p. 756.
99 John Paul II, 'Address to Polish intellectuals', p. 738.
100 ibid., p. 738.
101 ibid., p. 759.
102 On the occasion of the homily at Tarnow on 10 June 1987. As in 1983, the cardinal-primate of Czechoslovakia, Monsignor Tomasek, had not received permission from the government of his country to go to Poland, whereas the new primate of Hungary, Monsignor Laszlo Paskai, was present.
103 During the homily at Wawel cathedral in Cracow on 10 June 1987.
104 'Address to Polish intellectuals', p. 738.
105 ibid., p. 738.
106 'Homily for the beatification of Michal Kozal', Polish text in the *Osservatore Romano* for 16 June 1987, French translation in *La Documentation Catholique*, p. 755.
107 ibid., p. 755.
108 'Wawel homily', Polish text in the *Osservatore Romano* for 13 June 1987, French translation in *La Documentation Catholique* p. 743, (our emphasis).
109 'Homily for the beatification of Michal Kozal', p. 754.
110 Even though, in enumerating the important events of his pilgrimage at the general audience given on 17 June, the Pope mentioned only in the penultimate position the talks he had had with the president of the council of state, after having mentioned in the same sentence his visit to the royal castle in Warsaw (Italian text in the *Osservatore Romano* for 18 June 1987, French translation in *La Documentation Catholique*, p. 760).
111 Jan Krauze, 'The people must feel master in their own house', *Le Monde*, 10 June 1987.
112 Quoted by Henri Tincq, 'At Tarnow, the Pope took up the cudgels for rural Solidarity', *Le Monde*, 12 June 1987.
113 Address by General Jaruzelski on 14 June 1987', Polish text in the *Osservatore Romano* for 16 June 1987, French translation in *La Documentation Catholique*, p. 758.
114 ibid., p. 758.
115 John Paul II, 'Speech to seamen at Gdynia on 11 June 1987', Polish text in the *Osservatore Romano* for 15 June 1987, French translation in *La Documentation Catholique*, p 745.
116 ibid., p. 758.
117 John Paul II, 'Address of 12 June 1987 at Czestochowa', Polish text in the *Osservatore Romano* for 15 June 1987, French translation in *La Documentation Catholique*, p. 752.
118 There are in all three references to the geographical framework of Poland in General Jaruzelski's speech; it mentions the Rivers Bug and Order and twice uses the word *frontier*, contrasting the 'just frontiers' inherited from the Second World War with the 'challenge of confrontation that has lately been heard close to our western frontier'.

As for the Pope, he did not use the term, even though the government, by allowing him to go to Szczecin, very much hoped to hear him speak about the 'regained territories' on which it bases part of the legitimacy it boasts.

119 'Homily at the mass for the workers of Gdansk on 12 June 1987', Polish text in the *Osservatore Romano* for 15 June 1987, French translation in *La Documentation Catholique*, p. 749.
120 John Paul II, 'Homily at the mass for the workers of Gdansk on 12 June 1987', Polish text in the *Osservatore Romano* for 15 June 1987, French translation in *La Documentation Catholique*, p. 749.
121 John Paul II, 'Address to the conference of bishops on 14 June 1987', Polish text in the *Osservatore Romano* for 17 June 1987, French translation in *La Documentation Catholique*, p. 757.
122 'Homily at the mass for the workers of Gdansk', p. 749. In his speech of welcome, General Jaruzelski had on the contrary done his best to play down these Agreements, saying *inter alia* 'National agreement is not a question that can be settled by a single decision, a single act; it isn't a sheet of paper with this or that signature at its foot.'
123 ibid., p. 749.
124 'Speech to seamen at Gdynia', p. 745.
125 Ibid., p. 745.
126 John Paul II, 'Address in reply to the farewell speech by General Jaruzelski on 14 June 1987', Polish text in the *Osservatore Romano* for 16 June 1987, French translation in *La Documentation Catholique*, p. 760.

Conclusion

1 Adam Zagajewski, *Solidarité, solitûde*, Fayard, Paris, 1986, p. 44.
2 Georges Mink, '*Les Orientations de valeurs dans la sociologie est-européenne*', lecture given at the seminar conducted by Georges Mink and the author at the Ecole des Hautes Etudes en Sciences Sociales, Paris, 16 March 1987.
3 Robert Bellah, 'Civil Religion in America', *Daedalus*, 96, Winter 1967, pp. 1–21.
4 Ewa Morawska, 'Civil Religion vs. State Power in Poland', *Society*, vol. 21, no. 4, Butgers – The State University, New Brunswick, N.J., May–June 1984, pp. 29–34.
5 Narcel Gauchet, *Le Désenchantement du monde – Une histoire politique de la religion*, Gallimard, 'Bibliothèque des Sciences Humaines', Paris, 1985, p. III.
6 Of course other, more topical, factors have to be taken into consideration. For example, Josef Baniak, in an article entitled 'Dynamika powolan kaplanskich zakonnych w Polsce (1945–1982)' ('The dynamics of regular and secular vocations in Poland') (in *Kultura i Spoleczenstwo*, XXVIII, no. 3, Warsaw, p. 262) attributes the fact that the number of vocations to the priesthood doubled in Poland between 1978 and 1982 to the election of Karol Wojtyla.
7 See Jan Andrzej Klocowski, 'Religioznawstwo w szkole: zagrozenie czy szansa?' ('The science of religion at school: threat or opportunity?'), *Tygodnik Powszechny*, Cracow, no. 45/1958, 9 November 1986.
8 Alain Besançon, *La confusion des langues – La crise idéologique de l'Eglise*, Calmann-Lévy, Paris, 1978, pp. 83–4.
9 Jakov Jukic, 'La religion et les sécularismes dans les sociétés socialistes', in *Social Compass*, Louvain, XXVIII, 1981/1, p. 24.

10 In *Le Monde*, Paris, 15 October 1986.
11 And 200,000 in July 1987 (see *Le Monde*, 12–13 July 1987).
12 As, for example, the text published by the primate on 7 November 1984 on his return from Rome, in which he gives an account of his meetings with John Paul II and Monsignor Casaroli (in *Listy*, XV), Rome, February 1985, p. 47.
13 Without wishing to commit ourselves to hasty generalizations, we are bound to say that a strong attraction to the Orthodox religion is becoming apparent in the Soviet Union, particularly among the intelligentsia, doubtless closely connected with infatuation for Russian culture. There is also a noticeable rise in Islam, a national phenomenon as much as a religious one, in the Central Asian republics and an equally marked rise among young people of evangelical movements (Baptists, Pentecostalists) and oriental cults (Hare Krishna). For its part, the official press in Bulgaria has written about the proliferation of small, informal groups of young people, attracted to Eastern religions and fundamentalist Christian sects; and in that country which is traditionally the scene of heresies and esoteric mystical currents, there are once more Bogomils and adherents of Peter Danov, a philosopher who in the inter-war period founded a religion which combined Hinduism with Orthodoxy. In Romania, Baptist and Adventist groups are attracting a growing number of young citizens from the country districts, and Billy Graham's tour in 1985 well reflects the rise of evangelistic movements. Moreover, some members of the lower Orthodox clergy are ready to follow the path of Father Calciu and are rebelling against the state of the churches: Examples are A. Pop, expelled from the orthodox Church for having written a memorandum on the violation of religious freedoms, and N. Pescaru, who stood up for the Uniate Church. Catholics from the Banat and Transylvania have sent an open letter to the Pope to draw his attention to their wish to celebrate their religion in Romanian, whereas for some time the authorities have been trying to prevent church services being held in Romanian for fear lest the Uniates themselves should join the Catholic Church, having been forcefully integrated with the Orthodox Church in 1948. The increasing interest taken by young people in religion is also noticeable in the German Democratic Republic. The religious services for young people that take place each month in St Peter's church in Karl Marx Stadt are so many meeting points for East German Christians. At Dresden in March 1986 the general secretary of the YMCA (Young Men's Christian Association), which is proscribed in East Germany, spoke to a crowd of more than 1500. On all these matters, see Kathy Rousselet and Patrick Michel, 'La situation religieuse a l'Est en 1986-7', in *Traces*, Ed. Brepols-Lidis, Brussels, 1987.
14 *Le Monde*, Paris, 1 July 1986.
15 Le Seuil, Paris, 1979 (for the French edition).
16 Jerzy Turowicz, 'Kosciol i polityka' ('Church and politics'), *Tygodnik Powszechny* no. 12 (1865), Cracow, 24 March 1985. In an article published in *Kultura* (the organ of the Polish Unified Workers' Party) on 10 June 1985, Zygmunt Kaluzynski wrote: 'It is impossible to find a sincere, true, well founded objection to . . . Turowicz's text. There is only one – a very small one: it is against the Gospel.' And the author went on to write at laboured length in an endeavour to show that the Church was making use of God in order to sustain capitalism, concluding with the words: 'I suspect that the Church is falling into blasphemy.' Comment is of course superfluous . . .
17 For example, it is notable that both in East Germany and the Soviet Union many young people are turning to the evangelical churches, not so much for reasons of faith as in the search for political answers to the problems that are troubling them.

18 Raymond Boudon, *L'Ideologie-L'origine des idées reçues*, Fayard, Paris, 1986, p. 282. It might also be noted that the Marxism applied in Soviet-bloc countries no longer much in common with Marx's theories.
19 Michnik, 'Do not make religion into a synonym for opposition'. One has only to refer to the statements made by the policemen responsible for the murder of Father Popieluszko for confirmation of the hypothesis formulated by Michnik. On this subject, see Patrick Michel and Georges Mink, *Mort d'un prêtre-L'affaire Popieluszko: Analyse d'une logique normalisatrice*, Fayard, Paris, 1985, esp. pp. 212–14.
20 Clearly it is not without significance that the Hungarian episcopate has never succeeded in obtaining from the Vatican, and in particular from the Congregation for the Doctrine of the Faith, the clear and final condemnation of Bulanyi which it desired (unless one chooses to consider as such the two letters iron Cardinal Ratzinger published by *Uj Ember* on 14 June 1987 and preceded by a press release from the Hungarian episcopate bearing the signature of the new primate, Monsignor Laszlo Paskai. It is true that the prefect of the Congregation for the Doctrine of the Faith requested Father Bulanyi to change his position, but without setting a date limit for so doing.). On this matter, see Gwendoline Jarczyk, 'L'affaire Bulanyi rebounds', in *La Croix*, 4 July 1987.
21 General Jaruzelski made it clear by meeting the primate Monsignor Glemp in April 1986 and John Paul II in January 1987 how much he needed the Church as a mediator with a society that was persistently stonewalling his normalizing process. It is not impossible that he contemplated the Pope's third visit to his native country, in June 1987, both as a sign given to this resistance, a concession to the Church, and a mediating operation of the kind favoured by the Warsaw rulers.
22 It's all very well for the Vatican to describe such rumours as 'wild', but all observers believe that the fact that Russia was twice mentioned in the encyclical *Redemptoris Mater* was a message destined for Moscow, on the eve of the millenary of the baptism of Saint Vladimir, due for celebration in the USSR in June–July 1988. Nevertheless, such a journey is unlikely in the immediate future (see *Le Monde*, 2 September 1987).
23 *Literaturnaja Gazeta*, 4 February 1987.
24 The author states that the main characteristic of this model is that the religious situation may help to stabilize the system and enhance its legitimacy. None the less, Vrcan is still very reticent and acknowledges that there are some signs pointing to developments in that direction, which in any event is closely linked to the Orthodox Church.
25 Srdan Vrcan, 'Desecularization on agenda: three scenarios of religious change in socialist societies', in *Secularization and Religion: The Persisting Tension-Acts of the XIXth international Conference for the Sociology of religion – Tübingen 1987, 25–29 August*, CISR, Lausanne, 1987, p. 72.
26 Réforme et révolution dans les sociétés traditionnelles. Histoire et ethnologie des mouvements messianiques, Ed. Anthropos, Paris, 1968.
27 Michel de Certeau, *L'Absent de l'histoire*, Repères-Mane, Paris, 1973, p. 140.
28 Lech Walesa, *On chemin d'espoir*, Fayard, Paris, 1987, pp. 274–5.
29 ibid.
30 ibid., p. 288.
31 ibid., pp. 396–7.
32 Norman Davis. *A History of Poland*, Clarendon Press, Oxford, 1982.
33 C.G. Jung, *Essai d'exploration de l'inconscient*, Denoel, Paris, 1984, p. 117.
34 As Hegel said, 'mediation is equality with oneself in motion. It is the moment of death and of becoming'.

35 Gyorgy Konrad, *Antipolitics* Harcourt Brace Jovanovich, San Diego; New York; London, 1984, p. 37. The author states: 'If they cannot yet commit themselves publicly to this course, let them do it in small private committees. Let the American and European universities meet in Europe, away from the television cameras and without worldwide publicity. Let them sit down together at the café Florian in Venice, where a great European, Friedrich Nietzsche, loved to sit, and let them speak quietly and sincerely together.'
36 Michel de Certeau, *L'Absent de l'histoire*, Repères-Name, Paris, 1973, p. 136.
37 See especially *Religion and Social Conflicts*, Orbis Books, New York, 1982.
38 Olivier Carré, 'A propos de Weber et l'Islam', *Archives de Sciences Sociales des Religions*, no. 61/1, CNRS, paris, January–March 1986, p. 146.
39 Zbigniew Wierzbicki, 'Les Conflits accompagnant la sécularisation de l'écol – L'exemple du village de Zmiaca', paper read at the International Conference on the Sociology of Religions (Tübingen, 25–29 August 1987), typescript in the author's possession, p. 5.
40 Olivier Roy, 'Etat et société en Afghanistan', *Revue Française de Science Politique*, vol. 35, no. 3, Presses de la FNSP, Paris, June 1985, pp. 414–15.
41 Bruno Etienne, 'La moelle de la prédication-Essai sur le prône politique dans l'islam contemporain', *Revue Française de Science Politique*, vol. 33, no. 4, Presses de FNSP, Paris, August 1983, p. 719. Elsewhere, Etienne reports the opinion of a 'left-wing Noslem' with which perhaps many believers in the East could identify, substituting the word 'Catholcism' for the word 'Islam': 'For us, Islam is above all a method and not a closed, finished system. What matters is the goal pursued by Islam. At different times this goal can be attained by different forms of organization and social practices' (in *L'Islamisne radical*, p. 204).
42 Jacques Zylberberg, 'Crise de la socialisation on crise de l'organisation', in *Secularization and Religion: the Persisting Tension-Acts of the XIXth International Conference for the Sociology of religion-Tübingen 1987, 25–29 August*, CISR, Lausanne, 1987, p. 84.
43 Stefan Staszewski, in Teresa Toranska, *Oni-Des staliniens polonais s'expliquent*, preface by Jan Krauze, Flammarion, Paris, 1986, p. 190.
44 In *Istina*, XXVIII, Paris, no. 2/1983, p. 170.
45 Vaclav Havel, 'La communauté des ébranlés' (speech by the recipient of the Erasmus Prize 1986 at Rotterdam, November 1986), in *Lettre Internationale*, no. 12, Paris, Spring 1987, p. 16.

Postscript to the English Edition

1 See Michel de Certeau, esp. *L'absent de l'histoire*, Repères-Mame, Paris, 1973.
2 Jacques Zylberberg, 'La régulation étatique de la religion: monisme et pluralisme', paper read at the 20th International Conference on the Sociology of Religions, Helsinki, August 1989.
3 I have developed this theme in 'Messianisme polonais et histoire contemporaine' in *Le rêve de Compostelle*, Le Centurion, Paris, 1989, pp. 52–67.
4 Michel Maslowski, 'Foi et histoire – le modèle dynamique de la religion incarnée dans l'oeuvre d'Adam Mickiewicz', paper read at the *3rd World Congress of the International Committee for Soviet and East European Studies (ICSEES)*, Washington, DC 1985, typescript, p. 49.

5 As Jean Séguy wrote in a comment on Ernst Troeltsch, 'The superiority [of a religion] is demonstrated when the autonomy of the sacred strengthens that of the profane and when the two enter into a relationship of dialectic opposition', in *Christianisme et société – Introduction à la sociologie de Ernst Troeltsch*, Cerf, Paris, 1980, p. 47.

6 The course of events in the last few months has made these questions truly topical and of some urgency. See on this subject my articles 'La prétention à l'universel de l'Eglise polonaise', in *Le Monde*, 5 September 1989, and 'La Pologne, l'Eglise et la démocratie: Une transition délicate', in *Etudes*, February 1990, pp. 243–50.

Bibliography

The present study is on the borderline between at least two disciplines (political science and the sociology of religion), and several fields (development of the Church and of religion, development of Soviet-type societies), and it refers to concepts the mere definition of which has been the subject of many studies – such as totalitarianism, detotalization, desovietization, and so on.

It seemed neither desirable nor even feasible to offer an exhaustive bibliography for each of the disciplines, concepts or fields mentioned in our work. Taken to extremes, every book or article dealing with the situation in the Soviet bloc, the development of relations between Church and society, the concepts utilized by the sociology of religion or totalitarianism, to cite only some examples, would have a claim to inclusion. Arendt and Bourdieu, Weber and Durkheim, Marx and Lenin, but also Orwell and Kundera, are of course present in the background.

The solution chosen, to avoid overloading this bibliography, was generally not to mention works cited incidentally in the text and appearing as footnotes, and mainly to confine ourselves to listing works having a very direct bearing on the subject, whether relating to the subject as a whole or dealing in depth with a particular country.

I Sources

Most of the available information has been culled from the press, and in particular:

For Poland

Tygodnik Powszechny (Cracow)
Znak (Cracow)
Wiez (Warsaw)
Slowo Powszechny (Warsaw)
Chrzescijanin w swiecie (Warsaw)
Czlowiek i swiatopoglad (Warsaw)
Nowe drogi (Warsaw)
Trybuna ludu (Warsaw)

234 Bibliography

For Hungary

Uj Ember (Budapest)
Katolikus szo (Budapest)
Vigilia (Budapest)
Teologia (Budapest)

For Czechoslovakia

Katolicke noviny (Prague)
Rude Pravo (Prague)
Pravda (Bratislava)
Ateizmus (Prague)

In addition, there are the reviews published by emigrés (*Listy* (Rome), *Studie* (Rome), *Svedectvi* (Paris), for Czechoslavakia; *Kultura* (Paris), *Aneks* (London), for Poland, *internalia*) and the underground press or publications (*Informace o Cirkvi* and the *Petlice* publishers in Czechoslovakia, in particular). There are several hundred titles in Poland.

Abroad, there are several reviews devoted exclusively to providing information and analyses on the religious situation in the Soviet bloc:

Religion in Communist Lands, Keston College, Kent
Religion in Communist Dominated Areas, New York City
Istina, Paris
Altra Europa, Milan
CSEO Documentazione, Bologna
'Bulletins' of the Hungarian Institute for Sociology of Religion Press Service, Munich.

To this list may be added the 'Bulletins' of Radio Free Europe, Munich, which often contain useful information.

Other sources are:

La Documentation Catholique, Paris
The *Osservatore Romano*, Rome

There are also the reviews dealing with the situation in Eastern Europe, including:

L'Alternative followed by *La Nouvelle Alternative*, Paris
L'Autre Europe, Paris
La Lettre Internationale, Paris
specialist publications of *La Documentation française*

And those dealing with specifically religious issues, to mention only French-language reviews:

Etudes, Paris
Esprit, Paris
Project, Paris
Concilium, Paris

Also the daily press, including:

Le Monde (Paris)
Kurier (Vienna)
La Croix (Paris)

Texts of John Paul II

The texts of the Pope are of course published in the *Osservatore Romano*. In addition, there are numerous translations and other editions. *Documentation Catholique*, Paris, includes these texts in its French publications (no. 1900 dated 21 July 1985 for the encyclical *Slavorum Apostoli*, no. 1857 dated 7–21 August 1983 for John Paul II's second journey to Poland, and no. 1944 dated 19 July 1987 for the third journey, for example).

II General bibliography

1 Studies or essays on the relationship between politics, religion and society

Berger, Peter, *La Religion dans la conscience moderne*, Ed du Centurion, Paris, 1971.
Berger, Peter, *Affrontés à la Modernité*, Ed. du Centurion, Paris, 1980.
Berger, Peter, *The Social Reality of Religion*, Faber & Faber, London, 1969.
Bertrand, Michèle, *Le statut de la religion chez Marx et Engels*, Editions Sociales, Paris, 1979.
Besançon, Alain, *La Confusion des Langues – La crise idéologique de l'Eglise*, Calmann-Lévy, Paris, 1978.
Bourdieu, Pierre, *Choses dites*, Ed. de Minuit, Paris, 1987.
Calvez, Jean-Yves, *La Politique et Dieu*, Le Cerf, Paris, 1985.
Certeau, Michel de, *L'Absent de l'histoire*, Repères-Mama, Paris, 1973.
Cipriani, Roberto (ed.), *Legittimazione e società Armando editore*, Rome, 1986.
Cipriani, Roberto (ed.), *La legittimazione simbolica*, Morcelliana, Brescia, 1986.
Desroche, Henri, *Marxisme et religions*, Presses Universitaires de France, Paris, 1962.
Ferrarotti, Franco (ed.), *Sociologia della religione*, Ed. Borla, Rome, 1985.
Garrigues, Juan Miguel, *L'Eglise, la société libre et le communisme*, foreword by Alain Besançon, Commentaire Julliard, Paris, 1984.
Gauchet, Marcel, *Le Désenchantement du Monde – Une histoire politique de la religion*, Gallimard, 'Bibliothèque des Sciences humaines', Paris, 1985.
Maduro, Otto, *Religion and Social Conflicts*, Orbis Books, New York, 1982.
O'Dea, Thomas, and O'Dea Aviad, Janet, *The Sociology of Religion*, Prentice-Hall, Englewood Cliffs, New Jersey, 2nd edn, 1983.
Portelli, Hughues, *Les Socialismes dans le discours social catholique*, coll. 'Eglise et société', Editions du Centurion, Paris, 1986.
Poulat, Emile, *Catholicisme, démocratie et socialisme*, coll. 'Religion et sociétés', Tournai, Casterman, 1977.
Poulat, Emile, *L'Eglise, c'est un monde*, Le Cerf, Paris, 1986.
Ratzinger, Cardinal (in collaboration with Vittorio Messori), *Entretiens sur la foi*, Fayard, Paris, 1985.

2 Multi-country studies and general works on Soviet-bloc countries

The 'American Association for the Advancement of Slavic Studies' publishes the *American Bibliography of Slavic and East European Studies*, an indispensable working tool, now with its European extension, the *European Bibliography of Soviet, East European and Slavonic Studies*, Editions de l'Ecole des Hautes Etudes en Sciences Sociales – Institut d'Etudes Slaves, Paris (in colloboration with: Main Library and Center for Russian and East European Studies, University of Birmingham, Alabama; Staatsbibliothek Preussischer Kulturbesitz, Osteuropa Abteilung, Berlin; Bibliothèque Royale Albert 1er, Brussels; Oost-Europa Instituut, Universiteit van Amsterdam, 7 vols published (1975 to 1981)).

Studies on the contemporary religious situation in Eastern Europe

Adrianyi, Gabriel, *Die Führung der Kirche in den Sozialistischen Staaten Europas*, Johannes-Berchmans Verlag, Munich, 1979.
Beeson, Trevor, *Prudence and Courage – La situation religieuse en Russie et en Europe de l'Est*, Le Seuil, Paris, 1975. Original English, *Discretion and Valour*, Collins, London, 1974.
Bociurkiw, Bohdan, and Strong, John (eds), *Religion and Atheism in the USSR and Eastern Europe*, Macmillan, London, 1975.
De George, Richard, and Scanlan, James Patrick (eds), *Marxism and Religion in Eastern Europe* (papers presented at the Banff International Slavic Conference, 4–7 September 1974), Sovietica, D. Reidel, Dordrecht-Holland and Boston, 1976.
Gsovsky, Vladimir (ed.), *Church and State behind the Iron Curtain, Czechoslovakia, Hungary, Poland, Romania and an Introduction of the Soviet Union*, Praeger, New York, 1955.
Kiraly, Bela (ed.), 'Tolerance and Movements of Religious Dissent in Eastern Europe', *East European Quarterly*, Boulder, New York, 1975.
Miller, R. F., and Rigby, T. H. (eds), *Religion and Politics in Communist States*, Occasional Paper no. 19, Department of Political Science, Research School of Social Sciences, Australian National University, Canberra, 1986.
Ramet, Pedro (ed.), *Religion and Nationalism in Soviet and East European Politics*, Duke University Press, Durham, N. C., 1984.
Schneiderman, S. L., *Between Fear and Hope*, Arco Publishing Company, New York, 1947.
Schreiber, Thomas, 'Les problèmes religieux en Europe Orientale (1945–70)', *Notes et Etudes Documentaires*, Documentation Française, no. 3790–1, Paris, 1971.
Staszewski, M. T., *Stosunki miedzy Panstwem i Kosciolem w europejskich krajach socialistycznych* (Church – state relations in the socialist countries of Europe), Warsaw, 1976.

Special numbers of reviews

Concilium, no. 174, Beauchesne, *Paris*, April 1982, 'Religions et Eglises en Europe de l'Est' (esp. N. Greinacher and V. Elizondo, 'Entre l'adaptation et le refus. Le difficile chemin de l'Eglise dans le Deuxième Monde', pp. 7–14; E. Andras, 'Le Cultural Lag de la société et de l'Eglise en Hongrie dans l'après-guerre', pp. 21–30; W. Piwowarski, 'Le problème de l'Eglise populaire en Pologne', pp. 31–44; G. Frater, 'La séparation de l'Etat et de l'Eglise dans les sociétés socialistes de l'Europe de l'Est', pp. 57–64; E. Andras. 'La situation des prêtres en Hongrie', pp. 105–12; M. Tomka, 'La transmission de la foi', pp. 121–6; L. Hajek, 'Les deux visages de l'Eglise en Tchécoslovakie', pp. 127–31). *Social Compass*, XXVIII, Louvain, 1981/1: La religion et les fonctions de l'Eglise dans les sociétés socialistes' (esp. J. Jukic, 'La religion et les sécularismes dans les sociétés socialistes', pp. 5–24; Srdan Vrcan, 'Changing Functions of Religion in a Socialist Society', pp. 43–62; J. Marianski, 'Dynamics of Changes in Rural Religiosity under Industrialization', pp. 63–78; M. Tomka, 'Le rôle des Eglises instituées de Hongrie dans un contexte de chamgement', pp. 93–112).

Articles or papers read

Hebly, J. A., 'Churches in Eastern Europe: Three Models of Church-State Relations and their Relevance to the Ecumenical Movement', discussion paper prepared for AASS National Convention in Kansas City, October 1983, roneo.

Michel, Patrick, 'Les religions, facteur de déstabilisation', *Problèmes politiques et sociaux*, La Documentation Française, Paris, no. 491, June 1984.

Michel, Patrick (in colloboration with Georges Mink), 'Religion et société en Europe du Centre-Est – Elements de réflexion', in 'L'Urss et l'Europe de l'Est – édition 1986', *Notes et Etudes Documentaires*, La Documentation Française, Paris, 1986, pp. 13–30.

Ramet, Pedro, 'Religious Ferment in Eastern Europe', *Survey*, XXVIII, no. 4, Winter 1984, pp. 87–116.

Papers presented at the International Conference on the Sociology of Religions:

Religion et religiosité, athéisme et non-croyance dans les sociétés industrielles et urbanisées, Proceedings of the 11th International Conference on the Sociology of Religions (Opatija, Yugoslavia, 20–24 September 1971), Ed. CISR, Lille, 1971 (esp. A. Swiecicki, 'La foi religeuse des jeunes en Pologne', pp. 87–106; A. Pawelczynska, 'Les attitudes de la population rurale envers la religion', pp. 107–21).

Métamorphoses contemporaines des phenomènes religieux, Proceedings of the 12th International Conference on the Sociology of Religions (The Hague, 1973), Ed. CISR, Lille, 1973.

Changement social et religion, Proceedings of the 13th International Conference on the Sociology of Religions (Lloret de Mar, 1975), Ed. CISR, Lille, 1975.

Symbolisme religieux, séculier et classes sociales, Proceedings of the 14th International Conference on the Sociology of Religions (Strasbourg, 1977), Ed. CISR, Lille, 1977 (esp. A. Swiecicki, 'Situation de la sociologie des religions en Pologne comparée à celle des autres pays socialistes d'Europe', pp. 411–37).

Religion et politique, Proceedings of the 15th International Conference on the Sociology of Religions (Venice, 1979), Ed. CISR, Lille, 1979 (esp. Zdenko Roter, 'La politique et la religion dans un pays socialiste (on their post revolutionary relationships)', pp. 95–119).

Religion, valeurs et vie quotidienne, Proceedings of the 16th International Conference on the Sociology of Religions (Lausanne, 1981), Ed. CISR, Paris, 1981.

Religion and the Public Domain, Proceedings of the 17th International Conference on the Sociology of Religions (London, 1983), Ed. CISR, 1983 (esp. A. Swiecicki and T. Woloszyn, 'Etat, conscience, religion, dans l'approche d'ensemble et dans la pratique de la prise des décisions par les Polonais prenant part à la messe', pp. 343–56; M. Tomka, 'Problems in the identity-formation of the Catholic Church in Second and Third World Societies', pp. 151–76).

Religion et Modernité: Survie ou réveil, Proceedings of the 18th International Conference on the Sociology of Religions (Louvain, 1985), Ed. CISR, 1985.

Sécularisation et Religion: La persistance des tensions, Proceedings of the 19th International Conference on the Sociology of Religions (Tübingen, 1987), Ed. CISR, 1987 (esp. V. Vrcan, 'Desecularization on Agenda: Three Scenarios of Religious Change in Socialist Societies', pp. 79–84).

National identity and religious identity in East-Central Europe

Bibo, Istvan, *Misère des petits Etats d'Europe de l'Est*, L'Harmattan, Paris, 1986.

Cywinski, Bohdan, *Ogniem Probowanie* ('Tried by Fire'), Papieski Instytut Studiow Koscielnych, Rome, 1982.

Groupe de travail sur l'Europe centrale et orientale – Bulletin d'information, MSH-EHESS, no. 3, Paris, July 1980 (esp. the beginning on 'Religions et identités culturelles en Europe centrale et orientale: le cas du catholicisme et du protestantisme', pp. 74–156).

'Les Eglises chrétiennes dans l'Europe dominée par le IIIe Reich', Actes du Congrès de Varsovie (25 June–1 July 1978), *Miscellanea Historiae Ecclesiasticae*, IX, Bibliothèque de la revue d'histoire ecclésiasique, fasc. 70, Ed. Nauwelaerts, Brussels, 1984 (esp. G. Adrianyi, 'Die Kirchen in Ungarn während des 2. Weltkrieges', pp. 129–54; S. Smalik, 'L'Eglise catholique en Slovaquie dans les années 1939–44', pp. 259–70; and the whole of part two of the proceedings, which deals entirely with Poland, pp. 273–450).

L'Héritage chrétien de la culture européenne dans la conscience des contemporains, Intern (Rome, 21–3 April 1986). Fondazione Giovanni Paolo II, Istituto Polacco di cultura christiana, Rome, 1987 (esp. the lecture by J. Dloczowski and the papers read by J. Ziolkowski, P. Czartoryski, H. Wozniakowski and A. Stankowski, among others).

Questions et Débats sur l'Europe centrale et orientale, MSH-EHESS, no. 4, Paris 1985 (esp. the discussion on 'Identité ouvrière et conscience nationale', pp. 8–84).

Szucs, Jeno, *Les Trois Europes*, L'Harmattan, Paris, 1985.

Also, for the contemporary history of East-Central Europe

Brown, Archie, and Gray, Jack (eds), *Political Culture and Political Change in Communist States*, Holmes & Meier Publishers, New York, 1979.

Fejtö, François, *Histoire des démocraties populaires*, 2 vols, Seuil, collection 'Points' Paris, 1972.

3 Studies on the Pope and relations between the Vatican and Soviet Europe

Cardinale, Hyginus Eugene, *The Holy See and the International Order*, Colin Smythe, London, 1976.

Daim, Wilfried, *Le Vatican et les pays de l'Quest*, Fayard, Paris, 1971.

Dunn, Dennis J., 'The Catholic Church and the Soviet Government (1939–49)', *East European Quarterly*, Boulder, Columbia University Press, New York, 1977.

Dunn, Dennis J., *Détente and Papal-Communist Relations (1962–78)*, Westview Press, Boulder, Colorado, 1979.

Hammel, Wolfgang, *Die Ostpolitik Papst Johannes Pauls II – Beziehungen zwischen Kurie und Ostblock*, Verlag SOI, Berne, 1984.

Maqua, Mireille, *Rome-Moscou, l'Ostpolitik du Vatican*, Cabay, Liège, 1984.

Milcent, Ernest, *A l'Est du Vatican – le papauté et les démocraties populaires*, 'Rencontres/International', Cerf, Paris, 1980.

Mourin, Maxime, *Le Vatican et l'URSS*, Payot, Paris, 1965.

Stehle, Hansjakob, *Die Ostpolitik des Vatikans, 1917-75*, R. Piper, Munich, 1975.
Stehle, Hansjakob, 'Church and Pope in the Polish crisis', *The World Today*, Oxford University Press, April 1982, pp. 139–48.
Wenger, Antoine de, *Rome et Moscou (1900-1950)*, Desclée de Brouwer, Paris, 1987.
Williams, Georg Hunston, *The Mind of John Paul II - Origins of His Thought and Action*, Winston Press, New York, 1981.

III Bibliography by countries

1 Poland

General history

Davies, Norman, *God's Playground - A History of Poland*, vol. I, *The Origins to 1795*, vol. II, *1795 to the Present*, Clarendon Press, Oxford, 1982.
Davies, Norman, *Histoire de la Pologne*, trans. from the English by Denise Meunier, Fayard, Paris, 1986.
Kieniewicz, Stefan (ed.), *Histoire de Pologne*, Panstwowe Wydawnictwo Naukowe, Warsaw, 1972.
Leslie, R. F., *The History of Poland since 1863*, Cambridge University Press, Cambridge, 1980.
Walicki, Andrzej, *Philosophy and Romantic Nationalism - The Case of Poland*, Clarendon Press, Oxford, 1982.

On comtemporary Poland

Gora, Wladyslaw, *Polska Rzeczpospolita Ludowa 1944-74 (The People's Republic of Poland 1944-74)*, Ksiazka i Wiedza, Warsaw, 1974 (official point of view).
Rollet, Henry, *La Pologne au XXe siècle*, preface by Jean Laloy, Pedone, Paris, 1984.

Religious history of Poland

Bibliografia historii Kosciloa w Polsce za lata 1944-70 (Bibliography of the history of the Church in Poland in 1944-70), vols 1, 2 and 3 (7,740 references) *za lata 71-2* (years 1971-2), vol. 4 (1,643 references), *za lata 73-4* (years 1973-4), vol. 5 (3,303 references) ATK, Warsaw, publication commenced in 1977.
Castellan, Georges, 'Dieu Garde la Pologne!' Histoire du catholicisme polonais (1795-80), Robert Laffont, Paris, 1981.
Les contacts religieux franco-polonais du Moyen-Age à nos jours - Relations, influences, images d'un pays vu par l'autre (Proceedings of the international symposium organized by CNRS, GRECO, no. 2 and the Centre Interdisciplinaire l'Etudes des Religions of the University of Lille III, Lille, 5–7 October 1981), Editions du Dialogue, with the participation of CNRS, Paris, 1985.
Kloczowski, Jerzy (ed.), *Chrzescijanstwo w Polsce* (Christianity in Poland), Towarzystwo Naukowe Katolickiego Uniwersytetu Lubelskiego, Lublin, 1980 (17 maps); trans. into French by Karolina T. Michel, *Histoire religieuse de la Pologne*, Le Centurion, Paris, 1987 (very large bibliography at the end of the volume).
Meysztowicz, Valérien, *La Pologne dans la chrétienté - Coup d'oeil sur mille ans d'histoire (966-1966)*, Nouvelles Editions Latines, Paris, 1966.

Working documents. Texts of the Polish episcopate and of the primate

Listy pasterskie episkopatu Polski, 1945–74 (Pastoral letters of the Polish episcopate), Ed. du Dialogue, Paris, 1975.

Listy pasterskie prymasa Polski, 1946–74 (Pastoral letters of the primate of Poland), Ed. du Dialogue, Paris, 1975.

Wyszynski, Stefan (Cardinal), *Un évêque au service du peuple de Dieu*, preface by Cardinal Garrone, texts trans. from the Polish by Maria Winowska, Editions Saint-Paul, Paris-Fribourg, 2nd edn, 1970.

Wyszynski, Stefan (Cardinal), *Kosciol w sluzbie Narodu, Nauczanie Prymasa Polski czasu odnowy w polsce*, serpien 1980-maj 1981 (*teksty autoryzowane*) (The Church in the service of the nation. Teaching of the primate of Poland on national renewal, August 1980 – May1981), 'Corda Cordi' and press office of the Polish episcopate in Rome, Rome, 1981.

Wyszynski, Stefan (Cardinal), *Zapiski wiezienne* (notes from prison), Ed. du dialogue, Paris, 1982.

Prymas Tysiaclecia (The Primate of the Millenary), special issue of *Nasza Rodzina*, Ed. du Dialogue, Paris, 1982.

On the personality and action of the former primate of Poland

Kulesza, Ewa, *La Victoire de l'espérance: Idées et action du cardinal Wyszynski*, Institut d'Etudes Politiques de Paris, Mémoire de DEA d'Etudes Soviétiques, sous la direction de M. Bernard Michel, Paris, October 1982.

Lewandowski, Jerzy, *L'Eglise et la Nation polonaise selon le cardinal Stefan Wyszynski*, Peter Lang, Berne, 1982.

Micewski, Andrzej, *Kardynal Wyszynski, Prymas i maz stanu (Cardinal Wyszynski, Primate and Statesman)*, Editions du Dialogue, Paris, 1982.

Raina, Peter, *Kardynal Wyszynski (Cardinal Wyszynski)*, 2 vols published, Poets and Painters, London, vol. 1, 1979, vol. 2, 1986.

Contemporary developments in Poland and Solidarity

Blumsztajn, Seweryn, *Polonais, Juif, membre du KOR et de Solidarité, Je rentre au pays* (in collaboration with Patrick Michel and Georges Mink), Calmann-Lévy, Paris, 1985.

Bromke, Adam, *Poland: The Protracted Crisis*, Mosaic Press, Oakville, Ontario, Canada, 1983.

Brumberg, Abraham (ed.), *Poland: Genesis of a Revolution*, Vintage Books, New York, 1983.

Cywinski, Bohdan, *L'Experience polonaise*, Editions universitaires de Fribourg, Fribourg, 1985.

Czarna ksiega censury PRL (The Black Book of censorship in the People's Republic of Poland), 2 vols, Aneks, London, 1977 and 1978.

Dziewanowski, M. K., *The Communist Party of Poland – An Outline of History*, Harvard University Press, Cambridge, Mass., 1976.

Esprit, no. 1, Paris, 1981, 'Pologne: un défi, un espoir' (special number including articles by K. Woycicki, A. Michnik, J. Kuron, P. Michel, P. Thibaud, A. Smolar, C. Lefort).

Esprit, no. 3, Paris, 1982, 'La Pologne emmurée' (special issue including articles by C. Castoriadis, F. Dubet, J. Ellul, M. Heller, C. Lefort, J. J. Lipski, I. Kemeny, P. Thibaud, A Touraaine, M. Wieviorka).

Holzer, Jerzy, *Solidarnosc (1980–1)* (Solidarity), Kultura, Paris, 1984.
Karpinski, Jakub, *Count-down – The Polish Upheavals of 1956, 1968, 1970, 1976, 1980* . . ., Karz-Cohl, New York, 1982.
Le programme de Solidarnosc – Texte integral des thèses élaborées par le Congrès des délégués à Gdansk le 7 octobre 1981, Presses universitaires de Lille, 1982.
Les Temps Modernes, nos 445–6, Paris, 1983 (special issue entitled 'Pologne').
Pomian, Krzysztof, *Pologne: Defi à l'impossible? De la révolte de Poznan à Solidarité*, éditions ouvrières, 'Enjeux Internationaux' series, Paris, 1982.
Potal, Jean-Yves, *Scènes de grèves en Pologne*, Stock, Paris, 1981.
Raina, Peter, *Political Opposition in Poland (1954–77)*, Poets and Painters, London, 1978.
Staniszkis, Jadwiga, *Pologne: La Révolution autolimitée*, notes and introduction by Jean-Yves Potel. trans. from the English by Noelle Burgi, Alain Brossat and Alain Wallon, PUF, Paris, 1982.
Toranska, Teresa, *Oni – Des staliniens polonais s'expliquent*, Flammarion, Paris, 1986.
Touraine, Alain, Dubet, François, Wieviorka, Michel, Strzelecki, Jan, *Solidarité – Analyse d'un mouvement social, Pologne 1980–1*, Fayard, Paris, 1982. Walesa, Lech, *Un chemin d'espoir* (autobiography), Fayard, Paris, 1987.
Zagajewski, Adam, *Solidarité, Solitude*, Fayard, Paris, 1986.

Statistical data on the Church and Catholicism in Poland

Zdaniewicz, Witold, *Kosciol Katolicki w Polsce (1945–78) Duchowienstwo i wierni, miejsca kultu, zgromadzenia zakonne (The Catholic Church in Poland (1945–78), Clergy and faithful, places of worship, religious communities)*, Pallottinum, Poznan-Warsaw, 1979.
Zdaniewicz, Witold, *Kosciol Katolicki w Polsce (1945–82) (The Catholic Church in Poland (1945–82))*, Pallottinum, Poznan-Oltarzew, 1982.

Sociology and anthropology of Polish Catholicism (supplementary bibliography to Chapter 2)

Ciupak, Edward, *Kult religijny i jego spoleczne poldloze – Studia nad katolicyzmen polskim (Religious Worship and its Basis in Society – Studies on Catholicism in Poland)*, Ksiaka i Wiedza, Warsaw, 1960.
Ciupak, Edward, *Katolicyzm ludowy w Polsce – Studia Sociologiczne (Popular Catholicism in Poland – A Sociological Study)*, Ksiazka i Wiedza, Warsaw, 1973.
Ciupak, Edward, *Parafianie? Wiejska parafia katolicka (Parishioners? The Rural Parish)*, Ksiazka i Wiedza, Warsaw, 1961.
Kubiak, Hieronim, *Religijnosc a srodowisko spoleczne – Studium zmian religijnosci pod wplywem ruchow magracjyjnch ze wsi do miaste (Religiosity and Social Environment – Study of the Changes in Religiosity due to Migration from Country to Town)*, Panstwowe Wydawnictwo Naukowe, Wroclaw-Crakow, 1972.
Pawelczynska, Anna, *Dynamika przemian kulturowych na wsi – Metoda badan glownych tendencji (Dynamics of Cultural Transformations in the Country – Method for Researching the Main Trends)*, Panstwowe Wydawnictwo Naukowe, Warsaw, 1966.
Piwowarski, Wladyslaw, *Praktiki religijne w diecezji warminskiej – Studium socjograficzne (Religious Practices in the Diocese of Warmia – A Sociographical Study)*, ATK, Warsaw, 1969.
Piwowarski, Wladyslaw, *Religijnosc wiejska w warunkach urbanizacji (The Effects of Urbanization on Rural Religiosity)*, Wiez library, Warsaw, 1971.

Piwowarski, Wladyslaw, *Religijnosc miejska w rejonie uprzemyslowionym (Religiosity in Cities in an Industrialized Region)*, Wiez library, Warsaw, 1977.

Piwowarski, Wladyslaw, (ed.), *Religijnosc ludowa - ciaglosc i zmiana (Popular Religiosity - Continuity and Change)*, Warsaw, 1983.

Piwowarski, Wladyslaw, and Zdaniewicz, Witold, *Z badan and religijnosca Polska - Studia i materialy (Research Relating to Religiosity in Poland - Studies and Materials)*, Studia socjologiczno-religijne, Pallottinum, Poznan-Warsaw, 1986, p.

Pomian-Sredenicki, Mciej, *Religious Change in Contemporary Poland: Secularization and Politics*, Routledge & Kegan Paul, London, 1982. *Religiousness in the Polish Society Life (Chosen Problems)*, Studia socjologiczno-religijne (3), The Sociological Research Institute of Religion, Pallottinum, Warsaw, 1981.

Wichrowski, Zygmunt, *L'Evangile dans un pays socialiste - La problématique de l'Evangelisation en Pologne (1945-81)*, Université des Sciences humaines de Strasbourg, Faculté de théologie catholique, Strasbourg, 1983 (third-year thesis, roneoed, can be consulted at the library of the Maison des Sciences de l'homme, Paris, under number TH 2987).

Articles

Adamski, Francisek, 'Postawy i praktyki religijne mlodziezy' ('Religious attitudes and practices of young people'), *Znak*, Cracow, 3 (261), 1976, pp. 385–405.

Adamski, Francisek, 'Funkcjonowanie katolickiego modelu malzenstwa i rodziny w srodowisku miejskim' ('How the Catholic model of marriage and the family works in urban surroundings'), *Znak*, Cracow, 230, 1973, pp. 1050–1069.

Eska, J., 'Socjologiczne znaki zapytania nad religijnoscia polska' ('The question marks of sociology about Polish religiousness'), *Wiez*, Warsaw, 11 (187), 1973, pp. 17–31.

Jerschina, J., and Ulasinski, C., 'Kierunki przemian religijnosci mlodziezy polskiej' ('Trends towards change in the religiousness of Polish youth'), *Kultura i Spoleczenstwo*, Warsaw, no. 4, 1985.

Kultura i Spoleczenstwo, XXVIII, no. 3, Polska Akademia Nauk, Warsaw, 1984, notably W. Piwowarski, 'Przemiany religijnosci ludowej w srodowiska wiejskim' ('Development of popular religiousness in the rural environment'), pp. 27–41, J. Marianski, 'Wspolzaleznosc postaw wobec religi i postaw godnosciowych' ('Correlation between the attitude towards religion and the sense of personal dignity'), pp. 43–60; F. Adamski, 'Sekularyzacja malzenstwa i rodziny' ('Secularization of marriage and the family'), pp. 205–15; K. Sopuch, 'Zroznicowanie stosunku do religii w zalenosci od niedtorych zmiennych struktury spolecznej' ('Variations in the relation to religion connected with certain variables in the structure of society'), pp. 197–203; B. Sciborski, 'Autoidentyfikacje religijne i laickie' ('Religious and lay self-identification'), pp. 191–5; A. Potocki, 'Organizacja zycia religijnego w dzisiejszej Polsce poludniowo-wschodniej' ('Organization of the religious life in contemporary south-eastern Poland'), pp. 217–38; A. Zakrzewski, 'Geneza i przemiany kulturotworczych funkcji Czestochowy' ('Origin and development of the culturally creative functions of Czestochowa'), pp. 239–50; J. Baniak, 'Dynamika powolan kaplanskich i zakonnych w Polsce (1945–82)' ('The dynamics of secular and regular vocations in Poland (1945–82)', pp. 253–66.

Majka, Jozef, 'La sociologie de la religion en Pologne', *Social Compass*, no. 10, 1963, pp. 453–76.

Majka, Jozef, 'Jaki jest katolicyzm polski' ('What is Polish Catholicism'), *Znak*, no. 141, 1966, pp. 272–93.

Michel, Patrick, 'Le catholicisme Polonais – Approches sociologiques', *Archives de Sciences Sociales des Religions*, CNRS, Paris, no. 49/1, 1980, pp. 161–78.
Michel, Patrick, 'Espace sacré et espace social: l'exemple de Zywiec (Pologne)', *Ricerche di storia sociale e religiosa*, Rome, nos 19–20, 1981, pp. 265–308.
Piwowarski, Wladyslaw, 'Le problème de l'Eglise populaire en Pologne', *Concilium*, no. 174, pp. 31–44.
Piwowarski, Wladyslaw, 'La religiosité populaire polonaise – Continuité et changement', *Concilium*, no. 151, pp. 69–80.
Piwowarski, Wladyslaw, 'Operacjonalizacja pojecia religijnòsc' ('Operationalization of the concept of religiousness'), *Studia socjologiczne*, no. 4, Warsaw, 1975.

Relations between Church, society and state

Barberini, Giovanni, *Stato socialista e Chiesa cattolica in Polonia*, CSEO Saggi, Storia, Plitica, Diritto, Bologna, 1983.
Bethell, Nicholas, *Gomulka – His Poland and His Communism*, Penguin, London, 1972.
Blit, Lucjan, *The Easter Pretender, Boleslaw Piasecki: His Time and Life*, Hutchinson, London, 1965.
Boniecki, Adam, *Budowa kosciolow w diecezji Przemyskiej (The Building of Churches in the Diocese of Przemys)*, Editions Spotkania, Paris, 1980.
Cywinski, Bohdan, *Rodowody niepokornych (The Genealogy of the unsubdued)*, Warsaw, 1971.
Gromek, Willy, *Polnisch Leben – Stimmen polnischer katholiken – Ausgewählt und übertragen*, preface by Carl Amery, Biederstein Verlag, Munich, 1969.
Kaminski, Franciszek, *Religione e Chiesa in Polonia, 1945-75 – Saggio storico-istituzionale*, Ceseo-Liviana, Padua, 1976, 157 p.
Ksiega Jubileuszowa 50-lecia Katolickeigo Uniwersytetu Lubelskiego (The Jubilee Book of the Catholic University of Lublin), Towarzystwo Naukowe KUL, Lublin, 1969.
Lenert, Pierre, *L'Eglise catholique en Pologne*, Editions du Centurion, Paris, 1962.
Martin, André, *La Pologne défend son âme*, Editions Saint-Paul, Paris-Fribourg, 1977.
Micewski, Andrzej, *Katholische Gruppierungen in Polen*, Kaiser-Grünewald Munich, 1978.
Michel, Patrick, *L'Eglise de Pologne et l'avenir de la nation*, Le Centurion, Paris, 1981.
Michel, Patrick, and Mink, Georges, *Mort d'un prêtre – L'affaire Popieluszko: Analyse d'un logique normalisatrice*, Fayard, collection 'Est', Paris, 1985.
Michnik, Adam, *L'Eglise et la Gauche – Le dialogue polonais*, Le Seuil, Paris, 1979.
Michnik, Adam, *Penser la Pologne*, La Découverte-Maspero, 'Cahiers libres' 377, Paris, 1983.
Morawski, Dominik, *Chrétienne Pologne*, trans. from the Italian by J. Joba, Editions France-Empire, Paris, 1981.
Nous Chrétiens de Pologne (collective work), Cana, Mémoire vivante, Paris, 1979.
Pace, Enzo (ed.), *La società parallela – Religione, resistenza e opposizione nella Polonia contemporanea*, Franco Angeli/Sociologia, 1984.
Pietrzak, Michal, *Prawo Wyznaniowe (Law as Regards Religion)*, Panstwowe Wydawnictwo Naukowe, Warsaw, 1982.
Popieluszko, Jerzy, *Kazania Patriotyczne (Patriotic Sermons)*, Libella, Paris, 1984.
Raina, Peter, *Jan-Pawel II, Prymas i episkopat Polski, o stanie wojennym (John Paul II, the primate and the Polish episcopate, with respect to martial law)*, Poets & Painters, London, 1982.

Solidarité résiste et signe (proceedings of the symposium 'Pologne: aout 1980 – décembre 1982. Originalité et dynamisme d'une société'), Nouvelle Cité, Paris, 1984.

Szajkowski, Bogdan, *Next to God . . . Poland – Politics and Religion in Contemporary Poland*, Frances Pinter, London, 1983.

Tischner, Jozef, *Ethique de Solidarité*, Librairie Adolphe Ardant, Criterion, Limoges, 1983. Tischner, Jozef, *Polski ksztalt dialogu (The Polish Way of Dialogue)*, Ed. Spotkania, Paris, 1981.

Tomsk, Alexander, *Catholic Poland*, Keston College, Keston, Kent, 1982.

Urban, Vincenty, *Duzpasterska dziejba kaplanow repartriantow na ziemach odzyskanych w latach 1945-70 (History of the Pastoral (activity) of the Priests Repatriated into the 'Recovered Lands' in the Years 1945-70)*, Wroclaw, 1972.

Zalecki, Marian, *Notre-Dame de Czestochowa*, adaptation by Dom Bernard Billet, trans. from the English by Bernard Crassous, preface by René Laurentin, Desclée de Brouwer, Paris, 1981.

Articles

Dembinski, Ludwik, 'Les choix politiques des structures confessionnelles en Pologne', *Revue Française de Science Politique*, XXIII, no. 3, Paris, June 1973, pp. 537–49.

Deptula, C., 'Z zagadnien kultu maryjnego w Polsce' ('Problems of the cult of the Virgin Mary in Poland'), *Ateneum Kaplanski*, 60, 1960, pp. 392–419.

Domenach, Jean-Marie, 'Société et Eglise en Pologne', *Esprit*, Paris, no. 10, 1976, pp. 339–52.

Hebblethwaite, R., 'Is the Polish Church a model for the universal church?', *Concilium*, no. 161, pp. 59–67.

Istina, nos 3–4, Paris, 1977 (13 documents on the defence of human rights in Poland and 8 documents on the new government regulations with regard to the Catholic Church in Poland, esp. K. Kakol, 'Press conference at Warsaw on 19 May 1976', pp. 332–7).

Istina, XXXV, no. 4, Paris, 1980, 'Le réveil Polonais' (P. Michel, 'Pologne: le foisonnement et l'inquiétude', pp. 305–7; P. Michel, 'Eglise et Etat en Pologne: la permanence d'un fragile équilibre', pp. 308–19; P. Michel (in collaboration with Allen J. Grieco), 'L'Eglise polonaise: un lieu de communication rénové face au monopole d'Etat', pp. 320–4; J. Turowicz, 'Dialogue, pluralisme et unité', pp. 325–32; K. Pomian, 'L'université volante', pp. 333–5; documents, pp. 336–49).

Michel, Patrick, 'Les cultes populaires en Pologne – Matériaux pour une symbolique politique', in *Archives de Sciences Sociales des Religions*, CNRS, Paris, no. 51/1, 1981, trans. into Italian in *La società parallela – Religione, Resistenza e opposizione nella Polonia contemporanea* (edited by Enzo Pace), Franco Angeli, Milan, 1984, pp. 170–207.

Michel, Patrick, 'Résistance face à l'inconnu', *Projet*, no. 175, Paris, 1983, pp. 419–26.

Michel, Patrick, 'Morale et société en Pologne: le discours de l'Eglise', *Revue d'Etudes comparatives Est-Ouest*, Paris, vol. 14, no. 1, 1983, pp. 121–34.

Michel, Patrick, 'Le système polonais et ses acteurs', paper read at the 2nd National Congress of the Association Française de Science Politique, Grenoble, January 1984, published in *Bulletin du Groupe de travail sur l'Europe centrale et orientale*, MSH-EHESS, Paris, no. 4, 1985, pp. 57–70.

Michel, Patrick, 'Institution catholique et intégrisme en Pologne', paper read at the symposium of the Association Française de Sociologie Religieuse, Paris, 26 November 1984, published in *Social Compass*, Louvain, XXXII/4, 1985, pp. 353–61.

Michel, Patrick (in collaboration with Georges Mink), 'La police polonaise comme instrument de normalisation: le procès de Torun', *Les problèmes de la crise en Pologne*, report for the research project Les crises des systèmes de type soviétique study no. 12, published in French, English and German, Cologne, Index, 1986.

Michel, Patrick, 'Y a-t-il un modèle ecclésial polonais?', *Archives de Sciences Sociales des Religions*, CNRS, Paris, no. 62/1, 1986, pp. 81-92.

Morawska, Ewa, 'Civil Religion vs. State Power in Poland', *Society*, vol. 21, no. 4, Rutgers – The State University, New Brunswick, N.J., May–June 1984, pp. 29-34.

Nowak, Stefan, 'Valeurs et attitudes du peuple polonais', *Pour la Science*, no. 47, Paris, 1981, pp. 12-23.

Les Quatre Fleuves, booklet no. 13, Beauchesne, Paris, 1981 (esp. Cardinal Macharski, 'La vie chrétienne dans les temps difficiles', pp. 7-16; S. Wilkanowicz, 'La signification de la Pologne pour les chrétiens d'Europe', pp. 17-22; J. Mirewicz, 'Jean-Paul II dans le drame du catholicisme polonais', pp. 23-8; J. Wozniakowski, 'Le pluralisme en Pologne, hier et aujourd'hui', pp. 29-36; J. Turowicz, 'Le rôle de la presse catholique en Pologne', pp. 37-46; L. Kolakowski, 'La leçon Polonaise', pp. 47-56; A. Michnik, 'Une leçon de dignité', pp. 57-64; J. Kloczowski, 'Un entretien sur Solidarité', pp. 79-88). 'Spotkanie Prymasa z ksiezmi Archidiecezji Warszawskiej – 7 grudnia 1982' (Meeting between the primate and the priests of the archdiocese of Warsaw – 7 December 1982), in *Zeszyty historyczne*, no. 64, Instytut Literacki, Paris, 1983, pp. 206-18.

Szuba, Zdzislaw, 'Biskupi polscy xx wieku' ('The Polish bishops in the 20th century'), *Zycie katolickie*, Warsaw, no. 5-6, 1983, pp. 23-4.

Turbacz, Marek, 'Kosciol a kommunizm w Polsce' ('The Church and communism in Poland') *Kultura* no 4/451, Paris, 1985, pp. 1551-9.

Vaucelles, Louis de, 'Les relations Englise-Etat en Pologne', *Etudes*, Paris, November 1979, pp. 449-60.

Witkowski, Beata, 'Stosunek Episkopatu Polski do niektorych zalozen ustrojowych Polski Ludowej' ('The attitude of the Polish episcopate to certain principles of the political system of the People's Republic of Poland'), *studia Religiologica*, leaflet 3 (DXXIII), Warsaw-Cracow, 1978, pp. 83-98.

Official point of view

Godlewski, Jerzy, *Obywatel a religia – Wolnosc sumienia w prl (The citizen and religion – Freedom of Conscience in Poland)*, Ksiazka i Wiedza, Warsaw, 1977.

Godlewski, Jerzy, *Kosciol rzymsko-katolicki w Polsce wobec sekularyzacji zycia publicznego (The Polish Catholic Church facing the Secularization of Public Life)*, Ksiazka i Wiedza, Warsaw, 1978.

Godlewski, Jerzy, *Kontrowersje wokol swiatopogladu (Controversies on the World-view)*, Ksiazka i Wiedza, Warsaw, 1980.

Grzelak, Edward, *Z probelmatyki rozdzialu kosciola od panstwa (Problems of the Relations between Church and State)*, Ksiazka i Wiedza, Warsaw, 1980.

Marek, Ryszard, *Kosciol rzymsko-katolicki na ziemiach zachodnich i polnocnych (The Roman Catholic Church and the Western and Eastern Territories)*, Panstwowe Wydawnictwo Naukowe, Warsaw, 1976.

Markiewicz, Stanlslaw, *Kosciol rzymsko-katolicki a panstwa socialistyczne (The Roman Catholic Church and Socialist States)*, Ksiazka i Wiedza, Warsaw, 1974.

Markiewicz, Stanislaw, *Panstwo i Kosciol w Polsce Ludowej (State and Church in People's Poland)*, Ludowa Spoldzielnia wydawnictwa, Warsaw, 1981.

Markiewicz, Stanlslaw, *Wspoldzialanie Kosciola i panstwo w swietle teorii i praktiki* (*Cooperation between Church and State in Theory and Practice*), Ksiazka i Wiedza, Warsaw, 1983.
Opara, Stefan, *Marksizm a religijnosc* (*Marxism and Religiousness*), Ksiazka i Wiedza, Warsaw, 1980.
Piekarski, Adam, *The Church in Poland*, Interpress, Warsaw, 1978.
Piekarski, Adam, *Freedom of Conscience and Religion in Poland*, Interpress, Warsaw, 1979.
Tanalski, Dionizy, *Katolicyzm - Ewolucja ideologii* (*The Development of Catholic Ideology*), Panstwowe Wydawnictwo Naukowe, Biblioteka Problemov, Warsaw, 1978.

Articles

Godlewski, Jerzy, 'Stosunek Kosciola rzymskokatolickiego do inteligencji i jej spolecznej roli' ('The attitude of the Roman Catholic Church towards the intelligentsia and its role in society'), *Nowe Drogi*, no. 403, Warsaw, 1982, pp. 129–38.
Markiewicz, Stanislaw, 'Partia a religia' ('The party and religion'), *Nowe Drogi*, no. 407, Warsaw, 1983, pp. 26–36.

2 Hungary

Bibliography

Hainbuch, Friedrich, *Kirche und Staat in Ungarn nach dem Zweiten Weltkrieg*, Studia Hungarica (22), Ungarisches Institut München, Dr Rudolf Trofenik-Munich, 1982 (485 ref.).
Tomka, Miklos, 'A selected bibliography of Sociological Studies on Religion in Hungary (1945–79)', *Social Compass*, XXVIII, 1981/1, Louvain, pp. 125–41 (161 ref.).
The above two works contain a virtually exhaustive bibliography on the subject up to 1982. We shall therefore only supplement it here.

Religious history

Wandruszka, Adam, and Urbanitsch, Peter (under the direction of), *Die Habsburgermonarchie*, vol. 4: *Die Konfessionen*, Verlag der österreichischen Akademischen der Wissenschaften, Vienna, 1985.

Religious situation in Hungary

Andras, Emeric, and Morel, Julius, *Bilanz des Ungarischen Katholozismus*, Heimatwerk, Munich, 1969.
Andras, Emeric, and Morel, Julius (eds), *Church in Transition: Hungary's Catholic Church from 1945 to 1982*, Hungarian Institute for Sociology of Religion, 1983.
Andras, Emeric, and Morel, Julius (eds), *Hungarian Catholicism: A Handbook*, Hungarian Institute for Sociology of Religion, 1983.
Bozsoky, Paul, 'La longue nuit du clergé hongrois', *Etudes*, Paris, July 1972, pp. 99–115.
Bozsoky, Paul, 'Un tournant pour l'Eglise de Hongrie?', *Etudes*, Paris, May 1974, pp. 761–71.
Bozsoky, Paul, 'Chrétiens en Hongrie', *Etudes*, Paris, March 1977, pp. 401–16. 'Il caso

Bulanyi: scandalo di un'eresia o rinnovamento della Chiesa?' in *CSEO Documentazione*, XVII, 182, Bologna, July – August 1983, pp. 332–55.

Csanad, Bela, 'Lelkpasztorkodasunk a zsinat utan' ('Our pastoral life after Vatican II'), *Vigilia*, no. 5, Budapest, 1972.

Csanad, Bela, 'A katolikus valllasossag merese hazankban' ('Measure of Catholic religiousness in Hungary'), *Vigilia*, no. 5, Budapest, 1976, pp. 294–303.

Gari, Margit, *Le Vinaigre et le fiel*, Plon, Paris, 1984.

Gergely, Jenö, *A Katolikus Egyhaz Magyarorszagon (1944–71)* (*The Catholic Church in Hungary 1944–71*), Kossuth, Budapest, 1985.

Heller, Gy., 'A magyar papsag ma es holnap' ('The Hungarian clergy today and tomorrow'), *Teologia*, no. 4, Budapest, 1985, pp. 216–19.

La vie religieuse en Hongrie, a file compiled by *Conscience et Liberté*, no. 28, Berne, 1984, pp. 45–134 (esp. Laszlo Paskai, 'La vie religieuse des catholiques en Hongrie', pp. 94–8; Gyorgy Aczel, 'Les relations entre l'Etat et les Eglises en Hongrie', pp. 81–7; I. Miklos, 'Les problèmes actuels de la politique ecclésiastique', pp. 88–93).

Lukacs, Jozsef, 'Szekularizacio es vallaossag a szocializmusban' ('Secularization and religion in socialism'), *Vilagossag*, no. 1, Budapest, 1977.

Michel, Patrick, 'Eglises en Hongrie: Des croyants voués aux Catacombes pour cause de compromis', *L'autre Europe*, no. 1, Paris, 1984, pp. 35–7.

Michel, Patrick, 'En Hongrie, réforme économique et vide éthique', *Projet*, no. 185–6, Paris, 1984, pp. 675–80.

Mindszenty, Cardinal, *Mémoires*, La Table Ronde, Paris, 1974.

Muranyi, Mihaly, 'A vallasossag struktur ajanak es funkcioinak valtozsai' ('The structural and functional transformations of religiousness'), *Vilagossag*, no. 1, Budapest, 1977.

Nyiri, Tamas, 'Mire jo a keresxtenyseg?' ('What is the use of Christianity?'), *Vigilia*, no. 5, Budapest, 1977.

'I rapporti tra Chiese e Stato in Ungheria', *Ornamenti Sociali*, no. 7–8, Milan, 1985, pp. 561–8.

Ronay, Gyorgy, 'Hol tartunk?' ('Where are we?'), *Vigilia*, no. 12, Budapest, 1977.

Tomka, Miklos, 'Az egyhazak valtozo tarsadalmi szerepe – A hivatalos nagyegyhazah funkciovaltasanak modellje: a magyar tipusu fejlödesre alkalmazva' ('The development of the social role of the Church. A model of functional development of the Churches. Application to Hungarian-type development'), *Szociologia*, no. 2, Budapest, 1976, pp. 235–47.

Tomka, Miklos, 'A vallasi önbesorolas es a tarsadalmi retegzödes' ('Religious identification and social stratification'), *Szocologia*, no. 4, Budapest, 1977, pp. 522–36.

Tomka, Miklos, 'A Balance of secularization in Hungary', *Social Compass*, Louvain, XXVIII, 1981/1 (taken from the Hungarian: 'A szekularizacio merlege'), *Valosag*, Budapest, 1979/7, pp. 60–70.

Tomka, Miklos, 'Le role des Eglises instituées de hongrie dans un contexte de changement', *Social Compass*, XVIII, 1, Louvain, 1981, pp. 93–111.

Tomka, Miklos, 'Les rites de passage dans les pays socialistes', *Social Compass*, no. 2–3, Louvain, 1982, pp. 135–52.

Tomka, Miklos, 'Vasarnapok, unnepek, vallasgyakorlat – Megyezesek a templombajaras szociologiajahoz' ('Sundays, holidays, religious practice – some observations on the sociology of practicants'), *Vilagossag*, no. 5, Budapest, 1982, pp. 300–6.

Tomka, Miklos, 'Tarsadalmi valtozas – Vallasi valtozas (a mai magyar katolicizmus szerkezeti transformacioi)' ('Mutations in society – the development of religion (The transformation of the structure of contemporary Hungarian Catholicism)'), Szociologia, no. 3, Budapest, 1983, pp. 253–71.

3 Czechoslovakia

General history and religious history

Besides Wandruszka's work mentioned above, Macek, Josef, *Histoire de la Bohême (des origines à 1918)*, Fayard, Paris, 1984, can be consulted.
Michel, Bernard, *La Mémoire de Prague*, Perrin, Paris, 1986.

The religious situation

Frei, Bohumil Jiri, *Staat und Kirche in der Tschechoslowakei vom Februarumsturz 1948 bis zum Prager Frühling 1968*, IV. Dokumente und Tabellen, Verlag Robert Lerche Munich, formerly Calve'sche Universitätsbuchhandlung Prag, Munich, 1973, XIII.
Heneka, A., et al. *A Besieged Culture – Czechoslovakia Ten Years After Helsinki*, Charta 77 Foundation and International Helsinki Federation for Human Rights, Stockholm-Vienna, 1985.
Hlinka, Anton, *Liquidation de l'Eglise en Slovaquie*, trans. from the German by Robert Givord, Apostolat des Editions Paulines, Paris, 1981.
Krestané ä Charta '77 – Vyber Dokumentu a texta (Christians and Charter 77 – selected documents and texts) Index (7), Opus Bonum, Munich, 1980.
Priestervereinigung 'Pacem in Terris' – Eine kritische Analyse – Materialien zur Situation der Katholischen Kirche in der CSSR, vol. V, Sozialwerk der Ackerman--Gemeinde, Munich, 1983.
Rabas, Josef, *Kirche in Fesseln – Materialien zur Situation der Katholischen Kirche in der CSSR*, vol. VI, Sozialwerk der Ackerman-Gemeinde, Munich, 1984. p.
Rebichini, Andrea, *Chiesa, società e Stato in Cecoslovacchia (1948–68)* Ceseo-Liviana, Padua, 1977.
Zverina, Josef, *Odvaha byt cirkvi (The Courage to be a Church)*, Opus Bonum, Munich, 1981.

Articles

'L'Association *Pacem in Terris* – Un aspect des relations Eglise/Etat en Tchécoslovaquie', *Etudes*, Paris, January 1978, pp. 27–42.
Benda, Vaclav, 'Cattolici e politica in Cecoslovacchia', *CSEO Documentazione*, XIV, 150, Padua, May 1980, pp. 201–9.
Bottier, Albert, 'The Christian Peace Conference: 1958–83. A political overview', discussion paper prepared for AAASS National Convention in Kansas City, October 1983, roneo.
Cinoldr, F., 'Promeny vztahu katolicismu ke statu a moci' ('Changes in the relationships between Catholicism and the state and government'), *Nova Mysl*, Prague, January 1972.
'Eutanasia di una Chiesa', *CSEO Documentazione*, XVI, 175, Padua, September 1982, pp. 340–64.
Havel, Vaclav, 'Doing without Utopias', *Times Literary Supplement*, London, 23 January 1987.
Hejdanek, 'Le sens et la place du christianisme dans la société actuelle', pp. 65–70; and two documents on Charta followed by five on the situation of the Catholic Church).

Istina, XXII, no. 2, Paris, 1977, 'Hommage à Jan Patocka' (with contributions from B. Dupuy, J. M. Brunet Lacaze, P. Ricoeur, R. Jakobson and E. Borne on Patocka, Charta 77 and Human Rights in Czechoslovakia and two series of documents: 'La Charte 77 pour le respect des Droits de l'Homme', pp. 147–209; 'La situation de l'Eglise catholique en Tchécoslovaquie', pp. 210–72).

Istina, XXVIII, no. 1, Paris, 1983, 'Luttes pour les libertés en Tchécoslovaquie (1979–81)' (with contributions from E. Kalista, 'Le catholicisme dans l'histoire tcheèque', pp. 5–30; V. Benda, 'Le catholicisme et la politique', pp. 31–45; J. Trojan, 'En quoi l'Eglise est-elle irremplaçable', pp. 46–64; L.

Istina, XXVIII, no. 2, Paris, 1983, 'Luttes pour les libertés en Tchécoslovaquie (1979–1981) – Part Two' (with contributions from M. Hybler, 'Une réalité de façade'), pp. 115–18; J. Nemec, 'Les nouvelles chances de la liberté', pp. 119–30; M. Reichert, 'Le christianisme aujourd'hui et demain', pp. 131–4; and documents (pp. 146–234).

Kvasnicka, Bohumir, 'K procesu socialistickej integracie veriacich v Ceskoslovensku' ('The process of socialist integration of believers in Czechoslovakia'), *Ateizmus*, no. 3, Prague, 1978.

Pattaro, Germano (ed.), *Il dissenso religioso – La collaborazione tra cristiani, credenti non cristiani e non credenti nella lotta per i diritti dell'uomo e per la libertà di espressione nell'Europa dell'Est*, Marsilio Editori, Venice, 1977.

Ramet, Pedro, 'The Czechoslovak Church under pressure', in *The World Today*, Oxford University Press, September 1982, pp. 355–60.

Rulli, G., 'Processo contro laici e sacerdoti cattolici in Cecoslovacchia', in *La Civiltà cattolica*, vol. III, booklet 3193, Rome, June 1983, pp. 90–6.

Strmiska, Zdenek, 'Vysledky nezavislebo pruzkumu soucasnebo smysleni v Ceskoslovensku' ('Results of the independent survey of current opinions in Czechoslovakia'), *Svedectvi*, Paris, XX, no. 78, 1986, pp. 265–334.

Tandler, Nicolas, 'La politique religieuse des communistes en Tchécoslovaquie', *Est et Ouest*, no. 587, Paris, February 1977, pp. 47–52.

Tomsky, Alexander, 'Modus moriendi – L'Eglise catholique en Tchécoslovaquie', in *Communio*, vol. VII, no. 5, September–October 1982, pp. 76–89.

Trois documents secrets du gouvernement slovaque', *Est et Ouest*, no. 498, Paris, November 1972, pp. 439–44.

Chronology

REFERENCES	POLAND	CZECHOSLOVAKIA	HUNGARY
1944	7,170 diocesan priests		*3 March*: Josef Mindszenty becomes bishop of Veszprem
19 March: The Germans occupy Hungary
25 March: J. Mindszenty is appointed bishop by the prince-primate J. Seredi
June: The Sztojay government has the Jews confined in ghettos. The bishops protest
July: Admiral Horthy forms a military government. Hungarian defeats. Horthy asks the Russians for a cease-fire and orders the troops to cease hostilities. Bela Dalnocki Miklos's army joins the Russians. The Germans arrest Horthy and force him to hand over power to F. Szalasi, leader of the Arrow Cross movement
	22 July: Proclamation at Lublin of the Manifesto of the Polish Committee of National Liberation (PKWN)		
	1 August: Warsaw uprising begins
2 October: Watsaw uprising ends	*August–October*: Slovak uprising	*31 October*: The bishops of western Hungary protest against the new government
27 November: Arrest of Bishop Mindszenty
	3 November: Reopening of Lublin Catholic University in the presence of representatives of the PKWN and of the Soviety army
31 December: The Lublin Committee is recognized by the USSR (the Vatican recognizes only the Polish government-in-exile in London)		*21 December*: Debrecen provisional national assembly which appoints a provisional government. Formation of a Christian Social Party not permitted.

REFERENCES	POLAND	CZECHOSLOVAKIA	HUNGARY
			24 December: Beginning of siege of Budapest by the Russians
1945			
January: Yalta Conference	Results of conflict: Disappearance of 6 bishops, 2,030 priests and 243 nuns		*January*: The Russians capture the eastern part of Budapest. Cease-fire between the allies and the Hungarians, negotiated by Voroshilov
	17 January: The Red Army enters Warsaw		*30 January*: Rakosi, first secretary of the Hungarian Communist Party, arrives in Hungary
		February: The Red Army enters Slovakia	*15 March*: The provisional government adopts the law on agrarian reform (involving the expropriation of the greater part of the Church's wealth)
	24 March: Catholic weekly *Tygodnik Powszechny* (editor-in-chief: Jerzy Turowicz) appears		*29 March*: Prince-primate Seredi dies
		April: The American army enters western Bohemia	*4 April*: The whole country is occupied by the Russians alone
		3 April: Introduction at Kosice of the new Czechoslovak government and its programme	*5 April*: Papal Nuncio expelled
		4 April: End of Mgr Tiso's presidency	
		5 May: Uprising in Prague to liberate the city	*24 May*: First post-war pastoral letter of the Hungarian bishops
8 May: German surrender			

253

	9 May: The country is liberated. Beginning of a process which ended with the expulson of 3 million Germans
16 May: Return of E. Benes and the government to Prague. The Slovak national council nationalizes all the Church schools in Slovakia		
25 June: Charter of the United Nations		*June*: First plenary conference of the episcopate, presided over by the arch-bishop of Cracow, Mgr Adam Aspicha. Discussion of the consequences of the war.
29 June: Provisional government of national unity at Warsaw, recognized on 6 July by the United States and Great Britain	
17 July: Postsdam Conference begins
August: Atom bomb on Hiroshima		*20 July*: Return of the Polish primate August Hlond, with plenary authority from the Vatican
3 August: Arrest of bishop K.M. Splett, sentenced to eight years' imprisonment for 'activity directed against the Polish nation'
12 September: The provisional governments of national unity suspends the 1925 concordat	*September*: School reform
16 September: Pius XII appoints J. Mindszenty primate of Hungary
17 October: The bishops intervene on behalf of prisoners and protest against the collective reprisals undertaken against Germans in Hungary
4 November: General elections. The Smallholders Party gained
		11 November: Publication of the weekly *Tygodnik Warszawski* – in	*November*: Complete withdrawal of American and Soviet troops.

REFERENCES	POLAND	CZECHOSLOVAKIA	HUNGARY
	1946 its chief editor was the Minister of Education in the Polish government in London, Abbé Zygmunt Kaczynski	Nationalization of key sectors of the economy	57.7 percent of the votes, the Communist Party 17 per cent. A coalition government was formed. Z. Tildy, head of the majority party, became president of the Council of Ministers, which contained four communists *30 November*: The primate travels to Rome
	December: Publication of the weekly *Dzis i Jutro (Today and Tomorrow)* of the progressive Catholics (who were to form the Pax group)		
1946	*18 February*: The archbishop of Cracow. Mgr Adam Sapieha, was appointed cardinal		*January*: Nationalization of the greater part of the industrial sector *1 February*: The Republic proclaimed. President: Z. Tildy *21 February*: Mgr Mindszenty is appointed cardinal *12 March*: Law on 'penal protection of democratic public order and the Republic'. Formation of a 'left block' within the coalition. *23 March*: The CP relieves I. Nagy of his functions as Minister of the Interior and replaces him by L. Rajk, who starts a campaign against the Catholic schools
March: Winston Churchill's Fulton speech			
April: Opening of the peace conference in Paris			

13 May: Diplomatic relations between Prague and the Vatican re-established
25 June: Elections for the national constituent assembly
2 July: Gottwald heads the new government

July: The monthly *Znak* appears

August: Inflation overcome by draconian measures
Summer: Most of the Catholic associations are suppressed
Autumn: Discovery of a 'plot' to overthrow the republic, the aim being to weaken the Smallholders Party

September: Bishops' conference at which it is decided that the Christian Democrat Party no longer represents Catholics, who are forbidden to vote for programmes 'contrary to Christian ethics and teaching'

October: Peace treaty
November: Deportation of Hungarians from Slovakia to the Sudetenland begins

7 November: Mgr Beran appointed archbishop of Prague. He receives the Order of Merit for anti-Nazi activities
2 December: Trial of Mgr Tiso, Slovak ex-head of state, an ally of Hitler, opens at Bratislava

30 Catholic schools are authorized by the state
54 Catholic reviews

1947

February: New communist campaign against the Smallholders Party

REFERENCES	POLAND	CZECHOSLOVAKIA	HUNGARY
12 *March*: The Truman Doctrine	14 *March*: Letter from the bishops to the prime minister concerning human rights and Church–state relations Letter from the bishops on the eve of the first post-war elections, advising against voting for systems opposed to Christian principles		21 *February*: The Russians arrest the leader of the SP, B. Kovacs, for 'anti-Soviet activities' *March*: Trial of the 'conspirators'. Very heavy sentences passed
		April: Mgr Tiso sentenced to hanging	
			May: Nationalization of the leading banks 30 *May*: The president of the Council 'implicated' in the plot, resigns and is replaced by Dinnyes
5 *June*: Marshall Plan launched		2 *July*: The government accepts the Marshall Plan in principle 9 *July*: Marshall Plan rejected following pressure from the Soviets	*June–July*: Mindszenty goes to Ottawa for the World Marial Congress
			15 *August*: Opening of the marial year at Esztergom 20 *August*: On St Stephen's Day the Soviet rulers send official congratulations to the president of the Hungarian Republic 31 *August*: General elections. The government coalition wins 60 per cent of the votes (with the CP at 20 per cent). A Christian-oriented opposition party wins 16 per cent of the vote

September: The Cominform is set up		15 *September*: The interallied control Commission suspends its activities but the Russians remain in Hungary
		24 *October*: Mindszenty protests to the president of the council, Dinnyes, against attacks on freedom of conscience
		– The 47–8 budget gives substantial subsidies to the Churches
	November: Dissolution of the opposition parties (the Smallholders Party gives up opposition)	
1948		
	First arrests and series of trials of leaders of the Catholic hierarchy. Action Catholique and other Church organizations are declared illegal	
	25 *February*: The 'Prague Coup'. Although the Minister of Health was a Catholic, two measures were adopted against the Church: the quasi-confiscation of its lands in the agrarian law, and the closing of all Catholic schools and the ending of religious instruction in schools, with a state monopoly of schools	18 *February*: Soviet–Hungarian Treaty of Friendship
		March: More businesses nationalized, including Catholic printing firms
		Mid-June: Social Democratic Party merges with the Communist Party.
	15 *April*: Letter from the bishops to young Catholics warning them against atheistic, secular propaganda	
	30 *May*: Elections (single list)	*Mid-June*: Social Democratic Party merges with the Communist Party

REFERENCES	POLAND	CZECHOSLOVAKIA	HUNGARY
24 June: Berlin blocade	*24 June:* Letter from the primate of Poland to President Bierut dealing with the threats to Catholic education and with the young communist associations	*7 June:* Resignation of President Benes	*17 June–1 July:* Nationalization of the schools
		July: A priest subservient to the government appointed head of Caritas. The bishops forbid priests to adopt political commitments and ask the Minister of Health, Father Plojhar, to step down	*30 July:* Resignation of Tildy
			20 August: Collectivization of production announced in a speech by Rakosi
			September: Extensive reorganization of school and university education, beginning of a big purge of Party members
	22 October: Death of A. Hlond, primate of Poland		*November:* Censorship extended
	12 November: Mgr Stefan Wyszynski, bishop of Lublin, becomes primate of Poland		*End of December:* J. Mindszenty arrested, accused of 'high treason' and imprisoned at Budapest
10 December: Universal Declaration of Human Rights			

1949

| | | *January:* State monopoly on the non-periodical press and confiscation of all ecclesiastical libraries, suppressing forty-nine Catholic reviews | *Early February:* Trial of Cardinal Mindszenty. On 8 Feb. the primate was sentnced to life imprisonment |

259

		Spring: Formation of a movement of priests and laymen 'for peace', opposing the Vatican
March: The government complains about some sections of the clergy whom it considers 'hostile', but states it has no intention of curtailing religious freedoms or Catholic teaching in the schools		
	28 April: First meeting of the pseudo-movement Action catholique set up by the government	*April*: Rakosi announces, almost in so many words, the dictatorship of the proletariat
4 April: North Atlantic Treaty	*25–28 May*: 9th Congress of the Czech CP, signalling Russia's grip of the country	*15 May*: General elections. The unified list of the popular front wins nearly 100 per cent of votes
	15 June: Protest by the bishops against the arrests of several hundred priests and attacks on religious freedom	
23 June: Abolition of the Faculty of Law and Economic Science at Lublin Catholic University	*July*: Visas refused for Vatican officials	
30 June: Decree of the Holy Office forbidding 'joining atheist communism or any activity which might promote it'		*6 July*: The Court of Appeal confirms the sentence on Cardinal Mindszenty
6 July: Thanks to the primate, formation of a mixed commission of the government and the bishops		*20 July*: new constitution modelled on that of the USSR
August: 'Regulation' of Catholic associations		
21 September: Church-owned hospitals pass into state control		*5 September*: Cessation of compulsory religious teaching in the schools
September: Formation of the 'committee of patriotic priests' within the war veterans association (ZBOWID)		*End of September*: Rajk trial. Rakosi assumes full authority over the country
September: Soviet atomic bomb		
October: Law requiring government approval of all ecclesiastical appointments in the dioceses.		

REFERENCES	POLAND	CZECHOSLOVAKIA	HUNGARY
		1 November: Creation of a State Office for Ecclesiastical Affairs, priests will have to swear allegiance to the state, from which they will receive a salary. Henceforth the Church is considered as directly dependent upon the state. Building of churches or presbyteries is forbidden.	
	23 December: Monopolization of publishing houses and printing works. Creation of 'Pax' publishers whose 'progressivist' outlook is encouraged by the government		*21 December*: Lavish ceremonies for Stalin's 70th birthday *28 December*: Last nationalizations. All industry is now owned by the state. According to the official census, Catholics represent more than 70 per cent of the population.
1950	*23 January*: The Caritas organization is placed under state control		*1 January*: First five-year plan
	20 March: Law on the nationalization of the assets of confessional organizations *14 April*: Agreement between the government and the episcopate (in exchange for guarantees on religious activities the episcopate undertook to respect the com-	*February*: Clash between the Holy See and the government regarding ecclesiastical appointments (esp. in Slovakia) *March*: Final rupture of diplomatic relations between Prague and the Vatican *13 April*: Banning of the religious orders. The religious were assembled in concentration convents and their superiors were imprisoned.	*April*: Sjakasits, former leader of the Social Democrats, is arrested

261

munist government and to contribute to the reconstruction of the country)	*March–April*: Occupation of all monasteries. First large political trial against the religious for 'high treason and espionage'	*May–August*: Wave of arrests of former Social Democrats	
June: Beginning of the Korean war	*17 June*: The bishops' reserves concerning the *Stockholm Appeal* were described as an infringement of the April agreement	*9 June*: Beginning of large-scale deportations of religious	*1 August*: Formation of the 'Catholic priests for peace' movement, headed by Mgr Grosz
		14 July: Closure of all Catholic theological faculties except those of Prague and Bratislava	*30 August*: The Catholic bench of bishops signs an agreement with the state: The Church receives some subsidies and recovers some schools. The bishops recognize the new constitution
	12 September: Letter from the primate of Poland accusing the government, on behalf of the bishops, of violating the April agreement		*7 September*: Dissolution of the religious orders. There were fifty-three of them, with a membership of some 13,000 religious
	December: Pastoral letter from the bishops on the 'divine source of power in the Church of Christ'	*November*: Trial of Mgr Zela, bishop of Olomouc	
1951	*20 January*: Arrest of Mgr Kaczmarek, bishop of Kielce,	*January*: Show trial of the Slovak bishops	

REFERENCES	POLAND	CZECHOSLOVAKIA	HUNGARY
	accused of collaboration with the Germans and of spying. (He was rehabilitated in March 1957.) *26 January*: The authorities end the temporary status of the ecclesiastical administration over the 'Western Territories' and make chapters responsible for nominating capitular vicars *2 May*: Archbishop Wyszynski's first journey to Rome in his capacity as primate of Poland: the Holy See appoints some diocesan bishops (for Wroclaw, Opole, Gorzow, Gdansk and Warmie), but they cannot take up their posts because of government opposition	*April*: The government bans Mgr Beran from living in his Prague diocese Arrest of Mgr Tomasek (consecrated bishop in 1949 with the consent of the state). He remained in prison for three years	*February–March*: Party Congress *15 May*: Adoption of the Bill on the creation of the 'National Office for Religious Affairs'. I. Kosa, a member of the Central Committee, is put in charge *End of May*: New purge within the Party *15 June*: Beginning of forced deportation to the eastern parts of the country of 'enemy of the people elements' from Budapest and western Hungary *22 June*: Trial of J. Grosz, president of the bench of bishops since the arrest of the primate. He

July: An article in *Pravda* condemns the Vatican and 'the Polish Catholic clique under orders from abroad' was sentenced to fifteen years' imprisonment for plotting against the republic

21 July: The bench of bishops took the constitutional oath. The seminaries were closed

September: Father Plojhar, an excommunicated priest, launches the *Mouvement du clergé catholique pour la Paix* (MHKD), which replaces *Action catholique*. The aim is still to organize religious support for the policy of the government

24 November: Arrest of R. Slansky, general secretary of the Czech CP, following arrests of nearly 50,000 Party officials including V. Clementis, formerly Minister of Foreign Affairs

November: The economic crisis worsens. Religious instruction in state schools is given only to children who expressly ask for it, against much administrative harassment

1952

February–March: Letters from the episcopate to President Bierut on the draft constitution and in defence of the religious charitable organizations

9 March: Grandiose celebrations of Rakosi's 60th birthday

June: Formation of a Czechoslovak institute for the publication of political and scientific knowledge, responsible for anti-religious propaganda. A Catholic layman, Professor Otto Madr, is sentenced

REFERENCES	POLAND	CZECHOSLOVAKIA	HUNGARY
	3 July: Closure of the small seminaries and of some novitiates	to life imprisonment for 'spying on behalf of the Vatican'	*August*: Rakosi elected president of the Council
	October: The government does not recognize the new parishes created by the bishops and limits church building		*October*: Stalin calls Hungary 'the vanguard of socialism'
	November: The Katowice bishops are exiled from their diocese		
	December: Arrest of some employees of the Cracow Curia, accused of currency offences and of anti-state activities. Arrest of Mgr Baziak, archbishop of Cracow		*December*: Arrest of Mgr J. Petery, bishop of Vac
1953			
5 March: Death of Stalin	*12 January*: The primate, Mgr Wyszynski, is appointed cardinal	Bishop S. Trochta sentenced to twenty-five years' imprisonment for 'spying on behalf of the Vatican'	
	January: Big trial of Catholics at Cracow. One is condemned to death for spying		
	9 February: Government decree on appointments to positions in the Church	*14 March*: Death of Gottwald. He is replaced by Zapotocky	
	March: *Tygodnik Powszechny* ceases publication		
	May: *Non possumus* by the episcopate in reply to the decree on appointments		

17 June: Uprising in East Germany

June: World Congress of the 'Peace movement'
End of June: The meeting of the central committee reveals a trend to liberalization. Rakosi emerges weakened
2-6 July: Nagy replaces Rakosi, announces big changes in all areas and promises an end to the terror
20 August: General amnesty, end of deportations and measures of help to farmers
Spring: The sick Cardinal Mindszenty is moved to a prison infirmary

3 September: Khrushchev first secretary of the Soviet Communist Party

September: Warning letter from the primate to the 'patriot priests'. About fifty priests suspended
24 September: Letter from the primate to the Council of Ministers protesting about the trial of Mgr Kaczmarek
25 September: Internment of the primate Wyszynski, accused by the government of having used his power in the Church 'against the Agreement'
28 September: The episcopate places Mgr Klepacz, bishop of Lodz, at its head and issues a declaration on the internment of the primate
17 December: The Polish episcopate swears on oath of loyalty to the government in Warsaw

REFERENCES	POLAND	CZECHOSLOVAKIA	HUNGARY
1954		Intensification of atheist propaganda and attacks by the 'patriotic priests' against 'clericalism'	*May*: Third Congress of the Party, marked by conflict between Rakosi and Nagy
11 November: Khrushchev speaks about the 'errors of scientifico-atheist propaganda' and advocates a new line of conduct towards the Churches	*26 May*: Declaration by the episcopate on 'the defence of peace'		*June*: Many communists freed and disciplinary camps closed
	July–November: The theological faculties at Cracow and Warsaw are changed into state-run academies		*October*: Nagy announces further measures of democratization
			21 December: Rakosi violently criticizes the 'June line'.
1955	Some 2,000 Catholic bishops, priests and laymen are imprisoned		*22 January*: Rakosi denounces 'rightist deviationists'
6 February: Malenkov resigns			*Beginning of March*: The central committee denounces Nagy's stance, in the presence of Suslov
			18 April: Nagy is expelled from the Party and relieved of all his functions. His successor as president of the Council is under Rakosi's thumb
14 May: Signature of the Warsaw Pact			
	26 June: The Holy Office places one of Piasecki's works and the		

17 July: Geneva Conference begins

weekly Dzis i Jutro ('Today and Tomorrow'), published by Pax, on the Index

17 July: Cardinal Mindszenty's sentence is remitted, but he nevertheless remains under house arrest and can no longer act as primate. He is sent to Puspokszentlaszlo
2 November: Cardinal Mindszeny and Archbishop Grösz are moved to Felsopeteny, under 'monitored freedom'
6 December: central committee order against writers

1956

14–25 February: 20th Congress of USSR Communist Party
April: Cominform dissolved

16 May: Interned at Komancza, the primate composes the Vows of Jasna-Gora
28 June: Workers riot at Poznan

11 May: J. Grosz receives an amnesty and becomes Head of Catholic Church in Hungary

29 June: A book by B. Piasecki, president of Pax, is placed on the Index

July: Rakosi resigns and is replaced by Gero; Kadar is deputy secretary of the Party

26 August: Vows of Jasna-Gora at Czestochowa, with about a million of the faithful
22 October: W. Gomulka becomes first secretary of the Polish United Workers Party
26 October: Primate freed, returns

14 October: Nagy rehabilitated
23 October: Budapest uprising
30 October: Cardinal Mindszenty freed

REFERENCES	POLAND	CZECHOSLOVAKIA	HUNGARY
3 November: Pius XII's encyclical *Datis Nuperrime*, deploring the 'tragic events' in Hungary	to Warsaw and resumes his functions *October*: KIK ('Catholic Intellectuals' Club') formed *November*: A government/episcopate mixed commission formed *November–December*: The bishops appointed by the Holy See resume their functions in several dioceses (Katowice, Warsaw, Wroclaw, etc.) *7–8 December*: The 'Little Agreement' signed by the Mixed Commission annuls the 1953 decree on appointments and gives the episcopate certain guarantees, esp. as regards religious instruction *25 December*: *Tygodnik Powszechny*, edited by J. Turowicz, reappears *31 December*: New decree on appointments		*4 November*: Soviet troops intervene. Cardinal Mindszenty takes refuge in the American Legation, where he remained until 1971
1957 *6 January*: Joint declaration by Hungary, the USSR, Romania and Czechoslovakia on Nagy's 'treason'	*20 January*: Elections to the Diet and formation of a group of Catholic deputies 'Znak'. Triumph of Gomulka *26 January*: New taxes on churchmen and Church institutions – a 1949 decree abrogated (hindrances to religious events)		*End of January*: Campaign by Kadar aimed at discrediting the 1956 uprising and Cardinal Mindszenty who had taken refuge in the American Legation at Budapest

269

	9 *March*: Government decrees that Cardinal Mindszenty will never be allowed to carry out his duties because he 'incited rebellion against civic order' *End of May*: Mgr Grosz changes the 'movement of priests for peace' into Opus Pacis, and joins the organization himself	3 *May*: Great Novena begins at Czestochowa, preparing for the celebration of the millenary of the baptism of Poland 18 *May*: Primate Wyszynski receives the cardinal's insignia at Rome *August*: The copy of the image of Our Lady of Czestochowa begins to travel throughout Poland	7 *September*: A Vatican decree forbids clergy to take part in political activities on pain of excommunication *December*: Archbishop J. Grosz is decorated with the Order of the Banner for his 'activities in favour of co-operation between Church and state' *December*: First conference on 'contemporary problems in atheist education'. Approximately 10.5 million Catholics	*February*: The monthly *Wiez* begins publication 4 *August*: All religious services in schools forbidden	*March*: The Vatican excommunicates some priests who are Members of Parliament 17 *June*: Nagy executed

1958

1 *March*: Khrushchev president of the Council. Election of John XXIII

270

REFERENCES	POLAND	CZECHOSLOVAKIA	HUNGARY
	2 December: New law on marriage. Henceforward religious marriage has to be preceded by civil marriage		'Socialist' ceremonies are established to compete with religious ones, such as marriage and burial
1959	*4 April*: New taxes directed against the Church *May–June*: Seminarists once more liable for military service *3 September*: Pastoral letter from the bishops to parents and young people on the importance of religious education in families *12 October*: Letter from the Prime Minister to the episcopate informing it of the control over seminaries given to the Ministry of Education		
1960	*February*: Attempts at control in the seminaries *27 April*: Riot at Nowa Huta with bloodshed following a religious gathering *29 May*: More than 100 arrests at Zielona Gora when 5,000 demonstrators protesting against the seizure of a building managed by the Church clash with the police	*May*: Mgr Trochta granted an amnesty but forbidden to exercise his ministry until 1968 *11 July*: Constitution adopted. Article 32 guarantees 'freedom of religion'	

September: In view of the abolition of religious teaching in schools, the episcopate organizes catechism lessons in churches. Letter from the episcopate on the dangers of atheism *November*: The Church in the recovered territories has to pay rent for using Church buildings. The 'patriotic priests' intensify their activity		
1961 *15 May*: John XXIII's social encyclical *Mater et Magistra* containing some moderation of the condemnation of communism	*14 July*: Nationalization of Church property in the 'recovered territories'. Religious education in schools is declared illegal	
	13 August: Berlin Wall erected	
1962 *11 October*: Vatican II council opens *14–29 October*: Cuban missile crisis	*11 October*: Twenty-five Polish bishops are present at the opening of the council	*December*: Kadar becomes both Party secretary and president of the Council

REFERENCES	POLAND	CZECHOSLOVAKIA	HUNGARY
1963			
11 April: Encyclical *Pacem in Terris*, exhibiting more flexibility in the rejection of communism			
	July–August: Attempts to control the teaching centres in churches	*May*: Mgr Casaroli pays a first (unofficial) visit to Prague	*July*: The government announces that it is no longer opposed to the appointment of new bishops to the six vacant sees
			Autumn: Searches for religious literature, confiscations and arrests
	28 August: Letter from the bishops proclaiming the right to religious education		
		2 October: Mgr Beran given an amnesty, but confined to house arrest	
	30 December: Mgr Karol Wojtyla appointed metropolitan of Cracow		
1964			
	January–February: The press attacks the primate for his sermon on the encyclical *Pacem in Terris* and for the interview given to *La Croix*	Mgr Beran appointed cardinal by Paul VI. The government allows him to go to Rome, on condition that he does not return to Czechoslovakia	Average age of bishops: 68.6–3,700 Catholic priests
	March: Death of Mgr Splett		
	April: Letter from the bishops on the new conciliar liturgy		
19 May: Creation of a secretariat for non-believers.			

Khrushchev is dismissed and replaced by Brezhnev as Party leader and by Kosygin as head of government		*15 September*: Signature of an agreement with the Vatican: appointments of bishops to be negotiated and five new bishops to be consecrated (for the first time in fourteen years)
1965	*27 January*: Letter from the bishops to the government, protesting against attempts to take control in the seminaries	
		18 February: Mgr Tomasek, appointed apostolic administrator of the Prague archbishopric, swears an oath of loyalty to the Czechoslovak state
		19 February: Mgr Casaroli and Mgr Beran leave for Rome (Mgr Beran died in May 1969)
	30 May: Departing from custom, the primate does not take part in elections to the Diet	
	13 November: The letter from the Polish bishops to the German bishops ('We forgive you and ask you to forgive us') unleashes a violent campaign of protest in the press	
1966	*7 January*: The primate is refused	Five bishops request retirement,

REFERENCES	POLAND	CZECHOSLOVAKIA	HUNGARY
	permission to go to Rome *12 March*: Letter from the president of the Council of State (Head of State) to the Holy See, explaining that a visit to Poland by the Pope is not desirable at the moment *17 April*: Cardinal Wyszynski severely criticizes Gomulka, and says he 'intends to play a political part' in the country *3–4 May*: Celebration of the millenary at Czestochowa, presided over by the primate acting as papal legate *2 September*: The militia confiscates the copy of the image of Our Lady of Czestochowa *31 October*: Leszek Kolakowski is expelled from the Party *13 December*: Bishops issue a statement on the danger threatening the seminaries		but negotiations for the appointment of their successors do not come to fruition
1967	*20 January*: The bishops protest against the closing of six seminaries	Some relaxation of the fight against religion, although in August the central committee sends secret instructions to the Party organizations calling for an intensification of the struggle against the Church	

25 June: Paul VI grants all the rights of residential bishops to the apostolic administrators of the recovered territories
End of June: Mgr Wojtyla is appointed cardinal

15 July: Pastoral letter from the episcopate on atheism
28 September: For the second time the primate is refused permission to go to Rome

5–10 October: The Six Days War

1968

8 March: Clashes between the police and students at Warsaw
21 March: Letter from the episcopate on 'these sad happenings' in reaction against the 'events of March'

27–28 June: At the 4th Congress of Czechoslovak Writers the Party policy is condemned by some writers who are members of the CzCP. Congress passes a resolution calling, *inter alia*, for less censorship and a review of the law on the press

January: A. Dubcek becomes first secretary of the CP. The 'Prague Spring' begins: All Catholics are freed
17 March: 23,000 Catholics send a petition to Dubcek demanding freedom for the Church
18 March: The State Office for Church Affairs declares that believers should enjoy equal rights
March: Censorship abolished. Plojhar, president of the Peace Movement of Patriotic Clergy, deprived of office
April: Preparation for the reopening of some monasteries
End of April: Mgr Tomasek allowed a two-week visit to Rome, where he is advised to wait before

REFERENCES	POLAND	CZECHOSLOVAKIA	HUNGARY
		giving the Dubcek government his support	
		May: The Czech episcopate meets at Velehrad, with representatives of the clergy and of all strata of the population; formation of Post-conciliar Renewal Movement	
		Early August: Church gives its support to Dubcek	
		21 August: Invasion by Warsaw Pact troops. Mgr Tomasek declares his unconditional allegiance to the legitimate Prague government	
	27 November: Bishops protest against the new draft penal code		
1969		*16 January*: Jan Palach immolates himself by fire in Prague in protest against the Soviet occupation. Over 100,000 attend his funeral	*23 January*: Agreement between the Holy See and Budapest on the appointment of four new bishops. Average age of priests: 63 yrs 8 months
		17 April: Dubcek 'is retired' and replaced by G. Husak, a Soviet stooge known for his anti-clericalism	
		15–18 September: International scientific symposium at the Carolinum in Prague to commemorate the 1100th anniversary of the death of St Cyril	
	15 December: Memorandum from the episcopate to the Pope on stabilization of the Church	*End of year*: Preparation of a campaign against the Church and religion	

organization in the recovered territories

1970

12 August: USSR-GDR Treaty of Friendship and Co-operation

December: Treaty between Bonn and Warsaw (Recognition of Poland's western frontier)
December: Riots at Gdansk and Gdynia (over 100 deaths)
20 December: E. Gierek becomes first secretary of the Polish United Workers' Party
23 December: The Prime Minister, P. Jaroszewicz, states that the government is aiming at normalizing relations between Church

June: Dubcek expelled from the Czech CP

13 October: Negotiations between Rome and Prague resumed after an interval of three years. Simultaneous resumption of suppression of religion. Numerus clausus applied in all faculties of theology

August: Letter of encouragement from Paul VI to the Hungarian people. Millenary of the birth of King St Stephen. Celebration of the anniversary for the first time in twenty-one years
September–October: Fresh negotiations between the government and the Vatican to replace Cardinal Mindszenty and raise the excommunication from the three priests who were members of parliament. But the Vatican refuses to yield because about thirty-five priests had been arrested in mid-September for 'illegal exercise of the pastoral ministry'

REFERENCES	POLAND	CZECHOSLOVAKIA	HUNGARY
1971	and state'. Letter from the episcopate to 'all the children of our common fatherland'		
	27 January: The bishops call on all Poles to pray for the country *28 January*: Letter from the episcopate calling for 'defence of the threatened nation' *3 March*: Primate sees the Prime Minister about normalization of relations between Church and state *27–30 April*: First official talks between the Holy See and the Polish government, in Rome *21 June*: Document of the Polish bishops: 'What is the meaning of normalization?'	*June*: Institute for Scientific Atheism founded at the Slovak Academy of Sciences *Summer*: The members of the MHKD, dissolved in 1968, form a new organization called Pacem in Terris with the object of keeping the Church under the patronage of the regime	
3 September: Four Power agreement on Berlin	*17 October*: Beatification of Father Maximilian Kolbe		*28 September*: Cardinal Mindszenty leaves for Rome *15 October* Rome ends the excommunication of the three priests in Parliament and leaves it to the Hungarian episcopate to judge the political activity of the clergy; the

1972

May: East Germany recognizes the frontiers of Poland

26 May: SALT 1 agreements signed

18 June: Bull of Paul VI *Episcoporum Poloniae Coetus* (creation of dioceses in the recovered Polish territories). Virtual recognition of the Oder-Neisse line

18 June: Paul VI reorganizes the ecclesiastical administration of Poland by creating new dioceses in the 'Recovered Territories' (Bull *Episcoporum poloniae coetus*). Bishops protest at difficulties encountered in obtaining permission to build new Churches

About a dozen theology students at Bratislava are sent down

November: Fresh negotiations between Rome and Prague. Partial agreement on the appointment of four bishops. A government survey in Slovakia reveals that 72 per cent of respondents say they believe in God

policy of mutual concessions has begun

25 February: Rejuvenation of the episcopate, including the appointment of Mgr Laszlo Lekai, formerly Cardinal Mindszenty's secretary, to the post of apostolic administrator of Veszprem. For the first time, 300 Hungarian pilgrims are able to go to Rome. The Foreign Minister meets Paul VI

1973

21 February: Mgr B. Kominek, archbishop of Wrocław, is made cardinal

27 February: Agreement confirmed on the choice of four bishops

REFERENCES	POLAND	CZECHOSLOVAKIA	HUNGARY
	March: The episcopate calls on the nation to champion religious life and sends the Diet a letter on reform of the educational system	*3 March*: The four new bishops are consecrated by Mgr Casaroli in Czechoslovakia itself. Eight of the twelve episcopal sees are still without capitulary vicars. Virulent anti-religious propaganda	
	May: Declaration by the episcopate on education and Catholic youth		*July*: Formation of the secretariat of the Catholic Committee for Peace, subject to the central committee of the Party and responsible for all domestic activities of Hungarian Catholics, including religious instruction and clergy training
	September: Publication of the monthly *W drodze* (*Let's Go!*) by the Dominicans		
6 October–11 November: Yom Kippur war	*12 November*: The Polish Foreign Minister is received by Paul VI		
1974		Intensification of anti-religious activity	
	13–20–27 January: Primate's first cycle of sermons, given in the Holy Cross Church in Warsaw	*January*: Priests sentenced for purely religious activities on the pretext of political crime	
	4 February: Official visit by Mgr Casaroli, secretary of the Church's Public Affairs Council		

	July: Talks at Rome and improvement in relations between the Holy See and the Polish government	
	July: Dissolution of all remaining convents, the nuns being sent to 'concentration monasteries'	
	September: Fresh negotiations between the Vatican and the government, though most Czechoslovak Catholics did not favour them. Constant persecution of religion, especially committed believers	
		December: New regulations regarding religious instruction in Churches (subject to certain conditions) and permission to print catechisms and to translate the Bible
1975		
	19–26 January: Second cycle of sermons by the primate at the Holy Cross Church in Warsaw	
	Beginning: Many attempts on the lives of priests, house searches and intimidations of all kinds. Circulation in Slovakia of samizdats denouncing religious persecution	*10 January:* After lengthy negotiations with the government, Paul VI is able to appoint five resident bishops and reorganize the Hungarian episcopal hierarchy. The average age of the Catholic hierarchy goes from 62.2 years to 59.4. Only two dioceses are without resident bishops
	February–March: Visit by Mgr Poggi, delegate of the Holy See	
	March: Virtual internment of theology students at Bratislava	
		6 May: Cardinal Mindszenty dies in Vienna
1 August: Final Act of the Helsinki Conference		
	8 September: The bishops state that they distrust 'hasty normaliza-	

REFERENCES	POLAND	CZECHOSLOVAKIA	HUNGARY
	tion' and denounce the 'covert, relentless war against faith in God and against the Church' Memorandum from the episcopate to the government on the subject of the constitution. One priest to every 1,750 persons; 91 per cent of Catholics		
			13 November: Prime Minister Lazar pays a private visit to the Vatican – the first visit by a Prime Minister of Hungary since the war
		December: More negotiations between Prague and the Vatican	
1976			
	9 January: Letter from the episcopate to the president of the Council of State re the new constitution *11-15-18 January*: Third cycle of sermons by the primate at Holy Cross *10 February*: The Diet adopts the amendments to the constitution. The deputy of Znak St Stomma abstains and loses his seat	*January*: Negotiations between Prague and the Vatican Intensification of anti-religious activity	*12 February*: Mgr Lekai appointed archbishop of Esztergom and hence president of the episcopal conference and primate of Hungary
		May: Mgr Tomasek appointed cardinal, though the decision was not made public	
June: European conference of Communist Parties in East Berlin	*June*: Strikes and demonstrations. The government decides not to increase food prices		

1977

3 September: In a speech at Mielec, E. Gierek thinks 'that there is a broad field of collaboration between Church and state in the achievement of important national objectives'

23 September: KOR (Workers' Defence Committee) is formed in Warsaw

February: The primate protests against the publication of a falsified text of his sermons at the Holy Cross Church

1 January: Publication of Charter 77, demanding respect for human rights

23 January: *Katolicke Noviny* publishes a statement by Mgr Tomasek distancing himself, on behalf of the entire episcopate, from Charter 77

27 June: Mgr Tomasek made cardinal, with government approval

August: Mgr Lekai attends the 41st world Eucharistic conference in the United States

14 April: Paul VI receives the Hungarian bishops visiting Rome. He raises the problem of the religious congregations

9 June: Paul VI receives Janos Kadar, first secretary of the Party. It was the first time that a Pope had received the head of a Communist Party. After this visit the regulations on religious instruc-

REFERENCES	POLAND	CZECHOSLOVAKIA	HUNGARY
			tion were relaxed somewhat, but the government's basic position remained unchanged
	29 October: Meeting between the primate and E. Gierek. The primate speaks about 'the economic catastrophe threatening the country'. 1 December: E. Gierek is received by Paul VI Publication in Polish of Adam Michnik's book *The Church and the Left – The Polish dialogue*	September–October: Meetings between delegates from Rome and from Prague. 1,600 parishes (one-third of the total) have no priest	
1978	6 January: Homily by the primate in Warsaw cathedral, Mgr Wyszynski speaks about the Church's main demands on the state 8–9 March: The conference of bishops discusses the situation of the country and asks the state to help the workers	10 January: Accord regarding the appointment Mgr Tomasek as archbishop of Prague. The ecclesiastical boundaries are changed, this amounting to a recognition of the Czechoslovak frontiers by the Holy See. However, the problem posed by the vacant episcopal sees is not resolved, nor of course that of attacks on freedom of religion 28 March: Mgr Tomasek officially installed as archbishop of Prague 11 May: Archbishop Tomasek prevented from visiting Austria August: Fifty-four Czechoslovak intellectuals issue an appeal to 'save two Czechoslovak bishops in	

danger' (Mgr Gabris and Mgr Corec) and to rise against the lack of religious liberty in their country

September: The Catholic Academy of Theology at Budapest introduces a system of correspondence courses for laymen. However, the registration formalities are rather forbidding

20–25 September: Cardinals Wyszynski and Wojtyla visit West Germany

16 October: Karol Wojtyla is elected Pope
22 October: The inauguration of John Paul II's pontificate is broadcast on Polish television

16 October: Election of John Paul II

2 December: Letter from John Paul II to the primate Lekai, emphasizing pastoral work. This letter is read in all churches and published on the front page of *Uj Ember*

1979
25 January: The Pope meets Gromyko
11 February: Proclamation of the Islamic Republic of Iran

24 January: Meeting between the primate and E. Gierek

6 April: The Pope receives bishops, priests and faithful at Rome. He is thought to have spoken about the accommodating attitude of the hierarchy towards the government
April: With four new appointments the Hungarian hierarchy is at full strength

REFERENCES	POLAND	CZECHOSLOVAKIA	HUNGARY
	8 May: The secretary of the episcopate announces the Pope's official visit to Poland	*May*: In a letter to Cardinal Tomasek, John Paul II calls on Czechoslovak Catholics to display 'courage and hope'. In the same month, two Catholic priests are sentenced for 'obstructing the monitoring of churches and religious organizations'	
	2–10 June: First visit of John Paul II to Poland		
	30 June: Mgr Macharski, archbishop of Cracow, appointed cardinal		
		21 July: The Church mourns the death following torture of Father Milan Goro, who had been sentenced to two years' imprisonment for 'opposing state control of the Church'	
	September: The episcopate affirms its 'willingness to co-operate with the state' but continues to demand 'recognition of the rights of Catholics'	*September–October*: Wave of intimidation and arrests of clergy and Czechoslovak Catholics	
		December: An appeal to the Pope is signed by 350 Catholics to draw his attention to the persecution of religion in Czechoslovakia	
25 December: Soviet troops invade Afghanistan			
1980			
	January: First issue of the *Osservatore Romano* in Polish		*January*: The last charges against Catholics are provisionally dropped

27–28 February: The bishops demand 'the right to truth and freedom in public life and to dialogue between the state and the nation'

May: The bishops call on the authorities to prepare reforms

July–August: Strikes *26 August*: Homily by the primate at Czestochowa. Mgr Wyszynski appeals to the maturity of the Poles and states that respect for rights (including the right to form trade unions) is one of the conditions of social peace
28 August: The primate receives a delegation of workers from the Gdynia shipyard
31 August: signature of the 'Gdansk Agreements' between the government and the strike committee
5 September: E. Gierek resigns in favour of St Kania

April: Letter from the Pope to Hungarian Catholics, dealing with the teaching of the catechism and with base communities

June: Trial of an 'opposition' priest
Autumn: Hunger strike by 120 students at the Bratislava seminary in protest against Marxist and atheist indoctrination by Pacem in Terris

24 September: Commemoration of the 1000th anniversary of the

REFERENCES	POLAND	CZECHOSLOVAKIA	HUNGARY
			feast of the holy bishop and martyr Gellert. A delegation goes to Hungary from the Vatican
	21 September: First radio broadcast of the mass on Sunday, in fulfilment of the Gdansk Agreements		
	24 September: The Government/Episcopate Joint Commission resumes work		
	21 October: Meeting between the primate and the new first secretary of the PUWP		
	10 November: After the independent trade union NSZZ Solidarnosc has been registered, the primate receives L. Walesa and Solidarity officials		
	16–17 December: Unveiling of the monument honouring the victims of December 1970, in the presence of representatives of the episcopate, the government and Solidarity		
		29 December: *Pravda* of Bratislava publishes a long article on 'the clandestine Church'	
1981			
15 January: The Pope receives Lech Walesa	*15 January*: A Solidarity delegation led by L. Walesa is received by John Paul II		
	6 February: With the mediation of the epsicopate, an agreement is reached between the government and the Bielsko-Biala strike committee		
	10 February: The episcopate comes out in favour of the right of agricultural workers to combine	*February*: A priest very active in the Church dies in suspicious circumstances and many priests are sentenced	

19 February: The primate blesses students after the formation of the Independent Association of Students (NZS)

2 March: At a meeting of the Joint Commission, the place of the Church in the media and the Church's role in the life of society generally is raised

12 March: The bishops issue an appeal for prudence

16 March: The Social Sciences faculty at Lublin Catholic University is reopened

March: Independent writers' and artists' associations are formed

19 March: Events at Bydgoszcz increase tension in the country

25 March: John Paul II sends a message to the Poles: 'You are responsible for our country'

26 March: The primate and the Prime Minister, General Jaruzelski, meet to discuss how to overcome the tensions in society

28 March: The primate receives the Solidarity negotiators

30 March: Agreement between the government and Solidarity

2 April: The primate receives the agricultural trade union (Rural Solidarity) before it was registered (on 12 May)

28 May: Death of Stefan Wyszynski, primate of Poland

March: Mgr Poggi goes to Hungary where he also visits the religious communities (which, with four exceptions, had been banned since 1950)

13 May: Attempt on John Paul II's life

1 May: Priests who are members of Pacem in Terris are officially con-

REFERENCES | POLAND | CZECHOSLOVAKIA | HUNGARY

POLAND	CZECHOSLOVAKIA	HUNGARY
	gratulated and given a considerable increase in their stipend	
11 June: Cz. Milosz is made doctor *honoris causa* of Lublin Catholic University		
7 July: The bishop of Warmie, Mgr Jozef Glemp, succeeds Cardinal Wyszynski as primate of Poland		
5 September: First national congress of Solidarity. Homilies by the primate and Abbé J. Tischner	*September*: Father J. Kordik, a member of Charter 77, is sentenced to a year in prison, suspended. The comparative clemency of the court may have been the result of representations made by Mgr Tomasek	*Summer*: Two priests are suspended for having come out in favour of conscientious objection
13 October: J. Czyrek, Foreign Minister, is received by John Paul II	*October*: Arrests and police raids proliferate with the aim of disrupting the underground press networks. Widespread persecution of Catholics	
18 October: General Jaruzelski, already Prime Minister, replaces St Kania as first secretary of the PUWP		
4 November: Meeting between General Jaruzelski, Mgr Glemp and Lech Walesa		
5 December: Meeting between Mgr Glemp and Lech Walesa		
8 December: The primate appeals to Walesa to avoid confrontation and to continue to talk to the government in a spirit of understanding		*December*: A group of priests asks Cardinal Lekai to lift these suspensions
13 December: Proclamation of martial law. Mgr Glemp appeals to		

young people to act responsibly and begs them not to engage in civil war
15 December: Letter from the episcopate withholding approval from martial law
18 December: John Paul II asks the government and the people to resume peaceful dialogue
23 December: Letter from the bishops to the Minister of Justice on the plight of internees

More than half of the priests in Czechoslovakia are members of Pacem in Terris
The Vatican statement condemning this organization is censored by the government
Spring: Many priests and religious are sentenced by the courts for having printed clandestine literature or 'hindering the oversight of the Church by the state'
March: a Charta document protesting against the persecution of religion

April: Three new bishops appointed and the hierarchy reorganized

1982

8 March: Declaration *Quidam episcopi*, forbidding priests to become members of 'associations of clerics pursuing political aims'

21 January: Formation of primate's aid committee for internees and their families
27 February: The bishops ask the government to end martial law

25 April: Meeting between the primate and General Jaruzelski
27 April: John Paul II receives the primate of Poland
June: The Polish and German episcopates ask the Holy See to

REFERENCES	POLAND	CZECHOSLOVAKIA	HUNGARY
	canonize Father Maximilian Kolbe and to confer the title of martyr on him *July*: *Przeglad Powszechny*, the monthly published by the Jesuits, reappears *August*: Ceremonies at Czestochowa. The primate sets out the conditions he considers indispensable for dialogue between the government and the nation *16 September*: The bishops conference withholds approval from all use of force *5 October*: The primate cancels his journey to Rome in view of the situation in Poland *8 October*: The trade unions are dissolved *10 October*: Canonization of Father Kolbe in Rome in the presence of an official Polish delegation *21 November*: In a homily, the primate claims the right of Catholics to take part in public life *31 December*: Martial law suspended	*August*: Several dozen priests resign from Pacem in Terris and Mgr Tomasek demands the dissolution of the organization *Autumn*: The government calls the capitular vicars together and makes them sign a document approving the activity of Pacem in Terris. Mgr Tomasek withdraws all religious sanction from the official Catholic weekly *Katolicke Noviny*	*Summer*: A Vatican delegate visits the Jesuits of Hungary and requests that they (and the other communities under interdict) be allowed to accept novices
November: Death of Brezhnev			

1983

21,643 priests (16,200 diocesan priests and 5,443 religious)

2 *February*: Mgr Glemp appointed cardinal

21 *March*: John Paul II is officially invited to Poland by the president of the Council of State
10 *April*: 40th anniversary of the Warsaw ghetto uprising. Solemn mass and homily by the primate
April: Meeting between the primate and General Jaruzelski
16–23 *June*: John Paul II's second visit to Poland. The Pope has two meetings with General Jaruzelski and receives Lech Walesa privately in the Tatras
22 *July*: Martial law finally rescinded, but a number of oppressive laws partially deprives this measure of its significance
August: The PUWP states that the Catholic Church is 'ideological enemy no. 1, the most dangerous troublemaker'

Campaign of intimidation to compel priests to join Pacem in Terris (some 500 priests are deprived of their livings)

14 *February*: Mgr Casaroli writes to the Czechoslovak bishops assuring them, on behalf of the Pope, that the Holy See is still willing to seek an agreement with the government

April: House searches and arrests in Bohemia-Moravia and in Slovakia in underground communities of Franciscans

August: All the Franciscan religious who had been arrested are released

September: Mgr Tomasek receives permission to attend the world synod of bishops in Rome

Beginning: Some bishops are worried about the attitude of the base communities, who are opposing the government, especially on conscientious objection

August: For the first time since the communists came to power, a Catholic retreat and teaching institution is opened

REFERENCES	POLAND	CZECHOSLOVAKIA	HUNGARY
	5 October: Lech Walesa is awarded the Nobel peace prize		
1984			
	5 January: Meeting between the primate and General Jaruzelski	*13 January*: Three Catholics arrested in Slovakia on a charge of having transported underground literature	
February: Death of Andropov	*13 March*: After crucifixes were removed from a school of agriculture, the bishops call for crosses in public places to be treated with respect. Thus begins the 'war of the crucifixes'	*28 March*: Violent attack on the Pope in the weekly paper of the Czech central committee of the Communist Party, *Tribuna*	
		April: A petition containing 30,000 signatures demands permission for the Pope to come to Czechoslovakia. An official invitation is sent to John Paul II by Mgr Tomasek	
	May: Father Popieluszko calls for a boycott of the June municipal elections		
	July: The Church distances itself from the government and recommends multiple trade unions	*July*: Two pilgrimages in Moravia and in Slovakia are undertaken by 15,000 Catholics 72 per cent of Slovak children are baptized	
July: A Soviet daily deplores the 'serious problems still existing in Poland, including the growing influence of the Catholic Church'	*4 August*: Meeting between the primate and Lech Walesa
19 October: Father Popieluszko abducted		

295

1985	3 November: 500,000 attend Father Popieluszko's funeral in Warsaw	Charter 77 reports on the oppression 17 years after the Soviet invasion. The document reveals the bitterness of the conflicts between state and Church	Some priests are elected to Parliament. Cardinal Lekai is given total freedom of movement
27 February: The Pope meets Gromyko	27 December–7 February: Trial at Torun of Father Popieluszko's killers	March–April: Campaign of repression against the Catholic press	
	7 February: Verdict (sentences confirmed on appeal on 22 April)		
10 March Chernenko dies			
March: Mikhail Gorbachev becomes secretary-general of the CPSU			
2 July: Encyclical Slavorum Apostoli	July: Adoption of a law, denounced by the episcopate, strengthening state control of the universities	July: Commemoration of the death of St Cyril and St Methodius. Events attended by 150,000 Catholics in Moravia and 100,000 in Slovakia	
	September: The press office of the Polish bishops issues a report on the Catholic press	September: 40,000 Catholics take part in a pilgrimage in Slovakia. Nine out of thirteen bishoprics vacant	September: Agreements on the participation of laymen in the work of the episcopate
1986		End March: 17th Congress of the CzCP. Party members are urged to 'intensify their propaganda campaign based on scientific atheism'	2,600 Catholic priests (compared with 4,000 in 1976)
April: Instruction centred on Christian freedom and liberation	April: General Jaruzelski and the primate have their tenth private meeting since 1981		
	31 May: Arrest of Z. Bujak, secret head of Solidarity		

REFERENCES	POLAND	CZECHOSLOVAKIA	HUNGARY
			30 June: Mgr Laszlo Lekai dies
	June: A majority of IMF members vote for the admission of Poland	*July*: A large crowd numbering 100,000 on the annual pilgrimage at Levoca in Slovakia Cardinal Tomasek states that 70 per cent of Catholic priests are forbidden to exercise their ministry or have been arrested	
	End June–early July: 10th congress of the PUWP		
	End July: Partial and conditional amnesty; Adam Michnik is freed		
	Summer: The Catholic Church calls for 'a month of sobriety'		
	31 August: Large attendances at Mass on the sixth anniversary of the Gdansk Agreements		
	5 September: After four years of negotiation with the government, the Church has to give up its scheme to assist private agriculture		
	11 September: Full amnesty for political prisoners		
	End September: Mgr Glemp meets the recently freed members of the opposition		
	14 October: Sentences on three of Father Popieluszko's four killers are reduced		
		5 November: A Catholic militant is sentenced to two years in prison for 'religious propaganda'. Ten out of thirteen bishoprics are vacant	
15–18 October: Meeting between Catholics and Marxists in Budapest			
	25 December: Mgr Glemp says there should be more citizen involvement in public affairs		
1987			
	13 January: General Jaruzelski is		

received by John Paul II at the Vatican

4 February: An interview given by Mgr Glemp is published in *Literatournaia Gazeta*

February: Agreement for the transfer of the Auschwitz carmel

March: A very sharp rise in prices, denounced by the Church

7 May: N.W. Loranc, propaganda chief of the central committee, is appointed 'minister of religious affairs' replacing M.A. Lopatka

8–14 June: Third visit of John Paul II to Poland

15 August: 500,000 of the faithful attend service at Czestochowa

August: The massive inflow of Polish refugees worries the Italian authorities. In circles close to the pope understanding is expressed, but also the view that 'Poles would have done better to have stayed at home'

30 August: The 7th anniversary of the signauture of the Gdansk agreements is celebrated without disturbances. At Warsaw, 6000 people attend a mass at St Stanislaw's church in memory of Father Popieluszko

May: Two Catholic priests lose their appeal against sentence for infringement of the regulations on the Churches

July: 200,000 take part in the Levoca pilgrimage

August: On the anniversary of the Soviet invasion, Charter 77 issues an appeal, *inter alia*, for release of persons prosecuted for their religious or civic beliefs

24–26 August: For the first time, a delegation from the French and German episcopates goes to Czechoslovakia

March: Mgr Laszlo Paskai succeeds Cardinal Lekai as primate of Hungary

14 June: *Uj Ember* publishes two letters from Cardinal Ratzinger on the 'base communities' and Father Bulanyi

REFERENCES

POLAND	CZECHOSLOVAKIA	HUNGARY
13 September: On the initiative of the 'Freedom and Peace' (WiP) movement, a hunger strike is staged by fifty-eight conscientious objectors in St Andrew's church at Bydgoszcz	*18 November*: The funeral of Bishop Julius Gabris, apostolic administrator of the archdiocese of Trnava, is held in Eastern Slovakia in the presence of a delegation from the Vatican led by Archbishop Achille Silvestrini and the Slovak Minister of Culture, Miroslav Valek. Talks on the situation of the Catholic Church in Czechoslovakia take place on 19 November	*September*: Foundation of the Democratic Forum by opposition intellectuals
26–7 September: Official visit by Vice-President Bush to Warsaw. Talks with Jaruzelski and Walesa		
8 October: Meeting of the Central Committee of the Polish Workers' Party. It is decided to organize a referendum on the proposal for economic reforms		
27 October: Solidarity's national directorate calls for a boycott of the referendum	*10 December*: in reply to a call by Charter 77, more than a thousand persons gather in Prague for a banned demonstration in honour of the UN International Human Rights Day	*16 December*: Changes in the Hungarian governments (mainly affecting the economic and social sectors)
29 November: Referendum. A majority of the Poles reject the reform, either by voting against or by abstaining		

1988

17 December: Milos Jakes succeeds G. Husak as leader of the Czech Communist Party

9 January: Showing in Warsaw, at the headquarters of the KIK, of M. Lozinski's film 'the witnesses', on the Kielce pogrom
1 February: Steep rise in prices. Big Demonstrations in Gdansk an Warsaw

10 March: Students demonstrate for the 20th anniversary of 8 March 1968

January: Dubcek's house-arrest ended

February: Campaign for the restoration of religious liberties and the signature, on the initiative of A. Navratil, of a petition calling for non-interference by the state in religious affairs, the reopening of a faculty of theology at Olomouc, the legalization of religious orders and freedom to teach and practise religion. 270,000 people, including Cardinal Tomasek, signed the petition. The campaign is severely denounced by Party organs *Rude Pravo* and *Pravda* (which published a series of articles on 'The underground church in the service of anti-communism'). Simultaneously, negotiations in Prague between a delegation from the Vatican and Vladimir Janku, Vice-Minister in charge of Religious Affairs, regarding the appointment of new bishops
6 March: Mass celebrated in honour of Agnes of Bohemia in Prague cathedral. Planned as a

January: Income tax and VAT introduced

15 March: A crowd of 10,000 demonstrates in Budapest to commemorate the 1848 uprising

REFERENCES

POLAND

20 March: Some sixty intellectuals send a letter to fifty-five Soviet intellectuals asking their help in establishing the truth about the Katyn massacre

25 April: The Polish authorities and the Vatican draw up a draft agreement on relations between the Holy See and Poland
26–30 April: The strike movement started at Bydgoszcz spreads to the Lenin steelworks at Nowa Huta and reaches Stalowa-Wola

CZECHOSLOVAKIA

ceremony in favour of religious liberties, it was attended by over 5000 persons. The petition calling for freedom of religion gathered more than 400,000 signatures
25 March: A demonstration in favour of religious liberties at Bratislava brutally put down

12 April: Representatives of the Czech government received at the Vatican by Archbishop Achille Silvestrini in order to settle the question of the vacant dioceses (ten out of thirteen, the last episcopal appointment having been made in 1970)
23 April: Mgr Tomasek comes out publicly in favour of the campaign for religious freedoms and denies that it is politically inspired. The petition reaches 500,000 signatures. On the same day, during a mass at the Vatican, John Paul II refers to the Czechoslovak primate as an 'extraordinary person'
28 April: Agreement between

HUNGARY

17 March: Forty-six independent personalities representing various trends within the democratic opposition launch the 'Network for free initiative'
23–24 March: Plenary meeting of the Central Committee of the Party and drawing up of the 'draft position statement', which aims to accelerate the reform process, but notes an ideological 'revival of support for bourgeois, conservative and anti-socialist views, and political and ideological indifference'

2 May: The movement spreads to the Gdansk shipyards

5 May: Police intervention against the strikers at Nowa Huta and Gdansk. An attempted mediation by the Church fails. The bishops publish a declaration of support

9 May: Start of negotiations between the strikers and the authorities under the auspices of Mgr Goclowski, Bishop of Gdansk

10 May: Adam Michnik, spokesman of the strike committee at the Gdansk shipyards, announces the ending of the strike

11 May: Government takes extraordinary powers to carry out the programme of economic reforms

28 May: Radio Moscow hints that the soviet NKVD might have been responsible for the Katyn massacre

19 June: Only 52% of Poles take part in the local elections

20 June: At the close of its plenary conference, the Polish episcopate demands the re-establishment of free trade unions and freedom of association

11-15 July: Official visit to Warsaw by Mr Gorbachev

8 August: Demonstration at Gdansk on the anniversary of the birth of Solidarity

Prague and the Vatican on the appointment of bishops

10 May: Fresh agreement regarding the appointment of three bishops at Prague and Trnava (they were enthroned on 11 and 12 June)

20 May: Opening of the national conference of the Communist Party (meeting for the first time since 1957)

14-21 May: Meeting of several opposition groups and clubs in a Budapest theatre, on the subject of press freedom. Formation of the first independent trade union under the communist regime by researchers at the History and Sociology Institute of the Academy of Sciences, the 'Democratic Trade Union of Unionized Workers'

22 May: As the National Conference of the Party ends, Janos Kadar is replaced by Karoly Grosz as leader of the party and the political executive is renewed. Imre Pozsgay becomes a member

16 June: Demonstrations on the 30th anniversary of the execution of Imre Nagy

29 June: Imre Pozsgay, leader of the reformers in the Hungarian Communist Party, is appointed Minister of State

21 August: 10,000 people demonstrate in Prague on the 20th anniversary of Soviet intervention

22 August: Sources close to the Vatican announce a visit to Hungary by John Paul II (without

301

302

REFERENCES

POLAND	CZECHOSLOVAKIA	HUNGARY
August: The miners of Upper Silesia begin a strike to demand legalization of the Solidarity trade union and wage increases. Encircled by the zomos, the Gdansk shipyards join the movement on 22 August *25 August*: M. Stelmachowski, president of the KIK and a close associate of the primate, meets Walesa at Gdansk after having spoken to A. Michnik, T. Mazowiecki and Father Jankowski at St Brigitte's church *27-28 August*: Extraordinary meeting of the plenum of the Central Committee of the Party, which agrees to enter into dialogue with the opposition but refuses to legalize Solidarity *31 August-1 September*: Meeting between Walesa and General Kiszczak, Interior Minister. End of the strike at the Gdansk shipyards. The Church agrees to guarantee the personal safety and job security of the strikers *6 September*: The OPZZ (official trade unions) demand the resignation of the Messner government *16 September*: Second meeting between Walesa and Kiszczak *17-18 September*: 40,000 workers		specifying a date) at the invitation of the bishops and the government of Hungary

go on pilgrimage to Czestochowa
19 September: Messner government resigns
26 September: Mr Rakowski becomes Prime Minister
30 September: The administration agrees to register an organization of Catholic students (Mloda Polska)
4 November: Official visit by Mrs Thatcher, who meets Walesa at Gdansk
13 November: Large demonstrations to celebrate the 70th anniversary of Polish independence are violently put down
30 November: Televised debate between Walesa and Alfred Miodowicz, president of the OPZZ
11–12 December: Lech Walesa in Paris, at the invitation of F. Mitterand
18 December: Formation of a 'civic committee' within Solidarity, made up of fifteen subject committees. Some people call this committee a 'shadow cabinet'

1989

19 January: The PZPR proposes the gradual introduction of a certain kind of trade union pluralism
21 January: Murder of Father

15–21 January: Large demonstrations commemorating the death of Jan Palach. *Rude Pravo* calls his suicide 'a dangerous, irrational and tragic act'. 800 summonses.

11 January: The Hungarian parliament adopts two new laws on freedom of association and of meeting

304

REFERENCES

POLAND	CZECHOSLOVAKIA	HUNGARY
Niedzielak, parish priest of St Borromeo, described by Cardinal Glemp as a 'fresh tragedy for the Polish Church'	*16 January*: Vaclav Havel is arrested *22 January*: Cardinal Tomasek sends a letter of protest to the government	
30 January: Father Suchowolec is found dead at his home in Bialystok. His bishop, Mgr Edward Kisiel, says that this death is 'tragic and mysterious'		
6 February: Opening of the round table between the government, the opposition and the Church. The episcopate is represented by Father Orszulik and Mgr Dabrowski	*21 February*: Vaclav Havel appears before the Prague court for 'obstructing public order' and is sentenced to 9 months in prison. On the same day Tomas Hradilek, spokesman of Charter 77, arrested for 'incitement to rebellion'	*10 February*: Meeting of the Central Committee of the HSWP. Discussion centres on a reassessment of the events of 1956 – was it a 'counter revolution' or a 'popular uprising'?
11 February: Mr Rakowski announces that the Party is giving up its monopoly of power		*11 February*: K. Grosz's report to the Central Committee mentions 'current tensions within Hungarian society'. The Central Committee agrees in principle on a transition to a plurality of parties, provided that the new parties 'accept socialism'. Drafting of political reforms intended to lead to presidential elections in 1990 followed by parliamentary elections
5 April: An agreement is signed after the round table, providing for Solidarity to be legalized once more, for a very restricted kind of pluralism, the establishment of a bicameral parliamentary system	*1–2 April*: Cardinal Lustiger pays a visit to Cardinal Tomasek. During a mass celebrated at the St Guy cathedral, the Archbishop of Paris says: 'The heart of Europe, which is a Christian heart, is beating in Prague'	

and the installation of a president of the Republic provided with extensive powers, and freedom of association

7 April: The Diet adopts the political and constitutional reforms

13 April: Meeting between Glemp and Jaruzelski and signature of an agreement on relations between Church and state, intended to open the way to the re-establishment of diplomatic relations between Warsaw and the Vatican

17 April: Legalization of Solidarity confirmed by the Warsaw court

18 April: Meeting between Jaruzelski and Walesa in Warsaw

19 April: Official visit to Rome by Walesa. The following day he is received by John Paul II at the Vatican

23 April: Meeting of the Civic Committee of Solidarity at Warsaw university, a 'public, secular place' as B. Geremek emphasized

May: Parliamentary elections in the USSR

June: Spring bloodshed in Peking

4 June: Overwhelming victory by Solidarity at the parliamentary elections described as 'semi-democratic'

May: Vaclav Havel freed

10 June: Agreement between the HSWP and nine opposition groups on the opening of a round table dealing principally with the transition to a pluralist democracy

13 June: The round table begins

REFERENCES

POLAND	CZECHOSLOVAKIA	HUNGARY
		16 June: Official funeral ceremonies for Imre Nagy
		24 June: Reorganization of the executive of the HSWP. Creation of a collegial management consisting of four members and nomination of Imre Pozsgay as candidate for the presidential election
		6 July: The Hungarian supreme court annuals the guilty verdict on Imre Nagy. Janos Kadar dies
		23 July: At a by-election Gabor Roszik, a Protestant pastor, supported by the Democratic Forum and Fidesz, wins more than 69% of the votes and beats the HSWP candidate
17 July: Re-establishment of diplomatic relations between Poland and the Vatican	*1 July*: Mass at St Guy cathedral in honour of Mgr Tomasek's 90th birthday. The congratulatory message sent to him by Milos Jakes asks him to support 'the attainment of the noble aims of socialist development'	*26 July*: The pope announces that he will visit Hungary in 1991
	Early July: A petition, *Some sentences*, demanding that the regime be made more democratic, is launched on the initiative of Vaclav Havel. 15,000 people sign	*30 July*: Billy Graham visits Hungary. Cardinal L. Paskai, primate of Hungary, publicly encourages Catholics to go and hear the Baptist preacher
	26 July: New agreement between the Vatican and Prague and appointment of four bishops. The Holy See considers this to be a 'first step towards normalization of the local ecclesiastical situation'	
24 August: Mazowiecki Prime Minister of a non-communist government	*4 August*: In an open letter to the government, Mgr Tomasek issues an appeal for non-violence and offers himself as a mediator between the Czech government and its opponents	
26 August: In the course of a speech at Czestochowa, the cardinal criticizes the Jewish community and jeopardizes the agree-	*7 August*: The Vice-President of	

ments entered into Geneva providing for the Carmelites to leave the Auschwitz site

26 August: Exchange of ambassadors between the Vatican and Poland

3 September: Cardinals Decourtray, Danneels and Lustiger criticize Cardinal Glemp's statements calling for a renegotiation of the Geneva agreements on the Carmelites at Auschwitz

6 September: Article by K. Gebert in *Polityka* condemning Cardinal Glemp's remarks, which 'could nourish anti-semitism in Poland'

19 September: Statement by the bishops' committee for dialogue with Judaism, calling for full observance of the Geneva agreements

20 October: Mazowiecki received in private audience by the pope

the government, Matej Lucas, receives Mgr Tomasek

21 September: Partial agreement between the HSWP and the opposition regarding changes in the constitution, the creation of a constitutional court, the introduction of new parties, the method of electing members of parliament and changes in the criminal code

7 October: Transformation of the Hungarian Workers' Socialist Party into the Hungarian Socialist Party, at the 14th extraordinary congress of the party. Democratic centralism and the dictatorship of the proletariat are dropped

9 October: Nyers elected leader of the HSP

18 October: Hungary becomes the 'Republic of Hungary'. Cardinal Casaroli sends a letter to the Hungarian prime minister saying that the Holy See 'declares its

307

REFERENCES	POLAND	CZECHOSLOVAKIA	HUNGARY
9 *November*: Berlin Wall breached	6 *November*: The PZPR decides to transform itself into a social-democratic party	17 *November* ('*black Friday*'): Demonstration started by students, brutally put down 20 *November*: As a sign of protest against police repression, 200,000 people march through Prague and call for the resignation of Milos Jakes. Vaclav Havel forms a Civic Forum bringing together twelve independent political movements 24 *November*: The entire leadership of the Czech Communist Party resigns. Milos Jakes is replaced by Karel Urbanek. In Wenceslas Square Vaclav Havel tells a crowd of 500,000: 'Time is no longer suspended; history is beginning!' 25 *November*: Cardinal Tomasek celebrates a mass in honour of St Agnes of Bohemia, who was canonized in Rome on 12 November, at St Guy 26 *November*: 750,000 people demonstrate in Prague. Vaclav Maly, organizer of the Forum meetings and a Catholic priest, recites the Lord's Prayer before the crowd 27 *November*: 24-hour general	willingness to re-examine a normalization of bilateral relations with Hungary' 15 *November*: Application for membership of the Council of Europe 26 *November*: Referendum on the election of the President of the Republic by universal suffrage

1 December: Meeting between Mr Gorbachev and John Paul II. Agreement in principle on the re-establishment of diplomatic relations

December: Revolution in Romania

29 December: Abolition of the leading role of the PZPR and re-establishment of the Republic of Poland

strike throughout the country

Early December: *Pacem in Terris* dissolved. The bishop of Trnava appoints a new editor-in-chief at Katolicke Noviny

3 December: Adamec introduces his new government, which is immediately rejected by Civic Forum

8 December: Agreement between the opposition and the communists on the formation of a new government of national union in which the communists will be in a minority

10 December: New government formed and G. Husak resigns

13 December: Abolition of the provisions of the criminal law relating to the restrictions on religious freedom. G. Husak asks to be relieved of his functions as a member of the Central Committee of the CCP. Agreement between Civic Forum and the CCP on the election of a president of the Republic within forty-five days. Vaclav Havel is the Forum's official candidate

20 December: Extraordinary congress of the CCP opens and Adamec is elected leader

21 December: The new deputy prime minister, Josef Hromadka, visits the Vatican and John Paul II

Early December: Foundation of an association of catholic students

REFERENCES	POLAND	CZECHOSLOVAKIA	HUNGARY
		appoints three more bishops. The government decides to disband the secret police *29 December*: Vaclav Havel elected President of the Republic	
1990			
		16 January: Official commemoration of Jan Palach's self-immolation	*9 January*: Re-establishment of diplomatic relations between Hungary and the Vatican *23 January*: Resignation of the Minister of the Interior, Istvan Horvath, following the scandal created by telephone tapping of members of the opposition *25 March–8 April*: Parliamentary elections
		21 April: Official visit by John Paul II to Czechoslovakia *22 April*: At Velehrad the pope announces that a special assembly of the synod of bishops for Europe will shortly be convened	*Early May*: The new parliament meets. Jozsef Antall is invited to form the new government.
	27 May: Solidarity wins in the local elections	*8–9 June*: Parliamentary elections, which the Civic Forum wins *Catholic hierarchy up to its full complement*	
18 March: Elections for parliament in the German Democratic Republic			
20 May: Elections for parliament in Romania			
10–17 June: Elections for parliament in Bulgaria	*August*: At the end of a long debate it is decided to introduce the catechism into public education		

Index

Academy of Catholic Theology of Warsaw, 65, 67
Aczel, György, 57
Adamski, Franciszek, 69
African Churches, 74
Agricultural Modernization Fund, 47–8
Aigner, Robert, 39
alcoholism, 89, 92, 93–4, 95, 168
anti-clericalism, 33
  in Poland, 80
anti-Semitism, 80
archaism
  and Messianism, 177
  of Polish Church, 85
archaism–modernity debate, 77
army and religion, 142
Ash, Timothy Garton, 11
Ateistichna Tribuna, 173
Ateizmus, 53, 54, 135
atheism, atheist propaganda, 72, 73, 86, 89, 135, 172–3, 182; *see also* Marxist-Leninist ideology and religion
atomic weapons
  treaty on non-proliferation, 35
Austria, 8

Balint, Andras, 56
Bango, J., 60
Barta, Father, 127

base communities, 181
  in Hungary, 38, 96, 99, 103, 118–22, 128, 176
beatifications by John Paul II, 145, 163
Beauvois, Daniel, 16
behaviour, religious-political, 104–7
Bellah, Robert, 171
Bengsch, Cardinal, 117
Beran, Mgr, 35, 38
Berger, Peter, 13, 19, 102
Bertrand, Michèle, 118
Besançon, Alain, 2, 173
Bibo, Istvan, 11, 32, 34
Bilak, Vazil, 142
Blachniki, Father, 84
Bohemia-Moravia, 7, 12, 27, 32, 33, 116, 195; *see also* Czechoslovakia
Bolshevik revolution, 3
Boniecki, Father Adam, 79, 82
Borisov, O. V., 2
Borovicka, Miroslav, 155
Boudon, Raymond, 175–6
Bourdieu, Pierre, 15, 129
Braudel, Fernand, 11
Brzozowski, Stanislaw, 79
Budapest meeting of Catholics and Marxists, 173–4
Bulanyi, Father Gyorgy, 107, 118–21
Bulgaria, 173, 177

Calvez, Father Jean-Yves, 173–4
Carré, Olivier, 182
Casaroli, Mgr Agostino, 30, 34, 35, 38, 81, 121, 139
Catholic University of Lublin, 65, 67
censorship, 23, 118
Central Europe, defined, 11–12
Centro Studi sull'Europa orientale, 14
Certeau, Michel de, 177, 181
Chalupny, 8
change
  political, 130
  social, 71–95
charismatic renewal, 85
Charter, 77, 40, 41, 116–17, 122, 125, 128–30, 183
Chmielowski, Albert, 145
Christ, dedications of buildings to, 109, 113–14, 185
Church, 11, 46–8
  in Africa, 74
  authority and discipline, 83
  cohesion and influence, 24–7
  in Czechoslovakia *see* Czechoslovak Church
  dependence on government, 24–7
  and ethics, 37, 59, 85, 86, 88–95, 122–3
  in Hungary *see* Hungarian Church
  image of, 1, 71
  intellectualization, 75, 100, 172
  international nature and role, 23, 157–9
  John Paul II and mission of, 158–61
  and man, 131, 152, 155, 158, 164, 168–70
  and Marxist-Leninist ideology *see* Marxist-Leninist ideology and religion
  and multiconfessionalism, 12
  in Netherlands, 75
  and nobility, 33
  persecution of *see* repression
  in Poland *see* Polish Church
  as power for stabilization, 139, 141, 144
  religious instruction, 23, 34, 73, 85; *see also* education
  resources available to, 23
  ritual, 85, 114
  ritualization, 100, 104, 107
  and Second World War, 7, 80
  and social change, 71–95, 188
  and social relations, 33–4, 95–101
  and sociology of religion, 62–3, 65–6, 67, 68, 69–70
  and state, 6, 10–11, 15–19, 20–31, 46–7, 140, 155, 160–1, 172, 175–6; *see also under individual countries*
  as totalitarian system, 6
  and first visit of John Paul II to Poland, 138–41, 144
church building(s), 99, 108–16, 185–9
  permits, 23, 99, 108, 112
Cisiec, 108, 112
Ciupak, Edward, 65, 66, 68
civil religion, 171–2
civil society, 10–15, 16, 17, 18, 20, 46, 116, 178, 181
  and freedom, 2
  in Poland *see under* Poland
  re-emergence, 5
  see also opposition
class, 32
  working *see* working classes
clergy, 23, 30, 171
  in Czechoslovakia, 40–2
  in Poland, 82–3
  see also episcopate
clericalism and Czechoslovakia, 9
collaboration, 23, 30, 44, 72, 89; *see also* Church, and state
communist regimes *see* Soviet-type systems
compromise, 24, 28, 29, 31, 34–6, 61, 104, 106, 117, 118, 119, 133, 144, 174, 175, 186
Concilium, 65
confessions, 85
confrontation, 28, 44, 121, 136, 139
  Polish, with Russia, 7–8, 145
  see also opposition
Congregation of the Doctrine of Faith, 119
conscientious objection, 97, 120, 121

conservatism, Eastern Church as model of, 71–85
consumerism, 36, 37, 52, 77, 98
Coufal, Father Premysl, 127
Cracow, illegal church, 99
Cracow University, 63, 65, 69
Csoregh, Eva, 54
cults, 109–16, 185–9
culture
  John Paul II and, 143, 152, 153, 154, 157–60
  and Polish Church, 45, 85, 114
Cyril, Saint, 156, 158, 159, 161
Czarnowski, Stefan, 66
Czech Brethren, 9, 122
Czechoslovak Church, 1, 7, 9, 27, 34, 96, 116–17, 123–8, 134–5, 174
  clergy, 40–2
  episcopate see under episcopate
  repression, 9, 24, 71–2, 98, 127
  and state, 24–7, 35, 36, 38–42, 71–2, 175
Czechoslovak Communist Party, 42, 155
  17th Congress, 172
Czechoslovakia, 1, 7–10, 12, 129–30
  Charter 77 see Charter 77
  demonstrations, 5
  freedom, 129
  human rights, 9, 117, 128
  nationalism, 4, 6, 7, 27, 32, 116
  opposition in see under opposition
  Protestantism, 7, 9, 128
  religious activity, 125
  resurgence of religion, 97–8, 99
  and Slav Pope, 42, 134–8, 142
  sociology of religion in, 50, 51, 52, 53, 54–6, 61–2, 69
  statistical information about, 13
  underground Church see underground Church
  Vatican and, 35, 39, 40–2
  see also Bohemia-Moravia
Czerkawski, Wlodimierz, 79
Czestochowa
  John Paul II and, 82, 83, 115–16, 151, 153, 163

  Our Lady of see Our Lady of Czestochowa
Czlowiek i Swiatopoglad, 66, 142

Danyi, Ondrej, 155
Darczewska, Krystyna, 65
Davies, Norman, 180
Deleuze, Gilles, 17
democracy, 148
desovietization, 1, 5, 101, 102, 178, 185
détente, 35
detotalization, 1, 5, 101, 102
disalienation, 1, 103
Dobrovsky, Josef, 9
Domenach, J.-M., 87
Doromby, Karoly, 138
Dubcek, Alexander, 38
Durkheim, Emile, 66
Dziennik Ludowy, 146

East–West conflict, 180–1
economics, Church and, 85, 87, 88–95
ecumenism, 78
education, 22, 44, 54, 57, 59, 60, 112, 172, 182; see also Church, religious instruction
Eliade, Mircea, 13
episcopate, 23
  Czechoslovakia, 24, 27, 39–40, 71–2, 116–17
  Hungary, 6, 7, 26, 27, 37, 38, 72, 73, 118, 119, 140
  Poland, 22, 27, 43–4, 75, 81, 95, 133; address of John Paul II to, 83, 153–5, 164, 169
ethics see under Church
Etienne, Bruno, 3, 16, 183
Euhemer Centre, 66
Europe
  East Central Europe as 'other Europe', 4–6
  John Paul II and, 150, 157; and re-catholicization and unity of 132–3, 137, 143–4, 155, 156, 159, 161, 165, 166
  unity, 184
European identity, 180–1

314 Index

fascism
  and Polish Church, 80
  Vatican and, 135
Feranec, Mgr Jozef, 39
Foucault, Michel, 17
Franciscans, 41, 114, 127
Franz-Joseph, Emperor, 6
freedom, 2-3, 157, 170, 183
  of conscience and worship, 21, 22, 117, 136, 174
  Czechoslovakia, 129
  Hungary, 36
  Poland, 76, 80, 82, 115, 137, 148, 151-3, 154, 162, 168
French Church, 75, 79

Gabris, Mgr Julius, 39
Garrigues, Father Juan Miguel, 1
Garton Ash, Timothy, 11
Gauchet, Marcel, 171-2
Gdansk
  John Paul II's speech at, 167
  and workers' movement, 88, 90-1, 94
Gdansk agreements, 90-1, 169
Gdansk University, 69
Gydnia, John Paul II's speech at, 167
Gebethner, Stanislaw, 63, 64
German Democratic Republic, 11
Gierek, Edward, 35, 47, 63
Glemp, Cardinal Jozef, 35, 44, 47, 48, 64, 82, 176
Gniezno, John Paul II's speech at, 134, 157
Godlewski, Jerzy, 66
Gomulka, Wladyslaw, 64, 112
Gondova, Helena, 41
good and evil, 149, 183-4
Gorbachev, Mikhail Sergeevich, 2, 172
government and Church *see* Church, and state
Gromyko, Andrei Andreyevich, 35

Halban, L. 65
Haraszty, Miklos, 38
Havel, Vaclav, 11, 129, 184, 185
Hegyi, Bela, 61
Hejdanek, Ladislas, 122

history, 148, 152, 153, 157
Horvath, Zsuzsa, 62
house churches, Hungary, 7
Hruza, Karel, 38, 39, 41
human rights, 2, 16, 134, 170, 174, 180
  Czechoslovakia, 9, 117, 128
  Poland, 84, 87
humanitarianism and Czech Brethren, 9
humanity, Church and, 131, 152, 155, 158, 164, 168-70
Hungarian Church
  episcopate *see under* episcopate
  and multiconfessionalism, 12
  and society, 72-3
  and state, 7, 24-7, 28, 29, 30, 36-8, 50, 51, 53, 72, 98, 104, 117-22, 139, 173, 176
Hungarian constitution 1972, Article 63, 21
Hungarian uprising 1956, 7-8
Hungary, 98, 128
  base communities, 38, 96, 99, 103, 118-22, 128
  decline in religious behaviour and values, 52
  freedom, 36
  future development of religion, 177
  house churches, 7
  liberalization, 51
  and national question, 4
  opposition, 117-22, 128
  Protestantism, 120
  repression, 30
  and Russia, 8
  society, 53
  sociology of religion in, 51-2, 53-4, 56-61, 62, 69, 172
  statistical information on, 13
  Vatican and, 35, 72, 73, 119, 176
  and visit of John Paul II to Poland, 138-41
Husak, Gustav, 174

independence
  Poland and, 153
  see also nationalism
independent press, 14

Poland, 5, 14
Informace o Cirkvi, 125-6, 127
intelligentsia, 31, 32-3, 78, 79, 80, 83, 129
  and John Paul II, 162-3, 165
interiorization of religion, 106, 107, 136, 141, 172
International Conference on the Sociology of Religions, 64, 177
International Labour Organization, 91
international public opinion, 1, 126, 162
  and visits of John Paul II to Poland, 136-7, 139, 141, 162
international relations, 6, 10
interviews, 14
Iran, 181
Islam, 4, 173, 181-2
Italy, 79
Ivanyi, Gabor, 118

Jablonski, Henryk, 146
Jadam, 65
Jankowski, Father, 88
Jaruzelski, General, 47, 64, 144
  speeches on visits of John Paul II, 149-51, 152-3, 164, 165-8
Jasna-Gora, 115-16, 145, 151-3, 154, 161
Jerschina, J., 172
Jijderveld, Anton, 13
John XXIII, Pope, 34, 140, 157
John Paul I, Pope, 1
John Paul II, Pope, 2, 24, 64, 78, 121, 130, 132, 176, 180, 185
  as Cardinal Wojtyla, 87, 193
  and Czestochowa, 82, 83, 115-16, 151, 153, 163
  and Hungarian episcopate, 6, 26
  and Lublin, 162, 165
  Messianism of, 19, 154, 156, 161, 165, 179
  reactions of Eastern Europe to, 42, 133-44
  symbolism, 42-3
  visit to Mexico, 136
  visits to Poland: first, 35, 83, 115-16, 133-4, 135, 136-44, 157, 162, 193; second, 125, 144-55, 158; third, 162-70, 176
Jozna, Peter, 54
Jukic, Jakov, 173
Jung, C. G., 180
justice, 157, 164, 168, 170, 174

Kadar, Janos, 35, 51, 57
Kadlecova, Erika, 39
Kakol, Kazimierz, 47, 52, 141
Kalinowski, Rafael, 145
Kanturkova, Eva, 129
Karacek, 98
Katolicke Noviny, 41, 116, 117
Kawecki, Zenon, 69
Kemeny, Istvan, 59
Keston College, 14
Khomeini, Imam, 182
Kis, Janos, 128
Kiss, Istvan, 59
Kloczowski, Jerzy, 114
Klusak, Milan, 5
Koenig, Cardinal, 117, 136
Kolakowski, Leszek, 3
Kolbe, Maximilian, 108, 112, 113, 145, 154, 163
Kollar, Jan, 9
Konrad, Gyorgy, 11, 12, 129, 180
KOR-KSS, 129
Kosciuszko, Tadeusz, 148
Kozal, Michal, 163, 165
Kozka, Karolina, 163
Kramar, Karel, 32
Krasinski, Count Zigmunt, 131
Krauze, Jan, 166
Krejci, Jaroslav, 56
Kubiak, Hieronim, 65
Kultura i Spoleczenstwo, 66
Kundera, Milan, 4, 11, 184
Kuron, Jacek, 129

Laborem Exercens encyclical, 155
laicization, 62, 66, 67, 87
land collectivisation, 182
language, John Paul II and, 151, 153, 158-60

Latin America, 181
  John Paul II and, 136
Lebeda, Jan, 41
Le Bras, Gabriel, 65
Lecomte, Bernard, 118
Ledochowska, Mother Ursula, 145
Ledochowski, Cardinal Mieczyslaw, 145
legitimacy, 17, 18, 153, 181, 187–91
  of Hungarian hierarchy, 140
  and Poland, 42, 43, 94, 138, 147
  and territorial integrity, 147
Lekai, Cardinal Laszlo, 26, 36, 71, 72, 73, 104, 119, 120, 121, 176
  and visit of John Paul II, 138–41
Lenin, Vladimir Ilyich, 22, 88
Lévi-Strauss, Claude, 108
Lewandowski, Father Jerzy, 86, 132
Lewin, Moshe, 10
Libelt, Karol, 32
liberalization
  in Hungary, 51
  in Poland, 76, 112
liberation *see* freedom
liberation theology, 3, 181
Ligachev, E. K., 173
Listy, 123
Literaturnaya Gazeta, 176
Lithuania, 165
Lopatka, Adam, 47, 79
Lublin, John Paul II and, 162, 165
Lublin Catholic University, 65, 67
Lucan, M., 40
Lukacs, Jozsef, 56–7

Macharski, Cardinal, 81
Maduro, Otto, 181
Maghreb, 183
Majka, Jozef, 65
Makkai, Laszlo, 36, 37
Maly, Radomir, 134
Maly, Father Vaclav, 128, 183
man, Church and, 131, 152, 155, 158, 164, 168–70
marginalization, of the Church, 19, 103, 116–18, 182
Mariavites, 79
Maritain, Jacques, 75

Marx, Karl, 118
Marxism, view of Polish Church on, 89
Marxist-Leninist ideology and religion, 1–3, 22, 47, 49–50, 72, 76, 88, 102, 135, 164, 173–4
Marxist sociology of religion, 53–61, 63–70
Mary, devotion to, 78, 81, 82, 109–16, 186
Masaryk, Tomas Guarrigue, 8, 9, 31, 32
mass consumption, 36, 37, 52, 77, 78
meaning
  religion and, 102
  and struggle for freedom, 183–4
Merle, Marcel, 152
Messianism, 131, 177, 179, 180, 190–1
  and John Paul II, 19, 154, 156, 161, 165, 179
Methodius, Saint, 5, 156, 158, 159, 160, 161
Mexico, 136, 181
MHKD, 39
Michel, Bernard, 32
Michnik, Adam, 11, 79, 80, 87, 174, 175, 176
Mickiewicz, Adam, 42, 180
Miesko I, Prince, 43
Miklos, Imre, 3, 12, 36–7, 57, 118, 120–1
Milota, Jan, 135–8, 141
Mindszenty, Cardinal, 27, 28, 29, 30, 31, 50, 73
Mink, Georges, 19, 171
Mirewicz, Jerzy, 86
Misztal, M., 68
MKS, 91
modernity, modernization, 18, 67, 71–101, 182
  and government, 77
  Vatican II and, 77
Moore, Barrington, 15
morals *see* Church, and ethics
Moravia, 5; *see also* Bohemia-Moravia
Morawska, Ewa, 171
Mounier, Emmanuel, 75
multiconfessionalism, 12, 32
Muranyi, Mihaly, 54, 60

nationalism, 4–5, 31–4
  Czechoslovak, 4, 6, 7, 27, 32, 116
  Polish, 4, 6, 32, 43, 82, 86, 88, 90, 94, 112, 114–16, 131, 171–2, 183; and John Paul II, 132–55, 161, 162–7
  and religion, 6, 18–19, 27, 185, 190–1
nationalization of religion, 33
Nazarenes, 120
Nemcova, Dana, 130
Nemeth, Laszlo, 59
neo-catechumenate, 85
Netherlands, 75
nobility
  and Church, 33
  and Protestantism, 114
Nossol, Mgr Alfons, 86
Novajesky, Frantisek, 41
Nowak, Father, 44
Nowak, Stefan, 68, 95
Nowakowski, 66

Oasis, 84, 96, 99
opposition
  and Church, 19, 23, 103–4, 106–7, 131, 174
  in Czechoslovakia, 42, 103, 116–17, 122–30, 174
  in Hungary, 117–22, 128
  in Poland, 5, 14, 79, 80–1, 83, 84, 89, 107, 129, 137, 138
  underground, 107
Opus Pacis, 23, 30, 104
order and security, 148, 150, 151, 167, 168
Orthodox Church, 23, 173
Orwell, George, 130
Osservatore Romano, 146
Otto, Rudolf, 13
Our Lady of Czestochowa, 42, 110, 112, 113, 114–16, 145, 153, 183

Pacem in Terris, 23, 24, 39, 40–1, 104, 117
Pacem in Terris encyclical, 34
pacifism, 97, 120, 121
Palach, Jan, 265
Palacky, Frantisek, 9, 32, 123

Pallottins, 65
Papacy *see* Vatican *and individual Popes*
Papal decree, *Quidam episcopi*, 24, 40–1
Papal encyclicals
  Laborem Exercens, 155
  Pacem in Terris, 34
  Pascendi, 79
  Slavorum Apostoli, 133, 154, 155, 156–61
paper rationing, 23
Pascendi encyclical, 79
Paskai, Mgr Laszlo, 73
Pasztor, Mgr Jan, 39
paternalism, 61, 82
Patocka, Jan, 122–3, 125, 128–9, 175
patriotism *see* nationalism
Paul VI, Pope, 35, 78, 140
Pax, 23, 78, 80, 89, 104, 106
Pax publishing house, 75
peace, 148, 157, 164, 168, 170
Peace Movement of Patriotic Clergy, 39
Pekar, Josef, 8
Pereira de Queiroz, Maria-Isaura, 177
persecution *see* repression
Piarists, 118–19
Piasecki, Boleslaw, 106
Pietrzak, Michal, 64
pilgrimages, 79, 85, 96, 111, 115, 116, 145, 174
Pimen, patriarch, 44
Piwowarski, Wladyslaw, 65, 66, 68, 96
Plater-Syberg, C. 79
Podgorny, N. V., 35
Poggi, Mgr, 42
Poland, 7, 138, 141, 155, 172
  anti-clericalism, 80
  Church *see* Polish Church
  civil society, 45, 133, 134, 146, 171
  conceptions of, in speeches on second visit of John Paul II, 146–51
  confrontation with Russia, 7–8, 145
  decline in religious behaviour and values, 52
  freedom in *see under* freedom
  human rights in, 84, 87
  independent press, 5, 14
  and liberalization, 5, 76, 112

Poland — *cont*
  martial law, 44, 144, 148
  nationalism *see under* nationalism
  opposition in *see under* opposition
  partition and religious practices, 33
  Protestantism in, 114
  social renewal movement, 88, 90–1, 133–4, 169
  society, 43, 45, 154, 171
  sociology of religion in, 51, 52, 62–70, 100, 142, 172
  source material for, 13, 14–15
  symbolism and politics in *see under* symbolism
  Vatican and, 35, 43, 44, 87, 112
  visits of John Paul II to *see under* John Paul II, Pope
police, 55, 56, 126, 127, 129, 176
Polish Academy of Sciences, Philosophy and Sociology Institute, 65
Polish Church, 1, 7, 132, 171, 190, 193–4, 195
  and culture, 45, 85, 114
  episcopate *see under* episcopate
  and fascism, 80
  future development of, 177–9
  and modernity, 74–85
  programme of work envisaged by John Paul II, 154, 165–6
  secular opposition and, 79, 80–1, 83, 84
  and society, 74–95, 96, 98–100, 171
  and state, 24–7, 28, 29–30, 35, 36, 42–5, 47–8, 50, 84, 89, 133, 137, 175
  unity, 83–4
  view of Marxism, 89
Polish constitution
  1952, Article 70(3), 21
  1976, Article 82, 21
Polish United Workers Party, 65, 66
politics and religion, 102–30, 136, 174–5
  behaviour and attitudes, 104–7
Polityka, 47
Popieluszko, Father Jerzy, 45, 83, 163
Potocki, Andrzej, 67, 69
Poulat, Emile, 3, 118

power, Church and, 17, 86–7
Poznan, speech of John Paul II at, 158
Prague Spring, 5, 9, 38, 39, 51
Pravda, 173
press
  Catholic, 14, 23, 41, 85
  independent, 5, 14
  underground, 14, 41, 44
priests *see* clergy
private land ownership, 182
progress, progressiveness, 75, 77–81, 168
Protestantism
  Czechoslovakia, 7, 9, 128
  Hungary, 120
  Poland, 114
Prusak, Peter, 54–6
PZPR (Polish Unified Workers' Party), 47

Quidam episcopi Papal decree, 24, 40–1

radicalization
  Czechoslovakia, 40–1
  Polish Church, 45
  Polish socialist movement, 79
Radio Free Europe, 14
Radwan, 65
Ratzinger, Cardinal, 3
religion
  as a breach in totalitarianism, 15–19, 101, 102, 185–96
  and culture, 158–60
  definition, 13, 185
  distinguished by governments from churches, 24
  function in totalitarian system, 96–101, 172, 186
  future development of, 177–84
  and politics, 102–30, 186–96
  relation to society and government, 20–1, 185
  and search for meaning, 102, 186, 189–91
  and social groups, 181–2
  and Soviet-type government, 21–7
  and symbolism, 34; *see also* symbolism

theory of, 98
see also Church
religious behaviour, 104–7
  decline, 52
  Poland, 85
religious beliefs, 6, 61
religious freedom, 21, 22, 117, 136, 174
religious identity, 32
religious indifference, 74, 99, 107
religious institutions, 62
religious practice, 71, 72
religious renewal, 10, 38, 78, 97–8, 99–100, 172, 180, 181
religiousness in Soviet system, 96–101
Rémond, René, 7
Renewal Foundation, 39
renunciation, 72–3
repression, 4
  and Charter 77, 129
  and churches, 2, 23, 52–3, 103, 126–7, 186, 188–91
  constitutional, 21–2
  Czechoslovakia, 9, 24, 71, 98, 127
  and development of base communities, 181
  Hungary, 30
Research Centre for Religion and Human Rights in Closed Societies, 14
resignation, Soviet government and, 4–5, 145
resistance
  churches and, 1–3, 35, 86, 96, 161
  Polish, 80, 88, 108, 145
  see also opposition
Rigby, T. H., 6
ritual, 85, 114
ritualization, 100, 104, 107
Rome, 158
Roy, Olivier, 182
Rude Pravo, 39, 41
Ryczan, 65

sacralization of the nation, 33, 34, 86
Safarik, Pavel, 9
saints, 85, 109–14, 187–9
scientific socialism, and religion, 18, 49–70, 137

Second World War and Church, 7
  in Poland, 80
secret police *see* police
secularization, 54–8, 59, 62, 63, 66, 67, 84, 87, 98, 182; *see also* laicization
security and order, 148, 150, 151, 167, 168
separation of Church and state, 21–2
sexual relations, 86, 94
Shcherbitsky, Wladimir, 135
Sienkiewicz, Henryk, 79
Sikorski, Wladyslaw, 63
Silesia, 80
Silhanova, Libuse, 129–30
Skarzynski, A., 47, 89
Slav Pope, 1, 2, 132, 133–44
Slavorum Apostoli encyclical, 133, 154, 155, 156–61
Slavs, 132, 137, 155
Slonimska, 65
Slovakia, 6, 9, 12, 99
  underground Church *see* underground Church
  see also Czechoslovakia
social change and Church, 71–95
Social Compass, 53, 65
social movements, 172
  Poland, 88, 90–1, 133–4, 169
social relations, 181–2
  and Church, 33–4, 95–101
Social Sciences College at Central Committee of the Polish United Workers' Party, 65
society
  civil *see* civil society
  relations with state, 31
sociology of religion, 13, 18, 49–70, 183
  methods and techniques, 65
solidarity, 167, 169–70
Solidarity, 3, 42, 43, 64, 75, 78, 82, 85, 91, 133, 144, 155, 169, 179, 180
  compared with Iranian revolution, 181, 183
Sopuch, Kasimierz, 69
sources, 13–15, 24
Soviet constitution, Article 52, 21

Soviet-type systems, 103
  as historical break, 6–10
  and nationalism, 4–5
  reaction to religious renewal, 172–3
  and religion, 11, 15–19, 21–31, 49, 103, 175–6, 185–96; see also Marxist-Leninist ideology and religion
  as totalitarian system, 6
Soviet Union, 172–3, 161
  John Paul II and, 132–3, 145, 150, 176
space, in speeches on visit of John Paul II, 149–50
Stalin, Joseph, 17
Stanislas, Saint, 146, 163
Staszewski, Stefan, 183
state
  and Church see under Church
  and John Paul II and General Jaruzelski, 152–3, 157, 163–4, 168, 169
statistical information, 13; see also surveys
Strmiska, Zdenek, 4, 8
Studia Religiologica, 63
subjectivity and John Paul II, 162–3, 165
surveys, 54–6, 59, 60–2, 63–4, 65, 69, 123–4, 142, 171
Swiecicki, Andrzej, 62, 63, 65
symbolism, 4, 12, 16, 17, 19, 34, 45, 46, 172, 177
  and politics in Poland, 17, 42–3, 68, 86, 87, 99, 107, 108–16, 129, 133, 145, 146, 163, 171, 182
Szucs, Jeno, 11

Tanalski, Dionizy, 75, 142, 143, 144
Tarnow, speech of John Paul II at, 163
time, in speeches on visit of John Paul II, 149–50
Tito, Marshal, 35
Tomasek, Cardinal, 25, 35, 38, 39, 41, 98, 117, 135, 174, 195
  and Charter 77, 40, 116–17
Tomka, Miklos, 38, 53, 57, 62, 72, 98, 172
Tomsky, Alexander, 40

totalitarianism, totalitarian systems, 6, 76, 87, 129, 146
  function of religion in, 96–101, 172
Touraine, Alain, 88
trade unions, 91, 155, 169; see also Solidarity
traditionalism, of Polish Church, 74–85
Trentowski, Bronislaw, 131
Tribuna, 42, 155
Trojan, Father, 127
Trojan, Pastor Jakub, 122, 124
truth, Church and, 46, 78, 131, 154, 168, 170
Turkey, 182
Turowicz, Jerzy, 131, 174–5
Tygognik Powszechny, 131

Ucitelske Noviny, 155
Ukrainian Greek Catholic Church, 173
Ulasinski, C., 172
underground Church, 7, 13, 14, 41–2, 96, 97–8, 99, 125–7, 183
underground opposition, 107
underground press, 14, 41, 44
United States, 181
  John Paul II and, 136, 150
unity
  of Europe see under Europe
  of Polish Church, 83–4
Usjoly, 112
Usmankhodzaev, I. B., 173

Vatican, 6, 19, 28, 30, 34–5, 133–70; see also under individual countries and Popes
Vatican II, 39, 74, 76, 77, 80, 84, 85, 100, 158
Velehrad, 5
Vigilia, 5
Vilagossag, 54, 56, 57, 60
Virgin Mary see Mary
VONS, 41, 128, 129
Voprosy Ateisma, 57
Vrana, Mgr Jozef, 39, 40, 106
Vrcan, Srdan, 177

Walesa, Lech, 48, 78, 177–9
Warsaw, John Paul II's homily in, 165–6

Warsaw Academy of Catholic Theology, 65, 67
Warsaw University, 65
   Political Sciences Institute, 63
Weber, Max, 66, 182
West, 184
   Church in the, 77, 84, 172
   documentary collections in, 14
   East European Churches in, 3, 41, 71, 75, 77, 78
   Pope and, 150
   and visits of John Paul II to Poland, 136–7, 139, 141, 162
Westernization, 180
   of Church, 132
Wierzbicki, Zbigniew, 182
Wilkanowicz, Stefan, 83
Wojtyla, Cardinal Karol, *see* John Paul II, Pope
Wola, 44
Woodrow, Alain, 118
work and religion, 88–95, 155, 168–9
working-class movements, 3, 75, 88, 90–1, 94, 169
working classes
   conflict with Soviet-type government, 49, 50
   and socialism, 136
Wyszynski, Cardinal, 43, 45, 47, 50, 82, 83, 116, 117, 132, 133, 153–4, 181
   and morals and economics, 88, 89, 90, 92, 93
   and Polish Church and society, 74, 75, 76, 77, 78, 83, 84, 85, 86, 87
   and politics, 25, 28, 29–30, 31, 63, 179

young people, 84, 99, 116, 120, 123–4
   and John Paul II at Gniezno, 134, 157
   and sociology of religion, 56, 57, 59, 60, 63, 67, 100
Yugoslavia, 35

Zagajewski, Adam, 171
Zawieyski, Jerzy, 80
Zdaniewicz, Witold, 65
Zdziechowski, Marian, 79
Zmiaca, 182
Znaniecki, Florian Witold, 66
Zverina, Josef, 116–17, 125
Zycie Partii, 47
Zylberberg, Jacques, 183, 188
Zywiec, 108–15, 185–9